Highlanders

A History of the Gaels

JOHN MACLEOD

SCEPTRE

First published in 1996
by Hodder and Stoughton
First published in paperback in 1997
by Hodder and Stoughton
A division of Hodder Headline PLC
A Sceptre Paperback

10 9 8 7 6 5 4 3

A CIP catalogue record for this title
is available from the British Library

ISBN 0 340 63991 1

Typeset by Hewer Text Composition Services, Edinburgh
Printed and bound in Great Britain by
Mackays of Chatham PLC, Chatham, Kent

Hodder and Stoughton
A division of Hodder Headline PLC
338 Euston Road
London NW1 3BH

John Macleod

John Macleod was born in Lochaber in 1966, and is the son of the Highland manse. He spent the seventies in Glasgow and the eighties in Edinburgh. After graduation he worked for BBC Highland in Inverness and currently writes a column for Glasgow's *Herald* newspaper. His work has featured in the Scottish and English press and in 1991 he won the trophy for Scottish Journalist of the Year. John Macleod lives in Harris in the Outer Hebrides.

SCEPTRE

Also by John Macleod

No Great Mischief If You Fall

For Iain Calum Maciver

preacher's kid

CONTENTS

✠

LIST OF MAPS

LIST OF ILLUSTRATIONS

⊹

Doune Carloway, Lewis, with brock. (*Derick Mackenzie*)

Carloway broch. (*Derick Mackenzie*)

Callanish Stones, Lewis. (*Derick Mackenzie*)

St Columba preaching to the Picts by William Hole. (*Scottish National Portrait Gallery*)

James Drummond, Marquis of Montrose. (*National Gallery of Scotland*)

The Landing of St Margaret at Queensferry by William Hole. (*Scottish National Portrait Gallery*)

Prince James Francis Edward Stuart, the 'Old Pretender' by an unknown artist. (*Scottish National Portrait Gallery*)

Prince Charles Edward Stuart, the 'Young Pretender' by Maurice Quenton de la Tour. (*Scottish National Portrait Gallery*)

Prince Charles Edward Stuart, attributed to Hugh Douglas Hamilton. (*Scottish National Portrait Gallery*)

James IV (1473–1513) by an unknown artist. (*Scottish National Portrait Gallery*)

James V by an unknown artist. (*Scottish National Portrait Gallery*)

James VI and I by Adam de Colone. (*Scottish National Portrait Gallery*)

James VII and II by Sir Peter Lely. (*Scottish National Portrait Gallery*)

William Augustus, Duke of Cumberland, attributed to Sir Joshua Reynolds. (*Scottish National Portrait Gallery*)

Dundee, Viscount of Claverhouse by David Paton. (*Scottish National Portrait Gallery*)

James MacPherson by unknown artist after Joshua Reynolds (*Scottish National Portrait Gallery*)

St Columba's Church, Aignish, Lewis. (*Derick Mackenzie*)

The monument to Charles Edward Stuart by Arnish, at the mouth of Stornoway harbour. (*Derick Mackenzie*)

PREFACE

✠

This book is a popular history of Scotland's Highlands and Islands. It makes no claim to be a work of original and exhaustive scholarship; but I have drawn on a huge variety of sources – far beyond the titles listed in the bibliography – and it is presented as an accessible introduction to the Highlands, their people, and all that has become of them through recorded time. Inevitably such a work is highly selective, and some intensely turbulent and complex events – such as befell the Highlands in the seventeenth century – have had to be greatly simplified. There is much recent and excellent writing on such specific periods of our past and the reader who would like to inquire more deeply into such topics is directed to these.

This book would never have been written but for the labours on my behalf of Mr Giles Gordon, my former literary agent. I am indebted to him and to his industrious successor, Mr Robert Kirby. I am grateful to Dr James A. D. Finlayson, and Rev Roderick MacLeod, both of Harris, and Mrs Margaret Morrison, of Scalpay, for the loan of certain books, Mr John Murdo Morrison at the Harris Hotel kindly supplied the authentic words of *Chi mi in tin san robh mi nam bhalach*.

The work was completed under certain most trying circumstances, and I am grateful for the forbearance of Mr Roland Philipps and all at Hodder Headline. But my special love and gratitude goes to all my friends, in Harris and beyond, who – by their warmth, their hospitality and their cheerfulness – did so much to make dark months brighter.

JOHN MACLEOD

Isle of Harris
April 1996

The Highlands and Islands

Pentland Firth

Thurso
Wick

Lewis
Stornoway

North Minch

Ullapool
Dornoch

North Uist
Harris

The Little Minch

Dingwall
Inverness

Portree

South Uist

Skye
Kyle of Lochlash

Aviemore

River Spey

Barra

Rhum
Eigg
Mallaig

Sea of the Hebrides

Coll

Fort William
Ben Nevis

R. Tummel

R. Tay

Tobermory

Tiree

Mull
Oban

Firth of Lorn

Jura

Sound of Jura

Islay

Campbeltown

0   50   miles
0   50   100 kms

CHAPTER ONE

✠

I Will See the
Great Mountains

O chì, chì mi na mòr-bheana
O chì, chì mi na còrr-bheana
O chì, chì mi na coireachan
Chì mi na sgoran fo cheò

Chì mi na coilltean, chì mi na doireachan
Chì mi na màghan bàna as toraiche
Chì mi na fèidh air làr nan coireachan
Falaicht' an trusgan de cheò . . .

O I will see, see the great mountains
O I will see, see the great mountains
O I will see, see the corries
I will see the misty peaks

I will see the woods, see the glades
I will see the fair and lovely plains
I will see deer at the foot of the corries
Enfolded in a mantle of mist . . .

From the song, 'Chi Mi Na Mòr-bheana', by John Cameron. Its traditional melody featured in the soundtrack of the 1983 feature film, *Local Hero*, much of which was shot at the beaches of Arisaig, on the West Highland coast.

SCOTLAND'S Highlands and Islands form over a fifth of the British landmass and encompass some of the most beautiful scenery in Europe. They include the highest mountain, the largest lake, and the biggest offshore islands of the United Kingdom. Every year thousands and thousands of visitors flock to Scotland, and over the Highland Line, to see Ben Nevis and to view Loch Ness in hope of sight of the monster, perhaps to cross the new bridge to Skye, perhaps even to cross the Sea of the Hebrides and tour the clean, windswept Western Isles. They come, to be sure, in search of beautiful landscape, glowing sunsets, golden beaches, the sweet clean air and sweet fresh water, the whispering forests and grim peaks high amidst wallowing mist.

The Highlands appeal because they are beautiful, and they appeal because they are different. The pace of life is slower, the weather vigorous and unpredictable, the landscape spectacular and even frightening. The Highlands have never known industrialisation (save in one or two small pockets) and Highland villages are quite different from the English equivalent: they are linear, stretching along a road or a shore, and not huddled about such features as church, pub and village green. Highland townships and ports, too, have each a manifest sense of community, apparent in our local press, on shop notice-boards, in the gossip at the grocer's, in the cheerful huddle of men and boys standing on an island pier each evening as the last ferry chugs in. And, of course, there is Gaelic, still widely spoken in Skye and the Western Isles, a language musical in its very enunciation, a language very different and very old.

But the emptiness, perhaps, draws visitors most: in all

this vast terrain, fewer people live than in the average London borough. (The Highlands and Islands send but six members to the House of Commons in London; they make up only one constituency for the European parliament, though their total acreage exceeds that of one or two EU member states.) In 1745, when Charles Edward Stuart raised the clans in a brave bid for his family crown, the Highlands held a full third of Scotland's population. Today, they contain less than a tenth. One can walk – or even drive – considerable distances in the region without sight of a single dwelling place. And there are many ruined settlements, many empty islands, where once families lived and toiled and sang and died, remembered only by the grassy ruins of their homes, and in the dusty notes of history.

To the jostled and weary of overcrowded Europe – or, for that matter, of the heaving bustle of southern England – such a place is a world apart, and many visitors come expressly to be refreshed in the blissful space and quiet of northern Scotland. But many, too, find a wonder – a sadness – in the silence and in the depopulation. They know something, perhaps, of Highland history: of St Columba and his work at Iona, of the clans, of Charles Edward Stuart and the terrible things done after his final defeat at Culloden. Most visitors have heard of the Clearances, the forced removal of many Highlanders from the communities in which they lived and the land on which they worked. And they would like to know more.

There is no shortage of writing on Highland history: far from it. The last twenty years in particular have seen a spectacular surge of interest in the field, and every year brings more titles on the market. But we live in a culture of increasing specialisation, and these new books all tend to focus on some particular and narrow field – the Clearances, the '45 Rising, the Hebridean emigrations that followed the First World War, and so on. There is a place for a popular, one-volume history of the region, taking advantage of much recent scholarship.

History, and Scottish history in particular, is a sensitive and indeed politicised field. It is only in very modern times that the study of Scottish history became a serious academic discipline. Before the Second World War it was treated with a levity, and imperial languor, that would be unthinkable today. Sir Walter

Scott began the tradition – continued, most notoriously, by P. Hume Brown – of a romantic, anecdotal history, replete with colourful tales of battle, such engaging myths as Robert Bruce and the spider, and centring heavily on the deeds of kings, princes, warriors, aristocrats, damsels, and so on. It was history without analysis, without interest in the culture of the poor and lowly, weirdly anglophile, tacitly hostile to Scotland's native Presbyterian tradition, terminating in 1707, when we had a union and all lived happily ever after.

The rise of Scottish nationalism, since the war, has changed all that. Hume Brown is no longer read in schools. Such as Rosalind Mitchison, Tom Devine and Michael Lynch have transformed the bibliography of the Scottish discipline. Inevitably the initial swing, as Scottish history was overwhelmed by angry young scholars, took the form of overreaction against the Scott and Brown tradition. Charles Edward Stuart is a good example. Scott romanticised him. Writers in Scott's tradition encouraged the reader to lament Charles Edward's failure, in a sentimental sort of way, while deploring his cause. The first wave of new historians pilloried Charles Edward, presenting his cause as anachronistic, as damned from the start, as a folly that had never hope of success and that wasted thousands of lives. Later historians, such as Bruce Lenman and Frank McLynn, have taken Charles Edward – and Jacobitism – much more seriously. They have not returned to the frothy, chivalric style of the past; but they have analysed Jacobitism as a credible political response to the Whig ascendancy, and assessed the '45 both as a political adventure and a military campaign. Today the Rising of 1745 is allowed a dignity in proportion to its final tragedy.

There remains an unfortunate snobbery in the discipline. One of the best, and most accessible, modern writers in the field of Highland history is Skye-based Dr James Hunter, allied closely to the political Left. He is linked to Labour front-bencher Brian Wilson, to Wilson's Skye newspaper, the *West Highland Free Press*, and to the newborn Scottish Crofters Union. Hunter is, surely, the definitive historian of crofting and his popular books on Highland history – beautifully illustrated – are the most readable in the field. But he has never been taken seriously in the groves of academe. Hunter is too popular; he has worked as a journalist, he actually lives in the Hebrides. Professor Thomas Devine of the University of Strathclyde has sniffily dismissed Hunter's work; it has 'not been generally accepted within the mainstream of historical scholarship'.

Highland history, too, is of political significance. There remains a prevalent sense, throughout the region, that the Highlanders are a people wronged. The Clearances, for instance, are still invoked whenever any threat to, say, the crofting interest is sensed. The oral tradition, in most Hebridean families, still abounds with dreadful tales of past hardship: tuberculosis, famine, emigration, eviction, and so on. A Secretary of State for Scotland, some thirty years ago, referred to the Highlander as 'the man on Scotland's conscience'. There is a gratifying guilt to be sensed in the halls of government. In fact the Highlands, this century, have done remarkably well out of Whitehall, and especially since the Second World War – not least in the sense of this obligation that the rest of the country owes them something. Crofters have been heavily subsidised. Generous aid has been given for the construction of modern, sanitary housing. Hydro-electricity, modern car ferries, new and mighty road bridges – all have been provided, and at huge expense to the Exchequer. Even the long-lived Conservative government, elected in 1979, did well by the Highlands though, from the 1987 election, not a single Tory MP was returned throughout the region. At a time of massive government cutbacks, in the nineties, some £9 million a year was made available by the Scottish Office for the support of Gaelic television broadcasting, funding TV programmes in a language spoken by fewer than 70,000 Scots.

Too much can be made of such government spending in the region. Highlanders pay taxes like everyone else; the amenities provided are enjoyed by visitors from all parts of Britain; and mortgage-interest relief in the Home Counties alone costs the state far more than all its subsidies and outlays in the Highlands. But there is a sense of grievance – a culture of whingeing – in the north and west of Scotland that at times is highly vexing. What particularly irritates is the frequent expression of anti-English sentiment, exacerbated in recent years by the widespread settlement of English families in the Highlands. (Fully 15 per cent of the population of Skye are of English birth.) There is a popular belief that the English are the villains of Highland history, that the English today are at the root of prevalent Highland problems. Certainly some English incomers show gross insensitivity to Highland mores; and the many English-owned holiday cottages, used for only a few weeks each year, have badly distorted local property markets. But, in truth, this is myth – and slander – masquerading as history. Highlanders, in their day, did the most terrible things to other Highlanders. And the most determined external foe, the agents of the worst oppression, were not the English but the Lowland Scots.

It is in that struggle – Highlander versus Lowlander – that Highland history is best defined in the present millennium. Lowland Scotland was already united round an independent Scots crown at the time of the Norman conquest of England, while the Hebrides – and most of the mainland Highlands – were in the grip of the Vikings and, at least in title, under the crown of Norway. When the Gaels at length threw off the Norwegian yoke, in the thirteenth century, something approaching an autonomous Gaelic realm was created under the rule of Clan Donald. This 'Lordship of the Isles', however, fell increasingly into conflict with the Scottish court, and the kings of the Stewart dynasty in particular. The destruction of the Lordship, by King James IV at the end of the fifteenth century, brought on a century of virtual anarchy in the Highlands and Islands. The seventeenth century found Stuart kings on the throne of England, and in their wretchedly incompetent rule of that country they increasingly deployed Highland clansmen in the waging of their battles against Lowland opponents. Overthrown and in exile, Stuart claimants sought repeatedly to regain the throne by use of their supporters in the Highland arena. The '45 was the last such endeavour; Highland troops came within two days' march of London. The Culloden disaster was succeeded by punitive measures and the final establishment of southern authority, and southern political mores, over the Highland region. And so on.

But how much simplification there is in that! Take the battle of Culloden. It is popularly viewed as a total military defeat for

Scotland, a primitive and well-intended host of natives overcome by a superior, technological force, who proceeded then on
wanton rampage and killing. In fact the battle of April 1746 was
much more complex. More Scots sided with the Hanoverians
than with the Jacobites; to Lowland Presbyterians the cause of
the Stuarts was both Popish and pernicious. Scots fought on
both sides at Culloden. And Jacobite defeat arose as much from
the idiotic choice of stance by their commanders as from
Cumberland's well-trained, well-fed and supremely disciplined
force. And the defeat was far from final. Many Highlanders
made good their escape; many more flooded to rendezvous at
Ruthven; most expected to fight on, and were willing to do so. It
was Charles Edward himself who threw in the towel, who fled
for his life and sent word to his bewildered followers that they
were to scatter for their own safety until he came back with the
French. And the atrocities of the Hanoverian force, terrible as
they were, made a certain dark sense in their own view of the
situation. They were in a strange, frightening, 'barbarous'
landscape. They did not regard the Highlanders as rational
human beings. A Highland force had come perilously close to
deposing the established monarchy and the lawful order. Cumberland and his troops determined, once and for all, to root out
any abiding elements of rebellion. Which, in brutal and atrocious fashion, they did.

Or take that other celebrated time of misery: the Highland
Clearances. Nothing in Scottish history arouses more passion,
or so quickly divides in argument, as that enormously complicated period. The Clearances – in the sense of forced evictions,
without compensation and often with great brutality – really
cover three distinct episodes. There were the Sutherland Clearances, early in the nineteenth century, when by planned programme hundreds of families were evicted from their homes so
that the land they had worked for generations could be rented to
Lowland sheep-farmers. There were the Hebridean Clearances,
much later – the South Uist and Barra evictions are the most
notorious – precipitated by the widespread famine of the 1840s,
the inevitable result of repeated failure in the potato crop. And,
when these massed and forced removals took end, petty clearances continued: families evicted from a home because the man

had caused offence; whole townships shifted from one end of an island to another.

Further, throughout all this time there was much voluntary emigration, at one time so heavy that, during the kelp boom, Highland landlords successfully agitated for government measures to restrict it, and so hold on to their workforce. Emigration was more than a reality: it was a necessity. A sustained time of heavy population growth, in many Highland districts, pressed hard on the land and its resources. There was much tension between crofters and 'cottars', the illegal squatters who increasingly crowded the grazing in their makeshift homes. When these were shipped abroad, the crofters were glad to see the back of them. But these are dangerous things to say in the contemporary Highland arena: the Clearances are now popular myth, with goodies and baddies, and grossly simplified both in folk memory and political rhetoric.

It is too glib, besides, to talk of the 'Gaels of Scotland', or to regard all Highlanders as Gaels. In strict geography, the isles of Orkney and Shetland belong to the region, but Gaelic was never spoken there. Gaelic, on the other hand, was spoken in Galloway as late as the seventeenth century; but Galloway lies south of the Firth of Clyde, and by no stretch of the imagination belongs to the Highlands. It is not even true to say that Highlanders are Gaels racially. Most Lewismen, for instance, are more Norwegian than Celtic. In any event, the Gaels were late arrivals on the Highland scene; the Roman empire had fallen before the first Gaels of Ireland settled in Dalriada.

The one abiding constant in history here, the arena of all its events, the enfolding, towering, grand reality that fires the finest Gaelic poetry and draws visitors from the world over, is the Highland landscape itself.

Geographically the Highlands are all the lands and islands north of the Highland Boundary fault, an irregular south-west to north-east geological rift from Helensburgh in the west to Stonehaven in the north. Yet much of the land north of this line is flat in the extreme – Caithness, Buchan and so on. Scotland's highest villages, Leadhills and Wanlockhead, are actually in the Lowlands. Some of the Hebrides, such as Tiree and Benbecula, are exceedingly low-lying. The great mountain ranges that give the Highlands their name lie to the centre and west of the region; the east coast – with the odd spectacular mountain, such as Ben Wyvis – is predominately flat.

In geography, culture and character the Highlands split into three distinct regions: the West Highlands, including the Hebrides; the East Highlands, from Nairn to Caithness; and the Central Highlands, largely the inland districts of the county of Inverness and the Highland parishes of Perth. Their varying character shows the danger of generalising about the Highlands. The Highlands are predominately treeless, but much of Highland Perthshire abounds in fine woodland. Crofting is the definitive land use of the Highlands, but the East Highlands see agriculture overwhelmingly in the hands of vast farms; in mainland Argyll there are very few crofts, for land reforms in the eighteenth century created hundreds of privately owned smallholdings. In the eighteenth century, the East Highlands were largely Episcopal by religion, the Central Highlands Presbyterian, western Inverness Roman Catholic . . . and there, and in many other respects, the complexity of Highland comment is made plain.

There are only a few major centres of population. The town of Inverness was at one time the fastest-growing conurbation in Britain; through the sixties and seventies it spread in all directions, in big (and generally attractive) housing developments. It is the premier shopping centre of the Highlands and a good base for exploring the east coast. Fort William is the biggest community in the mainland West Highlands. Stornoway, the capital of Lewis, is the only town in the Hebrides; over 10,000 people live in the town and its satellite townships, in what has been described both as the most English community in the Hebrides and the most Gaelic town in Scotland.

There are other towns of varying size – Oban, Invergordon, Wick, Thurso – but the great mass of Highlanders still live in villages, their economy founded largely on agriculture, tourism and the harvest of the sea. We may divide the region as a whole into distinct sections. Argyll, in the south-west, is the heartland of Gaeldom, though much of the county lies further south than Edinburgh. Here the Gaels first came from Ireland, in the early centuries of the Christian era. Here Columba launched his great missionary enterprise, at Iona. Argyll, strikingly verdant and fertile, has much soft and lovely scenery. Oban and Dunoon are the most substantial communities; Tarbert and Lochgilphead are also significant. Argyll is distinctive in certain cultural respects: it is the only Highland county, for instance, where the Scottish Episcopal Church has a strong indigenous following.

The Argyll Hebrides – Islay, Jura, Gigha, Colonsay, Mull, Iona, Coll, Tiree and such satellites as Luing – are lovely but much depopulated islands. Islay has been called the Queen of the Hebrides, for she is the most fertile of all. Gaelic is still spoken on Islay: it is all but extinct in others, especially on Mull, noted for very many years for its heavy English settlement. Islay and Gigha are served by the car ferries of Caledonian Mac-Brayne – a state-owned concern, operating a near-monopoly of Highland passenger shipping – from Kintyre; the other islands are primarily served from Oban.

The district of Lochaber has been, through generations, the theatre of some of the most dramatic events in Highland history; it is those parts of Inverness and north Argyll bordering Loch Linnhe and the southern quarter of the Great Glen. Fort William is the largest settlement in the mainland West Highlands, enjoying good road, rail and sea links with the south; the Corpach township, nearby, is the west-coast entrance to the Caledonian Canal. The area was heavily industrialised during and after the Second World War, but tourism is still important; in particular, Lochaber is a famed centre for the mountaineer.

Wester Ross, heavily indented by sea lochs, abounds in attractive seaside villages. For most tourists it is their point of departure for Skye, and the Outer Isles beyond. Kyle of Lochalsh, Plockton, Lochcarron, Gairloch and Ullapool are the main population centres, though the jagged coast makes north to south movement in the area most difficult. Wester Ross enjoys an equable climate, with the tempering influence of the Atlantic Drift: at Plockton palm trees grow, and the gardens of Inverewe – planted by Sir Osgood Mackenzie, best of Highland landlords, last century – attract thousands of visitors each year. Many have settled to live in Wester Ross, from the Lowlands, England and beyond, and communities such as Ullapool now have a lively, cosmopolitan feel – fine restaurants, bookshops, a thriving cultural life even in winter.

Skye, with its outliers – Raasay, and the Small Isles of Eigg, Rhum, Muck and Canna – is perhaps the most famous of Scotland's islands; the Skye Boat Song – written, in English, many years after the '45 Rising – is sung all over the world. A new road bridge now brings visitors to the island's spectacular mountain scenery, though competing ferries survive to Armadale and to Kylerhea. Portree, Broadford and Dunvegan are Skye's principal communities. Here, too, there has been much immigration, but, like Ullapool, the effect has been to enrich rather than to swamp. Gaelic survives here: there is a Gaelic college, Sabhal Mor Ostaig, at Isle Ornsay in Sleat parish, and Gaelic is still spoken widely, especially in the parish of Kilmuir in the north-west, which largely escaped the Clearances. Quiet and beautiful Raasay is well worth a visit, by the short ferry crossing from Skye. The Small Isles are served from Mallaig, but there is no car ferry link; indeed, only Canna has a usable pier.

The Outer Hebrides, or Western Isles, from Barra Head in the south to the Butt of Lewis in the north, run for many miles along the very frontier of Scotland. They are largely treeless and, apart from the border of Lewis and Harris, without mountain scenery. But their very remoteness – the shortest crossing, from Skye, still takes nearly two hours – has preserved the old Highland ways – Gaelic, religion, hospitality – here with more vigour than anywhere else. There are six major island communities – Barra, South Uist, Benbecula, North Uist, Harris and Lewis – and some smaller satellites still support busy people: Vatersay, Eriskay, Berneray, Scalpay and Bernera. Each island has its own character, and a fiercely defended identity. The islands are even distinct in religion, with marked contrast between north and south. Barra and South Uist are staunchly Roman Catholic. In Benbecula the people divide evenly between Protestant and Catholic. As one advances up the chain Presbyterianism dominates, with different denominations in the lead. Largely Presbyterian North Uist adheres, for the main part, to the Church of

Scotland. In Harris the Church of Scotland divides its spoils with the Free Presbyterian Church of Scotland. This body should not be confused with the Free Church of Scotland, by far the strongest denomination in fiercely Presbyterian Lewis. But there is no Ulster-style conflict. United by race and language, working alongside one another in croft and council, the people of the Outer Hebrides live most amicably; and though they worship apart, they unite happily at weddings and funerals.

The Western Isles have a strong crofting economy, with the local authority an important source of supporting employment. The military facilities at Balivanich are important to Benbecula. Fishing, and increasingly fish-farming, still account for many jobs. Harris tweed – which must, by definition, be woven in the Outer Hebrides of pure Scottish virgin wool, and at the weavers' own homes – is largely woven in Lewis, though the classic, truly hand-made, sheep-to-suit product is still best found in Harris itself. Tourism is of less importance here than in Skye and the mainland Highlands: the long sea crossings and high air fares do not encourage the day-tripper. Ferries link the chain at various points to Ullapool, Uig in Skye, Mallaig and Oban; there are links between Barra, Benbecula and Stornoway, and to Glasgow and Inverness. But the Western Isles economy is always parlous and emigration remains important: at any given time, over a fifth of the workforce is officially unemployed.

The North Highlands are two counties: Sutherland and Caithness. Sutherland, rugged and with much fine coastal scenery, is one of the saddest places in Scotland. Most of its communities were eliminated in the most notorious of the Clearances and the human economy has never recovered. It is a land of great sporting estates, of golf tourism (around Dornoch) and of fishing (Lochinver and Kinlochbervie). And it is a land of empty straths, mile upon mile of road without human habitation. Gaelic clings on by its toenails, in little places like Embo and Strathy. Gaelic vanished from Caithness very many years ago: it has more in common with Orkney – even such eastern counties as Banff and Aberdeen – than with the rest of the Highlands. Its very flat scenery gives great visibility, but can be disconcerting after a prolonged tour of the Highland region. The nuclear industry, centred on the pioneer plant at Dounreay, has been the pre-eminent employer for decades, but its future is uncertain and the Dounreay plant is being scaled down.

The East Highlands, Easter Ross and Inverness, follow the shore of the great Moray Firth and its three inland pups – the Dornoch, Cromarty and Beauly Firths. There is little crofting here, but huge and abundant tracts of farmland: here grow potatoes for Golden Wonder crisps, carrots for Sainsbury's, and so on. Soft scenery, clean air and water, and a magnificent climate make this an idyllic corner of Scotland – for those in work. The town of Inverness dominates the region. Here are founded most enterprises important in the direction of Highland affairs. Here is the seat of local government.

The political Highlands are hard to describe because of repeated boundary changes: in barely two decades there were massive reforms of local government. But the old county bounds of Argyll, Perth, Inverness, Ross and Cromarty, Sutherland, and Caithness are still vividly apparent in culture and in folk memory, and occur so often in the texts of history that the author still prefers to use them. In 1974 the county councils were abolished. The old county of Perth was split between two new regional councils – Tayside, and the grotesquely named Central – and most of Argyll vanished into the large Strathclyde region. All the northern counties were absorbed into the vast Highland Region; the Western Isles, however – for long split between Inverness and Ross and Cromarty – were at last given autonomy, in the new Western Isles Islands Council, Comhairle nan Eilean.

Highland Region survived the reforms of 1994, as did Comhairle nan Eilean, but the mainland subsidiary councils – Lochaber, Sutherland and so on – were abolished in the new single-tier system. Argyll, though, was largely resurrected, the district council of Argyll and Bute being promoted to new and independent status. Personality is important in Highland local government, and most wards are still held by Independent councillors. In parliamentary politics the same applies, and in general elections the region remains distinct. Labour has never done well here: the Western Isles constituency is their only

natural seat, thanks to crofter radicalism, though the present
Liberal Democrat MP for Caithness and Sutherland held it for
Labour for his first fifteen years in the House. Throughout the
fifties the mainland Highlands were solidly Tory, though two
successive members in Caithness and Sutherland resigned the
Conservative whip to sit as Independents. In 1964 the Liberals
won three Highland seats; they lost some ground to Nationalism
in the seventies, but in the 1987 election the mainland Highlands
voted solidly for Liberal or Social Democrat MPs, and the
Liberal Democrats swept the region in 1992.

In 1970 Donald Stewart won the Western Isles for the Scottish
National Party, committed to the goal of an independent
Scotland, and the SNP held the seat easily until his retiral in
1987, when the archipelago returned to Labour. At their high
point, in 1974, the Nationalists took over 30 per cent of the
Scottish poll, and threatened in every Highland seat; they won
Argyll easily, but lost it in their 1979 collapse. That same year,
however, the SNP's Winnie Ewing won the Highlands and
Islands division in the first direct elections to Strasbourg, and
defended it successfully thrice, with ever larger majorities; she
retires as Mother of the European parliament.

In their human geography the Hebrides are overwhelmingly
coastal and the Highlands as a whole largely so. Travel by sea
was, by far, the easiest way of getting round the Highlands and –
as late as the last decades of last century – the readiest way of
getting into them. So most Highlanders, then and now, live on
the coastline, or in the most fertile inland straths. Huge tracts of
Highland landscape – in the wastes of Sutherland, the plateau
of Knoydart, the Great Moor of Lewis – are quite devoid of
people.

Queen Victoria herself popularised what was afterwards
known as the 'Royal Route' to the county town of Inverness:
travel by steamer down the Clyde to Ardrishaig, up the Crinan
Canal by barge, another steamer up the Firth of Lorne and Loch
Linnhe, and thus through the Caledonian Canal and the lochs of
the Great Glen to the Highland capital. She did not do this for
fun, as a pleasure cruise; it was by far the quickest route of
access. Likewise, in 1745, Hanoverian commanders shipped
forces from Aberdeen to East Lothian, prior to the Battle of

Prestonpans; it was much easier than marching troops by road.
It was almost the end of the nineteenth century before the
Highlands were integrated into the rail network. It was after
the Second World War before road travel triumphed over the
railways and it was the sixties before road haulage, and short
car-ferry links, began rapidly to displace the steamers of David
MacBrayne Ltd – and their long voyages from Glasgow docks –
as the prime transport of heavy freight to the Hebrides. Not all
progress, though, is advantageous. Public transport has deteriorated greatly in the age of the private car; many Hebridean
journeys – like, say, a trip from Barra to Canna – could be
accomplished more conveniently, and rather faster, a century
ago than today.

There are two principal road routes into the Highlands from
Scotland's central belt: the A9, from Perth through the Central
Highlands to Inverness, and the A82, from Glasgow by Loch
Lomondside and the West Highlands to Fort William, at the
other end of the Great Glen. The mighty mountains and the
long sea lochs of the west, and the firths of the north-east,
greatly restricted movement by land until the construction of
roads; it was the eighteenth century before serious road construction began in the Highlands. Thus the West and East
Highlands evolved quite separately from each other. Thus
Lewis and Harris – though geographically the same island –
are of very distinct character; to all intents and purposes
different islands. The road over the mountains dividing them
is of very recent construction; the people are of different
appearance, very different accent, distinctly different Gaelic.
And their history progressed under two separate tribes of Clan
MacLeod; until 1974, Lewis and Harris were even in different
counties – Harris in Inverness, Lewis in Ross and Cromarty.

The rugged, infinitely varied scenery of the West and Central
Highlands is the work of rock and water.

The region, geologically, should be viewed as a great plateau
of rock; its western half submerged, with peaks emerging here
and there as islands. This plateau has, over generation upon
generation, era upon era, been gouged by water, wrenched by
quake, smelted by volcano, scraped by vast glaciers of crawling,

sliding ice. This plateau of rock is still well evident in the Central Highlands: the Grampian and Cairngorm country, traversed by the highway from Perth to Inverness. In the west – Glencoe is a good example, the Cuillin another – the rock has had much more of a battering and forms the archetypal, dramatic Highland scenery. Here are the highest mountains, the sharpest ridges, the wildest glens, the longest sea lochs.

The line of the western seaboard is deeply broken and indented, strewn with islands, scattered with coves, probed by these pointing fingers of the sea. And in the far north-west, the rock has not merely been scored and gouged, it has been flattened, as if by plane. Scourie, Kinlochbervie – Lewis for that matter – are low, humpy country, stripped to ancient, Archaean rocks like Torridonian sandstone and Lewisian gneiss. Glaciers did this, and on occasion there are spectacular proofs of how, once, another rock lay atop what survives today. Ben Nevis, for instance, is made largely of granite; but the summit is not granite at all – it is basalt. It crowns that great hill like brandy sauce on a Christmas pudding.

There is an agreeable craziness to Highland geology, reflecting violent volcanic and hydraulic activity over the ages. For one, there is the Moine Thrust, running from a southern toe of Skye to the eastern shore of Loch Eriboll, far north on Sutherland. Along this line the earth's plates shifted violently; north of it lie very old rocks – gneiss again – and, south, the Moine schists. Along the Moine Thrust line itself, like filling in a sandwich (as Fraser Darling and Morton Boyd put it, in their summary of Highland geology) is a band of Cambrian beds. Then there are all the jumbled rocks, old and new, throughout Highland districts: gneiss and sandstone, the Tertiary terraces of volcanic rock, the conglomerates around Stornoway in Lewis, the plugs of Durness limestone brightening the agriculture, here and there, in barren Sutherland.

The Tertiary volcanoes created some of the most spectacular Highland scenery. The Red Hills of Skye are rounded massifs of granite; the Black Cuillin, some miles to the north, are of gabbro, a coarse igneous rock, with wonderful grip for climbers. On Skye and Rhum old lava terraces have been shifted and wrenched through time to create creepy castellated scenery, like

the weird Quirang, whose spikes and spars look like the setting
for fantasy fiction, and the Old Man of Storr, a mighty pillar of
rotten rock. On Mull, the lavas were basalt; there are none of
Skye's epic features, but mighty terraced hills. Volcanic soil
makes excellent grazing for cattle; Kilmuir, on Skye, enjoys the
best grass in the island, and the grazing on Mull is so good that
(naturally) it was savagely cleared of its people in the last
century. By the time of recorded history the Scottish volcanoes
were long since cold and silent; though one very famous extinct
ring volcano remains: the glorious St Kilda, way out in the
Atlantic, with its towering sea cliffs and unique, isolated
ecology.

Calcareous, sedimentary rocks – sandstones, yielding good
arable soil – are naturally important in Highland agriculture.
Against the dominant heaths, bogs and gneisses, patches of such
land – pockets of Skye, Mull, Raasay, Torridon, Ardnamurchan
– give good farming, rich woodland, green pastures, hazel scrub,
an abundance of wildlife. And then, of course, there are the
great faults, where the joins of the Highland landmass are easily
beheld. The Highland Boundary Fault is one; the Great Glen
another. The latter divides the north and north-west Highlands
from the central and south-west Highlands. Running dead
straight, from Lochaber to Inverness, south-west to north-
east, it holds three long freshwater lochs, divided only from
sea and each other by little necks of land, and in the last century
they were linked by the Caledonian Canal.

Perhaps the eeriest Highland scenery is the scoured bare
country left by glaciation – the east coast of Harris, the far
north-west. The Highlands appear to have experienced four
glacial episodes, and these were survived long after by two
slowly shrinking ice-caps, from which glaciers still flowed,
clawing out glens and corries, smoothing mountains, removing
layers of soft rock, depositing boulders and debris as they
thawed. The end of these ice ages was followed by an upward
heaving of the earth's crust itself, free from the weight of these
masses of ice. Argyll, in particular, abounds in 'raised beaches',
once coastal, now many hundreds of metres inland, with good
fertile loam.

'The glaciers,' write Darling and Morton Boyd, 'have not

only carved and smoothed the countryside but have had a profound effect on the subsequent natural history.' Anyone who has seen the east coast of Harris – reminiscent of nothing as much as the surface of the moon – can appreciate that. In the mountain passes of the island – Glen Lacsadal, Bealach na Ceist – vast boulders still sit about the landscape where the ice dumped them all that time ago. Little lochs sit in hollows on the rock where the glaciers gouged out a resting place. And so on.

The Highland climate is a good deal more diverse, and interesting, than is often suggested. The wet and rain and gales of West Highland winters are notorious. Yet the prevailing weather in the East Highlands, around Inverness and the Black Isle, is probably the best in Britain. Tiree, in the Inner Hebrides, regularly tops the sunshine charts; it is so low that rain sweeps over it, and clouds seldom linger, and at least one visitor remarked that staying on this flat, very windy island was like 'living on an aircraft carrier'. Lochaber and Knoydart are very, very wet. Frost is rare in Wester Ross, but in the Central Highlands temperatures of $-25°C$ have been recorded, as recently as 1982.

Weather can vary from one side of an island to another; a mountain will have separate climate zones, and to the fanatical naturalist even the lee of a boulder has its own mini-climate. Yet there are general features to the Highland weather patterns.

The west coast is much wetter than the east, and the more mountainous a district the more rain it will endure. Heavy rain has three principal effects. Soil is apt to be water-logged and this makes arable farming difficult; a wet summer is especially bad for grain and hay. Then, because the evaporation cycle in the West Highlands is poor – more water falls than the sun and wind can dry – and because the soil is generally acid, organic matter does not decay into good loam, but instead forms peat. Peat can be dried for fuel, and is; but peat, without the softening of lime and potash, will not yield crops. The last serious impact of rain is erosion. In every spate, Highland burns and rivers foam brown with sediment. Valuable minerals and nutrients are washed from the land into the sea, never to return.

The west coast is milder than the east. It enjoys the softening impact of the Atlantic Drift, a steady current of warm water from the south-west, sometimes (incorrectly) identified with the Gulf Stream. Frost and ice are, therefore, rare on the west coast and snow, when it falls, does not lie long. But 'mild' is a relative term. The mean temperature of Fort William, for instance, is higher than that of Cambridge, but Cambridge has much drier winters and much hotter summers. Altitude makes a big difference. Plockton may be ice-free; the high road from Plockton to Applecross, round Lochcarron by the Bealach na Bo, is frequently snowbound. Many a hill climber has perished because he thought the pleasant winter day by his lochside hotel meant warm, comfortable conditions a thousand feet up.

The Highlands are windy and the Hebrides especially so. At the Butt of Lewis gusts in excess of 100 mph are recorded regularly. Winds make our weather and, if you can ascertain the direction of wind, you can make as effective a stab at imminent weather conditions as the BBC. (Islanders disdain the standard weather forecast, preferring the wind-centred shipping forecasts, though since the Great Hurricane of October 1987 – which British weathermen quite failed to see coming – BBC forecasts have erred on the side of pessimism.)

The prevalent wind is from the south-west; this is mild, damp, and apt to bring rain. Winds from due west are gusty and unpleasant. North-westerlies bring hail, wintry showers, and high-speed cloud patterns. The north wind is very cold, and could bring snow. The north-easterly is cold, nipping to skin and growth, but clears the skies and dries everything in sight. It is in the weeks of late April and May, when the north-easterly blows steadily, as a rule, for two or three weeks, that Hebrideans quit agriculture for a while and cut peat, for this wind dries it perfectly.

The south-easterly is the wind of good weather; warm, kissing air, blazing sunshine, high pressure, clear skies. In summer the ground dazzles and blazes in the sun. In winter, a day or two of this – despite the frost at night – does much to lift the spirits.

At these northerly latitudes, of course, light is significant. The short day of midwinter – and the thin, watery light even when the sun is up – is one dispiriting aspect of the Highland climate;

at winter solstice in the Western Isles, one has less than eight hours of daylight. The long hours of daylight, in summer, do much to compensate for the long winter and for summer's relative cool and wet. Growth is happily forced by the extra light; it is a superb climate for growing grass, soil permitting, and so the traditional Highland economy was a pastoral one, and cattle a man's historic wealth. And in the old Highland culture, people adapted to the bleak winter days: they stayed indoors, for the most part, and slept a great deal, and diverted themselves in song and music and story, and found strength in family and community.

Highland weather, in truth, boasts infinite variety, and is generally capricious. The day may start sunny and end atrociously. The visitor could walk the hills in shorts in October and crunch through frost in May. The sensible visitor does not come to the Highlands expecting the worst – long, settled periods of fine sunny weather are not as rare as he might think – but he should come with reliable waterproofs and a warm jersey or two, whatever the time of year.

There is no doubt that the prevalent weather in the West Highlands was once much drier and warmer. In the Eocene period, just before the volcanoes began to throw up interesting places like Skye, conditions were subtropical. There followed the first Ice Age, dated by geologists to the Pleistocene period, some 600,000 years ago. According to W. H. Murray, there have been to date four great glacial advances, 'all followed by retreats and by long-lasting interglacial periods of climate no less warm than now, when the earth could return to its life-encouraging self.' Their geological impact we have seen. It also made for exotic wildlife. Before the last Ice Age – a mere 20,000-odd years ago, according to the boffins – Arctic mammals wandered Scotland. They included reindeer, elk, giant deer, bears, lynx, lemmings, the woolly rhinoceros, the hairy mammoth. (Carbon-dating of one woolly rhinoceros, uncovered in Bishopbriggs, by Glasgow, aged the remains at 27,000 years.)

Then the last Ice Age began. And Scotland was covered by an ice-cap whose edge ran 2,000 miles from Iceland to Norway. When it ended, so much water remained locked in the polar cap that sea level was about 400 feet lower than today. A succession of climatic changes radically altered the flora and fauna of the Highlands. Yet, even as late as AD 1000, Lewis was covered in scrub forest, according to Viking saga. Skye and Mull were well wooded as late as the sixteenth century.

Two climatic waggles occur in the historic era. Around AD 1000, before the Norman conquest of England, the climate of Europe became freakishly warm, and remained so for two centuries. Vineyards could flourish 300 miles further north than they can today. But there was a comeback. The period from 1430 to 1850 was so cold it has been dubbed the Little Ice Age. 'On Scotland's Atlantic coast,' writes Murray, 'eye-witness reports were of storm damage by spray, bitter summers, the failure of harvests, and the wholesale destruction of woods on exposed land . . .' This was the age of long white winters, the world of Victorian Christmas cards, with inns and churches half buried in drifts of snow. In our own century, between 1890 and 1938, there was an oscillation; sea temperature rose by half a degree, and there were apocalyptic prophecies that the whole Arctic might thaw, the sea level rise and half the cities of Europe be inundated.

Over the last thirty years milk cows have all but disappeared from the crofts of Lewis and Harris. Crofters have had more and more difficulty foddering beasts over winter, summers being much wetter and the hay crop poor, often unharvestable. There is also anecdotal evidence that the sea level has risen a little in recent years; however, cyclical variations are to be expected, and it would require much more evidence, over a much longer period, before we could be sure of a profound and abiding change in weather conditions.

Man himself has done much to shape the environment. His most significant impact has been on woodland. Much of the Highlands have been deforested: timber felled for construction, and for charcoal burning, and the cleared ground turned over to grazing. Cattle – but especially sheep – are inimical to tree growth, and where they are allowed free rein forest does not return. There are no trees on Lewis or Harris today, beyond the parkland of Stornoway and private gardens, save for forlorn little things growing where grazing stock cannot reach – little islets in the lochs, clefts in the cliffs. After the great loss of forestry in the 'Little Ice Age', some landowners did try to restore woodland. One Duke of Atholl created the magnificent forests of Perthshire, aided by non-native species such as sycamore and larch. Most did not bother.

The modern red deer has survived by adaptation, a small and wiry thing of the moor, much removed from its tall ancestor of several centuries ago. Other animals, of course, have been deliberately exterminated. The pine marten has been extinct in the Western Isles since the turn of the century. The wild cat, *felix sylvestris*, was almost extinct when it was granted legal protection; the threat, now, is from interbreeding with domestic felines. The last wolf in Scotland was killed a few years before the '45 Rising. The last great auk, a large flightless bird, was killed in 1844 by frightened St Kildan fishermen: they had caught it in their nets, and thought it was a monster.

Starkly beautiful as much of the Highlands are, it is most important to grasp that this is a country despoiled and wasted by man. The boggy, treeless, rugged terrain is, as Fraser Darling lamented in his *West Highland Survey*, a 'devastated countryside', hugely deforested, and thus unable – in the prevailing climate and at this northern latitude – to be either fertile or productive. Man everywhere has destroyed trees, felled or fired them, and then filled the landscape with livestock, preventing any regeneration of forest. Without forest, whole ranges of flora and fauna vanished, or survived only in stunted, inadequate form.

Without the binding effect of tree roots, soil erosion stripped hills and glens of fertile loam. Since last century the despoiling has, if anything, accelerated. The coming of large-scale sheep farming, during the Clearances, led to rapid deterioration of Highland grazing. In our own era the red deer population has swollen massively. There are far too many deer in the Highlands today, and a comprehensive cull is long overdue. 'Devastation has not quite reached its uttermost lengths,' wrote Darling, 'but it is quite certain that present trends in land-use will lead to it, and the country will then be rather less productive than Baffin Land.' Darling penned this over forty years ago, but these trends continue; the widening monoculture of sheep and the lazy practices of sporting estates still impoverish Highland soil.

Darling, of course, was aware how attractive visitors find the Highland landscape in its present state. Such, he said, had to be educated to better understanding, to grasp the reality that they were not viewing the glens and bens and islands in their natural, first-framed state. Darling wanted rejuvenated agriculture, with renewed focus on cattle rather than sheep. He wanted planned reforestation, and especially the return of deciduous woodland. He wanted drainage of waterlogged soil; he wanted an end to such practices as muirburn (when heather is fired, at spring, to renew the grazing). To him, the typical Highland glen – bare, treeless, mossy, deserted – was a thing pitiable, even a place of horror. That horror was even better grasped by Hugh MacLennan, a Canadian novelist who visited Scotland in the fifties, and visited the district of Kintail, in Wester Ross, from which his great-grandfather had emigrated to Canada.

Kintail has some of the most splendid scenery in the Highlands. There are mighty mountains, like the Five Sisters, one of Scotland's highest waterfalls, deep and mysterious sea lochs, bonnie little villages nestling under the skirts of hills. The climbing in Kintail is among the best in Britain. The long descent of Glen Shiel, on the road to Skye, takes you through one of Scotland's most spectacular mountain passes: it is almost a cliché of Highland scenery – foaming river, burns streaming white, crags frowning from on high, often mist, generally rain. The road winds, turns and falls. Here and there the eye catches a tumbled ruin. Kintail enthralls most visitors. But it did not enthrall Hugh MacLennan. The sheer emptiness of this land – without people, without bustle, without activity – struck him in the most powerful fashion. Later that same summer he again met an empty landscape, in the North West Territories of his own country. But that emptiness was of a different kind. 'Above the sixtieth parallel of Canada,' MacLennan wrote, 'you feel that nobody but God has ever been there before you, but in a deserted Highland glen you feel that everyone who ever mattered is dead and gone.'

MacLennan was glad to return to his own land. Of course, his response to Kintail was coloured by knowledge of its history, and of the hardship that befell his own people in that miserable, chaotic time we call the Clearances. But the wild places of

Kintail are miserable in themselves to the sensitive eye of the ecologist. These banks and glens were once green, grazed by sturdy cattle and manured with their dung, tilled by families through succeeding generations, so that in high summer the land was bright in cornrigs, neatly stripped with bobbing oats and barley. And centuries before their day, there was widespread forest: birch, alder, oak, rowan. The forest vanished, for the most part, long ago. And many, many communities disappeared – simply ceased to exist – in the Highland Clearances. There are few trees now, no cultivated land. The sheep – 'hoofed locusts', John Muir called them – nibble hungrily at cropped rank yellow grasses; former meadows are now bog, the very soil sour, waterlogged and acidified.

The Forestry Commission, established after the First World War to renew Scottish timber, has of course planted many thousands of acres of forest: but this has overwhelmingly been woodland of the wrong kind – blank squares of uniform conifer, largely of non-native species such as Norwegian spruce. In many ways modern forestry practice has been the worse for the Highlands. Dense coniferous forest acidifies soil still further; it acidifies the rivers, with adverse effect on game fishing. Nothing grows on the floor of a tightly grown pine wood. Light is denied to the ground and it is rapidly carpeted with pine needles. In recent years the Foresty Commission has been greatly embarrassed by the vulnerability of a popular – but North American – species, lodgepole pine, to 'strike' by the Pine Beauty Moth. The voracious, horrible caterpillar of this species can kill a large plantation in a single season. In 1992 alone, two Lewis forests – at Aline and Garynahine – were destroyed by Pine Beauty Moth. Millions of caterpillars worked through summer with such vigour that it was said one could stand in a clearing and hear them munching. By year's end all the pines were dead. These ghostwoods, and others, still stand: a mute reminder to human frailty. Forestry practice is now changing, with greater emphasis on native species and deciduous trees in particular.

The feral mink of the Outer Isles are another pointed reminder of human stupidity. Mink farming was briefly trumpeted, in the fifties, as a bright wheeze for rejuvenating the local

economy. Like many a well-meant scheme for the Highlands, it
went wrong; the West Highland climate is too warm, and the
mink failed to grow fur of sufficient length and density to gratify
the fur trade. Many escaped, and when at last the scheme fell out
of favour some mink farmers simply set their stock free. In the
wild, they thrived. Mink are brave, hardy, resourceful – they can
swim considerable distances – and utterly vicious. Feral mink
now plague the whole island and have already crossed the Sound
of Harris to the Uists. They have wrought grievous harm on
ground-nesting birds – corncrakes, puffins and terns are greatly
reduced – and driven many despairing crofters, and crofters'
wives, from keeping poultry.

The present history concerns the principal Highland region, a
little smaller than the European parliament division: all the
Hebrides, Caithness, Sutherland, Ross and Cromarty, Inverness, Argyll, and Highland Perthshire. It is written with the
visitor to the Highlands in mind, and thus there is a strong bias
to the West Highlands and the Hebrides: to these the great bulk
of tourists come. The sharp reader will also notice repeated
reference to the Outer Isles, and to Lewis and Harris in
particular. There are good reasons for this. The Western Isles
are the Highland corner which the author knows best. Further,
it is where he lives. Further still, it is where traditional Highland
culture still survives most vigorously, where Gaelic is still widely
spoken and old ways are still followed. The Outer Isles, by dint
of their environment and culture, are also peculiarly accessible
to study: social trends here are apparent very quickly, and what
goes on in the Highlands as a whole is seen in the Western Isles
first. But, in every example given, or every story related, from
the Outer Isles, the reader can be sure it is typical of the region
as a whole – the local episode but one in a wider drama, the
individual personality typical of his day, the hard life of a
woman that expected, through the Highlands, for her time.
    Personality stamps all history. This work makes no claim to
be 'in the mainstream of historical scholarship', but it has taken
advantage of many works by experts in specific fields, and these
are gratefully acknowledged in the bibliography. Anyone who
wants a detailed and authoritative life of Charles Edward Stuart

should read Frank McLynn. The student of conflict between crofter and conservationist should see James Hunter, and so on. In such a general and wide-ranging sweep of two millennia in such a great region as the Highlands, it is hard to avoid personal selectivity or prejudice. The sharp reader will notice, for example, a strong bias towards traditional Highland Presbyterianism, and a corresponding disdain for rites Roman or Anglican.

But the author has sought always to be fair, even in religion, and he is perhaps correcting the general tone of most Highland topography and historiography – notorious for their ignorance of, and contempt for, the ways of the Highland people in sincere, evangelical faith, inclined to be uncritical of priests in the prelatical, sacramentalist tradition. Even today journalists tour the Outer Isles and come away with accounts of the local religion which, by their flippancy and silliness, could deservedly be condemned as racist. The secular mind can be gloriously innocent of its own subjectivity; the religious mind is always alert to the risk of prejudice.

Yet one must be careful. Roman Catholic priests did much to preserve Gaelic lore and song in the modern era; much survived, in Roman Lochaber, Morar, Barra and South Uist, into our own day – by way of tradition, music and tale – that perished elsewhere. The Celtic Church – though hierarchical in government – greatly advanced Highland civilisation. Nothing is simple, especially in history. And even this Calvinist, Presbyterian heart still wishes, in weaker moments, that Charles Edward had succeeded.

Some points of nomenclature or pronunciation should be made plain. Scottish Gaelic is is pronounced *Gah-lic*, not 'Gaylick'; that is the language of Ireland, though Irish is an even better name for it. Gaelic, yes, or 'the Gaelic language', but 'the Gaelic' is a whimsical and incorrect usage. Two counties, Inverness and Perth, also give their names to their capital towns: when the town rather than the county is referred to, it will be made plain. (One could avoid this problem by appending 'shire' to the county, but the suffix is really an English import: besides, consistency would require such grotesqueries as 'Sutherlandshire'.)

Alert readers will notice that the name of Scotland's most eminent royal dynasty is spelled 'Stewart' until 1603, and 'Stuart' thereafter. In fact they are really two different dynasties. The direct line of Stewart Kings, who spelled their name in the Scottish style, ended with Mary, Queen of Scots. She married Henry Stuart, Lord Darnley; he was her distant cousin in the male line (though much more closely related to her by shared Tudor blood) but wrote his name in the French fashion. Thus his descendants spelled it, from James VI's accession to the English throne in 1603, to the last of the line, Henry Stuart, Cardinal York, priestly brother to the Bonnie Prince, who died in 1807.

Two common misspellings of Lewis placenames – 'Callernish' and 'Stornaway' – are entirely wrong. Skye's famous mountains are the Cuillin, not the Coolin, still less the Cuillin Hills. A croft is a rented holding of land, not the house built on it. It was common to refer to all the Hebrides as the Western Isles, but – since the advent of Comhairle nan Eilean – the term has been applied exclusively to the Outer Hebrides; it has been the name of the parliamentary seat they exclusively compose since its creation in 1918. There are two lines of Clan MacLeod: Mac-Leod of Lewis, and MacLeod of Harris. The MacLeod of Harris title is still correct, and is used here throughout, though the seat of that clan chief has been at Dunvegan, in Skye, since the eighteenth century. Notwithstanding the claims of the clan society, the MacLeods of Lewis, and of Raasay, owe no allegiance whatever to John MacLeod of MacLeod, present chief at Dunvegan, and are not of his house.

It is gratifying, come to think of it, that even today such a minor matter can still rankle. But that, perhaps, is the strongest feature of the Highland psyche: a long, long memory. History here is much more than books. It is the oral tradition, things handed down from father to son, mother to daughter, grand-mother to child. Oral tradition should not be lightly dismissed. In many spheres – such as that notorious field, Hebridean genealogy – traditional knowledge or lore is more to be trusted than the early (and often inept) documentary sources. And they are still alive in Morar, who have family traditions of the '45; in Skye, whose forebears told of the Battle of the Braes; in the

Black Isle, who relate anecdotes of the Disruption. And far beyond – in Canada, Australia, the veldt of Africa, the suburbs of Glasgow – there are still to be found many who know something, eagerly treasured, of the history of their family in the old country, things unrecorded by historians, never found in books.

We have long memories. That is a great strength. And we hold great grudges. That is our worst weakness.

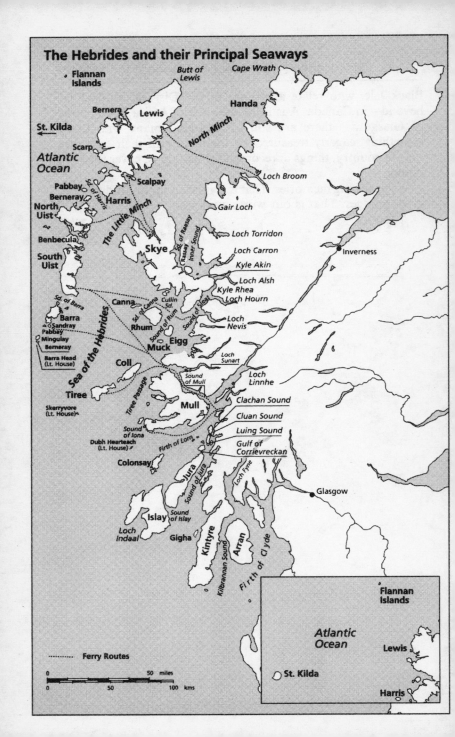

The Hebrides and their Principal Seaways

CHAPTER TWO

Holy Is Your Dream

Iomair ò, 'illean mhara
Iomair ò, 'illean mhara
Illean ò, hò ro èile
I mo ghaoil, gur naomh do bhruadar

Iomair ò, 'illean mhara
Iomair ò, 'illean mhara
Illean ò, hò ro èile
Rìgh 'na shuain a triall gu d'chala

Row o, boys of the sea
Row o, boys of the sea
Youths o, ho ro eile
Iona my love, holy is your dream

Row o, boys of the sea
Row o, boys of the sea
Youths o, ho ro eile
A king in deep sleep, making for your port

From 'Triall Mara Na h'I', 'Iona Sea Journey'. A Gaelic song of the 'Celtic Twilight' era, about the turn of the present century, by the late Kenneth MacLeod. Simpler and less sentimental than most.

IN THE BANK of a crumbling sand-dune, by the crashing Atlantic on a bay near Northton, by the south-west corner of Harris, are crushed an incredible mass of seashells. Ancient, white, long dead – mostly the shells of limpets – they break readily in your fingers. And if you are most fortunate, and probe for a while in this conglomerate, you might find something else, a brown fragment still more brittle – a shard of pottery.

This is a midden, a rubbish-heap, and these are the leavings of a people who lived here long, long ago. A team from the University of Leicester mounted an excavation here, some decades ago. They have yet to publish their results in detail, but we know that they uncovered several layers of occupation. They even found traces of a house, roughly oval in shape, some twenty-eight feet long by fourteen feet wide, built of boulders. When inhabited and kept in good order, the walls may have been six feet in height. There are holes in these walls, to accommodate wooden posts; they would have supported a light roof, probably sewn from animal skins. Charcoal and ash, surrounded by a circle of stones, mark this family's hearth.

'Pieces of animal bone, tools of deer-antler, bone and flint were scattered on the floor,' writes Bill Lawson, 'along with broken pieces of pottery, whose shape suggests that the people of the house belonged to the group of Neolithic people known as Beaker Folk, from the shape of their most common article of pottery.' And then there are the middens, composed of red peat-ash, and all those seashells, and the bones of animals, game and primitive livestock and birds. The grave of a small child was uncovered by the Leicester team.

This was one of the earliest settlements in the West Highlands; probably first occupied by man some three millennia before the birth of Christ. Successive generations of men and women lived here, and there is evidence that for a time the site was abandoned, then reoccupied. The later community, at least, must have been sophisticated. They kept sheep and cattle. They were able to make pottery; they probably grew crops. The original settlers were of the hunter-gatherer type; they killed things, and ate wild plants and fruits. Shellfish were evidently a mainstay of their diet.

People, if you can believe archaeologists and such things as carbon-dating, were in Scotland long before that. Tests on charcoal and other human artefacts found in Fife date the earliest traces of humankind in Scotland between 61000 BC to 4165 BC. There are traces of settlement at Kinloch, on the isle of Rhum, that are judged some 8000 years old. But the glaciers of the Ice Age, advancing and retreating, may well have destroyed evidence of earlier human life over much of Scotland.

The Hebrides, beyond doubt, were colonised much later than the mainland. W. H. Murray quotes a date of 3800 BC, from carbon-readings on sites such as Northton. This was in the mid-Atlantic period, when Scotland was a good deal warmer than it is now – some 4°F in mean temperatures over the present day. All the islands were thick with woods of birch and hazel. The great forests of the mainland swarmed with game and wildlife. Thus the earliest settlers – Mesolithic man – kept no animals and tended no crops, and could still live. They fed off wood, field and shore as they could, and there do not seem to have been very many of them; they seem to have been confined to the west coast of Scotland, including Argyll and the Hebrides. This suggests that they came from Ireland. It is reasonable to assume, too, that they could sail, or at least paddle. Life must have been precarious for those people. Their settlements were little more than camp-sites. They had hazards to contend with, too, unlikely to confront the Highland camper today – wolves and brown bears.

We can still identify these sites by those middens, especially evident on sandy shoreland like that of Northton, where drifting sand rapidly exaggerated the shape and size of the mounds. (Such mounds were often dubbed *sithean* by the Gaels, who

came so long after – fairy hillocks.) Interesting, if crude, tools
have been found: scrapers, chisels and choppers of chipped
stone, the odd arrowhead. Flint made the best tools, and flint
is not easy to find in the West Highlands. Mesolithic man did
rather better with bone. Needles, awls, pins, harpoons, that sort
of thing. If life for these people sounds as if it were nothing more
than a grim struggle for existence, there are notes of a lighter
side to their existence. Little cowrie shells have been found by
the hundred, each neatly bored with two holes, and evidently
made so for stringing into necklaces. So life was more than
limpet (though limpets are very good food; palatable even raw,
if you scrape off the entrails and munch the leathery foot).

They got about by coracle, a round craft of skins stretched
about a light frame. (Dug-out canoes would have been useless in
West Highland waters; they would have quickly foundered.)
Coracles and the curragh – a later development – would convey
Highland travellers for thousands of years to come. And Ireland
– only eighteen miles' passage from the Mull of Kintyre – had
much yet to offer the Highlands.

Neolithic man followed, some hundreds of years later, and
advanced civilisation. Spurts of human migration from Europe
to the great islands of Britain were thickening into a steady if
slow stream. These settlers brought skill upon skill. They knew
how to sow and raise crops, how to break the soil. They could
tend livestock. They tamed dogs. Above all, they could work
stone and metal. (The classical divisions are Neolithic, Bronze
and Iron Ages, but it was a good deal more blurred than that.)
Even the stone tools were of high quality. Neolithic man could
fashion flint axes so good he could fell trees with them. His
pottery, if coarse, was most functional. He tended sheep, cows,
pigs and goats. It is believed he originated in the east, in Asia;
that he moved westwards (perhaps in response to climatic
change, as the drying of grasslands later drove barbarians to
Rome) and that he moved into Europe up the Danube in one
direction, and along the Mediterranean coast in another, reach-
ing Ireland from Spain, and the Hebrides and the West Highlands from Ireland.

Their boats must have been huge. After all, they brought farm
animals, tools, their families. It is reckoned that a coracle of
thirty-two feet in diameter could have taken at least three tons of

cargo, including a dozen people and much livestock. They were
sufficiently skilled in navigation to exploit the tides of the west,
which would have borne a coracle northwards and inshore with
relatively little effort. But we speculate. Time and decay have
removed all but the imperishable evidence. We have no surviving coracles, or clothes, or utensils of wood and leather.

They lived in houses similar to the Northton type, but their
most spectacular memorials are their places of burial – the
chambered cairns, mighty things of drystone walling, and many
of these survive throughout the West Highlands. The best
examples are at Crinan, on the Kintyre isthmus. North Uist,
too, abounds in the stone monuments of these early peoples.
In these they laid their dead – sometimes buried, sometimes
cremated – and buried animals with them too, and ornaments
and pottery. They had religion of a sort; they evidently believed
those things could be of use in an afterlife. They also had
medicine and surgery. Skulls have been found with holes drilled
in them – perhaps to remove cysts or to relieve some kind of pain
– and, as the edges have healed, some at least survived these
operations.

But at Callanish stands the greatest memorial to the early
people of all. Callanish is a village at the head of Loch Roag, in
Lewis, and here is a world-famous circle of standing stones,
second in importance only to Stonehenge. (Indeed, stone circles
abound in that corner of Lewis; there are several more in the
Callanish area itself, as well as at Shawbost, Garynahine and
Achmore.) But the main construction stands on an elevated
knoll offering spectacular views of the district, out to the Park
and Uig hills, and over the townships of the Loch Roag coast,
and out to the Atlantic. The stones here are in the form of a
Celtic cross – a long cross with a circle surrounding the junction
– though they predate the Christian faith by at least fifteen
centuries.

The structure is complex in detail. In the centre is a roofless
chambered cairn. Below its base were found, on excavation in
1844, two stone beehive chambers which yielded tiny fragments
of human bone. These were topped by the two pillar-stones of a
dolmen, the table of which lay in the passage. (No other dolmens
are known of in Scotland, though there are good examples in
Ireland.) The Callanish stones, then, include a circle, this cairn, a

dolmen, the cruciform lines of the overall arrangement and a long aisle down the main avenue of stone.

The 1844 excavation was careless, and probably obliterated important details. At least thirty of the stones have vanished, over the centuries, though now and again a determined archaeologist has found one lying in the district, and triumphantly restored it to its right position. As the cruciform arrangement is somewhat skewed, it is even suggested that the structure has drifted in the peat. (At the 1844 excavation, no less than five feet of bog had to be stripped away to expose the full height of these megaliths.)

The thesis of drift is now generally disbelieved. But it remains a mystery as to what, precisely, these magnificent stones at Callanish were for. They obviously had ceremonial and religious significance to their builders. And the construction of the site would have required much labour and organisation; a highly ordered society once lived here. Much original and exciting work has been done on the Callanish stones in recent years, and it is now beyond dispute that the alignment of the stones is deliberately for astronomical measurement and observation. Events in the day and night skies, of remarkable complexity, can be plotted and tracked with great accuracy from using the stones as 'sights' from different angles.

The most spectacular such event – and one which, as demonstrated in magnificent photographs by Margaret Curtis, Callanish resident and the popular expert on the subject – is the rare Major Lunar Standstill, which happens only once every eighteen years. On this occasion the moon rises by the Park hills and moves dramatically along their silhouette, beaming from ridge to ridge; then along the Harris hills, still dancing, and finally to set behind the Uig hills. At a critical point in this movement – to viewers in the avenue of the main Callanish structure – a man standing on the high summit of the knoll, just beyond the tip of the stone alignment, is spectacularly framed by the huge, luminescent moon, as da Vinci's *Proportions of Man*. Thus, in ancient times, a priest may have appeared to the people gathered here, his detailed knowledge of astronomy, his skill in using these stones to predict and time such events, adding to the awe in which he was held.

So many standing stones and circles dot the Hebrides that,

even today, no complete list has been made. Three megaliths on the west coast of Harris – at Nisabost, Scarista and the offshore island of Taransay – form the points of a right-angled triangle, the angle far too precise to be mere coincidence. A mighty standing stone is the Clach an Trushall in the north-west of Lewis, within the township of Ballantrushal. It is surrounded by houses and crofts, but stands in open land; no man has dared claim this monument for his own. The Clach an Trushall is nineteen feet high, six feet wide and nearly four feet thick. Tradition relates that it was a place of execution; miscreants were backed up against it, and stoned to death. But it was old even when that was done. These lone stones probably were erected for calendar purposes. It has been remarked that the Nisabost stone (Clach Mhicleoid) and three other standing stones on North Uist, Benbecula and South Uist – even Clach an Trushall – are aligned towards Boreray, the highest point of St Kilda, occasionally visible on the western horizon. The sun, at times of equinox, sets behind Boreray as seen from these points, and the stones helped delineate the calendar.

The Callanish stones were once, perhaps, the centre of a cult and famed beyond Scotland; they may well be that 'Winged Temple of the Hyperboreans' of which Herodotus wrote, from which a priest named Abaros came, part of an academic exchange between the leaders of thought in Greece and Ireland.

In the first millennium before Christ, the Celts came to Europe. They were a travelling people, pastoral, driving their herds, and probably of Aryan origin, from the mountainous lands south of the Caspian Sea. The Celts were big, strong folk, generally red or fair of hair, their eyes blue. About 900 BC they mastered the use of iron, and established themselves in Austria, spreading from there across the whole of northern Europe. In the fourth century before Christ, they raided and sacked Rome – a humiliation the citizens never forgot. They were strong in northern France, in Spain, about Switzerland. The Romans called them Galli, or Gauls; even then, the Gaels had their name. Their language, known as P-Celtic, is the progenitor of the modern Celtic tongues. Some of the earliest Celts spoke another language entirely, which we know only by its Ogham script on assorted inscriptions; it is quite lost. It seems to have had no

Indo-European base, a linguistic freak, like the Basque language still surviving today.

They were already in Britain. A particularly formidable tribe of Celts, the Belgicae, arrived in the first century BC. They brought remarkable new skills. They had heavy ploughs, better able to break deforested soil. They used pottery wheels. They minted coins in gold. They were ruthless traders, and keen to export; they rapidly established a prosperous trade to the Continent, in metals, grains, and slaves. They were greedy for good land. They soon reached Scotland, and posed such a threat that a mighty range of stone forts and earthworks were thrown up against them. It is from this era that the oldest fortifications date.

It was in Ireland that the Gaels established hegemony, forming statelets, each with its own king. For their own defence, and better to act in concerted interest, these little kingdoms formed five great confederations. The names of these confederations still mark Ireland's ancient provinces – Leinster, Munster and so on – and the greatest of them all was in the north-west, the land of Ulster.

The Belgicae made such a pest of themselves to the Romans – both in supporting subversion in France, and as a centre of the Druidical religion – that in the reign of the Emperor Claudius the Romans finally invaded and conquered Britain. But they never succeeded in crushing Scotland. The first Scot in history is a man called Calgacus, and all we know of him is that he fought the Roman legions under Agricola in AD 84, in the reign of Domitian, twelfth of the Caesars. This battle was Mons Grampius, perhaps in Perthshire. Agricola was the first Roman to see the Hebrides; determined to sort Scotland out, he sailed right round it, through the Pentland Firth and south by Cape Wrath. Agricola won that battle at Mons Grampius, but with difficulty, and the Highland tribes continued a wearying campaign of guerilla warfare. The Roman empire reached its northern limits at the Antonine Wall, from the Forth to the Clyde, and apart from some outposts in modern Perthshire – Fortingall, Callandar – that was as far as Caesar reached in his war against the tribes of northern Scotland. These were a different breed entirely from the Gaels, fierce in battle, fond of hallucinogenic liquor. The Romans called them 'Painted Ones', or Picts.

The Celtic languages were already dividing from the P-Celtic root. The mother tongue we may call Classical Gaelic. Two distinct groups evolved, the Gadelic – from which we gain modern Irish, Gaelic and Manx – and Brythonic: modern Welsh, Breton, and the virtually extinct Cornish. The Gaels of Ulster spoke in the Gadelic tongue. These Picts were not illiterate. Their placenames still survive, and the names of their kings, and even some stone inscriptions. They must have been in Scotland long before the other Celts reached Ireland, and they too had obviously come, somewhere in the distant past, from these Aryan mountains. Perhaps they were among those first settlers from Ireland, millennia before. We will never know.

In this troubled time the building of forts continued. Some were of the dun type, and some were those curious 'vitrified' forts, the very stones melted and welded into a formidable mass by the heat of great fires. No one knows if they were deliberately processed thus in the building, or whether this vitrification was the result of being fired by enemies, but we do know that they are unique to Scotland. None has ever been found in England and Wales. There are mighty hill forts of the more traditional type: one survives at Dunadd, in Argyll. This was the capital of that kingdom of Dalriada, formed by the Irish Gaels when they began to colonise Scotland. And another fort at Craig Phadraig, Inverness, may have been the capital of the Picts. We shall read, shortly, of an important summit there between a Gaelic churchman and a Pictish king. The greatest fort of all is on Islay, the Great Mound, enclosing nearly three acres of ground. From here, after AD 300, a huge Irish expeditionary force marshalled to wage war of conquest on Argyll.

As for duns, like the standing stones no one has bothered to count them. The proliferation of 'dun' in placenames – Lewis alone must have a dozen Loch an Duines – shows they were ubiquitous. The walls of a dun might be ten feet thick and the structure some fifty feet in diameter. The walls had chambers and galleries. Many Hebridean duns were built on islets. All commanded fine views of the landscape about them. They were positioned to keep a watch on the coast; they were often built within sight-line of each other, and may have been able to signal by beacon. They were places of shelter in interesting times, when invasion and ransack were recurring hazards. But they certainly could not have withstood a long or determined siege, especially by a large force.

The finest duns were the brochs, like that at Carloway, built of stone and sited on commanding heights. They are also unique to Scotland. Nearly 500 are recorded, and their remnants still visible, about the coast. The structures, of cooling-tower outline, were of great internal complexity and the standard of masonry high. But only one broch – that at Mousa – has been found with an internal source of water: a spring or a well. They must have been designed for short-term use in times of great trouble, but this is disputed. Yet, without water, their sheltering inhabitants could not have borne long siege. (Mousa, fortunate in this regard, resisted siege by an Earl of Orkney as late as 1154.)

And it may well be that historians misunderstand the threat; that these brochs (which are found in the far north Highlands and Islands, and especially thick about Skye and the north-west of Lewis) were not built against Celtic migrants at all. Already, perhaps, the Scandinavian predators – the Vikings – were making their presence felt. There is some evidence for this, and there is some evidence against it, and the debate still engages the happy energies of many a Scottish and Celtic historian.

The Romans had taken a name home for these isles of the north-west, the isles viewed by Agricola and his fleet – Hebudes, as Pliny recorded it in the first century. And this lends support to the thesis that the Norsemen were already familiar with the islands of north-west Scotland. For it sounds like nothing so much as a phonetical rendering (blurred by the Latin accent) of Havbredev, pronounced 'Haubredey'. *Hav* is sea, *bred* is edge, and *ev* is island. And 'isles on the edge of the sea' is a pretty good description of the Hebrides.

Whatever was happening in the Outer Isles, the inhabitants of the southern Hebrides – and mainland Argyllshire – had other visitors to contend with. From 220 onwards, they were determinedly colonised by the Scots of Dalriada, a district of Antrim, in Ulster. For the large part, this movement was peaceful. The Scots and the Epidii – as the Celts of Argyll were known – had close links already, in trade and commerce. Their language was similar. It took the Picts some generations to grasp the mounting threat to their south-west, but by the fifth century Argyll had become a new realm, and named after the mother county –

Dalriada. By the fifth century, Dalriada was an independent kingdom of Gaelic-speaking Scots. And fired by a new religion, from the Middle East: faith in Jesus Christ.

What of the Druids? Little is known of this cult, save passing mentions by assorted Greek and Roman historians. They had a fascination with the afterlife, and reincarnation in particular. They are popularly remembered for their veneration of oak trees and the parasitical mistletoe, though these may not have figured as important symbols in Pictish Druidism. Julius Caesar, writing about his conquests in Gaul – as the Romans knew the greater part of France – speculated that it was this certainty in life after death which lent the Celts such valour in battle. The Druids in Gaul were given an extraordinary training, some twenty years; and to reach the highest level of ordination one had to undergo horrifying tests of physical and mental stamina. For example, an ordinand would be required to compose a song, and play it with instrumental accompaniment, to one of the many complex bardic metres – and the metre would be told him just before he was immersed, for a night, in a tank of cold water, with only his nostrils breaking the surface, and a boulder or two on his chest. When he was permitted to leave this uncomfortable bed, he had to play the song he had meantime been composing on the spot.

And so on. The highest tests of ordination were so dangerous, and of such a mortality rate, that only a handful of men dared to attempt them. These Druids are best remembered for their intellectualism. They were expert in the arts, in mathematics, in astronomy and philosophy. They were authorities in matters of law. Of their occult and religious practices we know virtually nothing. It is no doubt from them that such Highland superstitions as *deiseal* – the necessity of performing every significant activity or journey clockwise, from left to right – descends.

Some physical features of the Celtic culture survived into historic times, and are still of symbolic importance today. Tartan had already developed by the Roman occupation, with various patterns of striped cloth signifying a certain district, and the range of colours a certain rank. (A king might wear seven colours, a Druid six, a nobleman four, according to old tradition.) By modern standards, frankly, both Picts and Scots wore very little. They usually went bare-legged and wore only two overshirts or woollen tunics. Many wore undressed sheepskins. They had simple leather shoes. Inured to the cold, they stripped quite naked for battle, and went to fight with tribal patterns painted on their skins. The chiefs might go to battle on chariots, which the Celts manoeuvred with great skill. Their favourite weapon was the great sword; this survived as the Highland claymore, though by the '45 the name referred to a smaller basket-hilted blade. And they wielded short stabbing spears. They had small round leather shields – targes – but practised only mediocre archery; bows and arrows did become central to Highland warfare, but not to the same heights of skill as were attained in England.

They seem to have had a curious social structure. The clan system was already apparent, with territorial kings and chiefs presiding over free and classless men of equal right. (There was an underclass, of men and women enslaved as a punishment for offence, or incomers not of the tribe, but the poor aboriginals of some conquered territory.) But primogeniture, if understood, was not practised; under the old Celtic law of Tanistry, succession was linear. A brother, or even a cousin, had a stronger claim to inherit a title of power than a son. Transitions in power, then, were complex, and the death of a chief could trigger bloody wars.

Even more oddly, they had no institution of marriage. Men and women lived in what we would today call free love, and children were raised by the whole clan, and not as part of a smaller family unit. As paternity would have been a matter of much argument (had they greatly cared) succession to all offices came through the female line. Boys won independence from their parents at the age of fourteen, but were not counted men until they had grown a full circle of beard.

The system was aristocratic in many respects. Certain family lines were highly esteemed, and there was a royal class. But it was not feudal. A clan claimed common ancestry and kinship with the chief. Land belonged to no individual – certainly not the chief – but to the whole clan. Though office was hereditary, it was thus confined to families, not individuals. From a given number of men eligible, by birth, to hold some post of honour, the clan chose by election. The chief thus appointed was presented with cattle, chariots, and various goods fit to invest him and his immediate kin with the dignity of office. Though he had the right of jurisdiction – the power even to condemn to death – he could be deposed if found wanting.

It was not a bad system of government. All had dignity within it, in an era where elsewhere in Europe the gentry treated the peasantry as so much cattle. A clansman met his chief as an equal – regarding the office, not the man – and could speak bluntly with him, and to him. Male relatives of the chief would be designated chieftains, to construct a chain of command. He would even dub one his *tanistear*, the second, as heir-apparent – always an old and wise man; the Celts did not esteem youth and zeal in important office – but such appointment had to be endorsed by the clan, and a chief had still to pass election to assume office. Tacitus (who wrote the life of Agricola; he was his son-in-law) pinpointed one danger of the society. All enmities, as well as all friendships, were collective. If one clansman were to be insulted by a member, all were outraged on his behalf. Without wise chiefs, tribal warfare would be the result.

Law was administered by judges, 'brehons'; they were later known as brieves, and the office survived in Lewis – through a powerful family of Morrisons – until Reformation days. Confiscation of cattle was the general penalty; beasts forfeit went to the pursuer, or the chief. The brehons were granted glebes, and a proportion of fines, for their maintenance. Courts were always public, usually in the open air. For truly dreadful offences, both Scots and Picts would be impaled on stakes and burned alive.

But the Scots were in Dalriada, and fast expanding, and rapidly adopting the Christianity that was now firmly established in Ireland. Ireland today is a tragic land, divided socially, widely (if unfairly) mocked as culturally backward. It is hard now to imagine that, in the days we laughably insist on calling the Dark Ages, literacy and learning flourished in the Emerald Isle. While Europe wallowed in post-Roman squalor, Ireland was the one light of order, truth and beauty. And in Ulster especially there flourished good and able men, increasingly eager to spread the blessings of their civilisation to the benighted souls of north-west Scotland.

Conflict, at every level, was the result over the Irish Sea. Increasingly Scots and the Picts fought. The victory for Christianity, though, and the unifying of Gaelic Scotland, was not in the end to be won by claymore and targe. It was won by a missionary, and he came to Scotland, if we can believe tradition, expressly to flee from war, of which he had a deep and painful horror.

'That man is little to be envied, whose piety would not grow warmer amidst the sacred ruins of Iona,' wrote Samuel Johnson, after his visit to the island with James Boswell. Iona is a little island off the western extremity of Mull, and for century upon century has been a place of pilgrimage. It was from Iona, it seems, that the Gospel first became known in the Hebrides. It was through that Gospel, and through the life and work of the Celtic Church, that the Gaels conquered the Highlands. Within 500 years, the Picts – their history, their language, their race – had vanished as if they had never been.

Columba was holy, but he was neither soft nor effete. True, the name 'Columba' is Latin for dove, but this did not match his personality, which was quick to action, nor temper. In Gaelic he is known as Colum Cille. The name was probably conferred on him at his dedication to the religious life, in early childhood. His original name appears to be unknown. But we do know quite a bit about the saint; a long Irish eulogy was composed for him, in verse, shortly after his death, and at the end of the seventh century Adomnan – a later Abbot of Iona – wrote a biography in Latin. Both survive: they are vexingly short of specific detail about Columba's work, and big on piety and edifying anecdote, but from these sources virtually all we know of Columba is drawn.

Columba, born about 521 in Ulster – tradition says it was 7 December, and that he first drew breath near Lough Garten, Donegal – was of royal blood. His family, the Ui Neill, were widely feared as Ireland's most powerful rulers. His father was Fedilmith mac Fergus, whose great-grandfather had established the house of Tara as Ulster's ruling dynasty. And Columba's mother was Eithne, descended from kings of Leinster.

That is all that is known for sure of Columba's background and early life. He was forty-two years old when he came to Scotland, around 563, and Irish tradition – undocumented at the time – maintains his exile, in evangelistic service, was an act of penitence for his role in triggering a bloody Irish war.

Columba had always been fascinated by things religious and ecclesiastical. But he was of the seed of princes, warriors, robber-barons, and it repeatedly showed in his personality. The young Columba, if we heed Irish tales in the folk tradition, was at once a churchman and a politician. In his early twenties he is said to have established his first monastery. At the same time he played a part in the complicated disputes, turmoils and plottings of the secular realm. Around 563 came the vicious battle of Cul Drebene, between the Ui Neill and their massed enemies in Ulster. Legend ascribes the spark for this conflict to an act of plagiarism. It is said that Columba much admired a certain book, and asked its owner if he might be allowed to take a copy for himself. Permission was refused. Somehow, Columba abstracted the volume and – it must have been a Herculean labour – painfully copied it in longhand.

Word of this reached the owner. This was a time when books were valuable and their ownership a great matter of power and status. This fellow demanded that Columba's copy be surrendered. They went to law over it, and the judge found against Columba: 'to every cow its calf.' From this sprang war, and the battle of Cul Drebene, which left many Ulstermen dead, and Columba in agonies of guilt that haunted him for the rest of his life. He left Ulster, with twelve disciples, and sailed to Iona. He may well have been driven out – the Celtic Church would not have delighted in a cleric immersing himself in secular matters, especially if bloodshed had been the result – but for all this we have only tradition.

Now Iona, in our age and culture, seems a most remote and inappropriate place to base any movement. But that was a different world, where travel by land was laborious, where scarcely a road existed. The sea was the highway, and on channels between the Argyll coast – the kingdom of Dalriada – and Ulster focused the Celtic world. Besides, Iona – to the north of these waters – was well placed for Loch Linnhe and the Great Glen, with its chain of lochs up to Inverness; Iona was a convenient base from which to sally to Skye and all the Inner and Outer Hebrides and the entire western seaboard of Scotland. It was but a short sail from Ireland and little over a day from Crinan, at the isthmus of Kintyre, from which – by portage – the traveller could reach the Firth of Clyde and Arran, Bute and all the Clyde coast communities. Iona had another advantage: it was sufficiently far to the south to be, for the present, immune to the depredations of the Vikings.

James Hunter reminds us sharply that no one, then, thought of the Hebrides as peripheral. This was a world before cities, before industry, before roads. He calculates that today, the journey Columba took, from northern Ireland to Iona, would take at least two days, require three separate sea crossings and several hundred miles of road. In winter it might even take three days. But Columba's route – granted fair winds and long summer daylight – was less than a hundred miles and could have been done in one day.

Nor was Dalriada as alien a place to Columba as you might suppose. The people of Dalriada were kith and kin, speaking the same Gaelic language. Their ruler, Conall, was Columba's cousin. Columba had to visit him to negotiate the Iona mission; such matters were highly sensitive, and the people of Iona might not be entirely pleased by another descent of monks.

For Iona had a Christian community already. (There is an inveterate myth that Columba founded the Christian cause on that island, almost as ignorant as the surprisingly common notion that he brought Christianity to Scotland.) Little is known of this first monastery, though: tradition says it was founded by one Oran, whose thunder Columba stole. It is further, and colourfully, maintained that when Columba built his abbey Oran insisted on being buried alive in the foundations. After a day or two Columba grew concerned and opened up the work to see how Oran was. Oran declared he was doing just fine, so they walled him up again. We need not believe such nonsense.

The Gospel had been in Scotland since the second century; it sped rapidly through the empire after Christ's Ascension. Ninian had founded a mission at Whithorn in 397. Brendan of Clonfert had founded a little place on a Firth of Lorne island, Eilean an Naoimh, twenty-one years before Columba saw Iona. Moluag was already established on Lismore. Columba was not the first to bring the Evangel, but he was the first statesman of the Celtic Church in Scotland, and it was he who gave it, in the Hebrides and the Highlands, cohesion, vision and will. Through him, too, the Gaels took the country.

So Columba and his twelve followers sailed from Ireland,

almost certainly from Derry, out of Lough Foyle. They would
have made the voyage by curragh, a long boat of frame and skin,
with mast and lug-sail; it seems likely they took the passage up
the west coast of Islay, avoiding the dangerous tides and eddies
of the Sound of Jura. (In 1963, someone actually went to the
trouble of proving this by sailing a curragh on this Ireland-to-
Iona voyage himself.) The curragh, light and flimsy as it
appears, is in fact a formidable sea-boat: Irish fishermen used
them into the present century, and mighty voyages were made in
Columba's own millennium to the Faeroes, to Iceland, even
(almost certainly) to Greenland and North America. There is
tantalising evidence to that effect in the Irish chronicle of
Brendan. And would it not be wonderful to believe that the
Gaels beat even the Vikings to America, a millennium before
Columbus sailed the ocean blue?

Columba seems to have landed on Islay, and on Oronsay (a
tidal island off Colonsay) during the journey. It was a leisurely
enough passage. Is tradition true? Was this the driven, bitter
voyage of a man sick with shame and remorse? There is an
ancient Gaelic verse – often attributed to Columba himself –
describing, in much sentimental language, the pain of exile, as
the hero stands in the stern of the boat, gazing with 'soft grey
eye' to the vanishing hills of Ireland. Had he even been
forbidden to settle somewhere within sight of the hills of
Erin? He certainly passed the Mull of Kintyre, Gigha, and
Islay, and Jura, and Colonsay and Oronsay, 'from all of which
the Irish mountains can readily be glimpsed on the horizon,'
writes James Hunter, 'and made his landfall at last on Iona.
From there no part of Ireland can be seen.'

The Celtic Church is a much misunderstood body. The Roman
Catholic Church, in Ireland and Scotland, has seized claim to its
inheritance; but much in Roman practice would have appalled
the Celtic saints. In recent times the Church of Scotland – in the
form of the contemporary Iona Community, and all its irritating
hairy people – has allied the name of the Celtic Church to
pacifism, Marxism, vegetarianism, environmentalism, and
whatever New Age fad of political correctness fits the moment.

Whatever the Celtic Church was, it was not Roman Catholic.
The Christianity of western Europe was divorced from Rome at

the time of the fall of the Western empire – 410 – when assorted
Goths, Visigoths, Huns and Vandals overran the former ordered provinces of Caesar. So the Celtic Church – the Church
that, for some centuries, dominated Ireland and Scotland and
much of England – evolved separately. It was a good deal more
biblical, in its order and practice, than the degenerating Church
of Rome. The Roman Church was diocesan and episcopal, with
authority rigidly held through a hierarchy of bishops. At local
level it operated from a church, where mass was celebrated by a
single friar. The Celtic Church was Presbyterian and monastic.
It operated from monasteries – communities. These were
administered by an abbot – a *presbyter* – and he was assisted
by elders. There was an office of bishop – *episkopos* – in the
Celtic Church, but these had no precedence, no authority over
the abbots. They seem to have existed purely for consecration
and ordination ceremonies. The most obvious physical difference between a Roman and a Celtic brother would have been the
haircut. The Roman tonsure was the shaving only of the crown
of the head. The tonsure of a Celtic brother was the shaving of
the whole forehead in front of the ears.

It was not as organised a communion as the Roman Church.
This arm of Christianity was much looser, more fragmented, its
many communities and chapels united rather by a prevailing
ethos of practical Christianity and their sturdy independence
from Rome. The Celtic Church celebrated Easter on a different
date from the Roman communion. Its liturgy, too, was distinct.
Celtic bishops were ordained by only one consecrated bishop; in
the Roman rite, three were employed. The Venerable Bede
records (without detail) that their practice in baptism was at
variance with Roman ritual. The Celtic Church had high regard
for the Sabbath, and kept it strictly. The monastic life in the
Celtic Church always tended to the ascetic, though it did not
reach its later and notorious extremes for many generations
after Columba's death. But even the monasticism was tempered
by two features not common in Roman monasteries: a fascination with spreading learning and education, and an intense
passion for evangelism. Celtic communities were not fortresses
of refuge from the world; they were camps for its spiritual
conquest.

Above all, they acknowledged no head of the Church save

'Our Lord'; in this they anticipated post-Reformation Presbyterianism, and they certainly had no regard for the Papacy.

Celtic monasteries were simple buildings. Columba's church and monastic houses on Iona were built of wood and wattle, with an earthwork boundary high enough to keep the cattle out. The roofs were thatched. It is reasonable to assume that the abbey was on the same site as the present mighty stone buildings of Iona, which are of much later construction. Columba had but these twelve men to found his work. They would have been chosen specifically for skills in building, craft and trade. Once the premises were up and running, his Iona mission would have rapidly expanded; the normal community size for the Celtic Church was some 150 monks. Lay brothers wore a garb of leather. Clerics wore a gown of coarse, undyed wool over a white tunic, and only they bore the tonsure.

Many visitors view Iona as an ideal place for quiet, introspective, pious sloth. Columba did, indeed, take secret personal religion seriously – very seriously. But he was a man of action. He had come to Iona with a purpose. He 'sought to change the world much more than he ever sought to meditate upon it', says Hunter, quite rightly. But he portrays Columba as a figure still hungry for power, for authority, for influence. Even though Hunter does point out that the division between the ecclesiastical and the secular worlds of power was much more blurred then than now, that seems to me unfair. Columba burned with the Gospel. Columba would fire the hills and glens and isles of this strange north land with zeal for Christ, and in all he wrought in and from Iona this was his abiding purpose.

Iona offered more than geographical convenience. These Celtic missionaries always settled on fertile islands, and Iona – bare and windswept as it was – offers good *machair* grazing, that wonderful sward unique to the West Highlands and Islands. Machair is fine green turf, founded on white calcareous sands, every grain the crushed remnant of some shellfish or crustacean, rich in lime, able to soften and enrich the most thin and acid soil. All manner of herbs and plants thrive on it; sweet grass grows from it; in summer, machair smiles in a million flowers.

Though Hebridean winters are long, they are mild. And though spring comes late, the heat of summer can be intense, and daylight is so long – especially through June and July – that crops spring quickly from late beginnings.

The life of Iona, and the communities it spawned, was as practical as it was vigorous. Columba's Iona family soon expanded, as followers were attracted both locally and from Ireland. Each built his own cell, from wood and rush and clay, roofed with turf. There was work for all. Columba's community included church, refectory, a hostel for travellers, a common-room for relaxation, kitchens, a sick-bay, a library, a writing-house. Those not engaged in each department had much to do outside. Cattle were tended; crops sown, weeded, hoed, reaped, threshed, milled and stored. They fished in burn and sea. They crewed boats to bear travelling brothers and missionaries where they would, to fetch supplies, to export their surplus. Above all, they wrote, copying Scriptures – Gospels, Psalms – and from these the ordained brothers preached, in the Gaelic tongue, to the people about, and beyond. Foremost place was given, of course, to personal religion: prayer and meditation. Local children were taught to read, write, count and sing. Their parents were given instruction in fishing, in textiles, in agriculture, in animal husbandry.

Columba had a huge mission field at hand: the Picts, who still dominated the Highlands beyond Dalriada. Here he could put his old political and diplomatic skills to use. So he arranged a summit conference with the greatest Pict, King Brude himself, and on a day sailed from Iona round Mull, and up the Firth of Lorne, and up Loch Linnhe, and by portage and further sailing through the Great Glen – Loch Lochy, Loch Oich, Loch Ness – to meet the Pictish king, near Inverness, probably at his dun on Craig Phadraig. So he met King Brude and his chief Druid. Little is known of this meeting. We know that Columba required no interpreter, so either they knew Gaelic – or Latin – or Columba himself was fluent in their own tongue. There is no evidence that Brude himself was persuaded to embrace Christianity. Columba was probably too astute to press him. We do know that Columba, at length, went home with Brude's safe-conduct, and full permission from the Pictish sovereign to unleash his monks and preachers throughout the realm without fear of molestation. It was a remarkable achievement, all the more so because Picts and Scots were presently at war.

Soon monasteries and churches were rising throughout the Highlands. And beyond. It was an Iona monk, Aidan, who became the first Bishop of Lindisfarne, off Northumbria. Bathan, who had been one of Columba's twelve 'apostles', founded a community of his own, on Tiree. Donan was another of that twelve. He established a community at Eigg, in the Small Isles, and then he and all his followers were slaughtered by Vikings as they celebrated Easter mass; he was, then, perhaps Scotland's first martyr. Canice, or Coinneach, was with Columba when he met King Brude. This Coinneach is reputed to have built the first church – the first civilised thing – in what is now St Andrews. Drostan, of ascetic instinct, went to live in solitary meditation at Glenesk, before becoming the first Abbot of Deer, in the Buchan district of Aberdeenshire.

There was Finan the Leper, and it is said he (miraculously) healed a child of this leprosy by taking it on himself. Machar had come with Columba from Ireland too. He evangelised on Mull; became a bishop; went to evangelise the Picts of Aberdeenshire, and is said to have founded the Granite City itself. Certainly the church of Old Aberdeen is dedicated to him.

There was Maelrubha, perhaps the greatest Columba disciple of all. He was kindred to Columba; he had studied under Comgall of Bangor. Perhaps the foremost missionary to the Picts, he founded a noted community at Applecross, in Wester Ross, and from there based his missions. Many placenames in that area – Loch Maree, Mulruby, and so on – derive from him. Even today, the Gaelic name of Applecross – A Chomraich, sanctuary – recalls this good man.

Moluag founded a community too, at Lismore in the Firth of Lorne. He was in tradition both friend and rival to Columba. Another Bangor-educated man, he was actually a Scot, and his work was particularly extensive in the Hebrides as well as the West Highland mainland. The parish of Kilmallie is named for him; so are the two Kilmoluags, on Skye and Tiree. An admirer dedicated a chapel to 'St Luag' on the Harris coast of Loch Seaforth, according to tradition; there are ruins at the summit of the ancient burial ground in Maraig township, which are almost certainly its remnants. Moluag died at Rosemarkie, on the Black Isle, in 572.

Ronan was an Irish saint of the eighth century, who began his career at Iona. He was another Hebridean evangelist. A chapel was dedicated to him on North Rona, forty miles and more north-west of the Butt of Lewis.

And there were many, many others, their names unknown, their deeds unrecorded.

Columba himself did not spend much time on the missionary circuit. He did personally preach to a gathering of Picts, on at least one occasion, but most of his time he devoted to strict personal religion, to the administration (and discipline) of his community on Iona, and to the rare diplomatic foray. He returned to Ireland on several occasions – more evidence that should guard us against the tradition he fled the place in misery and disgrace. He founded another community in Ireland, in fact, at Murrow.

Columba was a great man, one of the greatest in the history of Scotland, for vision and achievement and sheer goodness. He attracted the admiration of none other than the Venerable Bede, ardent Romanist that he was. Writing centuries after Columba's death, Bede recorded that the monks of Iona had founded untold monasteries and churches in the wild lands of the Picts. But, 'Iona's monastery long held pre-eminence over most of the monasteries of the Scots, and over all the monasteries of the Picts, and was above them in community rule . . .' Of Columba himself, Bede wrote, 'this we know for certain, that he left successors renowed for their continency, their love of God and their observance of the monastic rites.'

Of course, the Celtic Church had been quite wrong about Easter, 'by reason of their being so far away from the rest of the world,' said Bede, with southern arrogance. But by his day Columba was long, long dead, the Celtic Church marginalised and increasingly eccentric.

Columba had made this little western island a centre of events: a place it would retain for some centuries. It became an ecclesiastical centre for all the northern British Isles. It became a steering place for history itself. In the time of Columba, the West Highlands made things happen. From the decline of his Christian tradition, things began to happen to them. The long and wretched course of the Highlands to passive victimhood had yet to begin. They could even aspire to educate and edify the English, whose land was overrun with immigrants, dark in illiteracy, half pagan, torn by a hundred petty feuds and wars, governed – insofar as England was governed at all – by a host of uncouth, violent, murderous robber-barons. The community of Columba could hear of dreadful things from England, and sigh at the poor folk of that vast and unhappy land, so far from the civilisation about Iona.

Here flowered diplomacy. Columba might receive a deputation of Welsh-speaking Britons from Strathclyde. And there would have been plenty of important visitors from Ireland. The clergy of northern England found their way here. (Northumbria, for some time, would look to Iona as its spiritual heartland, until Augustine of Canterbury took southern England for Rome, and at length southern England took Northumberland.)

Kings of Scots would, for generations after, be buried here. As all Pictland now venerated Iona – for its crops, its medicine, its art, if not for its faith – so it would be, in time, the more readily subsumed into the Scottish kingdom and under the Scottish crown.

Learning and the arts thrived on Iona. Its magnificent Celtic cross is among the most famed symbols in Scottish iconography. And then there are those wonderful manuscripts, the books and writings, lovingly copied by the finest penmen of that age – the immaculate script, the radiant illuminated capitals, the lovingly detailed illustration, the clarity and style of the written words themselves. The men of Iona did not merely produce religious writings; they copied, and preserved, all sorts of literature. In those sculptures, in that illustration, they also incorporated much, by way of symbolism, far older than Christianity.

There was, then, a wisdom to the Celtic missionaries: in bringing the Gospel to these lands, they did not insist on the extirpation of all else in art, language and culture. All that was evil, of course, that was idolatrous or vile, had to be repudiated. But folk legend, tribal tradition, old arts of healing, old poems and songs and story: these were encouraged. They were even set down on paper by the writers of Iona, to be saved for future generations. Some of those tales major in bloody warfare. Others are full of love, romantic and epic and erotic. But it is through these servants of the Celtic Church that we know, today, some of the oldest oral tradition in Europe: the legends of Deirdre, Finn, Cuchullain and Ossian.

So lore and legend survived, in daily life and through song and story sung by winter fires, lore and legend that has perished elsewhere. It was many centuries after the decline of the Celtic Church before meaningful religion – the power of Evangelicalism – would again explode in the Highlands. Some evangelicals tried to suppress the traditions and superstitions of the people (though not as many, nor with such a degree of success, as some historians might have you believe). To this day, then, something of other realms – second sight, and so on – survives, if very quietly, in the Highland culture.

Columba himself, that prince – 'the blessed man', as Adomnan usually calls him in his gloriously subjective biography – sought none of the pleasures of power and privilege. He accumulated no wealth. He wore the same garb as his disciples. He slept in the same bare sort of turf and stone cell as they. He played his own full part in manual labour. He, too, toiled in the writing-room. He may have relaxed in poetry; there are verses, still extant, ascribed to him in tradition, full of the sound of the sea and the cry of seabirds, and of very good quality.

He lived to the age of seventy-five, a good span. On a Saturday evening in the summer of 597, after a full day, Columba blessed some corn in a barn, did some copying, said goodbye to his pony, confided to an attendant that this would be his last day in our world, climbed to his favourite vantage-point to bestow a benediction on the island, and then repaired to his stone cot. At midnight he suddenly rose and ran into the church, where he collapsed before the altar; the brethren cradled him in their arms as he died.

W. H. Murray records, in his understated way: 'Columba's work made possible the union of the several parts of Celtic civilisation in Alba. From Fergus to James VI, sixty-three kings succeeded each other in 1,100 years, and forty-eight of these lie buried on Iona. For a thousand years after Columba's death, his island was everywhere known as *I-Chaluim-cille*, the island of St Calum. He, rather than Andrew, should have been the patron saint of Scotland.'

After the passing of Columba, Iona continued to flourish for some centuries. But the autonomy of the Celtic Church did not long survive. There was now a determined campaign from Roman bishops, in England and elsewhere, to make these brethren submit to Papal authority. The two traditions were in violent disagreement – the dating of Easter seems to have been the biggest controversy – and the one was scattered and diffuse, the other centralised, regimented, and at the heart of an empire. Above all, it had a Pope.

It was a bitter business. To the Bishop of Rome, and his minions, diversity could not be tolerated; the existence of another Christian system in Europe threatened their own stability and their own clout in matters temporal as well as spiritual. To be outwith the Roman communion was to be in sin. For the brothers of the Celtic Church, though, conformity to Rome would be an admission of past error. Things came to a head at the Synod of Whitby in 664. It is important not to make too much of this celebrated conference; but it was convened to decide – once and for all – the proper means for calculating Easter, and came down on the Roman system and against that used by the Celtic Church. So the Church of Northumbria grew distant from Iona, turned southwards, and was rapidly incorporated into the Roman communion. Scotland was now bordered, to its very gates, by Roman Catholicism. The Picts, too, were soon convinced of this Easter dating, and in 715 actually managed to impose the Roman Easter on Iona itself.

The decline of the Celtic Church was slow and the precise point of the death-rattle debatable. In the Hebrides the communities were increasingly harried by the Vikings, whose skills in shipping were improving all the while, and their voyages ever more epic and audacious. The Norman conquest of England completed final extinction of Celtic Christianity in that land. It was not long, too, before the Normans were in Ireland, and the English court soon well established in its dreadful hegemony over that great island.

It was a wedding that spelled the final death-knell for the Celtic Church in Scotland. By the eleventh century mainland Scotland was reasonably united under the monarchy of King Malcolm III, 'Malcolm Kenmore', who indeed bore the anglicised form of Columba's name. But Malcolm took for bride and queen an English princess, Margaret. This Margaret was a thoroughgoing Romanist, thoroughly English, and had nothing but contempt for the Gaelic language and the Celtic traditions. She pressed her husband into wide-reaching Church

reforms and innovations. She had churchmen brought before
her for earnest lectures on their failings. The wretched work was
continued by their son, David I. What remained of Celtic orders
on the Scottish mainland was assimilated into Roman monasticism.

The few, scattered survivors retreated into further extremes,
living as lonely hermits on sea-stacks, experimenting with
flagellation and other grotesque forms of penance. By the
end of the twelfth century, the Celtic Church had ceased to
be. The Highlands and Islands contended with less benevolent
warriors.

CHAPTER THREE

The Banner of
Red Olav

Ho bhan na ho bhan ho
Hi ho ro na hu bhan
Ho bhan na ho bhan ho
Air bhirlinn Ghoraidh Chrobhain

Fichead sonn air cul nan ramh
Fichead buile lughmhor
Siubhlaidh i mar eun a' snamh
Is siaban thonn ga sgiursadh

Ho bhan na ho bhan ho
Hi ho ro na hu bhan
Ho bhan na ho bhan ho
Air bhirlinn Ghoraidh Chrobhain

A' bhirlinn rioghail 's i a th'ann
Siubhal-sith 'na gluasad
Srol is sioda ard ri crann
'S i bratach Olaibh Ruaidh

Twenty heroes work the oars
Twenty valiant strokes
She will sail like a swimming bird
And the sea-spray powering her on

Ho bhan na ho bhan ho
Hi ho ro na hu bhan
Ho bhan na ho bhan ho
On the galley of Godred Chrobhan

The royal galley is she
Moving smoothly on
Satin and silk high on the mast
And the banner of Red Olav

From 'Birlinn Ghoraidh Chrobhain', by Duncan MacIain. Thus the glories of a Viking warlord are still sung today.

I N 794, ACCORDING to the Irish annals, the Vikings raided Skye and wrought much havoc. This is the earliest record we have of Norse assault on the Highlands, but it was certainly not the first. More and more the Vikings would descend upon the Hebrides, the West Highlands, the Northern Isles. They came at first to raid: later they came to settle.

To this day, the Gaelic of the northern Hebrides – and many of the placenames – show strong Norse influence. Indeed, but for the accidents of history, much of the north-west would be Scandinavian still. The Hebrides were under Norwegian, not Scots, sovereignty until 1266, and the isles of Orkney and Shetland lay under the Danish crown until the marriage of James III (who won them as security for his dowry; he married a princess of Denmark). The impact of the Norsemen, of their culture and ways on our region, cannot be exaggerated. Even those abiding symbols of Hebridean art, the Lewis chessmen – with their funny little faces, cross brows, sour mien – are of Norse execution.

But the early accounts of Norsemen in the Highlands and Islands are tales of atrocity and terror. Iona was repeatedly outraged, for the Vikings sought out churches and monasteries, where gold was kept for the illumination of documents, where communion vessels and fine raiment were used in worship, where corn and wine abounded. The Book of Kells – perhaps the finest surviving Celtic manuscript – was taken to Ireland around this time, expressly to be kept from Viking robbery. The Norsemen paid more visits to Iona, but islands further north took the brunt of their assaults.

It is hard to tell precisely when the Vikings stopped seeing the Hebrides as handy places for plunder, and began to settle in the region. At first they probably occupied the Scottish islands in summertime, as a base for raids on the mainland and elsewhere. Further, there was a population explosion back home. Norway was divided into twenty-nine hereditary kingdoms; under strict laws of succession, only one man could inherit each. These *fylker* played host to a fierce warrior culture. Status was a matter not of land but of how many fighting men one commanded. As economic recession, and rapidly rising population, overcrowded Norway, dozens of princelings and earls took to the seas, at the head of huge and well-armed bands of men, to engage in piracy, in the capture of slaves, in the pillage of whatever hapless land they might fall upon.

They reached Shetland first. Then Orkney. Then the Hebrides; from there they pushed north, to the Faeroes, to Iceland, to Greenland. And south, too, to the Isle of Man and to Ireland. As decades passed the Vikings hammered on all the coasts of Britain, and beyond. They certainly reached America, perhaps with Norsemen of Hebridean birth on board.

It is at this time that the Outer Isles begin to feature in written history. Rolf the Granger called at the Hebrides, around 876, on his way to that part of northern France we now, thanks to their influence, call Normandy. King Eric – who succeeded Harald the Fairhaired, when the latter abdicated in 930 – visited the Outer Isles; so did King Olav, who reigned from 968 to 1000. By his death, Jarl Torfinn Sigurdson was established as master of the Hebrides. In 1014, 'foreigners from Leodus' – Lewis Norsemen, under the banner of this Jarl – raided Ireland, according to an old manuscript.

What were these Vikings like? We have a popular notion of mighty, hairy, savage men, sailing in longboats with dragon-headed prows, springing ashore in their horned helmets with wild cries of ransack and rape. Much of this is endorsed in the tenor of Norse saga, like that happy boast of Bjorn Cripple-hand, or the verses of Egil Skalla Grimsson. These were men who exulted in the havoc they wrought. Egil hails his king as 'destroyer of Scots'; this generous personage fed corpses to wild beasts, gave dinner to the eagles, allowed the wolves to gnaw at the open wounds of the maimed and dying. 'Bitter is the wind tonight,' wrote one Gaelic scholar of this time, 'it tosses the white hair of the ocean. Tonight I fear not the fierce warriors from Norway.'

The Vikings did not have horned helmets; that belongs to Wagnerian opera. And their boats, though high-prowed, were for the most part too practical in purpose to feature fancy woodwork. But boats defined this people. The Viking name itself was taken from the creeks and bays – 'viks' – in which their boats lurked; indeed, the suffix survives in many a Hebridean placename – Crulivig, Marivig, Uig and so on. And the Gaels spoke of two races of Norsemen: the *dubh-ghoill*, or 'black foreigners', the Danes; and the 'white foreigners', *fionn-ghoill*, from Norway and Sweden. Most of the raiders on the north-west, however, were from Norway, and the Norwegian monarchy was by far the strongest power in Scandinavia.

The fear those men bred! Today that steady drying north-east wind, apt to blow in the Hebrides from late April through May, is a welcome thing: perfect weather for cutting peat, painting houses, airing linen, and performing a myriad chores after the long blustering damp of winter. A thousand years ago, the same wind struck dread in Highland hearts. It was the time for passage from Norway, when the longboats could be launched in a hundred fjords and set sail for Scotland, for 'the devastating of all the isles of Britain by the *Gals*' – by the 'strangers', or Gentiles, as the Annals of Ulster called them.

The Vikings affected our history in three regards. First: they finally broke the Celtic Church. Second: they forced (inadvertently) the unification of mainland Scotland. And, third, for three or four critical centuries they isolated the Hebrides (and much of the Highland mainland) from Lowland rule and from the development of feudalism.

The Vikings, to the Celtic monks and scholars, were more than killers: they were heathen fiends. In 825, in yet another Viking raid on Iona, they burst into the chapel where Blathmac – an abbot determined to maintain the ordinary, in extraordinary times – was calmly celebrating the sacrament. They had killed many men outside. They now killed men in the sanctuary. And they demanded, from this Blathmac, the silver casket wherein lay the relics of Columba himself. He would not tell

them its whereabouts (it had earlier been removed from the
abbey, and carefully buried). So Blathmac was slain where he
stood.

Shortly afterwards the relics of Columba left Iona, and were
entrusted to the care of brothers at Dunkeld, in Perthshire, on
which power in the developing Scottish state now tended to
centre. No wonder. In 795 Iona Abbey had been destroyed; in
802 it was sacked again; in 806 sacked once more (sixty-eight
monks were murdered on that occasion; the spot on the shore
where they fell is still known as Martyr's Bay). The atrocity in
825 was not the end either. As late as 986 the Abbot of Iona,
and fifteen monks, were slain on another shore. Yet the Iona
Community was repeatedly re-established, from its govern-
ment-in-exile at Kells, with a doggedness and courage that
excites admiration. (Kells itself was ravaged by the Vikings,
seven times.)

It was not the end of the Celtic Church, but it was the
beginning of the end. It became impossible to maintain coherent organisation. Nor can such difficulties have done much for
communal morale. From this time the Celtic clergy, more and
more, became solitaries, wanderers, hermits. They hid themselves away in isolated stacks and skerries. They cowered on tiny
islands, or in the remote rocks of big ones. Some even reached
the bleak Flannan Isles. Many had initially resorted to such a
lonely life in anger at the rising compromise with Rome, with the
concessions over Easter. Now it became a matter of survival. As
the Celtic Church disintegrated, and Scotland (not least in
response to the Viking horrors) finally married Scot and Pict,
the holy men formed a new, loose association, devoted to letters
and spirituality, the Cuil De – Companions of God. Long after
the reign of Malcolm and Margaret, long after Scotland had
knuckled under the Pope of Rome, the Culdees of the north kept
something of the old ideals and aspirations alive.

The Vikings, traditionally, were of the Teutonic faith. They
worshipped a pantheon of gods headed by Odin, and his son
Thor. Viking chiefs acted as priests – there was no clerical class –
and sacrificed horses, oxen and boars in wooden temples.
Occasionally, there was even human sacrifice. After death,
most Norse (so they believed) could pass to a better land, the
realm of Hel – daughter of a minor god – but the truly noble,

those slain in battle, ascended to Valhalla, there to feast and drink and be merry. Murray notes one curious feature of this creed: the gods were not thought immortal. 'A day far distant was foreseen when Odin and Thor would fall and Valhalla be destroyed by fire. In their place, the gods of a younger generation would govern a better world.'

But the Norsemen were, by nature, tolerant of other faiths. Christianity was in Iceland, and established by law, well before the eleventh century, when the Vikings converted wholesale to the new faith. What, then, lay behind the vicious raids on Iona, the slaughter of monks and priests, the wasting of churches, vestments, holy books? This was a reaction to another persecution – in Europe, by Charlemagne – of their own religion. The Holy Roman Emperor was determined to extirpate the Teutonic superstition. He burned temples, forced communities to convert at the point of a sword, slew the 'pagans' where he found them. In 782, after victory at Verden, he put 4,500 prisoners to death. Before then, the Vikings had taken no action against Christianity. For the next century, in the west of Scotland and elsewhere, they vented all their rage and fury on the followers of Christ, for the glory of Odin and Thor.

The Viking campaign was not without order. The islands were first occupied as summer bases; then, as the need for personal lands grew, they were settled, and if the natives of the islands made much protest they were put to the sword. The monasteries of the west coast they systematically destroyed. From the islands they moved into northern Scotland, and to eastern Ireland. But the Norsemen, apart from this vague plan of killing, conquest and settlement, had no coherent vision for Scotland, no unified leadership. Every Viking warlord was out for himself and his band of followers. Against this terrible but diffuse menace, Scots politics took a new twist. The Vikings finished the mission of Columba: they united the land.

For the Picts of the north, who had thrown off the Britons of Strathclyde, the Angles of Lothian and the east coast, even the Scots of Dalriada, could not apart resist the Viking threat. Pictish power crumbled, and in 843 Kenneth MacAlpine, King of Scots – who had Pictish royal blood, on his mother's side – deposed the last Pictish nobles and merged the kingdom. Two years later the Vikings sacked Paris. It was fortunate for King

Kenneth, and his new realm, that the Vikings had carried their
violent energies across Europe, and failed to concentrate on an
utter conquest of Scotland.

The Hebrides, though, were beyond the help – or the interest
– of the Scottish King. They were now cut off even from
Ireland. Within a generation the Scots themselves would know
the Hebrides by another name, *innse na gall*, Isles of the
Strangers, so completely Norwegian had they become. The
islands were now swamped by Norse settlers. This they owed to
a new King of Norway, Harald Haarfager – Harald the
Fairhaired – who, determined to attain supreme power, imposed a new and deeply unpopular feudal system on his
country. Rather than accept vassalage to this despot, thousands of Norsemen chose exile. From new bases in the Western
and Northern Isles, they began to harry the Norwegain coastline; it was not long before their former sovereign came to
avenge himself. In 891 King Harald raised a fleet and conquered all the Scottish isles. They fell under the Norwegian
crown – in name, at least – and for the next 370 years the
Hebrides were ruled by assorted Viking jarls.

This had one great historical consequence, though a near
millennium would pass before the conflicts it engendered would
explode in the turmoil of the Clearances. The Hebrides spent
four centuries clear of feudalism, which these jarls – viceroys,
really, quite autonomous of the Norwegian king whom they
honoured with their lips – never sought to introduce. The
classlessness of the culture endured. So did the communal
psychology of land use, and the clan system. But the Battle
of Hastings, in 1066, brought the French Normans to England;
they introduced a feudal order, and the marriage of English
princesses into the Scottish court – and the settlement, in
Scotland, of such noble Norman houses as that of Bruce –
brought feudalism to Scotland too. Scots kings still spoke
Gaelic, and would do so for some centuries yet, but the
divisions between Lowland and Highland Scotland now took
shape. When the Hebrides, and the West Highlands, were at
length subjugated to the rule of Edinburgh, and thence in time
to that of London, major conflict was inevitable.

For now, the Hebrides were Norse, and the chiefs were
Norsemen, and as the Norse purging relaxed and Gaels grew

from thralldom, and the two cultures merged, a most curious thing happened. The Norsemen begain to speak Gaelic. It was a very Norse Gaelic – full of Norse words and Norse phonemes – but, having embraced the Hebrides, the Hebrides embraced them, both by intermarriage between Viking and Gael, and in this adoption of the local tongue. It is the only time in history that a Celtic language, far from retreating and dying before an alien, intruding culture, has turned and overwhelmed a new and dominant influence.

Further, the Norse settlers created a monarchy. It was most unstable, but it was a monarchy. The 891 expedition of Harald the Fairhaired was led by the trusted Ketil. Having done the bloody work, this noble proceeded to cultivate the trust of the local power-class, and shortly proclaimed himself King of the Isles. He held this title for the rest of his life, defiantly independent of Norway. He failed, though, to establish a dynasty. But the title was revived. We know from Irish chronicle that Gofra MacArailt died as King of the Isles in 989. Then his Hebridean holdings were conquered by Sigurd, Jarl of Orkney. He lost them for a spell – a Ragnal MacGofra gloried in the rank at the turn of the century – but had won them back when he fell in battle in 1014. For twenty years the Hebrides enjoyed some sort of independence; then Sigurd's son, Earl Thorfin, conquered them yet again. He too died, though, and for a time the Hebrides were in thrall to a great Irish prince, Diarmad MacMaelnambo.

The agreeable notion of being King of the Isles had taken hold. One Godred, ruler of the Isle of Man, took the title. His son Fingal inherited it, but lost the isles in battle to another Godred, Godred Crovan – the White-handed – around 1077. This Godred Crovan was a son of Harald the Black and a noted warrior. In 1066 he played a commanding role in the Battle of Stamford Bridge, where King Harald of Norway fought King Harold of England. The English king triumphed, and the King of Norway died; but King Harold's triumph did not, of course, last long. William the Conqueror saw to that.

Godred Crovan survived Stamford Bridge, fled to the isles, took Man and much of Ireland, became king. He did not long enjoy power – the wily King of Norway, Magnus III, or Bareleg, deposed him – but seems to have died a natural death. He is one of Gaeldom's most celebrated Vikings; he founded a dynasty which survived for two centuries, and from his loins spring such notable Highland clans as MacLeod and MacAulay.

Godred Crovan's death, in 1095, triggered war between the Scots Norsemen and the Norwegian Norsemen. His heir immediately assumed a grand title, King of Man and the Isles. In the meantime the King of Scots, Edgar, presided over a realm of growing might and stability. King Magnus of Norway viewed these developments with concern. The rising independence of his kindred in the Hebrides could not be tolerated; nor could Scotland be suffered to reach a position where she might seize the islands for herself. So Magnus Bareleg paid his second visit to Scotland, in 1098, at the head of a mighty punitive expedition. It was the most fearful Norse invasion of all, and it was upon Norse settlers in the Hebrides, rather than Gaels, that it fell.

This Magnus was only twenty-five years old, and seems to have had a certain regard for Scottish customs; he adopted the kilt (thus his nickname) and it was worn in Norway for the next hundred years as a result. The unhappy Hebrideans were not treated to this tolerant aspect of his personality. Magnus, his fleet and his men, wasted Lewis, Uist, Skye, Kintyre, and all the Argyll islands. Bjorn Cripplehand – whose account 'reads as if he enjoyed the massacre from afar while basking aboard ship on a summer cruise', says Murray grimly – was with him. Cripplehand – the nickname suggests that he himself could play no part in the fighting; perhaps this fired the bloodlust in him – had a wonderful time. 'Fire played in the fig trees of Ljodus [Lewis],' he recorded cheerfully, 'it mounted up to heaven. Far and wide the people were driven to flight. The fire gushed out of the houses.' Nor did Magnus stop at Lewis. 'The liberal king ran with the fire over Ivist [Uist]. The *boendr* lost life and property. The king gained much gold.' Later, the glad wolf 'reddened tooth and claw in many a mortal wound within Tiree . . . the people of Mull ran to exhaustion. Greenland's king caused maids to weep south in the islands.'

Bjorn Cripplehand is often quoted, by writers who should know better, as giving account of how the Vikings won the Hebrides and crushed the Gaels. Far from it. The Highlands were long Norse by now. Cripplehand was spectator to a civil war, among the Norsemen themselves. And he loved every minute of it.

The very landscape of the isles today is a silent witness to that awful campaign. Today the Outer Hebrides are bare and treeless. Then they were densely wooded, with acres of low scrub and coppice. Cripplehand mentions fig trees; he was no botanist, but there was certainly abundant, if scrubby, tree cover on Lewis in his day. At any rate, Magnus Bareleg destroyed these forests, which had hitherto survived the needs of the population for wood and charcoal. They never recovered. An expanding population rapidly consumed what remained. The climate grew damper, colder, and the peat deposits thickened fast, and the trees did not grow again.

I have myself seen, in certain areas of Lewis bog, the ancient stumps and roots that may be remnants of the forest razed by Magnus.

The news from the Hebrides was not lost on the Scottish court. Edgar was quick to treat with King Magnus, and had no choice but to acknowledge Norwegian suzerainty over the Hebrides. He managed to avoid giving Magnus title to the mainland territories of the Norsemen, though these were considerable: almost all mainland Argyll, and all the Highlands north of Inverness, were under Viking settlement. The Norse King of Man, too, was forced to knuckle under Magnus. It was the second time in two centuries that the King of Norway had boxed his Hebridean cousins on the ears. His title to the Hebrides would stand for two further centuries. But the House of Man had only fifty more years of power in the Argyll islands.

About 1105, a woman in Ireland gave birth to a baby boy. Her husband was Gillebride of Clan Angus, the true (but exiled) King of Argyll, a Gael. He named the son Somerled; the boy's mother was Norse and, indeed, a princess, a daughter of the King of Man himself. The royal house had mothered their own conqueror.

Before we learn of Somerled's career, we should read something of his world, and the new order the Vikings had built in the Hebrides and much of the Highlands.

Norse colonial society was complex. It was also, in some

respects, oddly modern. There were three classes of men: the kings (princes might be a better word) who exercised power in, variously, matters military; matters marine; matters administrative; the tax-farming of tribute for Norway. Then there was the bulk of land-holders, the *boendr*. Bottom of the heap were the 'thralls', those enslaved by conquest. The indigenous Gaels of the islands, of course, started off the new order in this uncomfortable position. No doubt they were glad simply to be alive. Thralldom, and a recognised trade in slaves, was a major feature in Norse society. As late as the Treaty of Perth, in 1268, the Norwegian king – ceding the Hebrides to Scotland – made care to stipulate that the Norse settlers in the region should not be enthralled as a conquered race.

For free Norsemen, things were most democratic. Land was held in absolute title through inheritance, not by the goodwill of a feudal superior. You could bequeath it to your offspring. There was no rent, except civic (and on occasion military) services, those last also for the good of the community. A new settler had a right to water and wood, and to as much land as lay within a throw of a knife from the boundary of the park – bye-land – about his house, his *stadr*, as long as he fenced it all within a year. At the centre of every township – *tun* – was the main farm, *bolstadr*; the outlying pasture, beyond the bye-land, was the *saetr*. From these farmland names derive many Norse placenames in the Hebrides: Tolsta, Tong, Shawbost, Grimshader, are but four Lewis examples.

They were good farmers and unparalleled seamen. Their collective rights, on common pasture or fishing grounds, were administered by a constable, *hersir*, over a district, *herad*. Thus one island, the district – *na Hearadh*, the Herries, or Harris – of MacLeod, won its name. Measures of land were named and valued on a standard based on weights of silver. Every homestead paid one penny a year as *skatt*, rent; there are still pennylands in Hebridean nomenclature, like the township of Five Penny Borve, in north Lewis.

The Norse governed by a hierarchy of councils, or Things, dealing with different spheres of secular and religious life. In these every freeman had one vote. These could vote to grant (or withhold) supplies from the sovereign; thus he could not wage war (or make peace) without their consent. Their laws were based on a vigorous, democratic morality. Swindling was a serious crime, but a starving man who stole food would not be punished.

Women had surprisingly extensive rights; only in our own century have they recovered them. They could own property in their own right and had a recognised share in any marital holding. They could win divorce if a husband's ill-treatment or brutality could be proved; they themselves could be divorced for adultery, but otherwise a marriage bond could only be severed by mutual consent. Such enlightened aspects of Norse society show them much libelled in their historical reputation.

The Vikings had many skills. They enjoyed sports such as hunting, falconry, football and wrestling; they made music – on harp and viol – and delighted in verse and story. They excelled in artifice. Much of even their functional work was beautiful as well as useful. They could write – though they used a runic script, rather than the Roman alphabet, until their conversion to Christianity – but did not rate the art very highly.

For what their surviving sagas and chronicles lack in courtly elegance, however, they more than compensate in candid charm. Take this delightful description of Svein Asleifarson of Gairsay, a formidable settler in Orkney.

> This is how Svein used to live. Winter he would spend at home on Gairsay where he entertained some eighty men at his own expense. His drinking hall was so big that there was nothing in Orkney to compare with it. In the spring he had more than enough to occupy him, with a great deal of seed to sow which he saw to carefully himself. Then, when that job was done, he would go off plundering in the Hebrides and Ireland on what he called his spring trip; then back home just after midsummer where he stayed till the cornfields had been reaped and the grain was safely gathered in. After that, he would go off raiding again and never come back until the first month of winter was ended.

Above all, the Norsemen were masters of the sea.

The Viking longships were swift and powerful craft. They were clinker-built – with the planks overlapping – and double-bowed, with characteristic high prows. They were narrow in

beam, but drew only three feet of water. They were powered, for
the most part, by oar, and were readily manoeuvred in the
coastal narrows. If the wind was abaft they sped well under a
heavy square sail. But there was much variance in design. Ships
of the Gokstad type, Murray records, had a special keel that
allowed them to tack against the wind, if at a wide angle.
(Someone, in 1893, built a replica and successfully crossed the
Atlantic.) The fastest longboats were the *skutas*, where the
timbers were planed thin and tied with pine-root; nails and
metal fastenings were dispensed with, allying maximum light-
ness to maximum strength. The biggest boats would ply ten oars
a side. Shifts of rowers were necessary for very long voyages,
especially in contrary winds, when the boat might be rowed day
and night.

A typical Norse dragon-boat – a fighting ship – would bear a
crew of sixty; half to row, half to fight. Men bore the arms of the
day: axe, spear, hurling spear (or javelin), sword. Armour
consisted of helmet and jerkin of chain-mail. They had bows
and arrows too. This, then, was the Viking civilisation; and if
their name was at first synonymous with blood and terror, there
was much in the world they built in the Hebrides and Highlands
to excite our admiration.

To this world the young Somerled returned, about 1130, with
his father. They roused the people of Morvern and drove the
Norsemen out of mainland Argyll. Established as king, Somerled was quick to make peace with Olav the Red, the new King
of Man, and even married his daughter, Ragnild, a grandchild
of Godred Crovan himself. No one went to war with this Olav,
King of Man. The King of Man was deemed invincible; his
power was naval power, founded on his fleet of longboats, his
mighty rowers, skilled navigators and tough fighting men. So
Somerled bided his time, until Olav died, in 1152, and was
succeeded by his son Godred, who rapidly proved himself a
despot. Under Godred's yoke, the Hebrides soon looked to
Somerled for leadership.

Somerled was by inheritance a Gael, and his sympathies were
immediately with his Celtic inheritance and the old culture of the
isles. But he was also half Norse, and practical genius blended in
him with much political shrewdness. Godred and the Norse
pressed him on the west, from the Hebrides; at his back, in the

heart of the Scottish mainland, feudalism had begun to take root. Inertia was not an option. If Somerled did nothing, his little realm would fall to one power or another. But to break out, to be master of his world, he had first to master the sea. He knew much of seacraft already, and of naval warfare. He now applied himself to matters of marine engineering.

The traditional Hebridean galley was the *birlinn*, a long, heavy, cumbersome vessel, planks clinker-built and bound with thongs, driven by short oars. They were smaller, slower and more cumbersome than the longboats and no match for any serious Viking opponent. Somerled dwelt on the aspect of design long, and then began (secretly) to build a new fleet of ships, to a new design. For the Viking longboat had one remarkable weakness: it had no rudder. The ships were steered by a plank on the right-hand side of the stern; from this 'steering-board', indeed, we derive 'starboard'. Somerled's new ships had hinged rudders, and long helms. He also built fighting-tops at the masthead of his boats. He now had ships that could dodge and wheel and outsteer the Norse vessels in creeks and sea lochs; further, his archers could inflict much damage on enemies below at close quarters. He called these craft *naibheagan*, little ships, and it is said that he built a fleet of fifty-eight.

Godred was at length persuaded of the menace amassing in Argyll. He did not wait long to deal with it. A battleforce sailed to the Hebrides and, on 6 January 1156, the *naibheagan* and the Norsemen met off the west coast of Islay. They fought until dusk, and the Vikings were broken; the scattered survivors fled south. The men of Somerled were too exhausted, their little boats too battered to follow. But they had won. It was the first sea battle lost by Norsemen. Having held his ground, Somerled was careful not to risk a more perilous venture, nor to humiliate King Godred. He suggested, instead, terms, and the two kings made peace. The Hebrides were divided between them. Godred retained the Outer Isles, Skye and Raasay, with his kingdom of Man. Somerled took everything else: all the Argyll Hebrides, and the islands of the Firth of Clyde (these under the suzerainty of the Scots crown, at least officially) and added these to his existing kingdom. Somerled was Lord of the Isles, leader of the Gaels, head of a Gaelic state.

So, quietly, the Norsemen pass from history. In time, the Gaelic they had sought to suppress had actually overcome them, and the Norse tongue had died out in the Western Isles by the end of the fifteenth century. But Norse impact abides. Most natives of the Outer Hebrides are of Viking descent, especially in Lewis and Harris. Blood-grouping has shown strong links between the people of Lewis, Iceland and Norway. Men of the big, blue-eyed, fair-haired type can be seen – the Ness district of Lewis is noted for those tall, ruddy latterday Norsemen – and the Gaelic of the Outer Isles, notably in Lewis and, oddly enough, Barra, at the other end of the archipelago, abounds in Norse pronunciations and Norse loanwords. Boats in the Western Isles, of traditional type – the *sgoth niseach* is the best example, a distinctive little sailboat from the Ness district – feature Norse skills and design in their clinkered construction and high prows.

It is in topography, however, that the Viking era in the Outer Isles is most marked. 'There is hardly a hill in Harris,' writes Bill Lawson, 'of any eminence whose name does not end in -*val*, from *fjell*, the Norse word for a hill, and -*ay* for an island is equally common.' Roineval, Chaipaval; Pabbay, Berneray, Scalpay – all Norse names. The village names on the Harris coast are Norse: Sheilebost – Shell Township; Horgabost – Grave Township; Borve – Fort; Scarista – Skari's Farm. In Lewis, Francis Thompson observes that out of the 126 recognisable village names, fully ninety-nine are Norse. And another eleven are of Norse origin. There is an easy rule of thumb, by the way, to distinguish a modern Lewis settlement – like the new villages formed in the eighteenth and nineteenth centuries – from an old one. Old villages, such as Shader, have Norse names. A new village, such as Ballantrushal, next down the coast, has a Gaelic name.

The era of the Lordship of the Isles – virtually a Gaelic state, centred on Somerled and his successors, from their base in Islay – now has the aura of a golden age. It was a high point in Gaelic history; an era when the folk of the Hebrides and the West Highlands were under no alien crown, knew nothing of feudalism, and, together, had a certain standing in the world.

The Gaels in the Outer Hebrides – still, for another century, under Norse rule – prospered in their own way. The Gaels in Scotland beyond the Highlands did not. Queen Margaret had turned the court from Gaelic to English, and from the Celtic to the Roman rites. We have met her before, in that religious capacity, and she is still demonised as an anti-Gaelic, anglicising influence on the developing Scottish court. Certainly, if she ever learned a word of Gaelic, it is not recorded. Her sons were given vigorously English names: Edward, Edgar, Edmund, Ethelred, Alexander, David. The odd thing is that, though English by background, Margaret was no creature of the English court. She did not know the place. Her kindred, the House of Wessex – founded by King Alfred – had been overthrown by the Danes, then again by William the Conqueror. Margaret had begun her life in Hungary, of all places.

In her Romanising zeal she established a Benedictine monastery at Dunfermline. For these and other services she is memorialised by a famous little chapel at Edinburgh Castle; after her death, she was canonised. But Margaret's influence should not be overestimated in the decline of Gaelic Scotland. She was most baleful in matters religious; in things of state, however, Malcolm Canmore was not the sort of man to be moulded by a woman. Many forces were at work here, and the dominant theme was the need of the Scottish kingdom to survive both the Norse menace, and the possible threat from Norman England. So the King of Scots turned his back on Gaeldom. In 1098 he had actually made treaty with Norway, formally ceding the Hebrides to the Norwegian crown. Malcolm Canmore had overthrown and slain MacBeth; MacBeth was buried at Iona, and no Scottish king would follow him. Iona, for centuries, would be in a foreign land. The tongues of the Hebrides, to more and more Scots, became foreign tongues.

David, son of Malcolm and Margaret, was raised in England, and married a wealthy widow; this made him very rich, though in his possession of English land he made himself vassal to the English king. In 1124 he succeeded to the Scottish throne as King David I, and returned, bringing in his train near 1,000 Anglo-Norman adventurers – Bruces, Montgomerys, other noble folk – to whom he distributed land in great parcels, evicting its original occupants. A Scots king did not enjoy superiority of all lands, but English kings did; and David I thought in the English way. A new feudal order rapidly established itself. Gaelic, spoken throughout the land (except by the English border) lapsed within a generation.

The Highlands and the Lowlands fast drifted apart on three fronts. The nobility of one was Highland; of the other, Anglo-Norman. The language of one was Gaelic; of the other, Scots – more properly, Scottish English. And the order of one was free and independent; the other, hierarchical and subservient. So Somerled had feared for the future of his land. And, when David I died, in 1153, the ruler of Argyll had rallied the other Gaelic chiefs and approached the new king, Malcolm IV, wanting a conference, wanting to arrest the anglicising trend. They were coldly rebuffed. Then Malcolm IV began to demand the surrender of Somerled's mainland territory to the Scottish kingdom. After his resounding defeat of Godred, then – and after he had established his capital on Islay, and fortified the harbour at Lagavullin – Somerled decided to force the Scots king to treaty by a powerful show of strength.

In 1164 the King of the Hebrides sailed up the Clyde, at the head of a fleet of 160 ships, and an army of 10,000 men. With 5,000 men, Somerled marched to Renfrew and established camp, and received Walter Fitz Alan, another Norman – a Breton – who was Baron Renfrew, a steward to the King of Scots. The meeting was cordial, and afterwards all retired for the night. The next morning, Somerled was found dead in his tent. He had been murdered, and the schism between Highlands and Lowlands – which he had hoped to bridge, and had engineered a real chance of such healing – now became permanent.

His three sons divided the Hebrides. Ragnall got Islay, Kintyre, and his father's great fleet. Dougall took Lorne, and the other Argyll islands. Angus took Arran and Bute. Their authority was near-absolute; had they felt inclined to recognise any court beyond, it would have been that of Norway – a ready voyage by sea distant – rather than that of the King of Scots, far beyond sea lochs, mountains and roadless glens. As long as the Norse maintained a grip on good tracts of Scotland, this island triumvirate – of which Ragnall of Islay was princeps; his five successors would be kings of the Hebrides – could deem itself reasonably secure from Scottish interference.

This Ragnall – often known by the English form of his name, Reginald – did much good, and is especially remembered for his benevolence to the Church. He founded monasteries; he rebuilt churches and abbeys destroyed by the Vikings; the ruins of the nunnery on Iona, which he built, are among the loveliest in the Highlands. His son, Donald I, built castles rather than churches, and helped the Irish to fend off a Norman invasion. For this he was offered the crown of Ireland, which he declined. He preferred the Hebrides, and from him onwards his line and house were known as Clan Donald. These kings of the Isles had long reigns, and they were all – by dint either of innate wisdom, or the wisdom that lies in seeking and heeding good advice – good reigns.

But the times were turbulent. The Scots kings were no longer prepared to tolerate Norse occupation in any part of their realm. In 1196, King William the Lion threw the Vikings out of north Scotland. Alexander III, his grandson – one of that rare breed, a good and wise Scots sovereign – determined on war with the King of Norway. But King Haakon was not easy to provoke. At length, Alexander III stirred up various Highland nobles – the Earl of Ross and others – to make merry on Skye, and other islands; these attacks soon goaded Haakon to action. In 1263 he sent the last – and doomed – Norse invasion fleet to Scotland; in the late summer the ships anchored off Arran. If he had bargained on the support of the King of Clan Donald – which he might well have won – Haakon was outsmarted. King Alexander had seized the son of Angus, and was holding him hostage.

Alexander wasted a month of Haakon's time in negotiations. He wanted good strong October gales. The Vikings, unruly as ever, plundered the Clyde coast, and discipline grew slack. On the night of 1 October a fearful storm came screaming from the west. Longboat after longboat was smashed on the shore by Largs. Haakon had dithered too long. He ordered a landing, which the weather made most difficult; much of his invasion fleet had scattered to sea; more longboats burst on the shore as they tried to land troops, and many drowned. Before all his men were ashore, the Scots attacked. Haakon could render little support

from the sea, and his army suffered a crushing defeat. Haakon
narrowly escaped himself; he managed to secure a truce, and
limped northwards with his bedraggled armada. He lingered in
the narrows between Skye and the mainland (Kyleakin is named
for him) and made it as far as Orkney, where the Norwegian
king succumbed to fever, and died.

Alexander seized Skye and the Hebrides; three years later,
Norway was forced to cede these formally, in the Treaty of
Perth. Angus was cannily confirmed as king in the Hebrides; he
was king already, of course, but by granting title the Scots king
also hinted at power to remove it, and further that Angus was in
his vassalage. The Earl of Ross, who had proved most useful,
gained Skye and the Outer Hebrides; but lands in Skye, Lewis
and Harris were confirmed in the possession of one Leod, a son
of Olav the Black, who had been King of Man. This Leod had
two sons, Torquil and Tormod, who founded two distinct
houses: MacLeod of Lewis and Raasay, and MacLeod of
Harris and Dunvegan.

Then, in 1285, King Alexander died at Kinghorn in Fife; he
had been riding up a cliff path in the fog, and, unseen, his men
heard him cry; his broken body was found below a precipice. His
heir was a little girl, Margaret, his granddaughter, the Maid of
Norway. Edward I of England took note, and suggested, with
menaces, that she be betrothed to his own young son, Prince of
Wales. The Scots nobles reluctantly consented. But, on her
journey to Scotland, the little queen died at Orkney. Scotland
fell in turmoil as two rivals – Robert Bruce and John Balliol –
each made claim to the throne. With great folly, the Scots
sought an umpire to adjudicate the matter, that same King
Edward. And the Wars of Independence, which would cost the
nation dear, soon began.

Clan Donald, on Angus's death, elected a new king, Young
Angus – Angus Og. He was a personal friend of Robert the
Bruce, whose claim to the throne founded on his descent from
David I; he had a weaker claim than John Balliol, by strict
primogeniture, but Balliol – though enthroned by King Edward
– had put himself (and thus Scotland) in vassalage to the English
king; he had knelt in homage before him. Edward, though,
wanted more than vassalage: he sought the very union of
Scotland with his own kingdom, and to that end determined

to provoke John Balliol to revolt, by piling humiliation upon him. This Bruce did his best to exploit. But Bruce is one of Scotland's ambiguous heroes. At times he acted in support of Edward I. He certainly abandoned William Wallace. Then he, in turn, caught the nationalist bug; rose, failed, and fled. In a low point in his fortunes – defeated, friendless, on the run – the Bruce hid under Angus Og's protection, first in one MacDonald castle, then another. Meantime the *nabhaigean* harried English shipping, and even seized their naval base on the Isle of Man, on the eve of Bannockburn in 1314.

To that battle the Scots carried, in a gorgeously decorated reliquary of silver, a most precious relic. The casket can still be seen at Edinburgh Castle; it is empty now, but it contained little remains – hair, perhaps, or bone fragments – of Columba himself. So they believed. Bruce, famously, won Bannockburn, and the Scottish throne; nearly three centuries would pass before the independence of Scotland was again threatened. He was not slow to reward the Lord of the Isles. Angus Og won Mull, Coll, Tiree, Jura, isles forfeit from his kinsman, MacDougall, who had allied himself with the new king's enemies.

But King Robert I also demanded charters of the island chiefs – the papers showing that the crown had granted them title to their lands. This caused consternation. There were, of course, no such charters. There had been no kings about to grant them in the days when, by force of arms, the clans had seized and maintained territory from assorted foes and invaders. Bruce, then, issued such charters. So did his heirs, not to the clans, but to their chiefs. Thus the house of Bruce, Norman, feudal, remorselessly imposed a new order over the north and west.

Angus Og's son, John MacDonald, was granted charter by David II – Robert's son – to the isles of Gigha, Colonsay, Scarba, Skye, Lewis and Harris. John then made a happy marriage: through his wife, Amie of Garmoran, he won the Small Isles, the Uists, Eriskay and Barra and all their outliers. Thus he was king, *de facto* and *de jure*, of all the Hebrides. By the time he married again, King David III – a peculiarly unhappy, inept man – was dead. He died childless, and was succeeded by his nephew. Robert's mother, Marjorie, had been

David's sister; heavily pregnant, she had fallen from her horse, given birth to a son, and died. The child's father was one Walter, High Steward, of kin to that Baron Renfrew who, almost certainly, had contrived the assassination of Somerled.

The House of Stewart now ascended to the Scottish throne, in the person of Robert II, and for 400 years the scions of this fascinating, incompetent, and gloriously unfortunate royal house would exploit, torment and finally all but ruin the Highlands and Islands.

Robert II had a daughter, and the widowed John, King of the Isles, took her as second wife. In deference to his father-in-law's feelings, he stopped calling himself king and resumed the title Lord of the Isles. Yet, still, the realm of Clan Donald expanded. John's grandson, Donald II, became Earl of Ross; this took in all Ross, and much of Inverness too. The Lord of the Isles was now superior over the Atlantic coast, from Assynt to the Mull of Kintyre, and all the isles of western Scotland off that shoreline. Princes of Clan Donald could treat, as sovereigns, with other sovereigns – kings of England, Scotland, Ireland, even France – and they did. They even had to divide their empire, for purposes of adminstration, and centres were duly established in Islay, Mull, Skye and Lewis.

By 1420, at the height of the Lordship's influence, the Highland clans were established in the flower of their prosperity and pride. There were four clans of Donald descent, whose chiefs won charters from their lord: Clan Ranald (whose base might best be described as the Catholic Highlands: the districts of Uist, Benbecula, Barra, Eriskay, Moidart, Arisaig, Morar and Knoydart are Roman Catholic even today). Clan Donald held Sleat – the southern wing of Skye – and North Uist. Clan Iain held Ardnamurchan, with lands on Islay, Jura and Mull. Clan Iain Mhor were strong on Islay. Then there were other clans, not of Donald blood, but also granted charters of the Lord of the Isles.

Clan Gillean held Morvern and Ardgour, and the smaller Argyll Hebrides. Mighty Clan Leod held west Skye and Harris (the *siol Thormod*: Norman's seed), Lewis and Raasay (*siol Torquil*), Glenelg, Assynt and Gairloch. There was a Clan Neil of Barra. There was a Clan Neill of Gigha. Clan MacPhee had Colonsay; Clan Mackinnon, north Mull and central Skye. The little Clan MacQuarrie had Ulva and Gometra, western satellites of Mull.

The Lordship had distinct ceremonies of inauguration and charter, not all of Christian origin. Land was conveyed when the lord kneeled on Clan Donald's Stone of Destiny – not to be confused with that at Scone – and chanted a rhyming formula. This stone used to be kept on an islet in Loch Finlagan, Islay; in 1380, with the territory much expanded, it was shipped north to the more central isle of Eigg. This stone was not, like the Stone of Scone, a squared boulder upon which a sovereign sat. It was a slab, some seven feet long, in which a footprint had been carved. When he was inaugurated, MacDonald, Lord of the Isles, placed a bare foot in this, covenanting himself to walk in the wisdom of his fathers. A bishop presented him with a white wand, to symbolise the just rule of law, and a great sword, reminder of his duty to defend that justice and his people. Thrice the Lord of the Isles turned sunwise; thrice he brandished the great sword; thrice the gathered company of chiefs and men roared *MacDhomhnuill*. Priests celebrated mass, and there followed days of feasting and good times, at the cheerful expense of the Lord of the Isles.

A footprint similar to that Stone of Destiny (which has long since vanished) is carved in the rock of an outcrop at Dunadd, once capital of Dalriada, and where the Gaels from Ireland ordained their kings. Beside it is the clear carving of a boar, and words in ogham script – the lettering first devised in fourth-century Ireland – which no one today can interpret. So the rite of placing a bare foot in stone, to swear continuity with the past and faithful adherence to the ways of forefathers, is most ancient – older, probably, than the Christian faith in these islands.

The great tragedy of Gaeldom, of the Highlands and of the Hebrides, was the failure of this great realm to establish itself as a secure and abiding political state. At the dawn of the fifteenth century the Lordship of the Isles was, to all intents and purposes, an autonomous monarchy. A hundred years later, it had collapsed; the isles and glens under the heel of Edinburgh, the clan system sickening to the cancer of feudalism, the very title subsumed into the courtesy honours of the heir to the Scottish throne. There were many factors at work. It is not easy

to keep control of a realm consisting largely of a vast and
scattered archipelago. And the forces of trade, commerce and
education always pulled towards the mainland and the cities.
But the internal decay of this Highland polity was most
significant in ending the epoch. The Highlanders might call
MacDonald *buachaille nan eileanan*, shepherd of the isles – he
had, after all, given them peace, stability and wealth for over 300
years – but all power tends to corrupt.

MacDonald's realm was already losing democratic vigour. To
help him govern his vast sphere, the Lord of the Isles had a
council of fourteen chiefs: they met on Eilean na Comhairle –
Council Isle – in Loch Finlagan. On the great isle of Eilean Mor,
beside it, and connected by causeway, was MacDonald's capital:
a house with a great hall, and a dining hall, and stables, and
guardhouses, and a presbytery for clerics; servants' quarters, a
guest-house, and so on. According to Donald Monro, Dean of
the Isles in 1549, this council comprised 'four of the greatest
nobles, four thanes of lesser estate, and four great men of the
royal blood of Clan Donald'. The nobles were MacLean of
Duart, MacLean of Loch Buie, MacLeod of Harris, and
MacLeod of Lewis. The four thanes were MacKinnon, Mac-
Neill of Gigha, and MacNeil of Barra; another seems to have
taken his seat by rotation, from a number of gentry at this social
level. The royal princes were Clanranald, MacIain of Ardnamurchan, Clandonald of Kintyre, and Clan Alasdair Carryche
of Lochaber. The Abbot of Iona, and the Bishop of the Isles,
made up the rest.

There would have been much variance in this number over
time. But the prime function of the Council of the Isles was as a
court of appeal. The islands had their brieves, and their courts
of justice, and each clansman had the right to take his case as
high as this council. There its powers took end. It had not the
authority of the great Thing of the Norsemen. The days when
clansmen chose the chief, or chiefs their king, had perished.
Primogeniture – a key principle, of course, of feudalism – now
held sway. The Council of the Isles was a supreme court, and
nothing more. It had no executive role in the Lordship. It had
no power to withhold supplies for any military campaign,
however ill-conceived, nor to ratify (or block) such treaties
as MacDonald might strike. The Lordship, in fact, had no

checks and balances to its authority; its survival depended on
the good judgement and character of the sovereign lord
himself.

In truth, the Lordship of the Isles had acquired all the powers
of absolute monarchy. It was a benevolent monarchy, no doubt;
MacDonald took little interest in the minutiae of individual
islands and parishes, and it was not in his interest to squeeze
them for tribute. The men of the line, too, were remarkable for
even temper and cautious spirit. But increasingly they were
swollen by the trappings of feudalism. And there was no
powerful class or group of men to balance their judgement.
The chiefs, dependent on MacDonald for charters of land,
would do his bidding. Even the Church had lost its spirit. It
was still held in great awe by the people, and the dread of
excommunication was a powerful weapon against a sovereign
prince: he might laugh in Rome's face, but his people would not,
and they might then be driven, for terror of soul, to cast him
down. But the energy of Columba, the vision of the Celtic
Church, the manly rigour of those early saints, was no more.
The Church in the Highlands and Islands grew ritualistic,
formal, amoral. Clergymen lay in sloth, and grew fat. In the
looming crisis they would do nothing to rally the Gaelic spirit.
And now, in true tragedy, the power of the Lords of the Isles
reached its apogee, in the opening decades of the fifteenth
century, just as their one-time faculty for political judgement
deserted them completely.

The bid for the Earldom of Ross, in 1411, was a move carried
off with tactical success – Donald did win the earldom – but in
strategic failure. He took advantage of the exile of James I –
when the third Stewart king succeeded to the throne, on the
death of Robert III, he was a boy incarcerated in the Tower of
London – and prepared a mighty host. No fewer than 10,000
men marched with Donald II on north-east Scotland – and the
population of the whole land at this time has been reckoned at
800,000. The Lord of the Isles feared that the king's uncle, the
Duke of Albany, might seize Ross for himself; he had custody of
the infant heiress, and was regent in the king's absence. But the
campaign was really a swaggering mission to intimidate the
Scottish executive.

The Highland army did well. They marched from Morvern,

and took Inverness, and then scythed through the north-east, crossing the Spey and into Aberdeenshire. Great was the consternation before them. Some thought that Donald II intended to seize the very throne of Scotland. Nor was he at pains to dispel such an impression. He may at least, as James Hunter suggests, have dreamed of deposing Albany from power and becoming regent himself. But at Harlaw, by Inverurie, in the summer of 1411, the great Highland army was defeated. It was not a rout, nor a disaster. They were able to retreat in reasonable order back to the glens of the west. Donald II, in due time, was recognised as Earl of Ross. But the power that the Lord of the Isles had once wielded in Scotland at large was manifestly gone. At Harlaw the brief hope of regaining it, of enhancing the place of the Gaels in Scottish affairs, vanished for ever. Failure in this badly dented MacDonald prestige. He had failed to shake the crown.

The battle, too, did much to demonise the Gaels in southern eyes. There is still a monument at Harlaw – erected by local folk many years ago – honouring the Aberdeen burghers who marched out to resist the 'caterans'. A cateran, says James Hunter, was a 'freebooter, a bandit ... The Gaels were considered aliens now in Aberdeen; uncouth and uncivilised aliens at that.' A priest – John of Fordun – had, in 1380, already articulated in pen the thoughts rising in many a Lowland breast. 'The Highlanders and people of the islands, however, are a savage and untamed race, rude and independent, given to rapine, ease-loving, clever and quick to learn, comely in person but unsightly in dress, hostile to the English people and language and, owing to this diversity of speech, even to their own nation.' They were also, he declared, exceedingly cruel. He was not alone in his prejudice; similar views of Highlanders, indeed, are still heard today.

For a while the Scots monarchy was in such chaos that the Lord of the Isles could indulge in much daring and audacity. The House of Stewart was bedevilled, through two centuries, by a succession of premature deaths, infant kings and long periods of minority, while assorted regents and robber-barons governed the land (badly) or took to arms against one another. Possession of the latest boy-king meant possession of the reigns of power. Men would kill for it.

James I was the first to grapple with the Lord of the Isles. In April 1424 he returned, at last, thirty years old, from English exile, with a good English wife – a granddaughter of John of Gaunt – and a generous bundle of grudges to bear and scores to settle. James I rather appeals, despite the extreme aggression of his ruling style. He was a superb athlete. He was true Renaissance man, able to paint and draw, to play a variety of musical instruments, to indulge in a variety of skilled crafts. He was also an excellent poet; the verses he penned for his wife still survive.

But his reign was characterised by the sweeping imposition of taxes, a ferocious bid to curb the Scottish nobility, and much tactlessness and arrogance. James I was brutal; he was also, at times, dishonourable. Once King James felt himself secure, he moved against his principal opponents. In 1425 he summarily executed four leading nobles – the first state execution for over a century – gaining three earldoms for himself, and further annual revenue of over £1,000. But it cost him the trust of Scotland's political class.

The Highlands, too, were in the king's sights. In 1428 Highland chiefs were summoned to meet the monarch at Inverness. In a disgusting trick, he arrested fifty of them on arrival. Some were put to death. But Alexander, Lord of the Isles, humiliated the king by successfully escaping; for three years king and lord wrestled in cold war and minor atrocities – if the burning of Inverness to the ground can be so described: one of Alexander's spectacular escapades – until the Lord of the Isles beat the royal army at Inverlochy, Lochaber, in 1431. The king had the last laugh: in a grotesque ritual, Alexander was at length paraded before him in the Edinburgh church of St Giles, clad only in his underwear, making obeisance on his knees. But Clan Donald power remained an unbroken reality in the west. And the Inverness manoeuvre was stupid as well as wrong. James had shown he could not be trusted. In 1437 his continuing assault on baronial prerogatives finally provoked a palace plot. The king was cornered and brutally murdered in his apartments at Perth.

James II was but a baby when his father died; he grew up and was showing some promise when, in 1460, an exploding cannon killed him as the king's forces besieged Roxburgh

Castle. He in turn was succeeded by his six-year-old son. This king, James III, has been described as the most gifted – and most unpleasant – of the Stewart monarchs. Scotland did rather better under his minority than she fared once he took direct command himself. He defied the contemporary norms of kingship. He prefered music to athletics, and religion to warfare. Critically he much favoured the company of low-born friends to the society of Scottish nobles. A blacksmith, a tailor and a musician were honoured by him; a mere architect, one Cochrane, was even ennobled as an earl. Though married – and he fathered an heir – James may have had a sexual interest in these friends; there are hints of royal perversion in contemporary accounts, and his career has clear parallels with that of Edward II of England, another unhappy king. The king was foolish enough to debase the coinage, and all the time screwed as much by way of tribute and emolument out of the Scots as he could.

He also had two adult brothers to contend with, the Earls of Albany and Marr, and no love was lost between them. Marr was imprisoned, and died suspiciously. Murder was spoken of. Albany fled into exile. Trouble always seethed somewhere in the realm. There was only one accomplishment of note in this wretched man's personal reign. In 1472 he was able permanently to annexe Orkney and Shetland to the Scottish crown; his father-in-law, King of Denmark, had defaulted on the dowry for which they were comfort.

The chaos of minority periods gave abundant opportunity for the head of a Highland empire to sport himself as he would. But, in 1462, John II, Lord of the Isles, went too far in brinkmanship. He made a secret treaty with Edward IV of England: its terms were nothing less than the dismemberment of Scotland. John would win the north; Edward the south. This may have been bravado rather than serious intent. John II made no move on the Highland mainland. But, in 1476, parliament in Edinburgh learned of this. The land, titles and rights of the Lord of the Isles were made forfeit.

A great army was raised; John, a foolish man, had enough sense to submit. His son, Angus, did not, but Angus was a master of warfare. Thrice in succession he beat the mainland armies of the Scots king. He openly repudiated his father, and

sought the Lordship for himself. Clan Donald, and the Highlands, split between them, and all fell. Angus and John met in
vicious sea battle off the coast of Mull – Bloody Bay, it is still
called – and Angus won. Shortly afterwards he was murdered.
Then, in 1488, King James himself was killed, in a spectacular
coup. His own heir, a stripling of but fourteen, was willing
figurehead to a revolt against him. The king beat off the rebels
at Stirling Bridge, but the prince escaped. Battle was renewed
at Sauchieburn. The royal army was defeated. And the king,
who had fled to cower in a barn, was murdered by someone
posing as a priest. His son succeeded him as James IV; for the
sake of decency, of course, there had to be an inquiry into the
late king's demise. But parliament found no culprit, nor any
explanation more convincing than that 'the King happinit to be
slane'.

The reign of James IV got off to a shaky start; he was not
crowned for two years, and for the rest of his life he bolstered his
position by encouraging a cult of kingship. But he proved
perhaps the most capable Stewart of all. He rapidly shook
off the shackles of minority. In 1493 – still only eighteen – he
brought John II, Lord of the Isles, south in chains, put him on
trial, and destroyed him. The Lordship was abolished. The title
was passed to the heir to the Scots throne. (It is still one of the
Scottish titles of the Prince of Wales, along with Baron Renfrew,
title of that steward who had betrayed Somerled.)

James IV – who perished, with the 'flower of Scotland' at
Flodden, in 1514 – was the last great King of Scots. He was able,
humorous, shrewd, brave, courtly, friendly. He had much
generosity of character. He made various Highland tours,
and made an excellent impression: he spoke Gaelic fluently.
But, in so completely destroying the Lordship, James IV made a
bad error of judgement. Nothing was established in its place. He
could have stripped the lord of mainland possessions and left
him to govern the Hebrides, where he was a threat to no one and
a force for stability. But he abolished the office; worse, in 1499
he conferred lieutenancy of the isles to the one man the Highlanders and Hebrideans could not stand – Campbell of Argyll.
Argyll, and his lieutenants, were so widely deemed unprincipled
bandits that they could command no respect. The Scottish
court, its king and its nobles, were too remote to wield any

significant influence. Without the restraint of Clan Donald, without the salting of a lively Church, without any popular controls, the Highlands soon collapsed into anarchy. The new century would be remarkable in Highland history for its disorder and misery.

Radical Highland historians, such as James Hunter, would argue that the crown charters to personages, like chiefs, had been none other than grand theft: the stealing of the land from the Highland people. The result was the rapid development of Celtic feudalism: differing in some regards from Anglo-Norman feudalism, but feudalism still. These chiefs drifted gently away, generation by generation, from the old patriarchal ideal to a belief in (and exercise of) their own absolute power over the people. The people of the Highlands and Islands took a long time to grasp this. It was only as the chiefs degenerated to absentee landlords, when they actually forsook the Gaelic language itself – by the end of the eighteenth century – that ordinary Highlanders realised what had happened. But, even today, there is in many parts of the region a touching faith in the essential benevolence of power and authority.

For now, the chiefs of new character – free from the enlightened despotism of MacDonald – fell to gleeful and incessant warfare. The history of the Highlands through the sixteenth century, and through much of the seventeenth, abounds in tales of cruelty and massacre that would have appalled the very Norsemen. There was battle upon battle, war upon war, atrocity upon atrocity. Warfare and catte-rustling were the only fields of endeavour. Clansmen marched to war on behalf of their insatiably martial chiefs. Farmwork was neglected, the poor terrorised, their homes repeatedly burned, their beasts repeatedly driven away, their stuff repeatedly stolen. It would have made Columba weep. Some fields of endeavour lapsed entirely: the arts, organised commerce, anything beyond the most feeble and superstitious religion. Agriculture was arrested in development: it would be the nineteenth century before the Highlanders forsook their poor little cows and wooden hand-ploughs. Education ceased all together, save for the sons of the gentry; it would not be revived for 200 years.

From this era, from 1500 to 1745, come perhaps the best-known tales of hard Highland men and their derring-do. This would be the high season of Gaelic romance; but, apart from the assorted princes, chiefs and warlords, it would be a day of untold woe for many ordinary Highland people.

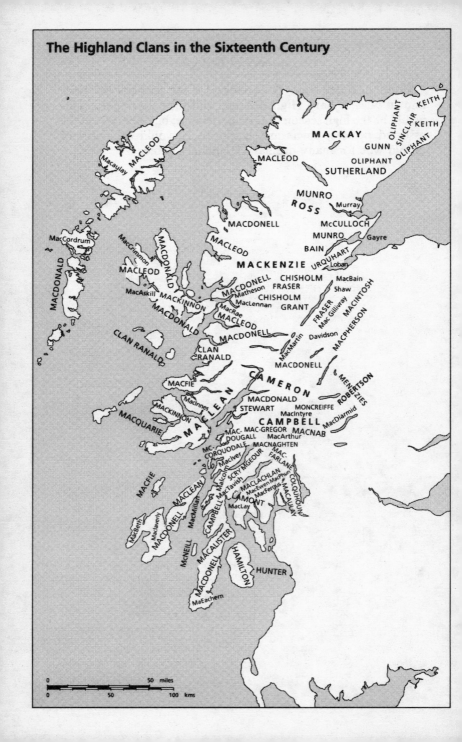

The Highland Clans in the Sixteenth Century

MACLEOD

Macaulay

MACLEOD

MacCordrum

MacCrimmon

MACDONALD

MACLEOD

MacAskill

MACKINNON

MACDONALD

MACDONALD

MACDONALD

CLAN RANALD

MACFIE

MACKINNON

MacInnes

MACQUARIE

MACLEAN

MACFIE

MACLEAN

MC-CORQUODALE

MaCBeth

Maclaverty

MACDONELL

MacMillan

CAMPBELL

MacTavish

LAMONT

MacLay

MCNEILL

MACALISTER

MACDONELL

MaEachern

HAMILTON

HUNTER

MACKAY

GUNN

OLIPHANT

SINCLAIR

KEITH

KEITH

MACLEOD

OLIPHANT

OLIPHANT

SUTHERLAND

MUNRO

ROSS

Murray

MACDONELL

McCULLOCH

MACLEOD

MUNRO

Gayre

BAIN

URQUHART

MACKENZIE

Loban

MACDONELL

CHISHOLM

MacBain

Matheson

FRASER

Shaw

MacLennan

CHISHOLM

MacRae

GRANT

MACLEOD

FRASER

Mac Gillivray

MACINTOSH

MacMartin

Davidson

MACPHERSON

MACDONELL

MENZIES

ROBERTSON

CAMERON

MACDONALD

STEWART

MONCREIFFE

MacIntyre

MacDiarmid

MAC-GREGOR

MACNAB

MAC-DOUGALL

MacArthur

MACNAGHTEN

MacIver

MAC-FARLANE

Malcolms

SCRYMGEOUR

MACLACHLAN

MacEwen MacPhun

COLQUHOUN

MacFergus

MACAULAY

0 ____ 50 miles

0 ____ 50 ____ 100 kms

CHAPTER FOUR

Ye Hielands and
Ye Lawlands

Ye Hielands and ye Lawlands
O whaur hae ye been?
They hae slain the Earl o' Moray
An hae laid him on the green

He was a braw gallant
An he rade at the ring
An the bonnie Earl o' Moray
He micht hae been a King

O lang may his lady
Look frae the Castle Doune
Ere she see the Earl o' Moray
Come soondin' through the toun

O wae unto thee, Huntly
An wherefore did ye say
'I bade ye bring him away
But forbade ye him tae slay'?

He was a braw gallant
And he played at the glove
But the bonnie Earl o' Moray
He was the Queen's true love

O lang will his lady
Look frae the Castle Doune
Ere she see the Earl o' Moray
Come soondin' through the toun

Romantic ballad composed for the Earl of Moray, after his murder by the Earl of Huntly in 1592, the first real crisis of the personal reign of James VI. Save that the Earl of Moray was indeed good to look on – 'bonnie' – the song bears little resemblance to the truth of the event.

THE PERIOD from the fall of Clan Donald to the Rising of 1745 is one of the goriest in Highland history, and something of its character may be grasped from these lines of a contents page in a Victorian history of the Highlands and Islands:

Confusion in Scotland after the death of James IV . . . Insurrection of Sir Donald of Lochalsh . . . Who is supported by MacLean of Duart and MacLeod of Dunvegan . . . The Earl of Argyll sent against the insurgents . . . Further measures of the Privy Council against them . . . MacIain of Ardnamurchan supports the government . . . Strength of the insurgents . . . Some of them submit, and their example is followed by Lochalsh . . . Lochalsh projects a new insurrection . . . Apparently owing to the intrigues of English agents . . . He expels MacIain from Ardnamurchan, and seizes the Castle of Mingarry . . . His violence disgusts his followers, who desert him . . . Offers of Argyll, of the MacLeans of Duart and Lochbuie, and of MacLeod of Harris, to the Privy Council . . . The Earl of Huntly and the Clan Chattan . . . Two brothers of Sir Donald of Lochalsh are executed . . . MacLean of Duart takes the oath of allegiance . . . Feud between Lochalsh and Ardnamurchan . . . In which the latter and two of his sons are killed . . . And takes a protest regarding it . . . Death of Sir Donald of Lochalsh, being the last male of that house . . . Comparative tranquillity of the Isles . . . Increase of power of Argyll and the Campbells . . . Renewed disorders in the Isles, and their causes . . . Duart exposes his wife on a rock . . . And is assassinated by Campbell of Cawdor . . .

And so on: rebellion, battle, bloodshed; feud, battle, bloodshed; betrayal, battle, bloodshed; wife-exposing, battle, bloodshed. But the main political features are already apparent. The continuing estrangement of much of Gaeldom from the Scottish court. The readiness of English agents to stir up these quarrels. The rise and rise of Clan Campbell and their prince, Argyll. The developing hatred between the MacDonalds and the Campbells. And continued unrest, fighting, instability, piracy and disorder.

When his father died at Flodden, James V was seventeen months old. The tot was crowned a fortnight later; his mother, Margaret Tudor, had been named regent in the late king's will, but she was a sister of the English king, and the Scots nobles speedily substituted her with another ruler, the Duke of Albany. This Albany was a first cousin of James IV, and a very odd choice for a governor of Scotland. Raised in France, he could speak not a word of Scots, Gaelic or English. Of ferocious temper, he had a habit, when very angry, of dramatically flinging his bonnet into the fire. One man recorded that in two years Albany burned twelve bonnets; after this, he wearied of the Scots, and returned to France. The child monarch fell under the custody of the great (and ruthless) Douglas family; for fifteen years, then, his reign proceeded like most Stewart minority reigns before it – feuding amidst the nobility, assassination, jealousy, corruption and killing.

James V was seventeen years old before he was able to rule in his own right. He had it in him to be a very good king. He had all his father's spirit, coupled with Tudor charm. He had the Tudor red hair, too, and was generally of pleasing appearance. He had a remarkable memory for faces, and used to enjoy travelling the land *incognito*, fraternising with the common folk. So he was remembered, many years later, as the 'Poor Man's King' or, more aggressively, as the Red Fox. But James V had three weaknesses. His education, frequently interrupted, proved most inadequate: he was twelve before he learned to read English, and he never enjoyed fluency in French. Due in some measure to his wretched childhood, he had an abiding distrust of the Scots nobles, and they of him. His health was also fragile: he was prone to sudden and hysterical collapse, especially in circum-stances of adversity, and would be for that time quite useless. It may well have been that disorder known as porphyria, which is hereditary: his daughter, poor Mary, seems to have had it, and bequeathed it to her distant descendant, King George III.

The Highlanders had taken full advantage of the minority reign. One Clan Donald scion, Donald of Lochalsh, in 1513 proclaimed himself new Lord of the Isles. He was able to command, for a time, considerable support – he had the men of Mull and Skye at his back – and, too, enjoyed the encouragement (and perhaps the funding) of the English government. In this, though, he only provoked the Scots government in Edinburgh to proceed against him with all the more vigour. Lochalsh's character, too, was excessively vengeful; and when his supporters saw him set on the pillage and rape of such Highland territories as he gathered under him, they turned against him. But the biggest obstacle to Lochalsh ambitions was the rising house of Argyll.

Now there is a quaint Scotch myth in Highland history that goes like this. Once upon a time we had the Lord of the Isles, and the men of MacDonald – real, noble, Gaelic-speaking Highlanders, of charm and skill and honour and wit – governed the Hebrides and Highlands, and all lived happily. But the nasty king in Edinburgh grew jealous of Clan Donald's prosperity. He brought the Lord of the Isles down by means of assorted dirty tricks, and he raised up – as unworthy successors to Clan Donald lands and might – Clan Campbell, a mean, low-down, mongrelised, half-southern alien race, too clever for their own good. So noble Clan Donald was displaced by this bad lot, and Highland history was unhappy ever after.

This is most unfair to Clan Campbell, whose origins were just as Celtic and noble as those of Clan Donald, and who bred just as many agreeable and winsome characters, and who – by dint of a certain political realism – lasted a good deal longer.

The first Campbell of whom we learn in history is Sir Colin Mor Campbell of Lochow – an archaic spelling of Loch Awe, in north Argyll, where the ruins of Kilchurn Castle still stand. This Big Colin fell in battle in 1294; he drew descent from one Diarmid O'Duin, and in classical Gaelic the clan were known as Clann Duibhne, generally anglicised to Clan Diarmid. This Diarmid, in true Gaelic tradition, was a figure worthy of Greek myth: it is said that he slew the Boar of Caledon – a beast no doubt as ferocious as it sounds – and the modern Campbell crest still incorporates a boar's head.

The Campbell name itself appears to derive from the nickname of some progenitor – *cam beul* is a wry or twisted mouth – but the clan is certainly of ancient Irish origin, its lineage quite as aged as that of Clan Donald. But, in deference to this Big Colin, every Campbell chief in succession has since been known as *mac Cailean Mor*.

The main Clan Campbell was in Argyllshire, but their territories, and influence, were extensive, and various Campbell septs still survive. Nairn has its Campbells of Cawdor, and the Moray Firth village of Ardersier was – into our own century – known to many in the district as Campbelltown. Perthshire had the Campbells of Glen Lyon, and the Campbells of Breadalbane. All have their bit-parts in Highland history, but the Campbells of Argyll are by far the mightiest and most powerful bloc of all. And we know of their claims of Celtic descent from a royal charter they were granted in 1368: it is quite typical of the Campbells that they took good care to secure such title to their name and estates, and a sum of their whole polity that – in all they did – they allied themselves closely to the King of Scots and his government.

Bruce was the first to benefit: a son of Colin Mor, Sir Neil, and his own heir – another Sir Colin – fought with him in his campaigns, and the Campbells thus won royal favour, coming into their own after the triumph at Bannockburn. What made them great was their own common sense – they understood that power in the Highlands and Hebrides could only be secure under the blessing of the crown – and, by contrast, the degeneration of Clan Donald into political idiocy. The Lordship of the Isles might have continued for many centuries had the lord been content to operate a mighty sub-kingdom under nominal Stewart overlordship. Instead Clan Donald tangled with the king himself, parleyed with the English enemy, menaced such Lowland cities as Aberdeen. Nor could they learn from experience. As late as 1545 a would-be Lord of the Isles, Domnhull Dubh – Black Donald – was trying to cut deals with Henry VIII.

For Campbell services in the War of Independence this Sir Colin won the lands of Lochawe and Kilmartin – Lochow and Ariskeodnish, in the old style – and was thenceforth able to call himself Lord of Lochow: that was the whole of mid-Argyll between the Firth of Lorne and Loch Fyne. As the years went by, and they remained true, the Campbells amassed more and more land and might in old Dalriada. By the end of the fourteenth century they had acquired the Craignish district, the lands of Ardkinglas, Ardgartan on Loch Long, and Kilmun on the Holy Loch. In the fifteenth century, Inveraray and Kilmun won charters as burghs of barony, granting valuable commercial privileges. A collegiate church was founded at Kilmun. For help in mopping up the assassins of James I, the Campbells won the lands about Loch Riddon. They were awarded Otter from the MacEwens. When the Lord of the Isles was later forced to surrender Knapdale to the crown, they gained that too, and by now *mac Cailean Mor* rejoiced in the title of Earl of Argyll, conferred on another Sir Colin in 1457. The Knapdale award made him Keeper of Castle Sween. Knapdale included north Kintyre: in the sixteenth century, Argyll would enjoy the custody of Skipness Castle in that district, and all the lands about it.

Argyll soon received, too, the Lordship of Lorne, in exchange for some lands outwith old Dalriada he had gained by a fortunate marriage. The superiority of Glenorchy also fell to the Campbells, in circumstances which remain unclear (and dubious). In the meantime possessions in Nairn and Perthshire were bestowed upon assorted nephews and relatives. As the years passed by, more and more of the Highlands drew under the dominion of the Campbells of Argyll, and their various cadet branches. Others, of course, had to be displaced to make room for them; and chief among those we might count the Clan Gregor, driven from Glenorchy by the Campbell settlement there, and who – scattered amid the southern Highlands – became an increasing nuisance to their neighbours.

It was James IV who used the Campbells most effectively. When there was trouble in the region, they were put in charge of resolving it. When the crown took possession of forfeit lands, the Campbells were rewarded with them. Possessions and prestige amassed to the House of Argyll, and Campbells grew skilled too at making ruthlessly good marriages. And at every step they took good care to have suitable deeds, charters and warrants from king and Privy Council.

The whole crown policy of keeping the Highlands in order rested, too, on another great house – that of Huntly. They were the Gordons, and their origins were not Celtic, but Norman; they were the seed of yet another adventurer who had come north with David I, and by the time of James V the Earl of Huntly and his house dominated north-east Scotland, including much of Inverness-shire. Upon both families, Argyll and Huntly, the Scottish crown heaped lands and honours, and together they guarded the south country from the assorted Highland hosts, and maintained the unity of the kingdom. In 1509 James IV simultaneously made Huntly sheriff of the north, and Argyll sheriff of the west. These were mighty, brutal clans, but they were on his side, and would keep those who disputed his crown in the Highlands from posing any serious threat. The MacDonalds never understood this: they continued to defy the Stewart monarchy, and paid the due penalty, in forfeit lands and declining influence.

Nor were the Campbells people to cross. One Lachlan Cattanach MacLean of Duart decided he was tired of his wife. Perhaps there had been domestic strife; perhaps their marriage was barren; perhaps his eye had fallen elsewhere; perhaps he suspected her of plotting against his life. At any rate he had her marooned – by suitable henchmen – on a reef visible only at low water, in the hope, no doubt, that the flood-tide would sweep her away. Unfortunately for MacLean of Duart, however, a boat came by before the tide was sufficiently high, and the distraught woman was rescued. Even worse, she was no ordinary wife; she was a daughter of the second Earl of Argyll, and these were not in-laws to insult. The Campbells were shrewd enough to hide their feelings for a time. Then, on a visit to Edinburgh, MacLean of Duart was surprised in his lodgings by his brother-in-law, Sir John Campbell of Cawdor, and murdered.

And, as the minority of James V passed, and the king grew into maturity, the pattern continued: shifting allegiances among assorted Highland chieflings, the odd feud, the odd war, and the same depressingly familiar story. There was a long spat between the MacLeods of Harris and the MacDonalds of Sleat. Trouble arose in the isles of Islay and Jura. The Earl of Argyll descended upon them, and Alexander MacDonald of Islay rose in revolt; this time, provoking alarm in Edinburgh, he could call on the help of MacLean of Duart, though that family had long been ferocious rivals of the MacDonalds. The young James V immediately prepared a great expedition, with much training of troops and loading of ships; Alexander and MacLean decided to make peace with him, lest this force fall upon them. Then the Earl of Argyll . . . and so on, and so forth: imprisonment, hostages, times of peace, times of turmoil, and the odd vicious atrocity.

In 1540 James V, in the flower of manhood, paid a famous visit to the Hebrides. It combined something of a jaunt with an awesome show of force, and it followed a serious revolt by the MacDonalds of Sleat, in alliance with the MacLeods of Lewis, their clan chiefs being related by marriage.

The MacDonalds were under one Donald Gorm, and he dreamed of nothing less than elevating himself as Earl of Ross and Lord of the Isles – titles to which he had a tenuous if arguable claim. So MacLeods of Lewis and MacDonalds of Sleat made war in north Skye, seizing Trotternish from MacLeod of Dunvegan, and then Donald Gorm nipped over to Wester Ross, for Mackenzie of Kintail, the baron of that region, was away. Kinlochewe was laid waste, and then Donald Gorm besieged Eilean Donan Castle, the principal fort in the Kintail district. All was going well – the defences of the castle were weak – but Donald Gorm stayed rather too close, and was shot in the foot. It was a barbed arrow; in pain and rage, and without thinking, he ripped it out, and tore an artery. Despite the efforts of those nearby he bled to death. In a gesture characteristic of the inane battling of this period, his disappointed warriors burned all the Kintail boats they could find, then slunk back home.

The rebellion, such as it had been, was over: but James V was determined there would be no such follies again. He decided to awe the Highlanders by an impressive display of the might and resources of the crown. He would also gather a few chief trouble makers on the way, and take them on a little cruise for their edification and fear.

Twelve mighty ships were fitted for this voyage, bristling with cannon. Six bore the royal suite and troops under the personal command of the king. Three were laden with provisions. And one was put at the disposal of Cardinal Beaton; another for the conveyance of the Earl of Huntly; still another for the Earl of

Arran, heir-presumptive to the Scots throne. The cardinal, and both these lords, each joined the king in command of 500 men, not to mention assorted secretaries, manservants, minor gentry and the like. And one of the best pilots in the land, Alexander Lindsay, was detailed to wait upon the king and keep him regularly briefed on his observations at sea.

At the end of May 1540 the fleet sailed. They anchored by Orkney, where they were well entertained by the bishop, and revictualled; then they continued to Lewis, where Roderick MacLeod – chief – and some of his kin were invited on board to join the trip; it was made plain that refusal was not an option. Then they berthed by the north-west of Skye, and MacLeod of Dunvegan was constrained to board. They went round to stop by Trotternish – still unrepaired after the ravages of the insurrection – and here a nervous assemblage of chiefs waited to pay their respects, all of MacDonald descent: MacDonald of Glengarry and MacDonald of Clanranald were among the eminent. James V sailed on. At Kintail he collected MacKenzie. At Mull he took MacLean of Duart. At Knapdale he took on board MacDonald of Islay.

The expedition at length made Dumbarton, on the Firth of Clyde, where James V went ashore to proceed home to court by dry land; the fleet, and its alarmed and unhappy cargo, were sent back on voyage round the north of Scotland to Leith. At his leisure King James dealt with the prisoners. Terms were struck. Homage was made, some hostages were taken, and the Lordship of the Isles, and north and south Kintyre, were declared inalienably annexed to the crown. So peace fell on the Hebrides and the Highlands – for a time.

James V was the first King of Scots who had no Gaelic. But the fine natural harbour on the east of Skye, in the lee of Raasay, is still named for him, for he spent a night in this 'king's harbour' – Portree.

In 1542 an ill-chosen conflict with his uncle Henry VIII led to Scots defeat at Solway Moss. As James lay in prostration, and willed himself to die, word came that his queen had given birth to a little girl; she had earlier produced two princes, who had died in infancy. 'It cam wi' a lass; it'll gang wi' a lass,' he is said to have moaned, no doubt mindful of how the Stewarts had gained the throne through the daughter of Robert the Bruce. He was only thirty years of age; the child was seven days old when she inherited the crown.

The most striking feature of the sixteenth and seventeenth centuries in Highland history is the general air of arrested development. For the first hundred years or so, there was considerable internal unrest: prolonged periods of clan warfare, feuding, piracy, roving robber-bands, and so on. For the century and a half that preceded the '45, most of the disturbance arose from external events, notably the growing tendency of the Stuart kings, in their wretched government of England, to raise Highland armies against their enemies elsewhere. The ordinary people of the Highlands and Islands suffered much in these events, but their daily lot saw no improvement.

Agriculture remained frozen in a Norse time-warp. The *cas-chrom*, the wooden foot-plough, was the main instrument of agriculture, used to turn sods of ground for planting. It was not at all a bad tool. It gave twice the return for the same labour as the spade, and could be used on steep, wild, sloping land inaccessible to the horse-drawn plough. Twelve men working the *cas-chrom*, it was said, could turn an acre of land a day. (It was always men; its use was considered most indelicate for a woman.)

They had ploughs, but until the eighteenth century it was of a primitive type, requiring four horses and four men to its use; it broke the soil badly, and not to any depth. Used intensively, you ended up with a hard 'pan' underneath the tilled earth, which soon caused great difficulties with drainage. They had primitive harrows too, but the hoe seems to have been unknown.

Land was still worked by runrig, and this was a bad system in arable farming. You had no motive to dung and improve a piece of ground if another man would shortly be working it in turn. Runrig was justified in a highly communal society, where all joined together in the major tasks of land-work. In these perilous times, too, it made sense for violent days, when common defence and a constant watch on the seas were essential, and where survival from pillage and slaughter depended on all in a community being near to one another.

Fortunately the Highlanders of the day were primarily engaged in a pastoral economy, not an arable one. Cattle were their main activity, and cattle were everywhere. It is hard now to grasp how much the passing of these great herds has impoverished the land. Today the visitor sees the Highlands and Hebrides as predominately brown: all heather, bracken, sour grasses, assorted rank weeds. Three or four centuries ago, our earth was green. Cattle roamed everywhere, their dung enriching the soil, their grazing habits allowing the ground to breathe, and keeping down the coarser plants and sedges. It was the coming of vast flocks of sheep, at the end of the eighteenth century, which debased the Highland landscape.

In the sixteenth century, according to Dean Monro, the Hebrides grew oats and barley as their primary crop, with flax, rye, hemp and linseed in rather smaller quantities. Hay, oddly enough, was not gathered, and grass was not grown for this purpose. There seems to have been no awareness of its value in overwintering animals. It was still the general custom to slaughter such beasts in winter as one required for food – their meat then being salted down and stored – and turn the rest on to the open hill to fend for themselves. Such as survived until spring were, of course, pretty emaciated. In a bad winter most cattle died. A milk cow or two shared the house with the people in winter: these were often so weak by spring that they had to be carried out to the new grazing.

Grain, in those days, was uprooted by hand rather than reaped by sickle; this granted a longer straw for thatching, and meant that the grain continued to swell a little, rather than shrink. A variety of techniques were used for drying and thrashing it. Its grinding was a daily chore for women, and every house had its quernstones; the upper, convex, rotated on the face of the concave lower. It could take two women – one turning the quern, one feeding in handfuls of corn – four hours to grind a bushel of meal.

Porridge of oats and barley, or cakes – bannocks – of these grains: that was the staple fare of the people. The cows provided milk and cream, and simple cheeses were made. Some poultry was usually kept. Pigs, however, were seldom seen in the Highlands: they did not thrive in Hebridean conditions, and as biblical knowledge spread they were increasingly viewed as unclean beasts. Cattle were the primary export of the region: drovers came about continually, buying up beasts, and driving them south in great herds to the Lowland trysts.

At the time Dean Monro wrote, in 1549, the Highlands and Islands seem to have enjoyed great fertility: he writes repeatedly of vast harvests of corn; the phrase 'fertill and fruitfull' appears constantly. (It was a different world then in many respects: fifty more of the Hebrides were inhabited then than now.) By the time Martin Martin wrote, in 1695, the fertility of the soil had greatly declined, and harvests were poor, sometimes atrocious. What had happened was an oscillation of climate. The 'Little Ice Age' struck in its severity. Long bitter winters, short wet summers, and incessant storms battered the region for several decades.

It was probably in this chilly period that the black house, in the form in which it survived into our own day, was evolved. The black house was a drystone dwelling, the unmortared walls of double thickness, and the roof was thatched. Derivation of the name is uncertain; it is of English rather than Gaelic origin. It has nothing to do with soot or fires (although the cottages were very sooty inside; the open hearth sat in the middle of the earthen floor, without chimney). Most likely is that 'black house' was coined by way of contrast to the new 'white houses', which arrived in the eighteenth century, their walls mortared and generally limewashed. The black house, though built on principles dating back to the Bronze Age, had many virtues. It was snug, and of such smooth, low design that even on the stormiest night those inside heard no wind. Black houses were still to be seen, inhabited, in the Outer Isles as late as 1983.

For all their hardships, the Gaels enjoyed a world of much song and laughter. Highland women had songs for everything: for thrashing grain, for milling grain, for baking with it, for milking their cows, for nursing their children. In the long nights of winter, in song and tale all entertained each other. There were ballads, of romantic love, of historical drama, of the great Norse heroes and the Lords of the Isles and so on. Though illiteracy was almost universal, an astonishing wealth of lore and tradition survived, handed down from mouth to mouth and generation to generation, and even today there is much material still to be found, recorded from old men and women, and stored in the archives of Edinburgh.

For at least eight centuries Highlanders, both mainland and in the islands, wore the tartan plaid as their primary article of clothing. It was a great piece of cloth, some six yards by two, and reminiscent of nothing so much as the Roman toga. The Highlander wore it over an undershirt – a long light garment, knee-length – and he donned the plaid, *am breacan feilidh*, in rather complicated style: he put his belt flat on the floor (or ground) first, laid the plaid over it, and folded one end in pleats. He then lay over this and did up the belt around his middle, with the pleated end of the plaid becoming the kilt. The upper part of the plaid could be arranged in a manner of ways, usually by being drawn up over his back and left shoulder, and fastened by a pin or brooch, falling in folds over his left arm. His right arm was left unencumbered to manage his sword.

The plaid was a wonderful garment. Wet or dry, the thick wool kept a man warm in all weathers, and except in the most extreme of conditions he could sleep out in the open without shelter. On campaign, two or three Highland warriors might sleep together on the hill in a huddle, with multiple folds of cloth above and below them; marching through storm, folds of the plaid could be drawn over head and shoulders. Soaking actually improved the plaid; it drew the threads together, and they shrank into an even better windproof seal. The plaid gave great freedom to the limbs, on march and battle; it was far superior to trews in fording burns or tramping through wet undergrowth.

Trews were favoured for wear at sea or while riding a horse; they were skin-tight, so as not to chafe. Highlanders generally went barelegged, though, and wore footwear only in winter. Most of what we regard as the essential items of Highland dress – short open jackets, sporrans, bonnets and so on – were worn only by the gentry, or in a strictly utilitarian form by the common folk. Women wore their version of the plaid, a graceful thing called the *arisaid*, usually white, fastened by a high leather belt. A married woman always wore a simple head-covering. Mainland fashions attracted the wealthy Highland ladies after the late seventeenth century, but the *arisaid* survived, at least in the Outer Hebrides, well into the eighteenth.

Little can be said of the Highland policy of Mary, Queen of Scots. That unhappy woman arrived as a virtual stranger to her native land – she had left it when she was five, to spend most of her early life in France. Her last twenty years on earth, too, were in exile from Scotland, a prisoner of her cousin, Elizabeth Tudor, who eventually had the head off her. Mary's active reign in Scotland was but six years and characterised, for the most part, by cautious inertia and, latterly, dramatic incompetence.

Mary's reign was damned by three things. One was the Reformation, in full flood through western Europe; it broke in Scotland in 1560. More damaging, though, was the conduct of her guardians during the minority. The Scots council of regency agreed, under duress, to the betrothal of their tiny queen to the little son of Henry VIII; when the deal failed to be ratified (due, in fact, to the arrogant prevarication of the English king himself), Lowland Scotland was much battered by its southern neighbour in the outrages of the 'Rough Wooing'. Mary's mother, Mary of Guise, took charge as regent; the traditional image of her as a bloody scourge of Protestantism is unfair, and she was not without ability, but she was far too inclined to pander to French interests. For Mary was newly betrothed to the young Dauphin, heir to the French throne. So the little queen was borne off to France. And, when her husband succeeded as king – still little more than a child – she, and he, were proclaimed as rightful sovereigns of France, Scotland and England! For Elizabeth I now reigned in England; she was Protestant, she was damned as a bastard by Catholic Europe, and Mary was nearest to her in succession. Worse still – in a deal kept secret from the Scots – her husband was accorded the crown matrimonial; on her death, that made him rightful heir to the throne.

So, when Mary was mercifully widowed, and when at length she landed at Leith, in 1561, she was cordially loathed by Elizabeth and the English court, and generally distrusted by the Scots. She insisted on adhering to the Roman faith – though celebration of mass in her private apartments threatened to convulse her kingdom – and she refused to ratify the Treaty of Edinburgh, recently and tediously concluded; thus she maintained title to the English crown, and an abiding French involvement in Scots affairs.

Admirers of Mary concentrate on the first four years of her personal reign, until 1565; she consolidated her position with care, and won the respect of many, both for her great charm and a genuine natural tolerance in religion. Or was it a matter of cunning: the Roman Catholic queen following courses of conspicuous neutrality? There were two external pressures. Mary was mindful of the English succession, for Elizabeth remained unmarried and childless, and the Protestants of England were watching closely the Queen of Scots. Besides, Roman Catholicism itself was at a crossroads. The Council of Trent – in which her uncle, Cardinal of Guise, was heavily involved – deliberated through those years, redefining the Roman faith in the light of Protestant upheaval.

Mary travelled a great deal in Scotland, and there were long progresses. In two months of 1563 she covered 1,200 miles. She never saw the West Highlands, but she twice visited Inverness, where one noble, the Earl of Huntly, posed a serious problem. He was no Protestant rebel, far from it. His house, the Gordons, had long been pet-barons of the Stewarts in north-east Scotland and the Eastern Highlands. They, and he, were staunch Romanists; he has been called 'Pope of the north-east'. But, as the queen toured the area in 1562, he made a gesture both grandiloquent and monstrously stupid: he invited the sovereign to join him at a celebration of mass in his chapel at Strathbogie. Mass, beyond the queen's own household, was outlawed in Scotland. It had become thus a royal privilege, dearly held against the outrage of the political class: for Huntly thus to offer such to the queen was dangerous as well as insulting.

Mary made an example of the man: his acts threatened to trigger a full-blown religious war in Scotland, and, besides, Huntly offered her good occasion to show the English how well she handled Roman Catholic subjects. The cautious policy of the throne in matters religious had to be upheld, and it had to be seen to be upheld. So Huntly was condemned and outlawed. He was hunted down; he escaped royal forces, but died suddenly of a stroke. The Gordons were broken. The queen's half-brother, James – a natural son of her late father – was confirmed as Earl of Moray. Stability, though, was preserved in this far-flung region of Scotland; it was no mean achievement for a woman whose career never gave other evidence of shrewd political judgement.

Passion was the undoing of Mary. She made a marriage remarkable for its folly, to her distant cousin Henry Stuart, Lord Darnley. He was related to her both in the Tudor and Stewart lines. The marriage caused huge offence to Elizabeth, and much alarm in England, for Darnley's Tudor blood would strengthen Mary's

English aspirations. In human terms, too, the marriage was foolish. Darnley was as stupid as he was arrogant. He was grossly immature in his character – vain, tyrannical, selfish – and dissolute in his pleasures. Mary fell madly in love with him because he was very handsome and (like herself) extremely tall.

Still, the union gave Mary some kin at court, and a measure of protection against jousting nobles. It seemed better, to many, than the perils of a marriage to some foreign princeling. But the Earl of Argyll violently objected to the match. So did James, Earl of Moray. Their campaign failed and they fled into exile. In February 1566, Darnley, vastly swollen in pride and vainglory, defiantly embraced the Roman faith. Meantime the royal marriage had rapidly slid from passion to icy hate. A few weeks later he and some cronies – leading Protestant nobles – burst into the queen's tiny apartment at Holyrood, tore her Italian secretary David Rizzio from her side, and butchered him before her. The queen was heavily pregnant; the experience was horrifying. Rizzio was widely distrusted as a Romanising influence. Darnley (whose involvement is otherwise puzzling) might have been persuaded that the Italian had seduced the queen: her consort was stupid enough. It may well have been an attempt (by traumatic miscarriage) on the life of the unborn child, if not on that of the queen herself. But a son was safely born, in June that year, and named Charles James. The queen was delivered in a claustrophobic chamber of Edinburgh Castle, whence she had repaired for safety.

The royal marriage collapsed. In February 1567 Darnley was murdered in dramatic circumstances; Protestant nobles (who had hated him in life) now exalted him in death, and engineered sufficient scandal to drive Mary from the throne, installing her baby son in her place as King James VI. The queen was widely reviled as an adulteress, a prostitute, a very fiend of womanhood. But there was more to the coup than mere politics. Mary was shortly to reach her twenty-fifth birthday, her 'perfect age'. She would then be able to recover crown lands entrusted to Scots nobles during the minority. This the good men in question were eager to forestall.

She was forced to abdicate, then jailed in an island prison in Loch Leven, Kinross. But the queen escaped, and raised armed revolt with her lover and new husband, Bothwell. The rising failed, and she fled by ship for France. But, on passage through the Irish

Sea – in a hysterical change of heart – she ordered a landing in England. Mary was stupid enough to believe that Elizabeth, whom she had so often insulted, and whose wise counsels she had blithely ignored, would now rush to her aid and restore her to the Scottish throne. Elizabeth, though, was mortified by the unexpected and most unwelcome guest. She refused to receive her; Mary's release, however, was politically impossible. Within weeks the guest was a prisoner. For nearly two decades, under increasingly close confinement, the Queen of Scots was held fast, until events compelled her royal cousin to consent to her execution. But these two remarkable ladies – one the greatest queen, perhaps, of the Christian era; the other the most hapless – never met.

The latest infant monarch was crowned in July 1567, just three days after his mother's deposition, and for only the second time in Scottish history the name was adjusted: he was hailed not as Charles, but as King James VI. The service featured other innovations. The rites took place not in the Chapel Royal, but at the Church of the Holy Rood in Stirling. There was no anointing ritual. The former Roman Bishop of Orkney put the crown on the tot's head. John Knox preached a mighty sermon from the First Book of Kings. Afterwards the sovereign was entrusted to the Erskine family, and the schooling of such Protestant stalwarts as George Buchanan and Peter Young. For the first time in a land long used to minority reigns, physical possession of the child king was divorced from the exercise of power. The Erskines took little to do with the administration of Scotland. The Earl of Morton, regent until 1578, seldom saw the boy and had little interest in him.

James grew up, of course, without any memory of his parents, and never saw his mother again. Though Mary survived until 1587, he had no filial feeling towards her, and he cannot be blamed for that; from infancy he had been raised to view her as monstrous and wicked. When she was beheaded, after the Babington conspiracy, his protests were formal and muted.

James's legitimacy has been questioned. Before his birth – and, indeed, through his lifetime – there were whispers about his paternity. Was he in fact the son of David Rizzio? Much more serious – because, after all, it was through his mother that he took title to royal thrones – is the persistent suggestion that he was a common substitute, a changeling for an infant who had died shortly after birth. Many commented on James's strong resemblance to the Earl of Mar: had a baby of the Erskine household been smuggled into the birth-chamber? And, in the last century, the bones of a newborn were uncovered in Edinburgh Castle during renovations. Was this, in truth, the Stuart heir? The question is entertaining, but too dangerous for most to probe: it reflects on the legitimacy of all subsequent British monarchs.

James was weird of personality and grotesque in his appearance, an odd product of such glamorous handsome parents. He was short, his features coarse, his tongue too big for his mouth. His speech was thick, then, and slurred; he could not drink without it spilling down his chin. The king was bandy-legged, his limbs so weak that he could not long stand without leaning on someone's shoulder. He had rolling, goggling eyes, which those in his presence found intensely chilling.

Despite an education of determined piety – he was tutored by some of the ablest minds of the Reformation – he achieved manhood as a vicious, self-indulgent character. He ate and drank too much, though his table habits were disgusting; the King of Scots slobbered and drooled. He never washed his hands; merely wetted his fingers, and wiped them dry on the clothing of any in the vicinity. He had a morbid fear of assassination, scarcely fit in a descendant of the manly Stewarts – though how many, indeed, had died a natural death? He could not bear to see a sword drawn in his presence, and the clothes of King James were mightily padded, lest he be stabbed: this made him look fatter than he really was.

His language was indecent. He delighted in bawdy jokes and crude entertainments. As King of England, he enjoyed getting respectable ladies of the court so drunk that they at length vomited or collapsed. James VI is notorious for his homosexuality. He was seduced at the age of thirteen by a French cousin – who offered him, in fairness, the first real affection he had ever known – and, in old age, became increasingly pathetic in his dotings over gorgeous young men. He would intimately fondle these darlings before an appalled court; he wrote risible letters to the latest catamite, signing off with such endearments as 'your dear old dad and gossip'; the king would even justify pederasty by blasphemy. 'Christ had his John,' he said once, without a blush, 'and I have my Francis.' Yet the king married Princess Anne of Denmark, who bore him several fine children.

He was not a simpleton, though. King James was immensely learned, fluent in the classical tongues, bookish and pedantic. He wrote a great deal, and, being king, these heavy, tedious works were obediently published. He is best remembered for the *Counterblaste Against Tobacco*, but it was in his reign of England, and under his auspices, that the great Authorised Version of the Bible was produced. Of real political significance was an odd work, *Basilikon Doron*, in which the monarch outlined his ideas of kingship. Kings, he insisted, were ordained of God, not men. The sovereign was the Lord's anointed. He should be aloof, imperious, absolute. To the Almighty alone he bore account for all actions, and no mere people, no General Assembly, no parliament, had any right to check, scrutinise or control the monarch's actions. It was mediaeval nonsense; it proved the undoing of his dynasty.

The minority of King James VI was peculiarly turbulent for his land and wretched for himself. Regent Moray, one of the very few able and principled men in the realm, was murdered in 1570. The Reformation was far from secure. There remained a strong party loyal to the exiled Queen Mary. There were battles, riots, plots, a brutal siege of Edinburgh Castle by the forces of the regime. Regent Morton governed with grim efficiency, but he maintained order; above all, he established Protestantism. His downfall came not by statecraft, but by sodomy. In 1579 one Esme Stuart, a French peer and a distant cousin of the king, came to Scotland. This Stuart was very handsome, very charming and very cunning. He befriended the lonely, repressed teenage king; soon, he was in bed with him. James made him Earl of Lennox. The favourite worked rapidly to destroy Morton. His design was nothing less than the restoration of Mary and the restoration of the Roman faith. So Stuart bribed his way round court, and engineered an anti-Morton party. The wily regent was brought down by an old scandal. He was accused of complicity in the murder of Darnley, arrested, tried, and condemned to death. He died by a chop of his own 'Maiden', the primitive guillotine he had introduced to Scotland, the more efficiently to establish the Protestant order.

The ascendancy of Lennox and his gang did not last long. The

Protestants took alarm; the nature of his hold over the young king became known. In 1582 they resorted to a classic Scots strategem: they tore the king from the possession of the dangerous faction. James was hunting in Perthshire; at nightfall, he was persuaded to retire to a castle at Ruthven, which belonged to the shrewd Earl of Gowrie. On the morrow the young king tried to leave, and was detained at the door. He burst into tears. Those about him mocked. 'Better bairns greet than bearded men!' said the Master of Glamis. It was a jibe which James never forgot. Lennox fled to France, and died soon after. The new oligarchy restored a Protestant policy. England, not France, was cultivated in diplomacy. Harsh anti-Roman laws were passed. All the time, though, James waited for his chance. In 1583 he escaped from Falkland Palace. It was not long before he had established himself as ruler in his own right.

James's reign in Scotland was rather more confident than his subsequent administration of England. It was marked by two obsessions. One was Church government. King James detested Presbyterianism, established by the General Assembly in 1560, a key principle of the Reformation order. The Church of Scotland was to be entirely free of the royal decree. Its sole head on earth was the General Assembly. There were to be no bishops. Parishes were to be run by sessions, counties by presbyteries, and so on. James, naturally, resented the denial of such important power; besides, he was convinced of the divine right of kings. So there were spectacular confrontations between him and the Reformation leaders, chief among them Andrew Melville. 'Thair is twa Kings and twa Kingdomes in Scotland,' he boldly told his sovereign. 'Thair is Christ Jesus the King, and His Kingdome, the Kirk, Whase subject King James the Saxt is, and of Whase Kingdome nocht a king, nor a lord, nor a heid, but a member!' To James, of course, imbued with notions of his 'Divine Right', there could only be one realm, with himself at the head of it; his tussle with presbytery is a long and diverting tale, but outwith the scope of this book.

His other passion was the throne of England. By 1583 Elizabeth Tudor was fifty years old; it was manifest she would never now marry or produce an heir. James was her nearest kin, after his disgraced mother: he was young, fit and Protestant. The King of Scots was eager to be formally recognised as heir-presumptive.

This the wily old queen was too shrewd – and too fickle – to do. She granted him a pension, the better to further the interests of England (and herself) north of the Border. Meantime, James played dangerous games: he cultivated Catholic Europe, and hinted he might change his religion to win their support for England's crown. They were deadly, desperate times, when the rule of law in Scotland was perilous thin; when men took religion with a passion we find hard to fathom today; when they would kill for faith and murder for offence. The nobility behaved with extraordinary viciousness. In 1592 a feud grew between a new Earl of Huntly and a new Earl of Moray. It ended in the bloody, and cowardly, murder of the latter. Great was the grief and rage of his mother; in ghoulish mourning, she commissioned a portrait of the corpse, which lay unburied for six years.

But what of the Highlands? The Reformation penetrated the eastern districts a little; most of the region, though, remained Popish by profession and pagan for real. The disorder and chaos of earlier reigns continued. Piracy was a huge problem; ships of the Lowlands, and of other European realms, were regularly halted, boarded and pillaged by west-coast villains. Meantime assorted bandits, freebooters and rascals roamed the Highlands and the Hebrides, pursuing assorted causes of dubious merit, and preying upon the poor. They practised 'sorning', a predatory requisition of all they might desire by way of provisions – clothes, boats, grain and meal, livestock and so on. So the miseries of the ordinary Highland people were great.

The clan system continued to evolve along feudal lines. Succession to a chiefdom became hereditary rather than elective; there were exceptions to this, and on occasion a new chief considered particularly unacceptable would be deposed for another. Charters of clan land from the crown were, exclusively, to chiefs and their heirs; but the Highland belief that land belonged to all of the clan, and that the chief was but head trustee, would survive for many more generations among the common folk. Nevertheless they now increasingly levied rent. The tacksman class began to rise: smallholders, working farms held by rent from the chief, or sub-letting these farms (and stock) to others. Below them were cottars, arranged in townships – little clusters of houses, each with enough land to sow a boll of oats and keep a cow or two.

The brieves vanished around the middle of the sixteenth century, and full powers of heritable jurisdiction were assumed by the chiefs, as well as the portion of fines that once maintained the brieves. The chief had power of pit and gallows – the pit to drown women, the gallows on which to hang men. Clan elders had the moral authority, at least, to counsel and restrain their chiefs. Some chiefs were manifestly evil men; most, though, seemed to have governed with reasonable impartiality and good sense.

The system did not prosper from the prevailing cult of aggression and violence, physical courage was reckoned the most supreme of virtues, and those who aspired to succeed to a chiefdom trained from an early age in the arts of war, manly rigour and bodily exercise. Such a young man was expected to prove himself in combat, and if no suitable conflict was at hand for him then the Highlanders had no hesitation in triggering one: a raid on the cattle of a neighbouring clan, the least excuse seized upon for a feud. So there was much unnecessary battle. The odd anecdote has survived, through the centuries, to indicate notions of manhood at this time. One young chieftain, out with his men on campaign at night, and, like them, with no more tent than his plaid and the bare hillside, found himself unable to lay his head comfortably on the ground. So he scrabbled about for a small boulder, and pillowed his head on that. But he still could not sleep, for all about him rose the murmurs and grumbles of the men: what sort of weakling needed a pillow?

And there were the spoils of piracy. Clansmen in the Hebrides, especially, found a lucrative living in waylaying and looting ships unwise enough to pass through their waters. In the sixteenth century, of course, the problem was universal: every part of the British coast seethed with pirates. And the Inner Hebrides, especially, provided abundant hiding for the various outlaws, desperadoes, cut-throats, bandits and other delightful characters who decided to prosecute this agreeable trade. (On the island of South Rona, by Raasay, there is still a cove known as *Port nan Robaireann*.) Most of these men were outwith the clan system, and so immune from attack by rival clansmen; they made sure of that by avoiding local shipping and preying, for the most part, on Lowland, English and European vessels.

The most famous Hebridean pirate, however, was a clan chief –

MacNeil of Barra. The immodesty of this house is renowned: it was a MacNeil chief who had it trumpeted from Kisimul Castle to the nations, after his evening repast, 'The great MacNeil of Barra having supped, all the princes of the earth may dine!' This MacNeil became notorious as a terror of the seas. His ships ranged as far as west of Ireland, into the Atlantic, ravaging even the treasure-ships of Spain and Portugal, and the boats of Elizabeth Tudor. The princes of the earth suffered much. The English, the French, the Dutch enjoyed no peace. Complaints flooded in to the Scottish court. MacNeil was repeatedly outlawed – 'put to the horn' – but continued his happy business activities.

At length James VI had no choice but to act fiercely: he was now receiving hate-mail from the English queen herself, to whose throne he aspired and by whose pension he lived well. MacKenzie of Kintail was detailed to kidnap MacNeil, by a trick, and bring him before the king in Edinburgh. No doubt James had expected to see a robber-baron of villainous mien and bloodthirsty appearance. He was taken aback when, instead, MacNeil proved to be an amiable old man with long white beard. Nor was the Barra chief at a loss for words when bitterly reproached for his attacks on English shipping. These 'piracies', he said innocently, were but just toll on 'the woman who killed your Majesty's mother!' What could James do then but set him free? MacNeil's estates were declared forfeit, of course, but none had the nerve to sail on Barra and take them. Like many an old Highland rogue, the pirate chief died peacefully in his bed.

Typical of the mainland clans at this time – and of them all, perhaps, none is more dashing, and more bloodcurdling in its history – was Clan Cameron, lords of Lochaber. The part of the Camerons in Highland affairs is particularly important because their territory – at the southern end of the Great Glen, and at the north of the Firth of Lorne – fell between those beats of the great sheriffs of the Stewart monarchy, Argyll and Huntly. Each, at various times, forced homage from Cameron of Lochiel, as the chief became known: but none ever quite mastered the men of Lochaber.

There is, of course, no such loch as Lochaber, and the derivation of the name for that district is a discussion in itself. It is, though, generally agreed to be the lands north of Loch Eil, as far as Loch Arkaig, and north of Loch Leven, as far as Glen Spean. The name 'Lochaber' can be traced as far back as the thirteenth century; it has been convincingly argued, by Donald MacCulloch, that it derives from a loch which no longer exists, a swampy piece of water at the lower reaches of the River Lochy. A large bog is still found in the district, the plain known as Corpach Moss. MacCulloch makes out a good case that Lochaber means 'loch of marshes'.

The Camerons seem to have been an Anglo-Norman family – no doubt descended from yet another of David I's schoolmates – who were initially settled in Perthshire. These de Cambrons reached Lochaber through their connections with the powerful Atholl family. The Atholls had gained superiority in Lochaber through marriage with the Comyns, or Cummings, who were overlords of Lochaber and Badenoch until they backed the losing side in the War of Independence. When John, Lord of the Isles, was made ward of Lochaber, about 1335, he installed John de Cambron as his baillie in the district. De Cambron, with an eye to establishing himself and his line in the district, rapidly annexed the lands of Glen Loy and Loch Arkaig to the Lochaber policies, seizing them from Clan Mackintosh and so initiating a bitter feud that lasted until 1665.

There were other families in the district, of course, with title – in their own parcels – to all the lands of Lochaber. But the MacMartins, the MacSorlies, and the MacGillonies were soon persuaded to join in confederation with Clan Cameron: once Black Donald, the first great Cameron chief, had wed the MacMartin heiress, the Cameron pre-eminence was assured. Soon the remaining MacMartins, MacSorlies and MacGillonies had obligingly changed their name to Cameron. By the end of the fifteenth century even the king had recognised the position of the family, and that of their chief as Captain of Clan Cameron.

This Black Donald, Domnhull Dubh, we have met before; though generally styled eleventh of his line, he was the first true Cameron chief in Lochaber. At Harlaw in 1411 he was prominent on the side of the Lord of the Isles. Later, though, he broke from the MacDonald cause, and acquitted himself sufficiently in the king's service to win royal favour for his family.

Few Highland clans, though, had to fight more strenuously than the Camerons to retain their land. It was frequently confiscated from them, by a Lord of the Isles here, or a king there, and the Camerons had to pay penance (in years of faithful service) to win them back. Mackintoshes, Campbells, MacLeans and so on regularly seized great tracts of it, and had to be beaten out again. The Camerons have survived, through history, remarkable reverses. In 1546, allied with the MacDonalds, the Cameron men inflicted a terrible defeat on the Frasers at Kinlochlochy; the Fraser chief and his son were killed, and many of their clansmen. For this the Earl of Huntly fell on Lochaber, with Mackintosh support, bore away Ewen Cameron of Lochiel (and Ronald MacDonald of Keppoch) and beheaded them at Elgin.

Yet, through it all – death, murder, military defeat, failed rebellion, lost cause – the Camerons endured; a Cameron chief still owns most of the ancestral lands about Lochiel, and he still stays at their ancient seat of Achnacarry.

Tales of this line abound. An early Cameron chief, *Ailean an Creach* – Alan of the Forays: he was an infamous cattle-rustler – thrived in the fifteenth century, and led a gloriously lawless (and most profitable) life. In his old age it is said that Alan grew penitent, and no doubt anxious for the future of his soul. He decided to resort to a black rite known as *taghairm*, an ancient form of divination – nothing less than raising the devil himself to do your bidding. In the best tradition of this sort of thing, Alan consulted a local witch, and on her advice repaired to a suitably lonely field, beyond Banavie, and built a little hut. There he composed himself with a manservant and an unfortunate cat. A blazing fire was lit, a spit was run through some non-vital part of the cat's anatomy, and Alan began slowly to toast the wretched creature over the flames. Soon its screeches and wails attracted a great host of cats. Every mouser and moggie in the district soon surrounded the hut. There appeared, too, some huge wild-cats, and all insensate with rage, and all set to tear Alan and his companion to pieces. But Alan had his claymore, and with this he kept the assembled felines at bay, and all the time roaring to his ghillie, 'Hear you this or see you that, turn the spit and roast the cat!'

Then, just as the horrid chorus of crazed cats reached its crescendo, a gigantic black cat appeared in their midst: the Devil himself. He ordered the other cats into abject silence. He inquired of Alan why he tortured the animal. Alan said, 'I will release it if you will tell me how I can atone for my past misdeeds.' And the Great Black Cat said, 'You can atone and be forgiven by building seven churches in the Highlands, one for each of your great forays.' So the poor cat was released. It dashed away with a terrific screech, and plunged into the River Lochy, followed by all its brethren; this part of the river is still known as the Cat Pool. They were borne down by the current to a gentle bend where, suitably cooled, the cats swam ashore and melted into the night.

Alan of the Forays duly built his churches: at Kilmallie, Kildonan, Kilchoireil, Kilchoan, Arisaig, Morvern, and Kilkellan. But some, like Donald MacCulloch, maintain that the story is really that of his son, Ewen, first of the house to style himself 'of Lochiel', and who led a life of even more noted wickedness; it is said that, bereaved of his son, this Ewen – an old man – made pilgrimage to Rome, and that it was the Pope, not the devil, who ordered the building of seven churches. But it is also said that, having erected the walls of each, this Ewen told the workmen to stop: he had promised to build churches, he declared, but not to roof them. It was he whom, in 1547, Huntly captured and took to execution at Elgin. Still, the house of Cameron endured, and prospered; the house of Huntly did not.

Protestantism, and the king's dream of the great throne in Whitehall, inevitably anglicised the Scots court. Further, the myths of kingship – lovingly fostered by generations of Stewarts to bolster their mystical position – were now purged of Gaelic elements. The monarchy began consciously to distance itself from the Highlands, from Gaelic, from the traditions of Dalriada. A court poet, Alexander Montgomerie, now felt free to mock a Gaelic connection cherished as late as the reign of James V:

> *How the first Helandmen*
> *Of God was maid*
> *Of a horse-turd in Argyll*
> *It is said . . .*

King, and court, had a vision of union. Scotland and England would emerge from Elizabeth's death as a great, mighty, prosperous realm, united by the monarchy, by a common tongue and a shared religion. Even as Elizabeth lived, men thought, spoke and wrote of a coming British identity. Those who rebelled against such union could be readily tarred as regressives, savages, pagans – Papists, Borderers, Irishmen, and the Gaels of the Highlands and Islands. Not that all Highlanders were viewed as irredeemably alien. The king himself had found a class to commend in *Basilikon Doron*: 'that dwelleth in our mainland, that are barbarous for the most part, and yet mixed with some show of civility; the other, that dwelleth in the Isles, and are utterly barbarous, without any sort or show of civility.' The king felt himself in a dilemma. Should the Highlands be civilised? Or should they rather be conquered, its indigenous people slaughtered and broken, the land resettled by godfearing southerners? Decision was never a striking quality of James VI. For a time he resorted to the traditional device of his house in controlling the Highlands: lieutenancies were again granted Argyll and Huntly. The king thought of touring the region, like his grandfather, and various expeditions were planned – 1592, 1596, 1598, 1600 – but never took place.

King James decided on Spanish-style, state-licensed expeditions of conquest. The Highlands and Islands were quietly disowned by the ruling culture. The court and government tacitly swung to sanction any means, fair or foul, that might bring the north and west to 'civilitie' – kidnapping, blackmail, extortion, fire and sword, massacre. As the century ended the first adventurers were eagerly sailing forth, backed by dramatic new legislation and the eager hopes of their sovereign, for the rape of the Hebrides.

The new century was not long old when, on 24 March 1603, a horseman galloped through the gates of Holyrood Palace. He brought word that Queen Elizabeth was dead. Two days later, another messenger brought word from England's Privy Council, hailing James as their rightful king. With manifest delight he was soon over the Border, heading south for his vast new realm.

CHAPTER FIVE

Great Is My Sorrow

'S iomadh oidhche fhliuch is thioram
Side nan seachd sian
Gheibheadh Griogal dhomh-sa creagan
Ris an gabhainn dion

Eudail mhoir a shluaigh an domhain
Dhoirt iad d'fhuil an-de
'S chuir iad do cheann air stob daraich
Tacan beag bho d'chre

B'annsa bhith le Griogal cridhe
Tearnadh chruidh le gleann
Na le Baran mor na Dalach
Sioda geal mu m'cheann

Obhan, obhan, obhan iri
Obhan iri o
Obhan, obhan, obhan iri
'S mor mo mhulad, 's mor

Many nights wet or dry
In the wildest of weather
Gregor found me a little rock
For my shelter

Much beloved of the people
Yesterday they spilled your blood
And stuck your head on a oaken post
Away from your body

I had rather be with Gregor my love
Driving cows in the glen
Than with the mighty lord of Dalach
White silk about my head

Obhan, obhan, obhan iri
Obhan iri o
Obhan, obhan, obhan iri
Great's my sorrow, great

From the song 'Griogal Cridhe', in its modern arrangement. Many versions survive, but all stem from the original lament of the widow of Gregor of Glenstrae, after his execution at Kenmore in 1570 – yet another victim of the court's war on turbulent Highlanders, and Clan Gregor in particular.

THE SEVENTEENTH century brought the Stuarts to the throne of England, and the Union of the Crowns led, inevitably, to considerable union of executive. It was a century whose politics were marked by the Stuart obsessions: the divine right of kings, and the Romanising of religion. The upheaval and disorder that had been the fate of the Highlands for much of the previous century now spread through the British Isles. The three kingdoms were shaken; the Stuarts were twice dethroned, and on the second occasion dethroned for ever. But, in one of history's paradoxes, the Highlands – which they had so long misgoverned and abused – became a source of loyal fighting men, a theatre for some significant (and vicious) battles for the control of Britain. In this the people of Gaeldom manifested that peculiar Celtic genius, for committing all in support of a doomed cause just as all other sensible men were abandoning it.

King James I of England had some difficulty adjusting to his new realm. Its political order was entirely different. Nor did the enthusiasm of the people appeal to him; he was aghast at the crowds that jostled his progress down to London, clawing to be near him, to win his touch for the 'King's Evil'. It was a new experience for a man used to the familiar contempt of the Scots, and he found the pressing and the stares disconcerting. Assured by courtiers that the common folk wished only to see his face, he snapped, 'God's wounds! I shall pull down my breeches that they may see my arse!'

On the other hand, the Episcopal administration of the English Church was very much to his liking. And, as King of England, he was a good deal wealthier. The crown, even here, was sliding towards relative poverty – Elizabeth had only been able to maintain her state by selling off crown lands – but, in Scotland, finance had been a perennial royal problem, exacerbated by the repeated minority reigns and the seizure of dynastic lands and assets by assorted nobles. It had tempted some Scots sovereigns to acts of folly. And, for James VI in his Highland policy, it had brought him to countenance genocide.

Perenially short of money, the king – in the last years of the sixteenth century – promoted a company of Lowland gentlemen who have gone down in history as the Fife Adventurers. He encouraged them in a grand project: the occupation, colonisation and plunder of the isle of Lewis. James VI had remarkable notions of this largest of the Hebrides, whose primary resource was, and remains, peat. Lewis, he declared, was 'inrychit with ane incredibill fertilitie of cornis and store of fischeings and utheris necessaris, surpassing far the plenty of any pairt of the inland'. At the same time the pillage of the island – for all the world as if it were some part of the Indies – needed rather grander justification than the mere enrichment of the sovereign. So James got up an Act of Parliament.

The Scots parliament, then, solemnly set Lewis beyond the bounds of civilisation. Its people were pronounced 'voyd of any knawledge of God or His religoun', as folk 'gavin thameselfis over to all kynd of barbaritie and inhumanitie'. The Adventurers were granted all powers for 'ruiting out the barbarous inhabitantis'. There was no mention of the Act for converting these benighted heathen to Christianity. It was tacitly understood that they were to be put to the sword. Further, it was made known that the rest of the Hebrides and Highlands, in due time, would be civilised in like manner; no lands in the region were henceforth to be 'disponit in feu, tak or utterways bot to Lowland men'.

At the head of this glorious expedition was put the Duke of Lennox, the king's cousin. The commission authorised whatever 'slauchter, mutilation, fyre-raising or utheris inconvenieties' the great Lennox might deem fit for crushing or annihilating the natives of Lewis. Meantime, with an air to future profit, the king was already negotiating with the Marquis of Huntly to seize the rest of the Outer Hebrides, 'not be agreement with the country people bot by extirpation of thame'. In November 1598 the first landing was made at Stornoway – then a huddle of poor thatched houses – on the promontory of what is now Point Street; two other landings were essayed in 1605 and 1609. They did their best to build a 'prettie toun'. But they had not prepared for the wet wild climate, nor brought sufficient stores. Dysentery ran rife. And they were already under attack.

For the Lewis people resisted them with force and courage. Led by Neil MacLeod, they sacked the camps of the Adventurers; they drove off livestock, fired the new houses, fired stores of provisions, defeated armed men in skirmish. When the Adventurers sent word south for help, the messenger was caught at sea. Another messenger was sent; but scarcely had he left when the MacLeods descended on the 'toun' with 'two hundred barbarous, bluidie and wiket Hielandmen' on yet another attack. The folk of Lewis pirated their ships in the Minch, took Stornoway Castle – twice – and finally slaughtered the garrison. The adventure failed: had it not, James VI would have created in the Hebrides what he did so devastatingly in Ulster: a 'plantation' society of alien settlers, Lowland and English; the islands were thus spared vicious 'improvements', the creation of an aboriginal underclass, and centuries of racial hatred.

MacLeod of Lewis had bravely stood by his people and spared them this evil fate. As fitting reward, in 1610 James VI granted title of the island to Mackenzie of Kintail and all the rights he had bestowed on the Adventurers. But it took Mackenzie two long brutal years, with much plotting and treachery, to wrest Lewis from the MacLeods: at length he won, and they lost control of the island, which remained under the Mackenzies until the middle of last century.

And what of Clan Gregor? This dispossessed tribe fought desperately for land and place in the passes around Loch Lomond, Loch Long, Loch Katrine. In Glen Fruin, in 1603, they slaughtered dozens of their bitterest foe – the Colquhouns – and threatened to besiege and fire Dumbarton itself. So the king forced a draconian measure through the Scots parliament, seeking to annihilate the very name of Clan Gregor, confirming Campbell possession of their lands.

It was enacted, [writes John Prebble] that no man, under pain of
death, might call himself MacGregor, nor his children and his
children's children unborn. If he did so use that name he could be
killed like a beast at the wayside, with all his lands and possessions forfeit to his killer . . . Death was the sentence if more than
four of Clan Gregor met together, if they possessed any other
weapon than a blunt knife to cut their meat, but only, said the
Law in its clemency, if they persisted in calling themselves
MacGregor . . . Many . . . died in brutish killings, or of starvation, cold and despair. Later Acts dealt with the branding and
transportation of MacGregor women, and the Lords of the Privy
Council discussed (and finally abandoned) a proposal to send all
their children to Ireland . . . the lands they had once held passed
to the Campbells of Glen Orchy who had been most active in
executing Letters of Fire and Sword upon them. Nearly two
centuries later the penal Acts against Clan MacGregor were still
on the Statute Book, in the adult lifetime of Tom Paine, Edmund
Burke and William Wilberforce.

Meanwhile, King James thought – and, increasingly, grew –
most British. He dreamed of a dual monarchy; he was the first
and last king to attempt it. The early years of his English reign
were marked by a flood of coins, medals, flags, seals and
histories in the quest to forge a coherent British identity. His
popularity was greatly boosted, for a time, by the Gunpowder
Plot. A Roman Catholic conspiracy to blow up King, Lords and
Commons in one blast was the stuff of a propagandist's dreams:
but it was true, and could be proved.

The king pursued an appointments policy of remarkable
even-handedness. Some four-tenths of Whitehall appointments
went to Scots: patronage, honours and titles of every sort were
given out in similar proportion. The king wrote of the 'Ile', not
of the individual kingdoms. Yet in 1607 the English parliament
rejected his proposals of a full, incorporating union. An early
union flag, of odd design, was produced after eight heraldic
attempts, but it proved unpopular, and was nowhere seen after
the end of the reign. The English resisted the naturalisation of
Scots; they feared the impact of free trade across the Border.
The Scots parliament was fearful for itself; in the same year that
union proposals failed in London, parliament in Edinburgh saw
a fearful future as a 'conquered and slavish province to be

governed by a Viceroy or deputy'. The immediate problem, to most Scots, was the reality of government under an absentee monarch. James returned to Scotland but once, in 1617 – a visit angrily opposed by his English council, determined to anglicise the man. He was taken aback by the warmth of his reception. Trash and beggars had been cleared from Edinburgh streets for the occasion.

The old Stewart tactic – of setting clan against clan, chief against chief, and so keeping the Gaels divided and impotent among themselves – had long since put paid to any threat of a united Lordship of the Isles; but the policy was now proving wasteful and dangerous. Further, it was apparent from the failed Lewis experiment that the Highlands and Islands were neither profitable nor amenable to colonial endeavour. In the meantime the king's law was of little effect and his authority was openly mocked. Taxes remained unpaid and the gentry of the region were as estranged from court as ever.

James decided, then – upon the counsel of the wily Andrew Knox, Bishop of the Isles – to resort to the ways of his fathers. The chiefs had to be brought over to his side, and given the hope of royal favour. But first they had to be brought to hear him. Like his grandfather before him, he tricked them into boarding a ship. Bishop Knox was sent up to Mull in a great galleon, and the great chiefs of the West Highlands summoned aboard to hear a sermon. No sooner were they ensconced on their pews, so to speak, than the ship set sail for Edinburgh. They were released on condition that they attend a conference on Iona, and duly endorse certain statutes which Bishop Knox had drawn up for the king's pleasure, and so aid His Majesty in addressing the troubles of the realm and the commonweal of the people.

Their counsel and assistance thus – rather late in the day – being sought, the clan chiefs dutifully came to Iona, and in July 1609 they ratified a code of nine statutes, all designed to stabilise the Highlands and Islands and put an end to the ongoing feuds and wars. At the same time, one wonders what kind of spirituality filled the heart of this Bishop Knox: he referred to his flock, on varying occasions, as 'a falss generation', a 'pestiferous people' and given over entirely to 'barbaritie and wiketness'.

The Statutes of Iona may be summed thus. First: they were to maintain the Church and its ministers. Second: they were to establish inns, throughout the region, to spare the poor folk the burden of entertaining visitors. Third: chiefs were to keep smaller households, and maintain them out of their own means and not by predatory taxation of their people. No one was to be allowed to live in the Hebrides without a trade or income. Sorning – the greedy practice of fighting clansmen, who took food and supplies without payment – was now to be viewed as common thievery, and these sorners were to be punished accordingly. No wine was to be imported into the Hebrides; they were to brew their own ale. (King James knew of the growing taste in the west for fine claret: he also knew their skill at evading duty.) Any man who owned sixty or more head of cattle had to send his heir for education at a Lowland school. The use of firearms was outlawed. Bards were to be dissuaded from glorifying war in song and poem. And so on.

The statutes had a strong anglicising bent. James Hunter writes of them with some hostility. King James, after all, detested the Gaelic language: he thought it essential that the 'Inglishe tongue be universallie plantit and the Irish language, whilk is one of the cheif and principall causis of the continew-ance of barbaritie and incivilitie amongis the inhabitantis of the Ilis and the Helandis, be abolisheit and removit'. But his experiment at Stornoway had ended in ignominious failure. These statutes were a much more subtle way of achieving the same end. The southern education of chiefs' sons, and the prohibition of the bardic arts, would by themselves do much to dilute the Gaelic culture and detach the Highland nobility from the passion-springs of their people.

James VI might be accused of sanctioning violence towards Highlanders; but, as Michael Lynch points out, Highlanders already suffered plenty of violence from each other. What is striking is that the Statutes of Iona did not work. Most of the chiefs, having signed the statutes, returned home and ignored them. Half a century would pass before the Highlands' leader-ship class would begin to take them seriously. Some of the terms were stupid. The prohibition of wine did much to stimulate smuggling in the Hebrides: by the end of the eighteenth century, smuggling – and the production of illicit spirits – would be a major plank in the Highland economy. The insistence on English education was equally stupid; again, it would be the nineteenth century before the authorities accepted the folly of the policy. On the other hand, the anathema on sorning, and the establishment of inns, were measures designed to relieve the ordinary people of the region from great imposition and suffering – had they been properly implemented.

Old paths proved better. There were forced clearances of awkward mobs. We have seen the fate of Clan Gregor. And, too, the end of the MacLeods of Lewis. Frontier clans, such as Clan Campbell – staunchly Protestant, monarchist, with a degree of Lowland interest – spread themselves at the expense of such as opposed the king's peace. The Campbells supplanted the MacDonalds of Ardnamurchan, and the MacDonalds of Kintyre and the Isles fell victim to further tentacle branches of that great clan. But the policy benefited the Campbells, not the crown. Future Stuart sovereigns would rue the day that Argyll was made great.

The significance of the Statutes of Iona lay in the new nature of the pact between crown and chiefs. It was no longer a pact of terror, enforced by hostage-taking, execution and confiscation of land. It was an invitation to the Highland aristocracy to align themselves with the crown in a final acceptance of the permanence of Lowland sovereignty and the inferiority of their own Gaelic culture. In time, the chiefs accepted this. That is why, as James Hunter points out, the chiefs of Gaeldom survived when the chiefs of Ireland did not; that is why there is still a Cameron of Lochiel. The seventeenth century was not long advanced, either, before another curious change became apparent: the same clan chiefs whose fathers had for so long been at loggerheads with the Scots crown, and with the old Stewart monarchy, would now prove the king's most ardent supporters, to the point of following the house of Stuart long after it had been driven from the throne.

In 1625 James, old, senile, and increasingly ridiculous, died in London. His firstborn, Henry – a gifted and appealing lad – had died as a young man; the king was succeeded by his second son, proclaimed as Charles I. Charles was the last Scots king –

indeed, the last monarch in Britain – to be born north of the Border, at Dumfries, in 1600.

This king is one of the most baffling figures in history. Charles I was, in some respects, the most admirable of the Stuarts. He was entirely free of sexual fault, cleaving faithfully to his wife, Henrietta Maria, and was devout in personal religion. (His wife was his downfall, and especially the ruin of his sons; she was an ardent, bigoted, convinced Roman Catholic of the most dangerous sort, and would have burned Presbyterians at the stake given half the chance.) Yet Charles was also aloof, intensely private, afflicted with near-megalomaniac views on the nature of the monarchy, and quite unable to treat honestly with those he regarded as inferior. He also had a very bad stammer and was very small. He liked to collect van Dykes.

Charles I soon alienated the Scots in religion. They were still snugly established in Presbyterianism, and an ordered but relaxed liturgy centred on the preaching of the Word and marked by *ex tempore* prayer. Of this Charles heartily disapproved. He thought episcopacy more fitting – after all, in England he already appointed bishops – and was suspicious of the popular democracy in which the Kirk functioned at parochial level. In England the gentry filled local livings with pet clerics. In Scotland ordinary folk had a voice in the settlement of ministers. English liturgy – which centred heavily on the sacraments, and read forms – was very much to his taste. But Scots' worship majored on the preaching of intensely argued sermons. And the General Assembly ruled the Kirk in a spirit of proud independence, seeing itself as answerable to Christ alone, and not in any respect accountable to the crown in holy things.

This, Charles resolved, was a state of affairs which he would not put up with. The sad aspect is that he was not, instinctively, a tyrant, nor even a bigot. He was an intensely religious man who genuinely believed it was part of the onerous burden of kingship to regulate the religion of the realm, and to do so in an order that acknowledged His Majesty as an authority spiritual as well as secular. But his bungling, tactless, remorseless efforts to impose sacramental worship and Episcopal government on the Scots led to outrage, mayhem, the National Covenant – a charter, signed by leading Scots throughout the land, making plain their allegiance to the crown but even more to the Kirk as historically established – and, at length, to rebellion against the king.

Meanwhile – with his hapless government of England alienating the ruling classes in the shires – Charles I soon found himself with roaring rebellion there. The spark in England was the right of the sovereign to tax without the consent of parliament. The monarchy was now desperately impoverished, and scarcely able to function for lack of funds. But to seek money from parliament – to go begging – was to imperil the executive authority of the crown. Such difficulties required a cool brain at the top, the skills of Elizabeth Tudor or even James IV. Charles was no statesman, and so all the 'Ile' was soon convulsed in civil war.

The history of both civil revolts, in Scotland and England, is complex, inspiring, and at times highly confusing. The Cromwellians rapidly saw the merits of combining with the Covenanting Scots; the two conflicts became hopelessly intertwined, and at length the Scots were persuaded to hand Charles I over to the victorious Cromwellians in return for the promise that, as they sought, a national Presbyterian Church would be established throughout the British Isles, and that the king's life would be spared.

Charles I, and his allies, had one good base of cannon-fodder – the Highlands. His principal Scottish foe proved the house of Argyll, the house so historically blessed by Stewart monarchy, and enriched even by the king's late father. The king's loyal servant was James Graham, Marquis of Montrose, a brilliant 'Captain-General', who sped north to eliminate the Argyll threat. Montrose had actually signed the National Covenant – the copy bearing his signature hangs today in the Free Church College in Edinburgh – but, when it came to the chance of royal favour, he broke faith. He assembled a force of loyal Highlanders, Irish, assorted mercenaries and vicious freebooters, and by the end of 1644 was the king's man against the Covenanters.

Montrose was a brilliant general, one of the finest Scotland has ever produced. He grasped the reality of the struggle: that Royalist control of Scotland required the destruction of the Campbells' base in Argyll. Over Christmas and New Year, into

1645, Montrose and his troops laid that county waste. They then began to proceed up the Great Glen, to seize and sack Inverness, but were taken aback by news from the north. The Earl of Seaforth, a prominent Covenanter, was marching south with an army of 15,000 men. Montrose's force numbered but 1,500. Hard on these tidings came word from their rear, as the Royalist force reached Kilcumin, which we now know as Fort Augustus. The Marquis of Argyll himself was after them, with Lowland recruits over and above 3,000 raging Campbell clansmen. Striving to control their alarm, Montrose and his men marched a little further, to Stratherrick, where a message came from old Lochiel, chief of Clan Cameron. Argyll and his men had reached Inverlochy. It is said that this intelligence was given to Montrose by Iain Lom MacDonald, a celebrated Gaelic bard, from the Keppoch district of the Great Glen. Lochiel's sympathies were with the royal cause, but he was an old man, and had to watch himself: his own wife was a Campbell, and his grandson, Ewen – his heir – had been entrusted to Argyll's household for his education.

Montrose did not hesitate. He and his army turned about and – though born of desperation – pulled off one of the most audacious feats in the history of British arms. In a forced march that would sap even the hardest troops of our own day, the little army trekked back down the Great Glen, by the bordering mountains, over snow and through hail and rain and through foaming burns and rivers in spate. The Royalists left Kilcumin early on the morning of 31 January; they reached their destination, the mouth of Glen Nevis, in the twilight of 1 February. The precise route they took is still a matter of fierce debate; certainly it was arduous in the extreme. That night Montrose and his men rested. As dawn broke on 2 February, they fell upon the Covenanting army. The Covenanting force was superior, and they had not trekked miles of wintry mountain. Yet they quickly broke, after brave fighting. 'The rebels could not stand it,' wrote Montrose, 'but after some resistance at first began to run, whom we pursued for nine miles, altogether making a great slaughter.'

The Irishmen in Montrose's force were 'half-savages'; the Royalist clansmen had a hereditary, venomous hatred of the Campbells. (Some western clans had joined Montrose less from ardour in the king's service than their malice against the sons of Dermid.) There was no quarter. The battle became a rout; it ended as a bloody massacre. It is said that the rivers Lochy and Eil were dyed crimson by bleeding Campbells, as they piled frantically through in their flight for life; Montrose lost perhaps two dozen men; the Covenanters over 1,500, including their commander, Sir Duncan Campbell of Auchinbreck. Montrose's lieutenant, the murderous Sir Alexander MacDonal – Alasdair Mac Colla – was Auchinbreck's own nephew. But there was no hope for the Covenanter general. He was brought, bleeding and captive, before MacDonald, and offered these bare alternatives: death by the rope or death by the sword. '*Da dhui gun aon roghainn*,' said Auchinbreck grimly, 'two bad choices: one result!' He was beheaded by his nephew's hand.

Inverlochy, brilliant as it was, is perhaps the most shameful slaughter in Highland history, and that is saying much. The Marquis of Argyll has been pilloried for escaping: when battle broke, he was still aboard his galley, on Loch Linnhe, and once the tide of events became clear he ordered the crew to remove him from the vicinity. The sight of his fleeing ship certainly dispirited his troops, but by then Inverlochy was irretrievably lost, and the Covenanting prince had a moral obligation to preserve his own safety. There was another noted non-combatant, Iain Lom. Montrose demanded to know why he made no attempt to fight, and merely watched with keen interest. 'And if I were slain, who would there be to sing of the great victory?' laughed the bard. He composed a remarkable poem of triumph, and it won him a remarkable honour.

But the Royalist victory here did not win the war; the Covenanters enjoyed overwhelming support where it mattered: in the Lowlands. Charles I's Scottish defeat was, at length, total.

Divines duly composed, and parliament solemnly endorsed, that magnificent body of doctrine now known as the Westminster Confession of Faith, of 1647, still the subordinate standard of the Presbyterian Churches in Scotland today. But Cromwell had no intention of imposing presbytery on England. Though a Puritan, he was a congregationalist in Church government; he held that local churches should be entirely independent in determining standards of doctrine, discipline and worship. Nor had he any intention of sparing Charles I. The man was a menace. He was incapable of holding to a promise, of accepting the prerogatives of parliament. As long as he lived the king would inspire revolt and, if granted success, would surely avenge himself on those who had brought him down.

In 1649, to the horror of Europe and the revulsion of the Scots, Charles I was tried, condemned and beheaded. The Scots, then and now, can throw a nationalist switch when it suits them. They might well have executed Charles I themselves, had he been their problem. But for their king to die in English hands was an outrage in itself and a betrayal of their trust in particular.

The Scots promptly proclaimed his eldest son King Charles II. In 1650, in an extraordinary service at Scone – the youth was made to homologate doctrinal standards and catechisms more appropriate to a Presbyterian ordination – he was crowned. He marched south at the head of a northern host, met with crushing defeat at the Battle of Worcester, and – after some narrow shaves; at one point he had to hide in a large oak tree – made good his escape to France. The Scots, finally crushed at the Battle of Dunbar, were put under ignominious occupation by Cromwell's army. Montrose himself finally lost a battle, at Corbisdale; he was betrayed, taken to Edinburgh, tried and hanged.

It is hard now to grasp how permanent the Cromwell regime seemed at the time. Few expected to see the Stuarts return. All the British Isles soon prospered in a new environment of commerce, learning, science and seamanship. If Cromwell had lived a year or two longer, as Paul Johnson has written, he would probably have accepted the monarchy and founded his own dynasty; the Industrial Revolution would have come at the end of the seventeenth century, rather than a hundred years later, and we would now be in a twenty-first-century world, 'with all its wonders and terrors'. But Cromwell died in 1658, still only Lord Protector; his son Richard did not share his father's gifts, and in 1660 – amid national rejoicing – Charles II and all the family were invited to return.

Charles II was tall, dark, swarthy, superficially genial. He was

Doune Carloway, Lewis, with broch: a typical crofting township in the Outer Hebrides.

Carloway broch. Much of the stone has been removed over the centuries for other building projects; it has, though, given an interesting 'cut away' aspect, showing the elaborate chambering of the structure. The drystone building's survival to this degree, through nearly 2000 years, is tribute to the skill of its masons.

Callanish Stones, Lewis.

St Columba preaching to the Picts by William Hole.

James Drummond,
Marquis of
Montrose.

The Landing of
St Margaret at
Queensferry by
William Hole.

Prince James Francis Edward Stuart, the 'Old Pretender' by an unknown artist.

Prince Charles Edward Stuart, the 'Young Pretender' by Maurice Quenton de la Tour.

Prince Charles Edward Stuart, attributed to Hugh Douglas Hamilton.

James IV (1473–1513) by an unknown artist.

James V by an unknown artist.

James VI and I by Adam de Colone.

James VII and II by Sir Peter
Lely.

William Augustus, Duke of
Cumberland, attributed to Sir Joshua
Reynolds.

Dundee, Viscount of
Claverhouse by David Paton.

James MacPherson by unknown
artist after Joshua Reynolds.

St Columba's Church, Aignish, Lewis. An ancient place of worship,
long ruinous. Here the MacLeod chiefs of Lewis were buried. The
building is now threatened by the eroding sea.

The monument to Charles Edward Stuart by Arnish, at the mouth of Stornoway harbour. Here the Prince spent a miserable night while his agents haggled – without success – to charter a boat for passage to France. In the background, an oil-rig 'jacket' is under construction at Lewis Offshore Ltd.

New Shawbost, Lewis. This township, formed from a former tack by Sir James Matheson in 1850, is typical of the modern crofting township – as opposed to the old-style Highland clachan – in that houses march along a straight line of road, each house at the foot of its strip of allotted croft land.

Old home, Dalmore.

Interior of a black house on the Isle of Scalpay.

Free Church ministers at an induction in Bernera, Lewis *c*. 1980.

in truth hard, calculating and ruthless. He hated the Scots and he loathed Presbyterianism with peculiar passion. He was, famously, much given to the joys of sex, and spawned a litter of illegitimate children, many of whom he ennobled. Charles had little judgement in foreign affairs. He made a secret treaty with Louis XIV of France; its terms included the king's secret conversion to the Church of Rome. Thus he found Popery 'a convenient shroud to die in'. He was one of the most amiable monarchs in our history, yet the most amoral and vicious.

Charles II was not long king when he hunted down and put to death the surviving principals in his father's downfall. They included the Marquis of Argyll, who had at length destroyed Montrose, who had presided over the young king's enthroning at Scone; who had genuinely believed that the life of Charles I would be spared. 'The King whose head I crowned,' he lamented on the scaffold, 'now sends me to a crown higher than his own.' Argyll's tomb lies in the High Kirk of St Giles in Edinburgh, across the nave from the bones of Montrose. They are tragic figures both: each was an honourable man, and Argyll a noble of simple and earnest Christianity.

King Charles was not without a certain charmed affection for Gaeldom. He knighted a MacLeod of Berneray, in Harris, for his valour at the Battle of Worcester. And Charles II was the only monarch, to this day, to have a Gaelic Poet Laureate – Ian Lom of Keppoch. But he was a Stuart, with Stuart obsessions. Soon he turned his attention on Presbyterianism. He sought, with a savagery that would have appalled his father, to impose, yet again, an Episcopal religion on the Scots. The second generation of Covenanters are, in some respects, less winsome than the heroes of the first. They included a few intolerant and bloodthirsty men. But there were very many men and women – brave, saintly creatures, who sought only the freedom to worship in their own tradition – put to bestial suffering, and death, at the hands of the king's men. Their hands were broken in thumbscrews, their legs shattered in iron boots. Women were staked on mud-flats and drowned by the rising tides. Men were hanged, beheaded, shot in front of their wives and children. And still they forsook the official, state-sanctioned services, holding secret 'conventicles' on the open moor and hill, listen-

ing to long, long sermons as if each might be their last. And, now
and again, government dragoons would swoop on them, and it
was.

To this day, in the hamlets of Ayr, Dumfries, West Lothian,
there are those who bitterly recall the House of Stuart and the
monstrous things inflicted on their forefathers in this time. And
in the Highlands, too – as we shall see when we come to its
evangelical history, and that minister of Evanton, Thomas Hogg
– the turmoil of the 'Killing Times' had its impact.

But, as Charles's nightmarish reign lengthened, the question
of the succession increasingly occupied high minds. His marriage to Catherine of Braganza proved childless. (She has often
been dismissed as barren; it is just as likely that the king himself
was sterile, if not impotent, from chronic venereal disease.) His
brother James, Duke of York, was heir-presumptive and a
Roman Catholic; he had converted to that sunny faith through
the influence of his mother. Though James's two surviving
children, Mary and Anne, were Protestant princesses – Mary
was married to his nephew, William of Orange – many feared
for their liberties if James ascended the throne. Charles had little
time for James. Rightly, he judged him a fool; he insisted that
the princesses be kept Protestant. But he was not prepared to see
the right order overturned; he would not put away his wife (of
whom the king was genuinely fond) and he would not disinherit
his brother, even for his own son.

For there was Charles's oldest bastard, James, Duke of
Monmouth and Buccleuch, whom many were eager to see
anointed as heir-apparent. This Monmouth was handsome,
articulate, and able in affairs (the English, perhaps, were less
aware of his murderous role in the repression of the Covenanters). A persistent rumour took hold that Monmouth was, in
fact, legitimate; that Charles had secretly married his mother,
the cheerful tart Lucy Scott. But Charles never confirmed this.
Perhaps it was true, and perhaps it was false. It is said that two
centuries later, in Victoria's reign, the Duke of Buccleuch –
Monmouth's direct descendant – actually found a copy of the
wedding certificate. 'That could cause a lot of trouble,' said he,
being a wise man, and no doubt a frequent guest at Balmoral. So
he burned it. The royal link was at length restored, in our own

century: Lady Alice Montagu-Scott, a descendant of Monmouth, married the Duke of Gloucester, third son of George V.

In 1685 Charles II died, weeping for Nell Gwynne the orange seller, receiving the sacrament from a Roman priest. His brother succeeded him as King James, II of England, VII of Scotland.

James was not without capacity. As Lord High Admiral he had proved competent in improving the navy. As Governor of Scotland he had superintended the repression of presbytery, with glum dignity, actually presiding over the torture of the king's enemies. But he was not as clever as his brother. He had no judgement. He was entirely without subtlety, cunning or statecraft. He took his cold, thrawn nature from his father and his fanatical Romanism from his mother. James's conversation was most curious. He once startled, then at length bored, a fine lady with an earnest and most tedious talk on such things as riding accidents, broken bones and dislocated shoulders. He had mistresses too, if exceeding plain. (Society wit Bishop Burnett wickedly remarked that the Duke of York's women were so ugly they must have been prescribed by his priests as a penance.)

James had sufficient wit to realise how precarious his position was. Mary Tudor, and the Massacre of Bartholomew's Eve, remained real in England's memory. Foxe's *Book of Martyrs* was read in every village in the land. London, in the latter part of his brother's reign, had been torn by anti-Popery riots. So, while defiantly practising his Roman faith, he made no effort to impose the old religion on his subjects. He spoke rather of liberty and tolerance. He plotted to reform the law to admit Roman Catholics (and dissenting Protestants) to public office. He was not long crowned when Monmouth revolted, raising the standard and making a bid for the throne. Few, to James's gratification, rose with him. The rebellion was crushed at the Battle of Sedgemoor; Charles II's bastard was found cowering in a ditch, and was shortly beheaded for treason. The execution was messy; it took 'five choppes'. Afterwards, someone realised there was no recent portrait of this aspiring princeling. They thought about it, sewed his head back on, and called in an artist to immortalise Monmouth's Stuart features.

As long as a Protestant succession remained certain, James

might – just – have had a stable and even fruitful reign. But then, in 1688, his queen, Mary of Modena, fell pregnant. She had been pregnant before, but no child had survived. (James's adult daughters were by his first wife, the rather common Anne Hyde.) At length, to the ecstastic joy of his parents, to the horror of his sisters, the glee of Romanists and the consternation of everyone else, Prince James Francis Stuart was born. He was a fine lusty child. He even survived the determined efforts of royal doctors, who insisted on feeding the baby doses of a weird mixture of wine, raisins and bran. Little James was promptly declared Prince of Wales; he eclipsed his older sisters in the succession, and he was baptised in the Roman Catholic faith.

King James now pressed on with his bid to win official tolerance; the first step to lead his land back to the Roman faith. He then did something very stupid. The Archbishop of Canterbury protested vigorously, and was promptly locked up in prison. At this point the wise ones of the land put their heads together. An invitation was sent to William of Orange, nephew and son-in-law of the king, to come over and defend popular liberties.

It was not conceived as a bid to see James deposed. Even William himself did not envisage such a prospect; at best, he had probably determined to force the king to release the archbishop, desist from his plans to Romanise England, and to raise his infant heir as a Protestant. Too late, James felt his position sliding. Naïve enough to think that Catholic Europe would dash to the aid of their royal brother, he sent frantic word to Louis XIV. But Louis XIV's religious zeal was no match for his complex political alliances in Europe. So King James, when William landed in England and marched on London, simply cut and ran. He was briefly captured. William (desperate to avoid having his tedious father-in-law on his hands) had quite a job to make it known that the old boy should be permitted to escape. The cage was left open, and James, wife and baby duly slipped to the Continent. The king was granted asylum by a guilty Louis XIV, and installed at the Palace of St Germain. The French court soon had the measure of James VII. 'When you listen to him, you know why he is here.'

After some reflection it was declared that the king had
absconded. Parliament further declared, then, that William
and Mary were now joint monarchs of England. Thus triumphed the 'Glorious and Bloodless Revolution' of 1688.

It was another year before the Scots caught up. They met in
Convention in 1689, having thoughtfully written to both James
and William asking for their positions to be put down on paper.
James's letter was so characteristically arrogant, so crass, that
without hesitation the Convention endorsed the monarchy of
King William III and Queen Mary II.

In the reigns of Charles II and James VII a Cameron chief had
played a colourful part. We have heard of this man already,
Ewen Cameron; that child whose Campbell custody had constrained his grandfather in 1645. He grew to be one of the most
celebrated Highlanders of his era, the epitome of Highland
gallantry and bloodthirstiness. His career is worth a little
study. Black Ewen – Eoghann Dubh – was born in 1629 at
Kilchurch Castle, Loch Awe, for his maternal grandfather was
Sir Robert Campbell, of the house of Argyll. Young Ewen was
raised at Letterfinlay and spent much of his youth as a virtual
hostage for the good conduct of the Lochaber folk; he succeeded
to the chiefdom at the age of eighteen, and speedily made his
escape from Inveraray, where he had been in the custody of the
Marquis of Argyll. Soon he and the Cameron warriors made a
real nuisance of themselves to the forces of Cromwell. The
Camerons were raised for Charles II, after the execution of
his father in 1649; they even fought – with Ewen at their head –
at the Battle of Worcester in 1651, which ended with Charles's
flight to exile. It was largely to curb their activities that a
government fort was first built in Lochaber, around which
grew up the town known today as Fort William.

In 1652 the Earl of Glencairn raised the Royalist revolt, and
Black Ewen joined this effort, winning a letter from his exiled
king. 'We are informed by the Earl of Glencairn with what
courage, success and affection to us you have behaved yourself
in this time of trial, when the honour and liberty of your country
are at stake. Therefore we cannot but express our hearty sense of
this your courage, and return you our thanks for the same.'

There are many stories of Black Ewen. In 1654 he was enraged to learn, as he and his officers met at Corpach, that government troops were busy felling trees at Achdalieu – his own trees – for the building of the new fort, and without his permission. So, without ado, he and his party set off from Corpach to fall upon the rascals. There were 150 in the wood-cutting party – armed men too – and only thirty-eight clansmen, but the Camerons had the advantage of surprise. They fell on the southern troops with bloodcurdling cries, wielding big swords and Lochaber axe. The fighting was fierce, and Ewen soon found himself in difficulty. He was at grips with a big Englishman, well skilled in swordsmanship, and presently this man had the Cameron chief pinned helplessly to the ground. At first Ewen was able to bind his foe's arms in a desperate embrace; then the Englishman got a hand free, and reached back for his dagger.

Ewen had only one chance, and he took it. The Englishman's throat was bared, so he sank his teeth into it. Sank them deep, and tore, like a wild animal, and that was the end of his adversary. It was, said the formidable old rogue many years later, the 'sweetest bite I ever tasted'.

But the Royalist cause had that year to be abandoned, for lack of funds, and Ewen was fortunate in the terms he got from Cromwell's generals: his men were allowed to keep their arms, and he even won an amnesty on back taxes claimed by the government.

It was Black Ewen who ended, at long last, the feud with Mackintosh, by legalising the Cameron possession of Glen Loy and Loch Arkaig in written treaty. By then he was Sir Ewen, knighted by a grateful Charles II for his services during the Cromwell era.

In an engaging sequel to the Achdalieu horror, Sir Ewen paid a trip to London after this honour from the king, and – in the course of his stay – went for a shave to a barber's shop. The barber soon sensed that his knightly client was both a Scot and a Highlander. 'You are from the north, sir?' he inquired. Sir Ewen replied in the affirmative: did the barber know anyone up there? 'No, and I don't wish to – they're savages. Do you know that one of 'em tore my father's throat out with his teeth? Now, if I had that wretch's throat as close to my razor as yours . . .'

Lochiel left as rapidly as was decent: it is said he never dared visit a barber's shop again.

In 1680, according to Pennant, Sir Ewen killed – with his own hands – the last wolf seen in the Highlands; more likely it was the last in the Lochaber district. He is supposed to have overcome the beast near the head of Loch Arkaig. And now, in 1689, he had better fights to wage: the Stuarts were in trouble again, and loyal Sir Ewen was principal military adviser to their commander at the Battle of Killiecrankie. Soon, at that Perthshire pass, an angry and determined army marshalled to restore the old line of Scotland, yet again, to its throne.

For one Scots noble, John Graham of Claverhouse, Viscount Dundee, had responded to Convention's decision with outrage. Claverhouse had prospered in the old regime. Spiritual heir to his distant kinsman, Montrose, he was handsome, dashing, most loyal to the House of Stuart, most zealous in episcopacy. Claverhouse is today romanticised, thanks to the writings of Sir Walter Scott and John Buchan, as 'Bonnie Dundee'; he is remembered in a jaunty song of that title. Scots of his day had another view of him. During the 'Killing Times', Claverhouse had personally hunted down a Covenanting fugitive, John Brown of Priesthill, to his family home; the house was surrounded by dragoons, and Brown dragged forth, where a dragoon blew his head off before his wife and small children. 'What think ye of your husband now?' asked a gloating Claverhouse of the weeping widow, as she scooped up pieces of skull and brain. 'I aye thought much of him,' she said, 'and now mair than ever.'

But this Claverhouse was a brilliant general. And he had a very shrewd grasp of Highlanders and Highland soldiery. They could readily be raised, in their hosts, at the orders of clan chiefs. They were not trained, disciplined soldiers, capable of being honed into an ordered fighting machine. But they were very brave, very tough, and very, very aggressive. Furthermore the English – even the Lowland Scots – were terrified of them. John of Fordun's propaganda still ran deep. It was said that the Highlanders drank blood and ate babies. And Killiecrankie – steep, wooded, mysterious, creepy – suited well traditional Highland tactics.

So Claverhouse raised his force, and marched on the Lowlands. He knew best how to exploit Highland soldiers. They should attack from high ground, racing down a slope, for maximum psychological value. The terror was heightened by their wild, plaided appearance and the distinctive war-cry of the Gael – a high, savage whooping sound, which would surface, much later, in the history of America, as the 'rebel yell'. The Pass of Killiecrankie was the chosen route to the Lowlands; there, they confronted the forces of government.

As the Cameron men waited to charge, their chief suddenly realised he was the only man among them wearing shoes. So he took them off, tossed them away, and dashed barefoot with his men into battle. It is said that, in the typical Highland politics of the day, Sir Ewen's son was at Killiecrankie too – on the other side, as a captain in the Scots Fusiliers, with the government army under General MacKay, a native of Scourie in Western Sutherland. MacKay, it is told, teased young Cameron, saying, 'There is your father with his wild savages. How would you like to be with him?' Young Cameron replied, 'It doesn't matter what *I* would like, but my father and his savages may be nearer us tonight than *you'd* like!' So it proved, and MacKay's army was routed.

The first Jacobite battle was victorious. The forces of 'King Billy' were beaten and scattered. But a stray government bullet slew Claverhouse in his moment of triumph. With their general lost, the success went for nothing and the Jacobites of Scotland scattered.

It was in Ireland, in 1690, that any realistic hope for James's restoration ended at the Battle of the Boyne (a triumph for King William, by the way, which excited the Pope to order torchlit rejoicings in Rome). James never returned to his native land. 'Dismal Jimmy', as the Scots had long ago dubbed the lugubrious monarch, sulked on at the Palace of St Germain. His old age was brightened by the birth of a daughter, Mary Louise – 'La Consolatrice' – and by the death of his daughter, Mary II, from smallpox in 1694; this last gave the frightful old man evident pleasure. He grew ever more intolerant, ever more rabidly Roman. On his deathbed, in 1701, he exhorted his teenage son never to forsake the Roman faith, never to forget that kings were chosen by the will of God, not the will of men.

Thus was born that movement we call 'Jacobitism'. James is the Greek form of Jacob; Jacobus is the Latin form of James, and the supporters of the exiled King James and his heir were thus the 'Jacobites'. Their cult would dominate Scots – and Highland – affairs for sixty years. And, if you have studied the foregoing at all, you will surely see why the Stuarts so divided Scotland, why so many dreaded their return, and why – having twice and thrice lost their throne – (through Mary, Charles I and James VII) no Stuart was ever to regain it.

Yet loyalty to the exiled dynasty remained a powerful force. Highland clans had fought for them so often, throughout the century, that loyalty was now bred into much of the Gaelic culture. Besides, in religion – predominately Episcopal, some Roman Catholic – the clansmen had little in common with the Presbyterian Lowlands. Nor was King William, or any of his successors, a man calculated to inspire Highland loyalties. Thus the government of King William moved swiftly to command some base of allegiance; in their zeal, they went a little too far, and in 1692 the new regime was but little embarrassed by one of the most dishonourable incidents in Scottish history – the Massacre of Glencoe.

After the 1689 débâcle, the chiefs of the Highland clans were ordered to swear an oath of loyalty to the new regime; and the deadline for this was 31 December 1691. MacIain, chief of the MacDonalds of Glencoe – a small sept of the great Clan Donald; they were a peaceable little tribe, fervently Jacobite, but most hospitable and kindly – like the other Highland chiefs, was loath to take this oath, and sought permission of the exiled James VII. It was nearly year's end before the old fool sent word of approval from France. Then MacIain made a tragic – but entirely honest – mistake. He thought he was required to be sworn at Fort William, and set off for that garrison; there, he was told that, in fact, the rite had to be performed at Inveraray, a long journey to the south. It was after New Year before MacIain reached that place, and duly took the oath before the sheriff. His tardiness was quite innocent; but it was all the excuse required for an administration eager to take bloody action on some Highland rebels, *pour encourager les autres*.

And the order was from very high up. Some implicate William himself, quoting documentary evidence. 'William Rex – as for MacIain of Glencoe, and that tribe, if they can be well distinguished from the rest of the Highlanders, it will be proper for the vindication of public justice to extirpate that set of thieves. W.R.' But the wording of the document is odd. Why should the king mark his name twice? It could be a *post facto* forgery. More likely the king signed it – or a document which, afterwards, was slightly 'improved' – under a deception from his Secretary of State in Scotland, John Dalrymple, Master of Stair. Stair seems to have told the king that MacIain had defied the edict utterly; William probably never realised that the old man had, indeed, taken the oath of loyalty. And the wily Stair saw, too, the propaganda advantage of the notorious antipathy between Campbell and MacDonald: the event could be passed off as another Highland atrocity between warring clans.

A band of Campbells of Glen Lyon were entrusted with the task; they arrived in Glencoe, to 'put all to the sword under seventy'. Even more repulsively, they met with a warm welcome, and were freely lodged by the MacDonalds after the chief, Campbell of Glen Lyon, made an outrageous fib: Fort William was full up, he said, and they needed accommodation. And was not his niece married to a son of MacIain? So he and his men were graciously received. On the night of 12 February, Campbell received secret order to proceed; he was told expressly to kill the 'old fox' and his sons. In the small hours, the Campbells fell on their hosts. The old man was murdered in bed. His wretched wife was dragged out, her rings torn from her fingers by a man's teeth, and then – stripped naked – she was thrust into the blizzard, where she was found dead the following day. But the killing was botched. Somehow most of the MacDonalds had sufficient warning to flee, and the whirling snow gave them ample cover. Only thirty-eight were killed, but these included two women and two children. Others died in the snow as they struggled to reach the refuge of Appin. The snow delayed a party of government troops, who had intended to cut off the escape route entirely; but for the weather, the slaughter would have been fearful.

Stair was highly annoyed by the subsequent outcry: Scots

everywhere were aghast. After three years of plaint the king was forced to appoint a commission of inquiry; Campbell of Glen Lyon, it found, had merely obeyed orders; Stair, it held, was the man responsible. But nothing happened to him. The king later made him an earl; by then all was known, and, whatever prior knowledge William had enjoyed, nothing can exculpate him in this. In March 1692, barely a month after the outrage, this future earl had written, 'All I regret is that any of the sort got away, and there is a necessity to prosecute them to the utmost . . .'

At the end of the seventeenth century the Highlands and Islands contained a full third of Scotland's population. The Gaels were then spread throughout the region in a much more even manner than today; Inverness, for instance, was a very small town, but every glen and nook of the county supported a little community. The Clearances had yet to lay vast tracts of northern Scotland waste. These people were not crofters. Crofting had yet to come. People lived in clachans – townships – and still worked the land communally, reallocating strips and plots from year to year in the runrig system.

The housing was very poor. They lived in houses of the black house type but, generally, inferior even to these. Many were built of turf, not stone. Very few therefore survive, even in ruin. People and animals huddled together in the one space, often black with soot from the rain dripping through scanty thatch, their bodies harbouring an interesting variety of insect life, their diet consisting largely of grains and dairy produce and, as a rare treat, salt meat, salt fish or game. Quite often, to flavour oatmeal, they would bleed a cow and stir the blood into that. And they lived in that strange social structure known as the clan system, increasingly feudalised.

Now there is a lot of nonsense believed about the old days of the Highland clans. Folk read that the Clan Cameron held Lochaber, and immediately think of Lochaber as being a county populated entirely by Camerons, and all clad in the Cameron tartan, and all under the benevolent rule of Lochiel himself, kinsman to each and every man in the district, loved by all and inspiring devotion and service wherever he went, and all – chief, chieftains, peasants – holding the land in common.

The Camerons did dominate Lochaber, as we have seen, and Lochiel was their chief. And most folk did wear tartan, of a sort; checked or plaid woollen cloth. But few could afford tartan of the gay colours we expect today, and they would have found the idea of a uniform tartan – specific to their name – quite risible. Most of the 'name' tartans sold in Scotland today are Victorian fakes, invented by clever folk cashing in on the cult of Balmorality. And a good many folk in Lochaber, who would have looked on Lochiel as their chief, were not Camerons at all. They were MacLeans, or MacMasters, or MacQueens, or MacMartins, or whatever; but they were under his authority, because they lived in his territory.

The Highland clan chief was not quite a landlord, as we understand the term today; he would not have thought of himself as owner of, say, half of Ross-shire in the same way as he owned his mansion. But he had something much more mighty, and dangerous: 'heritable jurisdiction'. He had the power of law-enforcement. He had full power of pit and gallows. He could hang or imprison any he chose. He could evict from land. He could burn a man's roof over his head. He could even sell people into slavery abroad (as two dreadful Highland chiefs tried to do in 1739). To this end the chief sat over a hierarchy of power. Every hamlet had its constable, and every district had its tacksman. A tacksman was a tenant farmer – the name has nothing to do with revenue-raising – and held his land on the condition of carrying out certain services, such as 'raising the clan' for any military (or, more often in Lochaber, cattle-rustling) venture the chief might propose.

The 'fiery cross', ignited and carried about to rally clansmen to the standard, is a myth too. It was lit – in some places – but then dipped in cattle blood, and left to smoke and smoulder noisomely. More often, when the chief wanted the men of the district 'out', the tacksmen were ordered to go and order them out. And if the good folk proved reluctant, the firing of a thatched roof or two tended to suggest immediate co-operation.

All this may conjure up a picture of a Highland clan chief of this era as a massive, hairy, forbidding Ben Nevis of a man, given to much whisky and tossing gnawed bones over his shoulder, roistering into the night like some mediaeval robber-baron. If this were ever true, by the Jacobite era the clan chiefs were civilised, even sophisticated men. Most had been abroad – Paris, Florence, Venice – and could speak French, sometimes Italian. They certainly all spoke English. Their sons were highly educated and their daughters accomplished in drawing, embroidery, music. Their homes were furnished and decorated to a comfortable standard for the day. The Highland chief was more apt to drink claret than whisky.

They were inclined to vanity. A chief went nowhere – certainly not to Edinburgh or London – without his *tail*, a retinue of big and faithful men, always including a piper and perhaps a bard. He himself was apt to dress colourfully. He would stalk about in garish tartan, hats of blue velvet, tall feathers, buckles and trimmings of gold or silver, often bejewelled; pistol and powder-horn and dirk at his belt – a veritable 'parakeet', as one mockingly described the typical chief in his gaudy garb.

They were apt to boast. There is the story of a MacLeod of Harris chief who dined with the king – probably James V – in Edinburgh. 'Have you ever seen a finer banqueting hall,' teased the monarch, 'did you ever see bigger candlesticks, a larger table?' MacLeod insisted that he had, and that if the king ever came to feast with him at Dunvegan in Skye he would see wonders indeed. The king duly visited. One night he was taken to the top of one of the strange Skye plateaux known as MacLeod's Tables; there, a mighty feast was spread about on cloths, and a hundred clansmen, tall and handsome, encircled them, holding flaming torches aloft for illumination, as the stars and borealis glittered in the indigo sky. So the king lost the bet.

These were the Highlands at the turn of the eighteenth century. And in this vast and rugged realm – a land apart – the writ of Edinburgh, far less London, still counted for little. Power lay with the chiefs, and whoever cultivated these wonderful princes could soon have thousands of fighting men at his disposal. The chiefs, by and large, were isolated from Lowland Scotland at one vital cultural level – religion. Most were Episcopal, or Roman Catholic. The common people followed a sacramental religion of a sort, and in many districts were so theologically illiterate and so little churched as scarcely to know in what tradition they were baptised. Presbyterianism had taken little substantive hold in the Highlands, beyond the Black Isle and Caithness. In the Outer Isles, especially, lazy and worthless ministers sat in vast parishes, scarcely carrying out the most formal functions of the cloth. Roman Catholic missionaries from Ireland were already regaining the folk of Barra and Morar – nominal Protestants – for Mother Church. Everywhere – contemporary writers always note it, in tones of horror or pity – people wallowed in poverty.

The Revolution Settlement had restored the Church of Scotland, broadly on the same lines as it is found today: Presbyterian, Protestant, free of 'patronage' – the system whereby feudal superiors, or landlords, appoint ministers – and committed to the Westminster Confession of Faith. Throughout lowland Scotland assorted Episcopal appointees were kicked out of manses and replaced with sound Presbyterian men. But, in the Highlands, ministers appointed under episcopacy generally remained. When the induction of a lawful minister was attempted in the parish of Gairloch, the district was convulsed in riot.

There was another factor too. The gentry apart, few in the Highlands could speak a word of English. The Gaels of the north remained a force apart from the rest of Scotland, from Britain, still relatively intact in their culture, still willing enough to sally south for the fallen House of Stuart. The remote forces of government had yet to realise, and to confront, the threat the Highlands posed to the new order of affairs. There would be more Jacobite risings before they did.

There is one last tale of Black Ewen. On the morning of 22 December 1715, when he was a very old man, the Cameron chief awoke and announced to his wife that King James – 'James VIII', the Old Pretender – had landed in Scotland. Lady Cameron, naturally, decided he was havering; but the old fellow was so insistent that, to humour him, the news was solemnly announced: fires of rejoicing were lit, and all Lochaber toasted the king's health in claret and whisky. And, sure enough, word duly came that, on 22 December, the Old Pretender had landed secretly at Peterhead.

Sir Ewen Cameron of Lochiel died in 1719, in his ninetieth year, and is buried in the grounds of the Kilmallie church. Lord

MacAulay would later call him 'the Ulysses of the Highlands'; another has called this Cameron 'the epitome of a Highland chief, arrogant, emotional, stiff with pride and extravagantly brave'.

His grandson, in his day, would fight for another Charles Stuart – and pay the price.

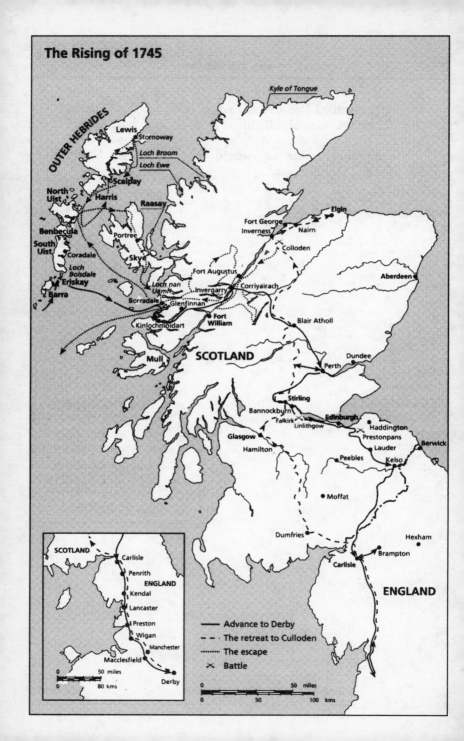

The Rising of 1745

OUTER HEBRIDES

Lewis
Stornoway
Loch Broom
Loch Ewe
Scalpay
North Uist
Harris
Raasay
Benbecula
Portree
South Uist
Coradale
Skye
Loch Bolsdale
Eriskay
Loch nan Uamh
Barra
Borradale
Glenfinnan
Kinlochmoidart

Kyle of Tongue

Fort George
Inverness
Nairn
Elgin
Colloden
Fort Augustus
Invergarry
Corriyairach
Aberdeen
Fort William
Blair Atholl
Dundee
Perth

SCOTLAND

Mull

Stirling
Bannockburn
Falkirk
Linlithgow
Edinburgh
Haddington
Prestonpans
Lauder
Berwick
Glasgow
Hamilton
Peebles
Kelso
Moffat
Dumfries
Hexham
Brampton
Carlisle

ENGLAND

SCOTLAND
Carlisle
Penrith
ENGLAND
Kendal
Lancaster
Preston
Wigan
Manchester
Macclesfield
Derby

0   50 miles
0 80 kms

——— Advance to Derby
– – – The retreat to Culloden
·········· The escape
✕ Battle

0   50   miles
0   50   100 kms

CHAPTER SIX
The Undefiled Blood

Hug o laithill ohoro
Hu o ro 'n aill leibh
Hug o laithill ohoro
Seinn o horo 'n aill leibh

Moch sa' mhadainn 's mi dusgadh
'S mor mo shunnd 's mo cheol gaire
On a chuala mi 'm Prionnsa
Thig 'nn do dhuthaich Chlann Ranaill

Grainne-mullaich gach righ thu
Slan gun till thusa Thearlaich
'S ann tha 'n fhior-fhuil gun truailleadh
Anns a' ghruaidh as mor naire

Nam faighinn mo dhurachd
Bhiodh an Diuc air dhroch caramh
Gum biodh buidsear na feola
Agus corcach m' a bhraghaid

When I wake early in the morning
Great is my joy and my song
Since I heard that the Prince
Was coming to the country of Clanranald

Better than all other kings are you
A happy return to you, Charlie
In him is the fine undefiled blood
In his face wonderful modesty

Were I granted my wish
The Duke would endure much woe
The vicious butcher would be
With the rope about his neck

From 'Hug O Laithill Ohoro', a song of the '45, by Alasdair MacDonald – Alasdair mac Maighstair Alasdair – who fought in the army of Charles Edward Stuart.

WILLIAM OF ORANGE did not long survive his father-in-law. In 1702, as he was out riding, his mount stumbled on a molehill and the king took a bad fall, breaking his collar-bone; soon afterwards William – never strong; he had bad asthma – died from pain and shock. Happy Jacobites raised glasses to the 'little gentleman in black velvet', whose earthwork had brought down a usurper. William left his kingdoms in deep unease. The succession was far from certain and most expected an imminent Jacobite rebellion: it seemed likely that 'King James VIII' would yet sit in the Palace of St James.

The marriage of William and Mary had produced no issue. Her sister Anne, however, had demonstrated magnificent fecundity, but all the valiant labours of her womb had been in vain. The princess had borne no fewer than seventeen children to her bovine husband, Prince George of Denmark, but almost all had perished within hours – or days – of birth. It appears that Anne had some gynaecological defect; whatever, though only forty-two at her succession, she was already an old and bitter woman. One son, William – Duke of Gloucester – attained the ripe old age of eleven, but this lad had various disorders, including hydrocephalus, and could not walk unaided. At the turn of the century he died. William was widowed; Anne and George no longer brought forth. Once the last daughter of James II and VII was dead, nothing stood between James Francis and the throne. The Pope had already recognised him as rightful king. So did all Roman Catholic Europe.

To the end of their days, Mary II and Anne refused to believe that James Francis was truly their brother. The tale was got about in society that the baby had been secreted into the queen's childbed by means of a warming-pan; that he was the unknown bastard of some poor woman in the stews of London. (As a result of this *fama* it was thereafter required that the Home Secretary attend all royal confinements; the custom survived until the birth of the present Prince of Wales, when George VI sharply ordered an end to it.) In 1701, then, the English parliament passed the Act of Settlement, ending the uncertainty by a defiant wresting of monarchy from the dictates of genealogy. After Queen Anne, all the descendants of Charles I – and a good few others from the loins of James VI – were debarred from succession. If the queen died childless, the throne would pass to the Electress Sophia of Hanover, daughter of Elizabeth of Bohemia, daughter of James VI. There were at least thirty-four people living with a better claim to the throne – Protestants, too, some of them – but a Hanoverian succession suited best the schemes and purposes of William of Orange.

The warming-pan story is nonsense. There is no doubt that James was his parents' child; he resembled them both closely, and grew up with some of his father's regrettable character traits. The sad thing is that he would probably have made a very good king. He was wise, moderate, humane, and kindly. As his previous siblings had died in early childhood, so he proved most fit and vigorous; he lived to a good age and – had his lot in providence been better cast – would have been the longest reigning monarch in British history. But he was resolutely, adamantly, Roman Catholic; he was, like his grandfather, extremely shy, and in close family relationships he was too inhibited and serious for his own good.

Nothing could shift the Romanism of the exiled Stuarts. The young prince had been made to swear, at his father's deathbed, undying fealty to the 'true religion'. The old king was not long dead when his widowed queen had begun eagerly to seek – and count – the necessary number of attributable miracles to gain his canonisation. King William, mindful of the great perils in bypassing the Pretender's strong dynastic claim – and well aware that he was, in truth, his father's son – negotiated discreetly with the prince's court. So, later, did Anne. Would the Stuart claimant not, for the sake of his three kingdoms, embrace the Protestant faith? But he was set. Bolingbroke, one of Queen Anne's chief ministers – and a fly, shifting figure in the complicated intrigues of the day – at length gave up on the Pretender. 'England would as soon have a Turk as a Roman Catholic for a King,' he exclaimed, but he had quite failed to persuade James Francis. For young James was as mulish, and as sanctimonious, as his late father. Nothing could bring him to see how devastating a Roman Catholic profession was to all his hopes.

Scotland did not long thrive after the Revolution. The Glencoe disgrace demonstrated, as nothing else could, the abiding failure of crown policy towards the Highlands: cajoling one month, threatening the next, a hostage here and a bribe there and an exemplary atrocity there. Religious trouble seethed, between ministers of the restored Presbyterian order and the Episcopal clergy they displaced across the land: much injustice was done, and considerable ill-feeling aroused, and the smarting Episcopalians became one of the strongest blocs of support for the exiled Stuarts.

The 1690s were marked by the spectacular – and humiliating – failure of an important Scottish venture, the Darien project. Determined to reap colonial wealth, the Scots parliament and the business community had invested heavily in a settlement scheme for Panama, in the New World. Their vision of colonial bounty collapsed in mismanagement, disease, and disaster. It had been billed to the Scots as a miracle cure-all for their economic malaise. But it was denied English backing; neither venture capital from London's financial houses nor practical aid from English colonies in the region. Three-quarters of those in the first expedition to 'New Caledonia' died, of disease, hunger, and the assaults of hostile tribes.

A second followed in 1699; they were soon starving, could win no aid from the English West Indies, and at length surrendered to the Spanish. At home, the end of the century was marked by a succession of bad harvests and a long, merciless recession. In Scotland as a whole, in the closing years of the century, at least 5 per cent of the population simply starved to death. In places such as rural Aberdeenshire, the figure was nearer 20 per cent. The English Act of Settlement was a specific challenge to the Scots, who had expressly reserved in 1689 the right to determine the Scots succession. Many in high places were now convinced that Scotland could not survive without full, free trade to and from a presently hostile England. Access to colonial markets, to the wealth of the New World, was denied to the little land. There now seemed a real danger, on Anne's death, of a separate Scots monarchy – a Stuart monarchy – and full-blown war with the elephant next door.

Through this chaos, born of fear, lubricated with bribes, and largely engineered by the Scots nobles and their allies in banking and commerce, came the 1707 Union of Parliaments. The struggle to force Scotland into this unhappy wedlock is a long and most complicated story. It is often forgotten that it was a measure as loathed in many parts of England as in Scotland. Certainly the great weight of Scots feeling was against it. A quarter of the shires and a third of the burghs petitioned against union in the most hostile terms. There were riots in the streets. One active in the negotiations, Sir John Clerk, later admitted that the deal had been pushed through 'contrary to the inclinations of at least three-fourths of the Kingdom'.

There were twenty-five Articles of Union, but there was no provision for any appeal against their breach. In theory, both English and Scots parliaments ceased to exist, and a new parliament of Great Britain was created. In practice – to our own day – the British parliament would think, and behave, as the English parliament continuing. A good many of these twenty-five articles have been broken; there is no redress whatever for the aggrieved. The irony is that pressure for union grew out of intense but largely short-term factors. The pressures in Scotland, the grip of the Whig administration on affairs, the popular fear of war and Romanism, met for but a brief time. By the end of 1708, union would have been impossible.

Nationalism certainly spurred most Scots, at this time, to sympathise with the Jacobite cause. But other emotions were in play, and at times there seemed almost as many motives as there were Jacobites. Roman Catholics supported the Stuart claimant, but in Scotland they were greatly outnumbered by the Episcopalians. Oddly, the Protestant paranoia of the English was not nearly so strong in Scotland; the king's personal religion mattered little to most Scots, as long as he would leave their own Church affairs alone. Tories – the patriarchal class of the land, exiled from government by the Whigs – were inclined to favour a Stuart restoration. Some, thrown out of power and office because of their incompetence, corruption or viciousness, sought a return by the revolutionary road. And so on. A vague, bitter, anti-English sentiment was the strongest charge of Jacobitism, a sense of national sell-out.

As long as Queen Anne lived, the monarchy had sufficient legitimacy – just – to stave off the threat from overseas. Her reign was as troubled, and unhappy, as her life. Scots rued it for the union of 1707 and the restoration of patronage on the Scots Kirk in 1712 – the first explicit violation of the union deal, and a measure stripping power from the Church courts and consolidating it in crown and gentry. She was the last British monarch to deny the royal assent to an Act of Parliament. Such Jacobite attempts as sputtered regularly through Queen Anne's reign – 1702, 1709, 1712 – came to rapid grief. And then, in 1714, she died, so obese that her coffin was almost square.

She had outlived the electress by a few months; to the crown there now succeeded Sophia's son, Elector of Hanover, who styled himself King George I. The succession was hugely unpopular. Throughout the British Isles, the mob jeered and derided the arrival of this alien princeling. Had the titular King James landed in London the day his sister died, he would have been carried to the throne by force. And in Scotland the feeling was even stronger. As George I was proclaimed in Inverness, the town crier could scarcely be heard for the mocking fury of the massed magistrates. Luckless officials cried, 'God save the King,' but were drowned by still louder cries of, 'God damn 'em and their King.' At word of Queen Anne's death, the garrison of Edinburgh Castle panicked: they knocked down the bridge at the gate, dug a moat and built a drawbridge. In Scotland the government felt under siege. The administration launched on a panic-stricken purge. Almost a fifth of all Justices of the Peace in Scotland were stripped of rank and office, on suspicion of Jacobite sympathy.

But James did not appear: timing was never a Stuart forte, and James Francis had no tactical sense whatever. Everyone knew rebellion was coming. Many – certainly most Scots – thought it would succeed. Few thought the union would survive it. George I was dull, German, and unpopular. He took little

interest in the affairs of Britain. He had been born in Germany
and would die in Germany. He never learned to speak English
and, on the rare occasions he met his ministers, discussed their
concerns in halting dog-Latin. For such a man few would fight
and none would gladly die. But when a rising did come, in 1715,
it was both inept and ludicrous: amid the most auspicious
conditions, the Jacobites succeeded, like Lincoln's Burnside,
in wresting defeat from the jaws of victory.

The '15 was not really a Highland adventure: its heartland was
in the north-east Lowlands of Scotland, a realm Episcopal or
Roman in religion, whose aristocracy aligned themselves with
the Stuart cause, where the common folk were overwhelmingly
in favour of the old line. (But in the Lowlands, too, there was
strong support.) Even Presbyterians favoured a Stuart return.
Yet again, as demonstrated throughout the previous century,
the Scots had an entirely different view of the monarchy from
the English. Sovereignty, not religion, was their concern. Of all
the Stuart risings, the '15 had the strongest base: it was a massive
and popular rebellion, needing not even the landing of a Stuart
prince to launch it, but merely one to raise himself up as a leader.

That leader, calamitously, was the Earl of Mar. He was a
failed and disillusioned career politician, who had been active in
securing the union, a former Secretary of State for Scotland. In
1709 Queen Anne had sacked him. Nor had Mar won preferment from the new king. So, 'fair scunnered', he cast in his lot
with Jacobitism. Mar was an able politician – calculating, shifty,
mercurial, dishonest – but successful military revolt requires
other qualities, and Mar had none of them. His timing was
deplorable: he launched his adventure only days after the death
of Louis XIV of France, a monarch of strong Jacobite sympathies, and the rising flooded and ebbed without any practical
support from any foreign power.

He and his cronies raised the standard at the Braes of Mar,
Aberdeenshire, in September 1715. It had been conceived as a
neat geographical juncture between the north-east Lowlands
and the Grampian Highlands, but the real strength of Highland
Jacobitism was in the west, and this country was too far away
truly to rouse their passions or direct their movements. The
western movement south was a disaster. By October the clans
had failed to take Fort William or even Inveraray. They

abandoned their separate march and joined Mar's main force in
Perthshire. He had taken Perth on 14 September; Inverness fell
quickly, and all Scotland north of Forth rallied to the Jacobite
cause. Everything had been in his favour. But, at Perth, he
dillied and dallied, and his armies waited and waited. What was
desperately needed was a dramatic battle, ending in resounding
Jacobite victory. It came far too late, at Sheriffmuir, on 13
November. A mere 1,000 government troops, under the Duke
of Argyll, easily held off the much stronger force of Mar; the
inconclusive battle effectively ended the rising.

On 22 December James Francis himself landed at Peterhead.
By then it was all over. A goodly rising of Jacobites in northern
England had come to nothing, falling to defeat at Preston. The
clans were already scurrying home and making their peace with
the government. The Pretender's coronation at Scone went
awry; it is not even clear if he was actually crowned at all.
He was also exposed, to disappointed Scots, as a prince sadly
short of drive and charisma. He was a glum, uninspiring figure,
with much of the pomposity of his beheaded grandfather. 'Can
he speak?' asked some who beheld the poker-faced, silent
Pretender. In March 1716 he scurried back to the Continent.
To Hanoverian joy, he was expelled from France by the new
regime and forced to settle in Rome itself, a propaganda coup
for his enemies in Britain.

For those familiar with the horrors that followed Culloden,
government measures after the '15 surprise in their mildness.
Proposals to build large military barracks – at Glenelg, Fort
Augustus and Inverness – came to nothing. The Disarming Act
of 1716 banned the carrying of weapons in public, not their
possession; in any event, only the loyal clans obeyed it. The
creation and arming of a Highland force loyal to the government would have made sense, but Whitehall had a distrust of the
Highlanders: no such brigade was formed, and the existing
Highland force – the Black Watch – was dissolved in 1717.
Estates were forfeited from prominent Jacobites, including
much Highland land; but after years of intrigue and haggling
most were returned.

Meanwhile Jacobite plot and enterprise continued, most
disabled by political intrigue, wrecked in the paranoia of the
Jacobite court, or defused by England's increasingly effective

network of spies. Sometimes a foreign potentate, such as
Gustavus Adolphus of Sweden, would die on the verge of
backing a great new Stuart enterprise. Or the 'Protestant
wind' would rise, and scatter the latest Jacobite fleet. In 1719,
though, another Jacobite initiative was launched on Highland
soil. The wind struck yet again, with lethal effect: a mighty
Spanish invasion fleet – twenty-nine ships and 5,000 men – was
scattered off Corruna. So an English invasion did not come off,
nor was the Pretender collected *en route* by this armada. Yet the
Highland advance-party, seeking landfall on the western seaboard, were blissfully unaware of this disaster. Two frigates,
with some 300 Spanish soldiers, berthed at Stornoway and
collected prominent Jacobites. Thus combined George Keith,
tenth Earl Marischal, and the Marquis of Tullibardine, great
Jacobites both, of some military experience, and each secretly
convinced of his own great vision and the other's essential
incompetence.

There is a comic-opera bathos to the '19. The two great
Jacobites fought and squabbled: daily councils of war were
reduced to shouting matches. They were unable to agree on
anything, even by what route they should march upon Inverness. They took possession of Eilean Donan castle, a pictur-
esque tidal fort by the confluence of Loch Alsh, Loch Long and
Loch Duich. Government troops speedily besieged them with
mortars, and a naval frigate or two, and the castle was reduced
to rubble. (The present building, much photographed and
famous, was largely built in our own century.) Their retreat
seaward was cut off; so humiliated already was this invasion
force that barely 1,000 clansmen joined their effort. They
included, to be sure, Rob Roy MacGregor, but the enterprise
was all but done. On 9 June it effectively ended in a trivial battle
at Glen Shiel, with not many dead. The disorientated Spanish,
cold and hungry, surrendered; they were well treated, and by
year's end they were back home.

The farce of the '19 did much to soothe government fear of the
Highland host. They were further misled by a report on the
'Highland problem', commissioned – by great ill-judgement –
from Simon, Lord Fraser of Lovat, in 1724. Lovat was a Roman
Catholic and a former Jacobite agent. He was a convicted rapist
and a man entirely devoid of ethical scruple. His report was

written to bolster his standing in London, advance his own territorial interests in the East Highlands, and attract government funds and activity to the benefit of his own neighbourhood. So he painted for London a picture of a Highlands and Islands torn by lawlessness (save for the good offices of chiefs like himself), united by common patriarchal interest to Stuart aspirations, its unstable clan society wild enough to threaten the British order but too savage to make that threat coherent and dangerous.

It was unjust, misleading and ill-informed, but London believed it. The truth of affairs in the Highlands was quite different. The clan wars were long over, blown out by the end of the seventeenth century. Clan society was, in truth, a stabilising force: such lawlessness as there was came from vagabonds, supporting themselves by cattle-rieving and freelance criminal activity. The clans had ceased to fight over land; Lovat himself was one of the last carpet-bagging adventurers. They no longer formed a solid Jacobite coalition or even an anti-Campbell coalition; some Campbell septs had actually risen in the Jacobite interest in 1715. Clan chiefs were now cutting deals with one another, agreeing peace and mutual protection. The abiding problem – every visitor in the period comments on it – was the grinding, inhuman poverty. Housing was generally deplorable. Stock was poor, agricultural standards low, the mass of the people unchurched. In winter, Highlanders regularly died of starvation. It was a land overwhelmingly in need of improvement, of cash investment; it got, instead, fortification.

In 1725 General George Wade was appointed commander of government forces in Scotland. He is most renowned for his roads: in the decade following his appointment, he built over 250 miles of them, plunging deep into the Highlands and up the Great Glen. A good many Highland roads are incorrectly attributed to Wade, but some stretches are still in use to this day, improved and metalled, of course. Wade perceived that the Great Glen was the key to the region: it was a natural barrier to any southern advance, and the obvious route of invasion to Inverness from the West Highlands. Wade's roads linked the various government garrisons, and major forts, to the south for supply of troops and ordnance and to each other for communication in crisis. A little warship on Loch Ness completed his *cordon sanitaire*. Forts were strengthened, and new ones built, such as that at Kilcumin, at the southern end of Loch Ness. Wade named this new keep Fort Augustus, after a son of King George II, who had succeeded his father in 1727.

Plots, conspiracies, and dreams continued to prosper at the Jacobite court in Rome; the lessons of the latest Highland failure ruefully absorbed. The Pretender was, by 1719, thirty years old, and mindful of the need to keep the Stuart line going. James Francis needed to marry: the bride must be both Roman and royal. His mother – a most meddlesome woman – had mercifully died in 1718; her interference in his affairs was done. But the prospects of James Francis were scarcely impressive, and agents of Britain toiled, at every turn, to frustrate the wooing of the 'Old Pretender'. At length, he won the hand of a Polish lass, Princess Clementina Sobieska, and – after epic adventures; the British pursued her and her Irish escort at every turn, and the party had to cross the Alps in the wildest conditions – the princess safely made Rome. By year's end they were married. At the end of the next year, 1720, she gave birth to a prince: Charles Edward Louis John Casimir Silvester Severino Mario Stuart. The delighted father created the infant Prince of Wales, and the child was baptised as his parents had been wed – by the Pope himself.

Charles Edward Stuart has had a raw deal in history. His admirers have had a bad habit of describing him as 'romantic', a word which today has distinctly effete overtones, and the aura of effeminacy is further enhanced by his best-known portrait, which makes the prince appear excessively pretty. (But he was only twelve years old when he sat for it.) His detractors have reacted against this abiding legend by dipping their pens in vitriol. The Prince has been done over as naïve, irresponsible, cowardly, quarrelsome, reckless, dishonest, selfish; they dwell happily upon the last, and increasingly wretched, decades of his career.

Charles had one great flaw: he could not cope with failure. As his life crashed into failure before his twenty-sixth birthday, most of his career was spent then in advancing disintegration. He was not, essentially, a strong and integrated personality. This must be put down to his childhood which was, for the most part, fearsomely unhappy. As the prince grew up his father grew increasingly melancholy and dark; resigned to the grim portion of his family, quite despairing of ever sitting upon the British throne. He found his elder son's brightness vexing, and his ever-bubbling hope infuriating. Bizarrely, even in early childhood, the prince and his father communicated by letter rather than face to face. Charles Edward's spelling was atrocious – he was probably dyslexic – and this gave ample ground for the parent to respond in terms of reproach and rebuke. The relationship steadily deteriorated. Charles Edward met his father in 1744, shortly before departing for his Scottish adventure; they never saw each other again, though the ageing Pretender lived for many more years. When it mattered most, in 1745 and 1746, the prince had great difficulty taking counsel from any older man; thus his father warped him.

Besides, the royal marriage had gone to ruin. Clementina was not a stable woman. After the birth of her second son, Henry Benedict, in 1724, she succumbed increasingly to neurosis and sick fancy. She developed anorexia, losing weight to the point where she ceased to menstruate. The family home was shaken by tantrums, scenes, and wild stormings and weepings. Clementina was convinced – quite absurdly – of her husband's adultery with a courtier's wife. (Her husband, though, was incurably uxorious: like his grandfather, he had a high and solemn view of marriage.) The royal marriage ceased, to all intents and purposes, to exist; Clementina sought refuge in a convent, and at length died, not an old woman, but certifiably insane. It is tempting to draw a modern parallel: it certainly scarred Charles Edward deeply, and it drove his weaker brother to introversion and homosexuality.

The accomplishments of Charles Edward Stuart, then, are remarkable. He was highly intelligent, and reached adulthood fluent in French, Spanish, and Italian; he spoke English, of course – with a pleasant Irish quality to it – and by Culloden he was able to converse in Gaelic. He was very tall and, by the standards of his day, extremely handsome. He was skilled in the saddle, in falconry, good with dogs. He was a keen swordsman and a superb shot. (When, after the loss of his hopes, and he was on the run over the Highland moors, the prince astonished his companions as a fowler; he seemed able to down a bird with every shot, time after time.) He vigorously enjoyed such sports as tennis and badminton. He was, though, quite unable to swim. And, even as a teenager, he showed a taste for drink.

While the father was plain, he was glamorous. While the Old Pretender was stoically grim, the prince was gay and effervescent. He cared little for religious observance; he was virtually agnostic. (In 1750, when it was far too late to make any difference, he actually converted to Protestantism, though he reverted to the Roman faith before his death.) Charles Edward was fun. He liked to dance, to make music (he was a fine cellist); he liked to party. He had, beyond all doubt, charm – the gift of making others feel good about themselves, the ability to make people do what he wanted. He could be very witty. He had a genius for the bright phrase, the courtly compliment, the gracious remark, the gently self-deflating *bon mot*. By 1739, this prince was in all but name leader of the Jacobite cause.

So he came to Scotland, in the summer of 1745. It was a reckless venture, and in many ways a makeshift gesture of defiance by a blithe and rebellious young man. It followed on the heels of another triumphant blast of the Protestant wind. France, early the previous year, had laid elaborate plans for a full-scale invasion of England, and it was to that end that the prince had come to France. But, in March 1744, the marshalling fleet had been struck by a wild storm off Dunkirk: twelve of the great vessels sank, seven with all hands. After that the French grew cautious. When Charles sailed for Scotland, it was less a serious attempt at launching a rising than a pre-emptive strike to force the hand of the French, who by now were at full war with England in the Low Countries. And the '45 Rising, unlike its predecessors, would be a Highland adventure from start to finish.

Charles had to finance the expedition himself, without foreign aid. Much of the cash he had from Aeneas MacDonald, an exiled Jacobite who ran a Paris banking house: it was by way of venture capital, bet on the prince and his adventure in the hope of fat returns come restoration to the throne. The rest the prince raised on credit, using his mother's jewels for security. With the funds thus gained, the prince bought twenty field guns, 3,500 assorted muskets and pistols, and some 2,400 broadswords. In June 1745 all this, and some hundred marines, were boarded on two ships at

Nantes, the *Elisabeth* and the *Du Teillay*. (The precise name of this latter boat is still disputed; some insist it was the *Doutelle*.) At any event, only she – with the prince, his companions and less than half the arsenal – made it to Scotland. The *Elisabeth* was crippled off the Channel coast and had to limp back to France, with all the soldiers and much of the weaponry.

His companions were a strange and seedy bunch. They included four Irishmen. John William O'Sullivan was one of those crawling inadequates who clung like leeches to the Jacobite court; he could boast some genuine military experience in Italy, but greatly exaggerated his skills and competence. The prince put far too much trust in him. Father George Kelly was an ordained parson of the Church of England, who had spent twenty years in the Tower of London for his part in the '15. He had a baleful hold over the prince, whom he knew perfectly how to manipulate for his own ends; despite Kelly's sufferings for the Stuart cause, he was a ruthless and wicked man. Sir Thomas Sheridan had been boyhood tutor to Charles Edward, an indulgent, kindly figure of little character, but whom Charles saw as a surrogate father. Then there was Francis Strickland, whom Charles can only have taken as an explicit snub to his grim parent: the Old Pretender had sacked this unimpressive hireling the previous year, and he had nothing else to commend him for the expedition.

And there were Scots: the Marquess of Tullibardine (who claimed to be the true Duke of Atholl, disputing the tactically important Atholl country with a Hanoverian occupier), and Aeneas MacDonald, coming out to watch his investment, and Sir John MacDonald, an eccentric, drunken rogue of an old warrior, whose company the Prince enjoyed. This extraordinary, and scarcely admirable, crew of companions were the far from glorious 'Seven Men of Moidart'. Some were to wreak great harm in the cause.

Without the *Elisabeth*, the party at length made landfall on little Eriskay, in the Outer Isles, in the heart of Jacobite country – MacDonald country, Roman Catholic country – and spent an uncomfortable night in the black house of one Angus MacDonald. As guest of honour, Charles Edward was made to sit on a stool, which meant his head was in the smoke; the rest made do with peats. After refreshment and rest, he sent word to the local chief. MacDonald of Clanranald refused to see him. He sent his regards and asked the prince, politely, to go back home. But Charles Edward pressed on, sailing to the mainland, landing at Loch nan Uamh, in the lovely landscape of Moidart.

At length he met with Lochiel himself. Lochiel refused to have any part in such a rash enterprise. Where were the French? Where were the ships, the provisions, the horses, the gold to pay the vast army seizing the throne would require? And he himself would incur huge personal risk: forfeiture of lands, estate, income, perhaps even his life if the rising came to nothing. Charles Edward promised that, even in failure, he himself would provide a living for Lochiel fully commensurate with such wealth as he lost. And he would put it in writing. But the chief of Clan Cameron refused to commit himself.

At length the prince said, dismissively, that for himself, *he* would press on; Lochiel could stay at home and read of his fate in the newspapers. This was too much for Cameron pride. With an oath, Lochiel pledged himself to the cause. He sallied forth to win other chiefs, and the die was cast. (Lochiel did not long survive the rising, but it must be noted that the prince honoured his promise; in French exile, Lochiel was granted a lucrative sinecure equal to the income of his forfeit estates.) So, on 19 August 1745, the standard was raised at Glenfinnan, some fifteen miles west of Fort William. Three MacDonald chiefs – Glengarry, Morar and Keppoch – turned out, with a mere 500 men; only Lochiel's arrival, with another 700, lent any hope to the enterprise. More, in the months that followed, would adhere again to the Jacobite cause, but there was a marked caution even at the height of the enterprise among the clan chiefs. Some came 'out' only after they had signed their estates over to their heir to safeguard the inheritance. Others stayed 'in' themselves, loyal to Hanover, but ordered a son 'out'. Thus bets were hedged. At least one clan chief marched forth to fight for Hanover while his wife, back home, directed operations in the Jacobite interest.

In fact, most West Highland clans would not stir for Charles Edward Stuart. Clanranald never changed his mind, though he was the biggest force in the Roman Catholic Highlands. Not a man from Barra and South Uist, staunchly Papist as they were, joined the cause. In 1715 Scotland had, for the most part, been warmly behind the Stuarts. In 1745 there was much fear, widespread indifference, and a good deal of ill-veiled hostility. It took time for the rising to gain any momentum. When Charles Edward and his force entered the Great Glen, they were joined by another 800 men – Glengarry MacDonnels, Stewarts from Appin – but the Jacobites had taken Perth before the Stuart force had risen much beyond its strength in 1719.

Nor could the prince count on the support of clans who had 'been out' in 1715. The Earl of Seaforth, over the Mackenzies and the MacLeods of Ross-shire and Lewis, had been badly burned in that episode; he refused, point-blank, to join the '45. Macleod of Harris and MacDonald of Sleat headed two of the biggest Jacobite clans. But that wily governor, Duncan Forbes – as Lord President he virtually ran Scotland, and to him more than any did the House of Hanover at last owe its throne – had a hold on these men. He knew that, in 1739, they had sanctioned the kidnapping of hundreds of Skye peasants to be borne away overseas for indentured service – virtual slavery. These poor people had been rescued in a port in Ireland. Of course, MacLeod and MacDonald had not been prosecuted for this outrage – yet. They wisely decided to give Charles Edward a very wide berth.

There is something pathetic, even obsolete, about the '45. In 1745 such a bid to restore a dynasty was already archaic. This was in the lifetime of Benjamin Franklin, Voltaire, Thomas Paine; men who would produce new and radical concepts of government. Besides, the British monarchy was no longer of executive force. Anne had been the last sovereign to withhold the royal assent. Under the indolent George I, Robert Walpole was able to establish the post of Prime Minister as the real head of government. George II was no fool, but quite happy to preside as figurehead over an increasingly corrupt Whig regime. Real hands-on government was of no interest to him. Party politics, a capitalist economy, the power of the House of Commons, a burgeoning executive of the gentry – these were new developments since 1688; a reality no Stuart triumph could have overturned.

The enterprise had no serious support abroad. International politics had become ever more secularised, and even Roman Catholic monarchs such as Louis XV did not greatly care who ran Britain: a Roman king would head a state just as dangerous a rival as a Protestant one. Jacobitism, at best, was a useful distraction; something to tie down British forces at home and give France a freer hand on the Continent. But the plans of this youth did not, in the court of Louis XV, promise to amount even to that. It would be late in the day, far too late, before the French suddenly realised the opportunity the '45 afforded them. For, incredibly, against all the odds, the rising nearly succeeded.

Charles Edward Stuart, within months, came within a few days' march of restoring his father to the throne. He reached the brink of success thanks to his own audacity. In his boldness, in the swiftness with which he drove his forces on, he anticipated modern warfare, running rings around the cumbersome military machine of that day which served the Hanoverian cause. And he also enjoyed momentum, a long, unbroken run of success as he headed south. Further, he was not greatly opposed. As many Scots stood against him as for him – more, probably. But these had no real heart for the struggle. General Sir John Cope, frantically raising volunteers for the defence of Edinburgh, mustered a mere 400 men out of a city of 40,000 people. By the next day, when they were due to march forth and fight Charles Edward, only forty-two remained. In London the regime was deeply unpopular. Had Charles Edward made it to the capital, all opposition might well have collapsed.

He took Scotland virtually without bloodshed. After the standard was raised at Glenfinnan, the clans headed not south by Fort William – where government forces waited in anticipation of a good fight – but east, through the mountain passes and by one of Marshall Wade's roads, and down through Atholl and Stirlingshire and straight into Edinburgh. For all Wade's endeavours, the government had neglected the Highland fortifications. Michael Lynch points out that the strong points of the Wade defence system were not the roads, but the garrisons they served; by 1745, these were undermanned, neglected, and ill-equipped for resistance. The Jacobites met no significant military force at any point. There was no battle in the north. Scattered government forces stumbled about the Highlands or dug themselves in at forts. A naval party reinforced Aberdeen. But, by year's end, Charles was master of Scotland.

The prince had been conferred with powers of regency by his father. So he promptly abolished, by decree, the Treaty of

Union. He paraded up the Royal Mile to an ecstatic welcome. Holyrood Palace was reopened, relit, and for a few short weeks rang once again with royal music, merriment and laughter. And a government army under Sir John Cope met with a humiliating rout at Prestonpans, on 20 September. They were surprised by a dawn attack, the Highlanders appearing on top of them after the traverse of an 'impenetrable' swamp. As news filtered down to London, hearts began to flutter; was this remorseless brigade, surely approaching, actually invincible?

It was the high point of Charles Edward Stuart's career; the happiest days of his life. He could have stopped there, secure in the kingdom of Scotland. Some of his supporters, afire with nationalism, urged just such a course. He and his administration were almost certainly secure. But he wanted more. He wanted London itself; all Britain and its possessions.

These weeks show the best of Charles's character. He was a humanitarian of the first order, as shown in the problem of Edinburgh Castle. The castle had not fallen; it was still in the hands of the government and an evil old general, and practically impregnable. The prince, naturally, ordered a total blockade of supplies. Word soon came from the castle that, should any interference be made with their provisions, they would open fire with big guns on the defenceless citizenry below. So the blockade was lifted. At Prestonpans the prince urged quarter for all who surrendered. He personally tended some of the wounded – of both sides. He reminded his companions, again and again, that he saw all in these islands as his subjects, worthy of his care and regard.

But he was young, a little reckless, and far too prone to make grand promises without substance. Charles Edward repeatedly assured his council of war that French aid was on its way – troops, gold, supplies. And he insisted that much of England was only waiting to rise on his behalf. There were Jacobites everywhere. He had letters from them. This did not convince Lord George Murray, his commander-in-chief – a fine general, if unimaginative. It has been said that, had the prince let Murray alone, he would have woken up to find the crown on his head. This is nonsense; Charles, by instinct, had probably a sharper grasp of strategy. But he was not honest with Murray, who in personality and solemnity was probably an irksome reminder of the prince's father. The relationship between prince and commander was not a good one. The outcome would cost them both dear.

An invasion of England required 5,500 men, at least. Such a force took time to raise; in the meantime, Highlanders were deserting and slipping back north, all the more encouraged in flight by their reluctance to cross the Border. When the prince's military council considered the matter, a decision to invade England was carried by only one vote. Most of the Highland chiefs were against it. Yet the essential strength had been attained. In November the prince, his council, officers and men marched south. Their progress was swift. Once over the Border, discipline remained firm; there were no further desertions. In a mere twenty-seven days they were at Derby. A few more days would bring the Highland invasion to London. Yet, though in town after town, village after village, the prince's advancing host met with courtesy, even welcome, it became apparent that many feared their presence. Scarcely a man would volunteer to join their ranks. At length the Jacobites simply seized whatever men they saw and pressed them into service. The prince's column was desperately short of bodies, heavy arms, gold, provisions. The English did not flock to the standard. There was no sign of the French.

When they reached Derby, only two or three days' march from London, the Jacobites knew little of the situation beyond. They did not know that they had already missed the bulk of the Hanoverian army, which had gone east of them and was stonking up to the north, lost and demoralised. They did not know that London was seized in a panic; that men were selling their goods and preparing to flee; that the city could rustle up only the merest rabble to stand between the prince and the palace. 'There never was so melancholy a town,' wailed society diarist, Horace Walpole, 'nobody but has some fear for themselves, for their money, or for their friends in the army . . . I still fear the rebels beyond my reason.' (It is said that George II himself was packing his trunks for a quick flight to Hanover. That is mere tradition – afterwards, of course, treasonable to say – but it is entirely possible.) Above all, Charles Edward and his council did not know that, at long last, the French had taken notice. Word of Prestonpans had reached them. Troopships were being prepared; all the stuffs and weaponry the Jacobite cause could desire were being bundled aboard.

At Derby, the prince's council of war lost their nerve. They confronted the prince. They would go no further. There was no sign of the English Jacobites. There was no sign of the French. A mighty government force, in all probability, blocked the London road. This was confirmed by one Dudley Bradstreet, who stepped in at a vital moment to warn of a strong army nearby – 9,000 men, between Derby and London. There was no such army. Bradstreet was a Hanoverian spy.

Lord George Murray had had enough of the prince. He was cold, courteous, but scarcely able to hide his contempt. In his panic, Murray had forgotten that vital military principle: concentration of force. The Jacobite position was much stronger than any in the room – save the prince, by instinct as much as stubborn pride – would admit. Further, retreat had another disadvantage: it would make plain to the government that there was, in fact, no co-ordinated pincer plan, no invasion marching from the north in common plan with a French invasion from the south. Yet all these arguments come with the benefit of modern knowledge and wistful hindsight. In the light of such information as they had, the prince's men had collectively – but understandably – lost their nerve. Charles Edward cajoled, begged, stormed and wept. To no avail. He should have done what he did in Lochaber; dismissed them with scorn and gone out to lead the clansmen to London himself, and if he had the ending of this story might – just might – be very different. But Charles Edward had not, at the last, the hard stuff of greatness within him. He caved in. He removed himself, weeping, bitter and sullen. On the morrow of the next day – to a moan from the clansmen as they recognised the terrain – the forces of the rising began their retreat north.

When word reached Paris, the French – naturally enough – stood down their forces and unloaded the supply ships. When word came to London, the mob that had quailed and shivered before – or dared to think of the positive aspects of a restored Stuart monarchy – wheeled in a frenzy of delight and mocking, and began to cry for blood, all the more viciously for their earlier terror. 'No-one,' wrote an exuberant Walpole, 'is afraid of a rebellion that runs away.'

The rising now became incoherent. The Jacobite council had no clear military objective in sight, save to return to Scotland, consolidate some sort of position there, and wait upon events. But they had lost their psychological advantage; besides, in their southern absence, they had lost Scotland. Edinburgh had been swiftly reoccupied. The armies of Wade and Cumberland had marched over the Border. As Charles Edward and his troops returned, weary and demoralised – despite one successful skirmish at Penrith, in Cumbria – few really saw much hope of a swift victory. They prepared for a war of attrition, and all the time the government was busy releasing forces from assorted European entanglements and landing them back in Britain.

The royal child, William Augustus, after whom Wade had named his new fort on Loch Ness, was now Duke of Cumberland, a much younger man than popularly realised. Indeed, the duke was younger than Charles himself, though grossly fat and of unattractive appearance. But Cumberland was a very shrewd soldier. He had made minute study of Highland fighting style and the Highland charge in particular. The Highland soldier charged from above, roaring, with shield – the targe – strapped on his left arm and a pistol in his right hand. The pistol was fired once, then discarded, and dirk or sword drawn. Highlander would fall on Redcoat, readily deflect his bayonet with the targe – after all, the musket was held on the Redcoat's right – and make his fatal thrust with blade. Couple this with that bloodcurdling cry, and it was small wonder that whole lines of government dragoons had simply turned and fled at Prestonpans.

Cumberland's solution was ingenious. He trained his men, day after day – and he was a ruthless martinet of a general – to hold their muskets on their *left*. He also resolved always to fight a Highland force on level ground. And he vowed to haul in plenty of artillery – cannon, grapeshot – and cut the clans to ribbons before they charged at all.

The débâcle of Culloden, on 16 April 1746, is so horrific that it scarcely bears description. The Jacobites could still inflict crushing victories; only weeks before, they had scattered a superior government host at Falkirk. But they had quite failed to follow up that signal victory. They retreated north, and further north, to Inverness, all the time dwindling from desertion, hunger and disease. The commissariat was in the hands of John Hay of Restalrig, a useless fool, who wrung his hands and complained and sighed as men dropped dead from hunger. And the prince himself was no longer that jaunty, optimistic figure of a few months before. He was a bitter, pessimistic, seething lout of a fellow, who now slept late most days, who often did not bother to shave, who made his loathing of Murray and other senior officers manifest to all, who was already finding a bumper or two of brandy in the evenings just the thing for wounded pride.

From Inverness a last, daring plan was proposed; Cumberland's army were only a half-day's march distant, at Nairn. Might the Jacobites not try a surprise attack, by night, and fall upon the Hanoverians in their tents? So, on the night of 15 April – the date was especially apt, as it was Cumberland's birthday, and perhaps the government troops had been permitted a drink or twelve – the straggling clansmen marched out. They were tired, worn, starving; some had not eaten for several days. A few more perished, from exhaustion and hunger, on the way. The force moved far too slowly. Dawn was upon them long before they were within sight of their target. Desperately, the officers ordered a retreat. Never did Charles Edward appear at his worst than on this moment. He exploded in anger and berating, and rode up and down the lines, calling imprecations on the men, prophesying disaster within the day.

Cumberland was moving fast behind them. Murray and the officers wanted to make a stand in the strath of the River Nairn, near the Cairns of Clava; good high ground for a Highland charge. Charles insisted – for reasons only he knew – that they must make a stand on the plain of Drummossie Moor, by Culloden House, the Highland home of Duncan Forbes himself. In this he was supported only by the daft O'Sullivan. Everyone was too tired to argue. So the Highland force took up their position, against government artillery, at the bottom of gently sloping ground, and in the full teeth of a bitter north-east wind. A long stone wall badly distorted the Jacobite line. There was a soggy bog between them and the government forces, over which they were expected to charge. Cumberland's lines were already forming. Shortly they opened fire. Shot and bullets tore into Jacobite ranks, mowing men down in lines. They screamed for the order to charge. But it did not come. (The prince, standing at a distant point, could not see what was happening. The communications, at any event, were deplorable; Charles Edward later insisted he had ordered the charge eight times before it was acted upon.)

As captain-general on this occasion, and by his reliance on the counsel of fools, Charles Edward himself must be held responsible for the Culloden débâcle. But the real tragedy lay in his failed relations with the wisest officers, and with Lord George Murray in particular.

The defeat was total, bloody, and murderous – for the men who were there; two-fifths of the prince's army were absent. The charge proved ragged; scarce a man made it alive to the government lines. The MacDonells of Keppoch initially refused to charge; they were still seething at being denied their favoured fighting position, on the right, which had long been a clan prerogative. Their chief, cursing, flung himself into the fray without them, and was felled almost immediately. Within minutes the Highlanders were in full flight. The wounded and dying were killed where they lay by gleeful government troops. (So were several Inverness schoolboys who had snuck off their lessons that day to come out and watch.) A thousand Highlanders fell.

There were plans to rally at Ruthven, but only a few battered dozens turned up. The prince told them to fly and make shift for themselves. He was going back to France, he said; he would return soon, with a host at his back, to lead them again. It was a precipitate decision, born of panic. Even after Culloden, there were still many willing to fight; the struggle could have continued. As late as mid-May, Lochiel was drafting plans for a summer campaign. But the figurehead of the movement had gone. With their commander in flight, the '45 collapsed.

'That fellow will do me more harm than all the Elector's army!' roared Charles at Derby, when Dudley Bradstreet solemnly lied of a 9,000-strong army between the Jacobites and London. How critical in history was the retreat from Derby? The panic of government generals, and of the government itself, is too well documented to be lightly dismissed. All the 'loyal' forces marshalled to confront the rising – in Edinburgh, Glasgow, London and elsewhere – melted away whenever a real fight seemed likely. It was a corrupt and cynical age and the resident regime was not one for which free men would die. The financiers of London were in panic, fearful for the future of the National Debt. Had the advance continued, there might have been a *coup d'état* before the prince had even reached London. Like General Monck in 1660, one of the military commanders – Wade, perhaps? – could have played kingmaker.

Charles, almost certainly, would have taken London. He, not his father – who by this point had all but given up on public life – would have supplanted George II as king. What we will never know is if he could have held his throne, and what like a king he might have proved. A Roman Catholic monarch would have had immense difficulty in holding the trust of the country. What is certain is that the Highlands would have been spared the horror shortly, after Culloden, to be released upon them.

Several months passed – months of much mishap, narrow squeak, heroism and near-comedy – before Charles Edward Stuart made his safe escape from Scotland. His zigzagging across Scotland still makes good reading today. Valuable time was bought for him, according to tradition, by one Roderick Mackenzie who, like the prince, was tall and fair; when he was cornered and gunned down by government troops, he had the presence of mind to wail, 'Oh, you have killed your prince!' The delighted soldiers cut off his head and sent it to Cumberland; he, in turn, despatched it to London for certain identification. In the meantime, word spread that the prince had been found and killed, and the hunt relaxed. By the time Mackenzie's head reached London, it was beyond recognition; more time was lost before Cumberland's men were forced to admit that Charles was still at large.

He skulked in Moidart; he made escape to the Outer Isles, and hid for a time in Benbecula, then in the wilder reaches of the Park district of Lewis. For a night or two he huddled at Arnish, near Stornoway, where his friends desperately tried to charter a ship. The scheme was detected, and the townsfolk sent word begging Charles Edward to leave, lest he bring the wrath of the government upon them. What is remarkable – and still heart-warming, even today – is that, despite the vast price on the prince's head (£30,000, a fortune for that time) not one in whom the prince placed his trust betrayed him. And only one man, Harris minister Aulay MacAulay, tried to capture the Young Pretender: word reached him of Charles Edward's presence in the isles. But the alarm was raised and the prince escaped.

Too much has been made of Flora MacDonald's part in aiding
Charles Edward. They were together only for a few nights – one
man, Donald MacLeod, was by his side, sharing his sufferings,
for months – and she was not greatly impressed by the Prince;
there was certainly no romantic interest between them. Her part
was to win him the vital pass – under the name and guise of one
'Betty Burke', an Irish maid – by which he was able to escape over
the Minch to Skye. They never met again. From Skye he made
good his escape to Morar, and from thence a French ship picked
him up – at Loch nan Uamh, where his mainland enterprise had
been launched only a year before – and took him to safety. Flora
MacDonald became rather a celebrity, and, though briefly jailed,
attracted some important visitors, including the Prince of Wales.
Later in life she emigrated to America, where two of her sons
perished, in the service of George III, in the War of Independence. She returned and made her home on Skye, where she was
visited by Samuel Johnson.

Charles Edward never, it appears, got over what – by his agency
– had been inflicted on the Highlands. He made repeated attempts
to interest the French and others to support a further bid for the
crown; but was adamant that the landing be in England, not
Scotland. A Scottish sideshow – an independent Scotland, even –
rather interested the French. A full-scale armada to England did
not. Charles was, at length, expelled from the land. Meanwhile, to
his fury – and with his father's blessing – Henry Benedict had been
ordained a priest of Rome, a Cardinal. Nothing could have more
emphatically spoken of Stuart surrender than that.

Charles converted to Protestantism in 1750, and made a
clandestine visit to London. He is even said to have been
present, *incognito*, at the coronation of George III in 1760. He
fathered an illegitimate daughter, Charlotte, who loved him to
the end of his days, perhaps the only person who really did. Even
her mother, Clementina Walkinshaw, finally wearied of him, of
his neglect and his drunken beatings; her life was especially
difficult in the paranoid Jacobite court, for her sister was
employed by the Dowager Princess of Wales, mother of George
III. Charles grew increasingly loathsome: fat, ailing, flatulent, a
topper of an alcoholic. He married late and calamitously, to
Louise of Stolberg. The marriage was a farce from the start and
within months she was openly cuckolding him. Their union

collapsed in the most acrimonious circumstances, with half of Europe laughing at him and the other half laughing at her.

'I will do for the English Jacobites what they did for me,' said Charles, in bitter old age, 'I shall drink their health.' And once, when visitors tried to draw him on memories of his great adventure, he was rapidly reduced to a weeping, incoherent heap. Charlotte was furious. 'Sirs!' she cried. 'What is this? Why! You have been speaking to him of his Highlanders!'

James, the Old Pretender, died in 1766. The Pope refused to acknowledge 'King Charles III'. The young hero of the '45 died, in wretched and prematurely senile distress, in 1788. Henry Benedict – 'Cardinal York' – struck a medal for 'King Henry IX' and left it at that. He was a gentle, sheep-faced bore of a fellow, and a pederast. Before his death, the last of the Stuarts entertained a son or two of George III; the Duke of Sussex afforded the old man great pleasure by solemnly addressing him as 'Your Royal Highness'. Cardinal York was ruined when Napoleon invaded Italy and he lost almost all his belongings; he died, in 1807, as the grateful recipient of a Hanoverian pension, and George IV paid for the handsome family tomb in Rome.

What remained of Jacobite claims to the British throne passed by primogeniture to the descendants of Henrietta, daughter of Charles I. The senior line is the royal house of Savoy, who occupied the Italian monarchy until after the Second World War; but their connection to the Stuarts comes by an uncle-to-niece marriage illegal under our law. The Duke of Bavaria, whose descent is not thus muddied, is generally accepted as the modern Pretender. A nineteenth-century Duke paid ironic homage to his little band of British supporters by bedecking his apartments in tartan wallpaper.

The last of the line by blood – Charles Rohanstart, an illegitimate son of Charles Edward's illegitimate daughter – was killed near Perth in a coaching accident, in 1854, and is buried in the grounds of Dunkeld Cathedral, within sight of the modern A9, where coaches and articulated lorries thunder by the moment into the most civilised Highlands.

That civilisation came hard.

CHAPTER SEVEN

The Everlasting Sea

An ataireachd bhuan
Cluinn fuaim na h-ataireachd ard
Tha torann a' chuain
Mar chualas leam-s' 'nam phaisd
Gun mhuthadh, gun truas
A' sluaisreadh gainneimh na tragh'd
An ataireachd bhuan
Cluinn fuaim na h-ataireachd ard

Sna coilltean a siar
Chan iarrain fuireach gu brath
Bha m' intinn 's mo mhiann
A riamh air lagan a' bhaigh
Ach iadsan bha fial
An gniomh, an caidreamh 's an agh
Air sgapadh gun dion
Mar thriallas ealtainn roimh namh . . .'

The everlasting surge of the sea
Hear the roar of the mighty surge
The thundering of the ocean is
As I heard it in my childhood
Without change, without pity
Sweeping up the sands on the shore
The everlasting surge of the sea
Hear the roar of the mighty surge

In the woods of the west
I would not want to wait for ever
My mind and my wish
Were ever in the little hollow by the cove
But those who were gracious
In act, in friendship and in mirth
Are scattered without protection
Like a flock of birds before an enemy . . .

From 'An Ataireachd Ard', by Donald MacIver, a native of Lewis, composed in Canada.

IN A WORLD WHERE the wild, rugged, misty scenery of the grander Highland landscape is universally deemed most beautiful, it is hard now to realise how modern such aesthetics are. Before the Romantics of last century – Byron, Wordsworth, Scott and so on – began their deification of nature untouched by man, beauty was the artificial. Beauty was the tended, the ordered, the planted. To such eyes the Highland landscape was quite horrid. It actually frightened them.

'I like not this place,' said Cumberland gloomily, in 1746, and he thought the Highlands 'a barbarous country'. To this land, as the smoke of Culloden drifted and died, he now determined to bring order and civilisation. He was a savage lump of a young man. The lash, the noose were frequently wielded on his ill-paid, reluctant troopers. He seems to us entirely devoid of the normal instincts of humanity. He could not see the Highlanders as human at all; even his own soldiers were to him but fodder, to be advanced and moved and forfeited at his most German will. Cumberland was of that type who, two centuries later, in the name of order and racial hygiene, would cram Jews and Slavs and gypsies and homosexuals into the gas chambers, and neatly tot up the work in a ledger at day's end, and feel but weary satisfaction at a job efficiently performed.

This royal prince now stood at the head of a massive army, in the heart of the Highlands. The Royal Navy was at his disposal; there were, besides, two large local militias. In London the mob – from the stews of Whitehall to the coffee-houses of the intelligentsia, even in the Palace of Westminster itself – clamoured for vengeance on those strange northern creatures who had so terrified them, not very many weeks before. 'For the first time the Highlands and Islands were at the mercy of the British government,' writes Bruce Lenman. Thus the strategy of Jacobite retreat had repaid the Highlands.

The quality of mercy was exceeding strained. The Prime Minister, Lord Newcastle, wanted the Highlands 'utterly reduced'; it was, to him, an utterly alien and dangerous state. Lord Chesterfield, Lord Lieutenant of Ireland, called for genocide. He cut off all food supplies from Ireland to Scotland. He wanted a naval blockade and a price to be put on the head of every chief. And he suggested a wholesale massacre of the Highland peasantry. Compared to many a voice in the streets of London, his demands were – if anything – moderate. What seems remarkable today is that all Scotland was tarred with the Jacobite taint. Most Scots were passively hostile to Charles Edward; more had fought against him than with him. One could argue, indeed, that Culloden had been a Scots victory – for Presbyterianism, for the Protestant succession, for the commercial and fiscal order. But a verse was now added to the national anthem wishing the king all power 'rebellious Scots to crush'. (This verse remained in the Church of England hymnal until the late 1980s.) And popular writers still talk of 'Scots' and 'English' forces at Culloden.

Cumberland and his officers now proceeded to pacify the region.

The atrocities had begun on the battlefield itself. The wounded were slain where they lay. So were those idle schoolboys. So were men lying asleep, men who had collapsed on the appalling retreat from Nairn, so drained and starved they had slept through the battle itself. A thatched cottage was surrounded, wherein lay maimed and dying men; the roof was fired, and they perished. Word was got about that written instructions had been found from Charles Edward, urging 'no quarter' upon his foes. This was completely untrue. But it inspired the Hanoverian troopers to fearful retribution. They advanced on Inverness, looting, burning, and killing before them. The Duke of Cumberland issued a proclamation to all rebels in arms, ordering these weapons to be surrendered, and for their bearers to fall upon the king's mercy. Only one clan duly obliged, so he felt free to sanction a general pogrom. All rebels found armed were killed on sight. (They included a good many trudging towards the authority of Inverness to surrender.)

As word got about, the Highlanders began running in the other direction. When, at length, they dared to creep back home, they found their homes ruined, their stock driven away, their tools and utensils stolen or irreparably smashed. Others were slow to learn. Eighty-four clansmen surrendered to Sir Ludovic Grant in May. Notwithstanding the terms agreed, they were immediately arrested and, many months later, such as had survived internment were transported to the Caribbean. These prisoners included James Grant of Sheuglie, who had fought on the Hanoverian side. He died on a prison-hulk at Tilbury. Centuries later, many black Jamaicans, including noted Rastafarian singers, still bear the Highland names of their poor exiled ancestors.

Throughout the length and breadth of the West Highlands flew this reign of terror. The isle of Eigg was laid waste. Men landed from the king's navy in the creeks and bays of Morar, Moidart, Arisaig, and continued the vicious work. The stately homes of chiefs and chieftains were ransacked and fired. Whole hamlets were razed from the map, many never to be rebuilt. Raasay, for two nights only, had sheltered the prince on his desperate flight after Culloden. So Raasay was pacified with particular zeal. Its MacLeod chief had had the sense to sign his estates over to his son before he left for the Jacobite cause; in law, then, the lands were not forfeited. But his fine house was destroyed. For weeks the work went on. Every house, hut and hovel on the island was levelled. Every beast and bird of livestock was killed or removed. Anything of the least value was taken. A blind girl was raped so savagely, by two soldiers, that she lost her reason. Before leaving, the Hanoverians destroyed every single boat.

The commander of the Fort William garrison, Captain Caroline Scott, had bravely resisted a Jacobite siege. He lost his honour in his subsequent conduct by the shores of Loch Linnhe. He led men about Lochaber, Ardgour and Appin, in a rampage of wasting and bloodshed. One day they paused, *en route* to burn the house of MacDonell of Keppoch (from whose family had come the king's Poet Laureate, less than a century before), to hang three Highlanders with the ropes of a salmon net. These men had been heading to Fort William to surrender their arms, in compliance with Cumberland's decree.

No one could have forseen such a vicious work. Reprisals after the '15 and '19 had been most moderate; and this should be said in mitigation of Charles Edward. Something about the '45 – probably its initial, remorseless advance through Britain – had horrified the capital city, inspired this feral lust for revenge. Still, some called desperately for moderation and prudence. Senior Scottish voices urged an end to the killing. With their leader gone and the passion spent, the Highlanders were as harmless as a dispersed urban mob. But, 'that old woman dared to speak to me of mercy,' said Cumberland contemptuously, 'as arrant Highland mad as Lord Stair or Crawford.' He was speaking of Duncan Forbes, to whose wisdom and cunning his dynasty owed more than it ever acknowledged.

Cumberland was quite glad to give up his command in August 1746. He was succeeded by the Earl of Albemarle, no less fervent in the continued thumping of an iron fist, deeply resentful of enforced sojourn in these savage northern parts. The killing, seizing, burning and stealing continued. Far from quietening the region, of course, they began to have the opposite effect. Where the state itself has turned criminal, all law and order rapidly collapses. Every bandit, footpad and thug of the Highlands was quick to take advantage of the bloody confusion. Vendettas flourished. Little warlords sprang up to impose their own order in the vacuum left by the exiled or broken chiefs. In the winter of 1746 to 1747, many who had survived this chaos now died from cold and starvation.

The distrust of Scots, even at the highest level, by the forces of central government prolonged the paralysis of safety and order. Local justices endured repeated meddling and harassment. Even in Aberdeen – easily the most loyal of all towns to the Hanoverian cause – the populace had to endure the contempt of an encamped army that beheld all Scots as traitors. The Earl of Ancram ordered general illumination on the night of the birthday of the late George I. In the small hours soldiers went on a general rampage, smashing every darkened window they saw, and much else. Ancram had to make humiliating apology to the burghers of the city.

More ordered steps were taken, of course, to introduce the

Highlands to the delights of civilisation. Mighty new forts were built, like the magnificent polygon of Fort George, built on the narrows of the Moray Firth to guard the maritime approach to Inverness. Thousands of miles of new military road were laid, and for many years after Culloden these were regularly marched by military patrols. (Latterly their main concern was cattle-rustling.) The Disarming Acts banned the bagpipes – 'engines of war' – and the wearing of tartan. How rigidly these provisions were enforced is doubtful; psychologically, however, the message was clear. The Gaelic culture itself was condemned.

It took a generation, and more, for some measure of normal law and order to be resumed, for the abolished 'heritable jurisdictions' to be replaced by something approaching the modern judicial system. All this time the Highlands were under effective military occupation. A sense of defeat pervaded the region – as, after the American Civil War, it would pervade the states of the Confederacy – which has never lifted. It added, more than any other single event, to that most dangerous aspect of the Highland character: the sense of being wronged, the belief that we are always being wronged.

Cumberland never won another battle, and no British regiment now flaunts Culloden among its battle honours. He lived to be godfather to the infant George IV, who would himself – in due time – come to Scotland, wrapped in tartan and flesh-coloured tights. But 'Baron Culloden' is still a subsidiary title of the Duke of Gloucester, grandson of George V and first cousin of the Queen, and a noted anti-smoking campaigner.

It was not so very long ago; now and again, one hears anecdotes showing how real it remains in folk memory. The present Lord Tweedsmuir, son of John Buchan, remembers a very old man visiting the family home around 1914. This old man, in infancy, had been nursed by an elderly English nanny from Derby, who could remember – as a tiny child – being terrified of Charles Edward's Highlanders. And Sorley Mac-Lean, the poet of contemporary Gaeldom, tells of his brother, Calum – a great folklorist who died, too young, over thirty years ago – who knew a very old man in Duirinish, a township north of Kyle of Lochalsh. This old man had known another exceedingly old man, who could remember seeing the fires blazing on Raasay.

And there are still a few, in the depopulated glens of Lochaber and the west, who have not forgotten what their forebears endured for Charles Edward Stuart in the rising of 1745.

So we come to that bitter period of history we call the Highland Clearances, and no chapter of Scottish history is more emotive, more controversial, more laden in myth, more enduring as a *leitmotif* in political rhetoric.

The prime causes of the Highland Clearances were socio-logical, cultural and economic. And the first thing to say about them – which remains highly unfashionable – is that, initially, the mass emigration of Gaels was voluntary, and to a large degree necessary.

By the early years of the nineteenth century the population of the Highlands had begun rapidly to increase. The reasons for this are obscure; one, probably, was the introduction of the potato. The staple food of the Gael had been such grain-crops as oats and bere (a primitive form of barley) and these had been highly vulnerable to the vagaries of weather. A cold wet spring, a wild wet summer and autumn led to poor harvest, winter famine and widespread death. Potatoes had reached the High-lands by the end of the seventeeth century: Martin Martin, Hebridean topographer, mentions them as a common enough crop in 1695. But it was after the '45, at earliest, before it was intensively grown as a staple food-crop. Clanranald introduced them in Uist in 1743, bringing seed-potatoes from Ireland. The people at first refused to grow them. When compelled, and the potatoes were duly dug, they flung them down, refusing to eat them. But it did not take long for Highlanders to see the glories of the tattie. It grew rapidly, flourished even in poor soil, and was remarkably insensitive to bad weather. Potatoes stored well, were easily prepared, readily cooked. By 1780 it was already the mainstay of the Highland diet.

Besides, Edward Jenner had discovered the principle of vaccination. Smallpox – now, in our own day, extinct – was, in those distant times, a murderously effective agent in popula-tion control. So people were apt to have very large families, insurance against this and other diseases. Smallpox vanished but the large families continued.

In the meantime profound social change continued. The clan

system, as we have seen, has been glamorised. It had also, increasingly, been contaminated by southern models; well before the '45, the chiefs were exercising an increasing feudal authority, on the lines of England, at odds with the old Gaelic culture. Hence men like Cameron of Lochiel and MacDonald of Clanranald had raised great armies for Charles Edward. This much parliament grasped. And, by abolishing the heritable jurisdictions, disarming the clans, and prohibiting Highland dress, the government neutralised the threat of rebellion. They thought they had put an axe to the tree of the clan system. So it proved; but not in the way folk in London had envisaged. They had only removed the feudal notions which actually impaired the old Gaelic civilisation. The clan system should, logically, have revived and strengthened. London won, in the end, not because of their laws, but because of the rapid corruption of the clan chiefs themselves. Celtic feudalism perished. Economic feudalism arrived.

After the '45 there was a huge demand for cattle. By the 1760s England clamoured for more and yet more Highland beef. The chiefs took full advantage of the trade, levying higher and yet higher rents, which filtered down through the tacksmen to the poor and still poorer below. The market collapsed at the end of the decade with a succession of bad harvests and thin stock. Famine stalked the Highlands again, with the poorest scouring the beaches for shellfish and seaweed. By now a full three-fifths of the chiefs had, to all intents and purposes, left the Highlands. They were absentee landlords. They had been schooled at Eton, Winchester, Oxford. They maintained fine houses in Edinburgh or London. They ran up big tailor's bills. They loved gambling. They no longer spoke Gaelic, those Highland princes, and increasingly they viewed their ancestral lands not as an inheritance to be cherished but as a source of cash to squander.

They appointed agents to screw as much money out of their estates as possible; these were called 'factors'. Their bosses still called themselves 'chiefs' – the title had a certain Gothic ring – but they were really now lairds on the Lowland model, like those Lowlanders to whom, increasingly, they sold parcels of Highland land. In the old order the chiefs had high notions of conduct: they governed as noble princes, in patriarchal style, and saw themselves as trustees for the people and for posterity.

If this new breed knew of such ideals, they laughed them to scorn.

That grand old Tory, Samuel Johnson, shrewdly saw the future on his Hebridean jaunt with James Boswell. 'The clans retain little now of their original character. Their ferocity of temper is softened, their military ardour is extinguished, their dignity of independence is depressed, their contempt for government subdued and their reverence for their chiefs abated . . . As they [the chiefs] gradually degenerate from patriarchal rulers to rapacious landlords, they will divest themselves of the little that remains.'

The greed of the new cattle-ranching, the doubling and trebling of rent, the instability wrought by repeated sale and re-sale of land . . . it was too much for the natural leaders of the people, the tacksmen. In the last decades of the eighteenth century they emigrated in huge numbers. Many took their tenants with them. In one twelve-year period – from 1763 to 1775 – it has been calculated that 20,000 people left the region of their own volition, largely for the Americas.

But a vast, unrecorded number went involuntarily too. Not driven out by landlords, but kidnapped, *en masse*, by the slave trade. Many of the poorest emigrants, lacking more than a few words of English, bound themselves to unscrupulous export agents, who sold them as beasts in colonial ports. These agents knew a good living when they saw it. There were seven slave-trading vessels cruising off the Outer Isles in 1774, poking into every creek in the hope of spying vulnerable peasants. If men, women and children could not be lured on board by false promises, they would fall upon townships and carry folk off by force. The captain of one ship, *Philadelphia*, took boys off the beach at Stornoway harbour. He did not even permit their parents on board to see them. Who had power to compel him? Lewis had no sheriff, no policeman, no resident chief, no magistrate of any sort – nothing but a factor to levy rent, and who probably cared not a fig for the plight of these youngsters.

A huge tide of voluntary emigration continued, and this began to excite the concern of men in authority. Westminster worried about the shortage of cannon-fodder; Highlanders were now valued, if only as infantry statistics, in the service of the

British state. Landlords began to fret about the loss of manpower in the kelp industry.

Kelp is, properly, a heavy, woody seaweed tossed up in mighty branches on western shores after the ferocious storms of winter; but in the context of its industrial application virtually any marine wrack or weed served to produce kelp, the rich alkaline ash left when seaweed is burned. MacDonald of Clanranald – a most inventive chief, as we have seen – brought the industry to Uist from Ireland, just as he brought potatoes. The ash was of great value in the production of soap, glass, and linen, and fetched a good crop. The creeks of Hebridean east coasts, the storm beaches of the west, were rich in heaps of suitable weed. Twenty-two tons of seaweed produced a ton of the lucrative ash. But there was a cheaper source of soda-ash – barilla, imported from the Mediterranean countries. The Highland kelp industry, in its early decades, was a solid rather than spectacular source of income. Then Britain entered a sustained period of war. From 1756 to the Battle of Waterloo in 1815, Britain was regularly cut off from supplies of barilla. At times – during the American War of Independence, and the great fight against Napoleon – she was at war with virtually all Europe. Even in peacetime there was a tax on barilla. The kelp industry boomed.

Its harvesting was a wet and difficult chore. The labourers waded waist-deep in freezing water, at low tide, or leaned from boats, cutting with sickles and billhooks. Creels of weed were laid ashore to dry in heaps. They were eventually burned to kelp in shallow pits – a skilled job. At the height of the boom, the landlord could win a price of £20 a ton. The Highlanders who produced the stuff might hope for £2.

A fortune was to be made – for the chiefs. But, first, they had to maximise the labour at their disposal. So quiet words were heard in London. Parliament moved, by force of law, to steeply raise the fare to America. The costs of immigration became prohibitive. Then, the landlords had to reorder the Highland economy to encourage the people to devote their energies to kelp. They rapidly realised that the best means to bring this about was to force them into controlled, below-subsistence agriculture. The common holdings vanished. The arable land, worked in collective runrig, ceased to be. The clachans were reshaped. Gaels, throughout the region, were allotted individual strips of land; perhaps two hectares drawn on a map, and a share in the common grazing on the hill. These holdings were often little more than sour bog. So the Highlanders, between breaking and dunging this land to make it fruitful, had to work at the kelp to survive. 'By limiting the amount of land at a family's disposal, by charging a high rent for that land and by paying extremely low prices for kelp, island lairds provided themselves with a workforce which was as much at their mercy, and as firmly under their control, as any set of slaves on a colonial plantation,' writes James Hunter.

The landlords had, in short, invented crofting. The revolt of the people at this new order – in 1803, two-thirds of Lord MacDonald's crofters in Skye were said to be planning emigration – had been blocked by London. 'The emigration is entirely stopped now, by Act of Parliament which puts it out of the poor people's power to pay the increase of freight,' recorded a smug factor of Lord MacDonald, laird of great tracts of Skye. Mighty fortunes were won for the landlords in kelp. But, 'the number and bravery of their followers no longer supports their grandeur,' sighed Dr Johnson, 'the number and weight of their guineas only are put in the scale.' The vast profits of kelp were spent in the cities, on high living and grand style and every form of waste and extravagance. Very little of this bounty was invested in the bays and islands where the fortune had been won. Rents were pushed as much as the landlords dared.

Besides kelp, there were other trades. Landlords experimented with linen-growing in the north-east Highlands. The coastal fishing began, very slowly, to take root in the culture; it would be well into the nineteenth century, however, before it grew to an important part in the northern economy. More promising was the distillation of whisky. Long the staple liquor of the Hebrides, it had been limited by the old economy – barley, after all, was a vital food-crop, and not much could be spared. The advent of the potato changed all this. The new rack-renting, and then some ill-considered legislation, further encouraged the expansion of the whisky trade. Grain shortages in these war-torn decades repeatedly provoked the government to prohibit distillation. So a happy black market of illicit stilling and distribution flourished. It became an industry of great importance. Whisky was even acceptable as a currency. The people of Pabbay, for instance, in the Sound of Harris, paid their rent in whisky. (It was a wonderfully fertile island, producing two harvests of grain a year.) It was illegal, and their landlord knew it was illegal, but he was happy to turn a blind eye. For the moment.

It was a mad, frenzied sort of time. The production and smuggling of illicit whisky boomed in the Hebrides as nowhere else in the land. As in Pabbay, landlords and factors everywhere connived in the business. As skill improved, much of the illicit spirit became superior in quality to the minimally produced legal stuff. Government measures to destroy the trade were inept. Heavy licences were charged on stills. Stills smaller than 500 gallons were banned by law. A duty of nine shillings and sixpence was levied on every gallon. Naturally, only the legal producers suffered from these regulations. At length the authorities saw sense. The duty was cut to a modest sum and a reasonable licence fee introduced. This brought most of the illicit distillers into the legal trade and smuggling died away.

Behind all this glamour, however, hung a dark reality: the near-total vulnerability of the Highland people to the vagaries of power and providence. They had lost, wholesale, their traditional leaders, the tacksman class, to America. Their titular leaders, the chiefs, no longer lived among them and felt not the slightest obligation for their welfare. The population still grew at a dangerous rate – by 1841 it would reach its peak and, contrary to present orthodoxy, this was not a healthy thing for Highland society. There were far more people than the land could, by itself, support. They were grossly dependent on one crop, the potato. Seaweed, an important manure, was collared for kelp. All were forced to neglect more arduous agriculture to immerse their energies in whisky and kelp.

In 1815, the Napoleonic Wars ended. And the tax on imported salt was dramatically lowered. Then great natural deposits of potash were found in Germany, and a new process was invented to produce very cheap soda from salt. The kelp industry collapsed. By 1823, a legal whisky industry had begun its rapid rise in mainland – predominately eastern – Scotland, and the Hebridean cottage-trade fell to pieces. The whole economy of the Highlands and Islands – with its swarming population, its greedy and heavily indebted landlords, its long-neglected husbandry of land and sea – now made shipwreck. Ruin faced everyone. Every single island in the Outer Hebrides was quickly sold. And only a handful of the Inner Isles remained in the possession of the old clan chiefs.

They, and the new southern landlords, now thought of sheep.

In the crazy order from 1770 to 1820, people mattered: landlords wanted rent, and landlords wanted labour. We have seen how neatly they adjusted the free market to suit themselves. Now their people were a nuisance. In the meantime a huge market had risen, throughout Britain and the empire, for wool and mutton. In the days of the cattle boom the landlords had ignored this. When kelp and whisky filled their wallets, they paid little attention – even as flockmasters of the south had begun to exploit Highland pastures, cattle-enriched for centuries, never before exposed to the massed munching of sheep. These men introduced the Blackface, then the more lucrative Cheviot. The Cheviot could weather the West Highland winter. It did not require to be folded at night. By 1810 the price of Highland sheep had quadrupled in forty years.

The landlords had begun to take note, even before the end of the whisky and kelp bubbles; sheep were much less labour-intensive than cattle, and spared more Highland hands for the busy trades. In the Hebrides the beef and dairy trades had disappeared entirely. Now, the Highlands were awash with unemployed men. And sheep were the only viable resource left. In much of southern Scotland, such agricultural change had already been implemented, with sheep-farmers moving in as the rural poor moved out. But this occurred gently, without force; besides, the swelling cities offered a new future, and new employments, to the rural peasantry; urban and rustic Scots, after all, spoke the same language. Yet it was not to the south country that the landlords looked. It was rather to the example of Sutherland where the Clearances, in all their barbarity and inhumanity, had begun in earnest.

Sutherland was the theatre of the most notorious of the Clearances. It was not, though, the first scene of clearance. Sheep-farming, and the removal of the peasant class, had been spreading into the Highlands since the 1770s, causing ever

greater hardship and misery as it spread north. In Ross-shire –
especially in 1792, the 'Year of the Sheep' – there had been
serious riots. But Sutherland is the best-documented scene of
Highland Clearance, and the work of eviction was done with
peculiar calculation and ruthlessness.

The Countess of Sutherland, owner of two-thirds of that
beautiful county – where thousands lived in a predominately
pastoral economy, tending cattle and growing crops in such
lovely green glens as Kildonan and Strathnaver – had married
well, to George Granville Leveson-Gower. He was Marquess of
Stafford, and he owned vast estates in England; he may well
have been the richest man in Britain. But his wife's dowry, her
lands in Sutherland, yielded a mere £15,000 a year in rent. This
exalted and honourable personage conceived a wonderful plan
for the improvement – his word – of the Sutherland estates. The
straths should be cleared of their inhabitants and given over to
Lowland sheep-farmers; one good sheepwalk would yield a
much higher rent than forty crofting families. The crofters
would, he declared, be retained on the estates, but transferred
to the coast and encouraged to take up fishing.

The work began in 1807. In 1811 Sutherland had 15,000 sheep.
By 1846 there were over 200,000. The credit for this achievement
falls to one Patrick Sellar, a native of Moray, factor to the house
of Sutherland. Sellar's name has gone down in the annals of
Highland infamy, and justly so. He had utter contempt for the
people of the county. He called them 'savages' and 'aborigines'.
He dismissed Gaelic as 'a barbarous jargon'. In 1814 he started
the grand design of his master in Strathnaver, which Sellar
wanted for himself. The people of Strathnaver were poor in
many respects. But their lives, if arduous, were happy. Their
black houses were better than some inhabited in the Outer Isles
even after the Second World War.

But the word came to quit. And the minister of that parish,
Rev Donald Sage, never forgot the horror of his last day
preaching in Strathnaver.

On the Sabbath, a fortnight previous to the fated day, I preached
my valedictory sermon in Achness, and the Sabbath thereafter at
Ach-a-h-uaighe . . . In Strathnaver we assembled, for the last
time, at the place of Langdale, where I had frequently preached

before, on a beautiful green sward . . . The still-flowing waters of
the Naver swept past us a few yards to the eastward. The
Sabbath morning was unusually fine, and mountain, hill and
dale, water and woodland, among which we had so long dwelt,
and with which all our associations of home and native land were
so fondly linked, appeared to unite their attractions to bid us
farewell. My preparations for the pulpit had always cost me
much anxiety, but, in view of this sore scene of parting, they
caused me pain almost beyond endurance. I selected a text which
had a pointed reference to the peculiarity of our circumstances,
but my difficulty was how to restrain my feelings till I should
illustrate and enforce the great truths which it involved with
reference to eternity.

The service began. The very aspect of the congregation was of
itself a sermon, and a most impressive one. Old Achoul sat right
opposite to me. As my eye fell upon his venerable countenance,
bearing the impress of eighty-seven winters, I was deeply
affected, and could scarcely articulate the Psalm. I preached,
and the people listened, but every sentence uttered and heard was
in opposition to the tide of our natural feelings, which, setting in
against us, mounted at every step of our progress higher and
higher. At last all restraints were compelled to give way. The
preacher ceased to speak, the people to listen. All lifted up their
voices and wept, mingling their tears together. It was indeed the
place of parting, and the hour. The greater number parted never
again to behold each other in the land of the living . . .

Sellar fell upon Strathnaver with his thugs and writs. The
people were driven from their homes, some of which were
burned to preclude their return. 'One could scarcely hear a
word,' one witness recalled, many years later, 'with the lowing of
cattle and the screaming of children marching off in all directions.' All 'was silence and desolation,' wrote another, 'blackened and roofless huts still enveloped in smoke, articles of
furniture being cast away as of no value to the houseless,
and a few domestic fowl scraping for food among the hill
ashes, were the only objects that told us of man. A few days
had sufficed to change a countryside, teeming with the cheeriest
sounds of rural life, into a desert.'

It has been calculated that over 8,000 people were uprooted
in Sutherland; the great plans for resettlement were, for the
most part, a fiasco. The scheme was not even profitable. The

proprietors, in the end, lost money. Sutherland, mocked Hugh Miller, had been 'improved into a desert'. And Sutherland, as James Hunter bitterly remarks, is a desert still.

For years Patrick Sellar did his master's work. This was the reality of the Highland Clearances. Violent assault: men, women and children beaten with staves, young women kicked in the genitals. Wanton destruction: the burning of houses and effects. Grand larceny: the seizing of cattle and other livestock, on the pretext of 'arrears of rent'. And wanton murder. In one home lay an ancient woman, over a hundred years old. She could not be moved. The family begged for that home to be spared, for that lady at the very least to be allowed to die in her native glen. 'She has lived too long, I say. Let the witch burn!' roared Sellar, and the thatch was fired, and the old woman was scarcely rescued; she died five days later from shock and burns.

He was put on trial for arson and cruelty, but acquitted. The jury, of course, was manned by his own contemporaries in Sutherland society. Sellar became a large-scale sheep-farmer in his own right; having enjoyed Strathnaver, he later retired to Morvern in Argyll and continued the business there. He benefited rather more from the Sutherland work than his employers.

Dark tales of the period are legion. On one occasion a terrified cat tried to escape the flames of a family home; it was caught, and thrown back in, and again it tried to flee, and again it was seized and hurled, and the men had good sport in this fashion until the cat at last was burned to death.

Some of Sellar's victims were crammed into new coastal settlements – Strathy, Bettyhill, Dunbeath – where the good countess expected them to learn fishing. 'I presume to say,' wrote Sellar, 'that the proprietors humanely ordered this arrangement, because it surely was a most benevolent action to put these barbarous hordes into a position where they could better associate together, apply to industry, educate their children and advance in civilisation.' In due time the Marquess of Stafford was further ennobled, as Duke of Sutherland. The work of eviction continued through the century. In 1842 Glencalvie, Strathcarron, was cleared. And so Sutherland continued to suffer.

The old parish church at Creich, in whose yard some of the

recipients of the Strathcarron 'improvement' had to camp for weeks until they were rehoused, still bears – etched on its old windows – the scratched names, initials and sentiments of these unhappy Sutherland tenantry. 'The people of Glen Calvie,' one anonymous hand etched, 'the wicked generation.'

The Leveson-Gower family still own much of the county. A mighty statue of the Duke atops the summit of a hill overlooking Golspie. Many today call for its removal. In the 1980s, Sutherland estate publicity observed that 'something very similar to the Clearances is still done today by local councils.'

The economies of sheep, and the efficiency with which Sutherland had been 'improved', now caught on throughout the Highlands. So vast were the Clearances, and so many were the communities lost, and so ill-documented is much of the suffering, that it is still hard to draw a whole and coherent picture. The memories of certain areas will suffice.

In Harris at the turn of the century the great mass of the population still lived on the rich grazings of the west and in the green islands of the Sound. The Atlantic coast of Harris is, for the most part, fine machair land – grassy sward, undulating inland from long white beaches, the wind sweeping in calcium-laden sand to sweeten and enrich the soil. The east side of Harris appals the stranger. It is bare, grim, lunar land: nothing but rock in great ribs and lumps, little save heather growing in the cracks. Man had never thought to live here. In the latter years of the eighteenth century Captain Alexander MacLeod had established a fishing industry in these barren Bays. He built harbour works at Rodel, but found most of the Harris tenantry most reluctant to apply themselves to that trade. The Bays were initially settled by fisherfolk from Skye, Lewis, and a very few Harrismen.

Through the kelp boom the Harris rents had been doubled, then trebled. When the trade went belly-up the rents stayed high. Captain Alexander had died in 1790. His son so despised the clan tradition that he actually adopted his mother's name of Hume. Harris, to him, was nothing more than a source of income. He replaced a sensitive local factor with one Robert Brown, a Lowlander, whose only concern was to gather good rent. And, if the people of Harris would not pay, he would replace them with those who would. North Harris was purged first. Then the township of Horgabost was cleared for a sheepfarm; it went to one Alexander Torrie, an Argyll man. The celebrated writer James Hogg, the 'Ettrick Shepherd' himself, had angled to win Luskentyre. It went to a man called Donald Stewart – his uncles already grazed the Park peninsula in Lewis – and it was not long before this Stewart began eagerly to seek further land for his Cheviots. His eye fell on the Scarista townships, on perhaps the finest land in Harris, where thirty families made a living. They were, of course, in arrears of rent. It was all the excuse Stewart, and Brown, needed. In 1828 Scarista Mhor and Scarista Bheag were cleared. The people were permitted to take only such chattels as they could carry. Even as they trudged over the shoulder of Druim Scarista, they saw the roofs of their houses burn behind them, and the factor's men pulling down the very walls. There was none to whom they could appeal. The parish minister himself had been bought off. He was to gain Scarista Bheag for his glebe, and cede the Borve lands to Donald Stewart.

The fortunate Harris folk made Cape Breton in Canada; to that dense and wooded land, indeed, the great mass of the island's people were delivered. Cape Breton is covered in trees. There they grow like virtual weeds. Most of these new settlers had never seen a tree in their lives. One family settled at Wreck Cove on the North Shore. It was mountainous, densely wooded country. Only the narrow strip of land along the shore offered any agricultural potential. This had first, of course, to be cleared of trees. It took the men a long, long time. There were accidents, and some died. But they planted potatoes and, when autumn came, these were harvested and buried in pits. Such they had always done in the blustery but mild winters of home. The Canadian winter came, and with it cold such as the Harris folk had never known. The ground froze solid. They could not reach their buried potatoes. They hacked and picked for a while, then lit great fires in a desperate bid to thaw the earth. But the crop was ruined. Many died that first winter.

There were still fish in the sea, and game in the woods. Slowly, the new Canadians won a living. Here, at least, they were for ever free from oppression, from seeing the soil they had tilled and enriched for generations being wrenched away for southern sheep.

Others, less fortunate, found themselves on wild coastal islands of Harris, like Scarp. And some went to the Bays, to villages such as Borsam, Manish, Finsbay, Kyles Scalpay. Here there was no grass, no soil, nothing but rock and peat. They had to make soil, these people, before they could grow and live. Day after day, week upon week, they carried seaweed from the shore, and dung from their cattle, and scraped peat from between the ribs of rock, and made dozens of tiny plots in this manner, some no bigger than a dining table. From these *feannagan*, these lazy-beds – and never was a name so inapt – they might, as Fraser Darling recorded, win two buckets of potatoes, a sheaf of barley, 'a harvest no man should despise.'

On Pabbay a community still thrived and they still made and sold illicit whisky. It took Brown a long time to remove them. He visited, time and time again, with an exciseman, in the hope of catching the people in the act of the dark trade. But the master of the cutter in which the officials sailed had struck a deal with the islanders: if the exciseman was on board, he sailed with a certain flag, giving sufficient warning for still and worm and so on to be hidden. Inevitably the day came when this master was absent; he had broken his leg. The relief skipper knew nothing of the arrangement. The boat sailed, with exciseman and without signal, and the islanders were done. Pabbay was cleared. Some families went to Cape Breton, some to the Bays, the bulk of them to Scalpay, a bare island in East Loch Tarbert, already overcrowded with other victims of the upheaval, affording no living but rock and heath and the sea.

In time the Scalpay folk would conquer the sea. A century later Scalpay would be among the most vibrant and wealthy West Highland communities. But this was a long way off. To relieve congestion, certain Pabbay families were forced to move again. Around 1886 they sailed up Loch Seaforth and settled in Maraig, formerly part of the Scalpay 'tack', a lush place by Harris standards, with curious geology affording much grass, and the ruins of the ancient chapel to Moluag. Pabbay, once the seat of the Clan MacLeod, a verdant jewel of the Hebrides, has never been resettled. Occasionally parties of Harris youngsters are permitted to land for summer camps. It belongs to an Englishman who maintains a single holiday house.

At the turn of this century, had you been able to drive from

Tarbert to Obbe by the west, you would have passed but four inhabited houses on the whole Atlantic seaboard of Harris.

In 1841, as we have seen, the Highland population peaked. In the Hebrides alone some 93,000 souls fought for a living. The crofting system was already failing. Holdings were divided, and sub-divided. They might not have security of tenure, but there was nothing to stop a crofter distributing his land to adult sons – 'cottars', such unofficial tenants were called. At the height of the kelp boom every hand helped. And there was always the reliable potato. But the overcrowding was gross. In one Skye township, twenty-two crofting families shared their land with twenty-five families of cottars. There were some 250 people in that hamlet, far more than the soil could maintain.

Scarista was one of the first Hebridean Clearances. In that same year, 1828, MacLean of Coll cleared the isle of Rhum, south of Skye. All 443 inhabitants went to America. They were replaced by 8,000 sheep, a flockmaster and some shepherds. Similiar Clearances were now under way throughout the islands. Mull was swept of its people to such a devastating extent that, today, it barely qualifies as Hebridean at all; the great mass of its inhabitants are by background Lowland or English. The parish of Uig, in Lewis, was likewise emptied – a good many folk removed to make a glebe for their new minister, Rev Alexander MacLeod.

The Clearances shock the modern mind because of their brutality, the large-scale theft, and the utter remorselessness with which people were compelled to leave their ancestral lands. The paradox is that, in large measure, the population transfers were essential. But, had it not been for the greed of chiefs and landlords, and their blockade on free emigration after 1800, the problem might never have arisen. This was untrammelled capitalism, and it was not even a free market; these men rigged the market, they made the laws, and at every level they had exploited, manipulated and compelled their Highland tenantry to live in a manner befitting their own interests.

The 'famine Clearances' of the Hebrides, though, have a horror all their own.

From 1835 the Hebridean potato crop had begun to fail, as the poor variety universally grown throughout the region fell to blight. From 1846 to 1848 the blight was universal and continuous. The devastation in the West Highlands became utter famine. Today this would be judged a national emergency. Action would be demanded from the state. The government in London did nothing. It granted no funds and no relief, though it did establish a Colonial and Emigration Department to compile statistics. Southern granaries overflowed with grain; little of it reached the north. The new Free Church, horrified by the situation in the Hebrides, deployed a ship, the *Breadalbane*, and this delivered repeated loads of food up and down the coast. But, even in 1850, when the blight struck again, Free Church leaders were still begging for government action. Highlanders were not only starving, they were freezing. They had no change of clothes. They went everywhere barefoot. Some made ragged garb from mealsacks.

A very few landlords bought and distributed grain. Some actually bankrupted themselves in the process – they included MacDonald of Clanranald, a descendant of the Lord of the Isles, whose house had been the last in the Outer Isles to show any humanity or initiative. MacLeod of Harris, too, did all he could. But the factor of MacDonald of Sleat, having bought a shipload in England for the hungry, promptly resold it at a large profit. None of it reached Skye. Others, fearful of pandering to idle scroungers, insisted that the mouths fed by charity had to work for their subsistence, and various 'destitution roads' in the Highlands date from this time. But very many Highlanders saw no help at all. Disease was quick to take advantage of miserable, undernourished people. A Uist minister never forgot the misery he beheld in those days. 'Deplorable, nay heart-rending. On the beach the whole population of the country seemed to be met, gathering the precious cockles . . . never witnessed such countenances – starvation on many faces – the children with their melancholy looks, big-looking knees, shrivelled legs, hollow eyes, swollen-like bellies. God help them, I never did witness such wretchedness.'

He thus described the classic symptoms of kwashiorkor, familiar from a dozen newsreels of Ethiopia in our own day. This was on the eve of the Great Exhibition and in the motherland of the British empire. Shellfish and seaweed, indeed, were all the food to be had in the Hebrides for the truly poor. But the diet is scarcely balanced. Many soon ailed with bloody dysentery. To this day, shellfish in the Hebrides are stigmatised as the food of utter poverty. Many will not eat them.

The lands of bankrupt Clanranald were bought by Colonel John Gordon, who was said to be the richest man in Scotland. His tenants, in Benbecula and South Uist and Barra, were surely the poorest. For the starving of these island the colonel had no answer but eviction. He described them as 'redundant', and it was in these evictions that perhaps the most nightmarish scenes of the Clearances were recorded. Furthermore, he could call on government help. The state had refused his kind offer of Barra as a penal colony – the island had cost him £38,050 – but gave him a large grant to arrange emigration.

Gordon's agents when the work began included – incredibly – policemen, equipped with clubs, guns, and snarling dogs. The tenants were ordered to assemble, upon pain of fine, to learn of their gracious landlord's solution to their problem; when they duly gathered, the policemen, bailiffs, press-gangs and hoodlums fell upon them. People were hauled bodily into open boats. Some fled to the hills and had to be hunted down like game. On Barra, every single crofter was evicted; all that they owned – cattle, furnishings, implements – was confiscated. Among those enthusiastically directing the work was the parish minister, Rev Henry Beatson, who 'may be seen in Castlebay directing his men like a gamekeeper with hounds'; the fellow who thus described this man of God likened the scene, that day, to a slave-hunt on the African coast.

The poor folk of Uist and Benbecula and Barra were taken, at length, to ports such as Glasgow and Liverpool and borne to Quebec. Some escaped, and their plight aroused national indignation; the good folk of Edinburgh were shocked by the appearance of Barra refugees 'in a state of absolute starvation'. In Canada, hardened officials had seen much of human misery; but even they revolted at the sight of these broken, bedraggled, verminous new arrivals, who squatted hopelessly in the gutters and huddled on the docks, who had nothing in all the world but in what they stood. Hebridean womenfolk, once renowned for their hospitality to strangers, hobbled about the streets of great Canadian cities, begging for bread.

That they had reached Canada at all was merciful. The best

ships of Britain's merchant fleet were reserved for things like tea, coffee, spices, tobacco, good cloth – these boats were watertight, in good order. Leaky old boats were relegated to the transport of timber. When they were too battered, swollen and creaking even for that – their hulls bound round with rope to keep the boards together, the decks leaking, mast and keel half rotten – they ended their careers carrying emigrants from Scotland, Ireland and the poor north of England. Between 1847 and 1853, at least forty-nine emigrant ships sailed from port, laden with these miserable people, and were never heard of again. They went to the bottom of the Atlantic, and their cargo with them.

A woman called Catherine MacPhee remembered these scenes in her old age.

Oh Mary Mother . . . I have seen . . . the people being driven out of the countryside to the streets of Glasgow, and to the wilds of Canada, such of them as did not die of hunger and plague and smallpox while going across the ocean. I have seen the women putting the children in the carts which were being sent from Benbecula and Iochdar to Lochboisdale, while their husbands lay bound in the pen and weeping beside them . . . the women themselves were crying aloud and their little children wailing like to break their hearts. I have seen the big strong men, the champions of the countryside, the stalwarts of the world, being bound on Lochboisdale quay and cast into the ship as would be done to a batch of cattle or horses in the boat, the bailiffs and the ground-officers and the constables and the policemen gathered behind them in pursuit of them. The God of life and He only knows all the loathsome work of men on that day.

In North Uist some fought vigorously to resist. Six hundred people faced eviction in 1849 in the district of Sollas, and such townships as Middlequarter, Dunskellor and Malaclete. They were poor, hungry, and had endured much hardship through bad summers and thin harvest. But they had refused voluntarily to remove, despite the offer of every assistance from landlord and the Highland Destitution Fund. At length thirty-three constables arrived from Oban to preside over their enforced clearance. There was a bad scene and four men were arrested. Some houses were de-roofed. The minister had to come and calm everyone down. These men were tried at Inverness, at length, and though found guilty the jury pled for leniency.

It was something of a watershed: southern opinion was now aware of the wicked work, and increasingly hostile. The judge, Lord Cockburn, decided to be lenient. 'They had nothing but the bare ground, or rather, the hard, wet beach, to lie down upon. It was said, or rather insinuated, that "arrangements" had been made for them, and in particular that a ship "was to have been soon" on the coast. But, in the meantime, the people's hereditary roofs were to be pulled down, and the mother and her children had only the shore to sleep on, fireless, foodless, hopeless.'

So the warriors of Sollas got a mere four months. Their people were removed to the south of North Uist, then to Canada, then Australia. Sollas was at length revived as a settlement. But the old community vanished for ever.

Not all landlords were of the Colonel Gordon class. On Skye, the two principal landlords – MacLeod and Lord MacDonald – did all they could to minimise the suffering, and quite deliberately ruined themselves in the process. MacLeod helped to establish relief committees in the Scottish cities, which in three years raised £209,000. To him the only solution, long term, was voluntary emigration. In 1851 he helped form a private Emigration Society on Skye, and this grew into a national organisation. The government's emigration office supplied vessels. The society paid for the passage of migrants. But MacLeod and MacDonald were still spending money on grain, until at last they were spending money they no longer had. So they went bankrupt. Thus they lost control of their affairs to receivers, who appointed ruthless factors. Further dreadful evictions now followed. And all the more efficient, through the benevolent organisation of MacLeod and the public.

The clearance of Suisnish in western Skye, on the good lands by Loch Slapin, was among the last in the Highlands. Eviction papers were served by Lord MacDonald's agents, and the factor insisted that this was 'prompted by motives of benevolence, piety and humanity'. The people were declared to be too far from church. Suisnish was to become another sheep-farm. Its people were bound for the colonies of Canada and Australia. So they were cleared, and put on something approaching a forced march to Broadford, where the ships lay off to take them away. A young man watched them go; he was Donald Geikie, who would become a geologist (and mountaineer) of distinction, and fifty years later he had not forgotten the sight.

> A strange wailing sound reached my ears at intervals on the breeze from the west . . . I could see a long and motley procession winding along the road that led north from Suisnish . . . There were old men and women, too feeble to walk, who were placed in carts. The younger members of the community, on foot, were carrying their bundles of clothes and household effects, while their children, with looks of alarm, walked alongside. When they set forth once more, a cry of grief went up to Heaven; the long plaintive wail, like a funeral coronach, was resumed . . . the sound seemed to echo through the whole wide valley of Strath in one prolonged note of desolation.

But 1854 saw perhaps the most revolting clearance of all, at Greenyards, in Strathcarron. On 31 March a detachment of policemen arrived – drunk – to execute eviction orders. They were met by a group of protesting women; their landlord, Alexander Munro, had personally denied rumours of impending clearance. Munro had lied. And the scene grew violent. A procurator fiscal, accompanying the detachment, told them to knock the women down and get on with the job. So they did.

Three men held and clubbed a woman of fifty, kicking her in the belly and the breasts; she shortly after went completely insane, and never recovered. A woman of forty was likewise beaten. Another lost sight and hearing as a result of this battering. Yet another, a full week later, still bore the clear print of hobnails on her breasts; constables had stamped on her. Her scalp was torn away; bones of her skull were crushed in. A woman who had borne seven children was battered to death. An old man of sixty-seven, a veteran of Waterloo, rushed to the assistance of these poor people, and was likewise knocked down and abused. Two terrified young boys were chased, and caught; one was hammered unconscious.

So resistance was overcome. The constables burned down the houses and Greenyards was cleared. And they took their victims back to Tain, where they were charged with rioting and disorderly behaviour.

Emigration was essential if the widespread suffering was to be relieved. But the rigour and arrogance with which these Clearances were enforced is without defence. Yet for many years the work went on: decisions, eviction notices, the arrival of violent men, the firing of thatched roofs, the destruction and seizing of property. Sometimes the evicted would return, broken of spirit, when all was quiet, to die of exposure by the blackened stones of their former homes. Few landlords had any notion of benevolence. The work was done for money, and for their own gain. Public opinion, from 1850 onwards, began to mitigate the dark work. But suffering continued.

Some communities endured the wretched experiments, fancies and fads of a rapid succession of landlords. By 1922, octogenarians on Raasay had lived through the ownership of the historic MacLeod chief; a West Indian sugar planter; that planter's son; a land-profiteer; a southern romantic who had read far too much Walter Scott; a *nouveau riche* industrialist and his family; a Lanarkshire iron firm and, at last, the Board of Agriculture. Villages were cleared and resettled at a whim. One landlord forbade the people of the island to marry without his permission; when a couple defied this ruling, and wed, he threatened any Raasay family who offered them shelter with eviction.

Throughout the Highlands there are tales and traditions of this time. Survivors of the era, eye-witnesses, lasted well into living memory. Not all the Highlands suffered in like degree. Lewis, save for the parish of Uig, escaped the Clearances without significant removal of populace. Its enlightened landlord, Sir James Matheson – who had made a fortune from the Chinese opium trade, a co-founder of Jardine Matheson & Co. – assisted voluntary emigration and invested much money on improvements; in particular, he established a thriving fishing industry.

But the thoughts of the generality of landlords still survive. 'Of late years the landlords have very properly done all they could,' wrote one Robert Chalmers, 'to substitute a population of sheep for the innumerable hordes of useless human beings who formerly vegetated upon a soil that seemed barren of everything else.' Chalmers was a child of his age. Many sophisticated souls nodded in agreement.

By the close of the 1860s the forced emigrations had ceased.
But clearance continued on a local scale, with tenants pushed
about – and crammed, in ever larger numbers, on to ever poorer
areas of land – as long as the landlords had the power to force it.
Mr Wood of Raasay, who saw the whole island as his personal
playground, introduced rabbits to that island, to improve the
sport. The creatures thrived and multiplied, ruining crops and
grazing. When he realised that the crofters were killing them,
Wood forbade them to touch a hair of a bunny's head, on pain
of eviction. He forbade the people to keep cats or dogs, lest they
too cull rabbits. Wood's luxurious lifestyle in Raasay House
included a man, employed full-time, to pick leaves off the lawn.
A child from Clachan was found playing in the grounds. She
was driven back to her parents and they were told if it happened
again they would be removed. The tot did find her way back,
and they were evicted.

Finally, Wood reduced the great bulk of Raasay to a sporting
ground. All its inhabitants, save for those directly in his employ,
were forced to settle in the barren north, on the island of Rona
and the bleak peninsulas facing it. It was a landscape every bit as
savage as that of eastern Harris.

Such men could afford to be tyrants. The crofters still had no
vote and they had not yet raised a class of leaders. The law
afforded them no protection. What particularly disgusts about
this period is that these terrors and innovations militated against
any proper stewardship of the ground. Sheep, over time, reduce
and impoverish land. They crop grass close with their teeth, and
only eat the sweet grass, leaving coarse and couch grasses, and
rank weeds, to multiply. They carry bracken seeds in their
fleeces. Their dung is of no manurial worth. For a few decades
the sheep did well enough in the Highlands, munching off the
capital in the soil left by generations of cattle. But the grazing
declined. So did the sheep. The advent of refrigeration brought
cheap meat from New Zealand and the Argentine to Britain.
The wool market glutted. The price of sheep fell, and landlords
turned increasingly to shooting and fishing as sources of income.
Queen Victoria had made the Highlands fashionable. All the
gentry wanted Highland holidays, and they wanted to kill things
while they were there.

The Highlanders, of course, were much mocked as feckless,

lazy, without initiative, loath to improve their houses or holdings. What few observers realised was that any attempt to better
what you had was pointless. There was no compensation for
improvement. Indeed, improvement attracted attention: it could
cost a man all he had owned. A family might break their backs
for twenty years dunging and fattening a croft, and then have it
seized. Or a township might toil to enrich a large area of
common grazing and, at a whim, suddenly be ordered to
move, *en masse*, to the other end of the parish (always, of
course, inferior). If you worked on your house, and made it
strikingly cosy and attractive, the factor was apt to take it and
bestow it upon another tenant to whom he owed a favour.

There is a saying in Harris, 'never boast of a Vigdale sheep!'
Vigdale is a wild glen in the north of the island, and one year the
lambs fattened there came to market in exceptionally good
condition. The factor noticed them – factors were always at
market, the better to snoop on their tenants' affairs – and came
over to pay kind compliments. What magnificent beasts. Such
quality. Where had they grazed? 'On the side of Vigdale,' he was
told. On the next spring the hapless crofters found the Vigdale
grazing denied to them. It had been added to the factor's
personal holding.

Incoming tenants suffered too. They were generally made to
pay the arrears of rent left by evicted predecessors. Often, once
they had parted with their cash, they would find grazing had
been seized for the factor's sheep or the landlord's deer. They
were forbidden to erect any barriers, any fences or dykes, to
guard their painfully grown crops from game. Their dogs were
apt to be shot by the gamekeeper. Many estates forbade crofters
to keep horses, and so they had to carry heavy loads on their
own backs. Many landlords, fearful that grouse and other fowl
might be disturbed, forbade tenants to pull heather or rushes
from the hill for thatching, so house roofs were everywhere
dilapidated and leaking. What could the crofters do? Protest
invited eviction. And complaint to the civil authorities – the
magistrates – was utterly pointless; these were the same lairds.

Why did they take it, these Highlanders? They endured it
because – in the words of a Sioux chief in America, who likewise
saw the ruin of his folk – 'the people's hoop was broken, and the
sacred tree was dead.' The old Highland culture had, in a matter

of two or three generations, been destroyed. The chiefs were
gone, or alienated. The tacksmen had vanished. Their new
landlords had no understanding of the tenantry, no interests
in their needs. All the upheavals, disruption and misery of these
decades had left the Gaels without any reference they recognised, any focus by which to judge their condition and articulate
their grievances. All the forces of government, establishment,
commerce, education and the press seemed against them.

And much was lost in that time, much of the Highland race,
with all their songs and verse and pluck and resourcefulness and
ability and gaiety, who vanished overseas, into new continents
and other cultures. In places such as Nova Scotia they arrived in
such volume that they created a new Gaelic culture. One
startling figure shows how vast and sweeping the work of
clearance had been. In 1901 250,000 Scots spoke Gaelic. In
Nova Scotia, Canada, there were that year counted a million
Gaelic speakers.

Yet the tide was now about to turn, and through a most
surprising agency – not education (though that was part of it),
not politics (though the widening of the franchise proved
significant), nor anarchy and Communism. The prime force
of renewal was the rise and triumph of evangelical religion.

It is important not to exaggerate the Clearances, nor to demean
greater horrors of our age in comparison. The Highlanders, for
all they endured, did not face the same savagery, or undergo
the same awful neglect, as the people of Ireland. To call the
Clearances 'the Highland Holocaust' is to insult the real
Holocaust and the 14 million Europeans who died in it.

Yet it was, perhaps, a holocaust of a sort. A burned offering,
not only in the smoke of thatch and sticks, but the destruction –
utter and irreversible – of ancient, irreplaceable things. In Uist
there was a celebrated family, the MacMhuirichs, hereditary
bards to Clan Donald, who had centuries before recorded on
ancient scrolls the heroism and glory of the Lords of the Isles.
They were a breed of extraordinary brilliance, learning and
talent. They ended in one Lachlan MacMhuirich, of South Uist,
who was still about in the 1790s, as the frenzy of kelp began the
ruin of his community. This MacMhuirich was illiterate, unable
to read or write in Gaelic. But, as a child, he had seen the once

cherished manuscripts of MacMhuirich chronicle cut up for a tailor's patterns.

Only two years ago a young woman from Cape Breton, of Hebridean descent, came to sing Gaelic songs on an evening in the Harris Hotel. Though she had never seen the Hebrides until that week, and her family had been Canadian for five generations, she had only to start a song for her Harris audience immediately to join in the chorus. But there were one or two Harris songs she sang which no one knew. The words and tunes had vanished to Canada with their lost kinsmen, 160 years before.

CHAPTER EIGHT
As Flow'r in Field

13 Amhlaidh mar ghabhas athair daimh
    is truas da leanban maoth,
    Mar sin da fhior luchd-eagal fhein
    Dia ghabhaidh truas gu caomh.

14 Oir 's aithne dhasan agus 's leir
    ar cruth 's ar dealbh gu ceart;
    Gur duslach talmhainn sinn air fad,
    is cuimhne leis gu beachd.

15 An duine truagh, a ta a laith'
    amhlaidh mar fheur a-ghnath;
    Mar bharr na luibh' air machair fos
    a ta e fas fo bhlath.

16 Oir ghabhaidh thairis osag ghaoith',
    's cha bhi e idir ann;
    'S chan fhaicear e san ionad ud
    an robh e fas gu teann.

                              Salm 103 13–16

13 *Such pity as a father hath*
    Unto his children dear;
    Like pity shows the Lord to such
    As worship him in fear.

14 *For he remembers we are dust,*
    And he our frame well knows,
15 *Frail man, his days are like the grass*
    As flow'r in field he grows;

16 *For over it the wind doth pass,*
    And it away is gone;
    And of the place where once it was
    It shall no more be known.

                              Psalm 103 13–16

THE PLAIN CHRISTIANITY of the Celtic Church did not long survive Scotland's submission to the Roman communion. By the time of the Reformation in 1560 little of vital religion – practical, spiritual, biblical – survived in the Highlands and Islands. All were nominally under the Roman faith. But ignorance, and the superstitious remnants of Druidism – and a certain fearful sacramentalism – were as much as most Highlanders knew of the world beyond. The priests performed their rites of mass in tiny chapels, emerging only when consecration was complete to flourish the wafer before the people. (Many such little churches can still be seen, ruinous, in the old burial grounds of the west.) Pagan rituals of a kind we would associate with Papua New Guinea had revived. The people of Ness, by the Butt of Lewis, still, in the seventeenth century, made an offering of beer to a sea god, one Shony, with the invocation that he might cast up abundant seaware for the spring planting.

Even more telling, and tragic, was what had become of Christianity in Applecross. Here Maelrubha had set up a Christian foundation towards the end of the seventh century. A true son of Columba, he travelled widely in the north-west, bringing the Gospel, imparting new skills to the people: literacy, music, agriculture, medicine. Maelrubha was a man of God. Yet, by the Middle Ages, the simple faith he had bequeathed to the people of Wester Ross had become an idolatrous cult. He himself was worshipped as a minor deity, and worshipped in barbarous rituals. On 25 August, each year, bulls were sacrificed to his glory. Offerings of milk were poured, in oblation, upon the ground.

The priests were firmly under the thumb of clan chiefs,

and generally clansmen themselves. As the old system degenerated into something approaching a feudal order, so the clergy paid their dutiful part. They often connived in deeds of slaughter and vengeance. It was not unknown for a priest to summon folk of a certain clan to mass, that they might be conveniently gathered in a spot for his own chief, and armed followers, to fall upon them in massacre.

Only three years after the Reformation, one Donald Munro was appointed 'commissioner of Ross' by the General Assembly, and was perhaps the first Protestant missionary in the Highlands. His labours seem to have prospered. A congregation in Tain grew to such an extent that Regent Moray himself presented the burgh with a fine pulpit. The new, reformed order abolished the mass, the celibate priesthood, elaborate Church music, enclosed orders and all the unscriptural innovations of Rome. The emphasis in worship was on preaching – in English, Scots or Gaelic, not in Latin – and only metrical Psalms were sung, also in the common language. John Knox and his followers laid great stress on education. All should be taught, at least, to read, write and count. They also outlined very sensible measures for public health and sanitation.

By 1574 ten ministers and twenty-five lay readers toiled in Ross-shire alone. Little is known of their work. For many years the Highlands would be chronically short of ministers and of Gaelic ministers in particular. The extraordinary delay in producing a full translation of the Gaelic Bible – it would be the nineteenth century before one was complete, and available at a price most folk could afford – greatly hampered the establishment of the Reformed cause in the north and west. It thrived earliest, and best, in Easter Ross, and in the Black Isle peninsula in particular. To this day Evangelicalism is strong in that area, in a continuous tradition for four centuries; it has long been dubbed 'the garden of the Lord'.

The turmoils of the seventeenth century – the Civil War, the 'Killing Times' – were felt here, though not with the same savagery as in Scotland's southern counties. Thomas Hogg, minister of Kiltearn, was deposed for refusing to submit to bishops. Rev John McKilligan, minister at Fodderty, immediately quit his charge. Evicted from his manse, he became an intinerant preacher – in increasingly cloak and dagger circumstances – to little groups of Easter Ross folk weary of the empty liturgy of episcopacy. Repeatedly hunted, harried, pursued, captured and beaten, McKilligan was at length confined in the dreadful prison of the Bass Rock, a grim islet in the Firth of Forth. His health broke in that place; he was freed, but only to die in 1689, as the Revolution came to Scotland, a martyr for civil and religious liberties.

After the Second Reformation the Church of Scotland had great difficulty in re-establishing itself in the Highlands. The Episcopal incumbents, who had occupied the main charges after the Restoration, proved adept in stirring up popular feeling against Presbyterian 'intruders'. Further, the issue was politicised by Jacobitism. The Jacobite chiefs were overwhelmingly Episcopalian. Their loyalty was to the exiled Stuart claimants, and to them Presbyterianism was but the House of Hanover at prayer. There were extraordinary scenes of violence. In 1716 the Presbyterian minister of Gairloch fled the district: his home had been repeatedly looted, his cattle driven off, his crops destroyed, his family on the brink of starvation. In 1720 the new Lochalsh minister was utterly prevented from preaching.

And in Killearnan the 'heritors' – feudal superiors, who under the laws of Establishment were obliged to support the ministry – refused any practical stipend or gift to the new Presbyterian minister. They were bigoted Jacobites. His manse was burned down. The people were excited into a frenzy, and threatened to kill him. During the '45, as Charles Edward and his men advanced through the region, Presbyterian ministers fled before them, and Episcopal curates briefly reoccupied many manses.

Many, many years passed before the 'gadflys' of episcopacy ceased to trouble the Reformed cause in the Highlands. The Scottish Episcopal Church retains real, indigenous strength only on mainland Argyllshire. In recent decades many new Episcopal congregations have sprung up – largely attended by English incomers – but these assemblies are in the main very small, and survive only because of the Church's policy of 'non-stipendiary clergy' for such charges – a caste of ordained but unsalaried priests, most in retirement from other and more lucrative callings. It is, today, a harmless and insignificant tradition.

In 1712 something had happened with grave implications for the cause of Christ in the Highlands. The government of Queen

Anne restored patronage to Scotland. Patronage had been expressly forbidden in the terms of the 1707 Articles of Union; that promise went the same way as such undertakings never to impose separate taxes on Scotland or close the Scottish Mint. Patronage is an evil of feudalism. In the Reformed order it was a firm principle that the people of a parish had the absolute right to elect – or, at the very least, to oppose by veto – the minister settled over them in holy things. Patronage removed that right; more importantly (for eighteenth-century culture was not greatly democratic) it weakened the authority of the Church courts. The superiors – the lairds – might now fill the 'living' with whatever creature they cared to choose; in fact, two-thirds of all livings were in the gift of the Crown itself. So the Church of Scotland became rapidly bound up with the ruling order in every parish: the ministers became tools of the chiefs and landlords, and this scarcely boded well for the region's spiritual good.

The English often mock Scotland's fragmented Presbyterianism. But the multiplicity of denominations arose entirely from patronage, an English concept imposed by English votes in an English-dominated parliament. Good men and women rapidly revolted against patronage in principle and the dreadful ministries it produced in particular. So they left in new, nonconformist, Presbyterian denominations. The Secession Church was formed in 1733. In 1745 the 'Cameronians' – ferocious laymen in the Lowlands who maintained the dissenting 'conventicles' from Covenanting times – were able, thanks to the accession of two refugee ministers, to form the Reformed Presbyterian Church of Scotland. (This still exists, though now very small.) Later the Relief Church sprang up. The Secession and Relief Churches eventually sub-divided into different and opposing factions, largely on the precise ramifications of the 'Establishment principle' – should or should not the state support a state Church? – and, later, on Calvinist or less Calvinist theology. They had little impact on the Highlands. But, in time, the hostility of the United Presbyterian Church – the merged, liberal mass of progressive factions from the Secession and Relief bodies – to religious Establishment would be of great significance in the north.

In the Highlands and Islands, patronage created a new class of ministers. These were the Moderates. They were agreeable to landlords, and in the main ministers of low quality. They were not stupid; many of the Moderates were men of high ability. Nor were they heretical; the Moderates were largely men of iron orthodoxy, happily endorsing the Confession of Faith, and keeping such doctrinal scruples as they had to themselves. What characterised the Moderates was their total disinterest in evangelism. Soul-winning was of no importance to them. They positively loathed 'enthusiasm', an earnest, fervent spirit in holy things. Further, they were apt to be lazy. Many took more interest in farming their glebes than in fulfilling the holy duties of office. They seldom preached and, if they did, their orations were as brief as they were vacuous. They were, of course, bound hand and foot to the landlords. When the Clearances began, few of these ministers raised a finger, or a protesting voice, against the iniquities wreaked upon the region. And among the Moderate ranks were not a few clergy of plain bad character.

In Easter Ross, good men still filled many a pulpit: men like James Fraser of Alness, Hector MacPhail of Resolis. But they were in a minority. Everywhere else abode, and now again preached, the Moderates. And these included men like Rev Alexander Simson, of Lochs in Lewis, who was an open drunkard, and men like that minister in Harris who turned a blind eye to the clearance of the west in exchange for a nice new glebe. The Highland character had no concept of secession. Nor were these evangelical ministers in Gaeldom prepared to lead people out of the Church. Increasingly laymen began to hold private meetings of exhortation and prayer, but these 'separatists', as they became known, still maintained sufficient link to the Established Church to qualify for sacraments. We shall hear more of these men.

In November 1779 a baby boy was born to James MacDonald of Reay. There was no minister in that parish at the time, and so MacDonald and his wife, with the infant in her arms, walked one December day into the neighbouring district in search of a minister and baptism. They met the local man of God on the moor, with his fowling-piece, out in search of game (in the pursuit of which he probably devoted most of his energy). He was not inclined to waste time in convening the kirk session and, horror of horrors, holding a service. With the butt of his gun, the cleric smashed the ice in a tarn and baptised the baby on the spot.

The child's name was John MacDonald and he is known, to Highland posterity, as the 'Apostle of the North'.

In the West Highlands, as this little boy grew to manhood, one evangelical ministry did prosper. The people of Lochcarron sat under Lachlan MacKenzie, a most vigorous Christian, and an engaging character of wit and energy. (MacKenzie brought about the conversion of one evil old woman, *Ceit Mhor* – Fat Katie – by running up a comic song about her, which he carefully taught to the village lads; it was soon widely sung in the district, to her shame and eventual repentance.) He bathed twice daily in the sea, every day, even in winter. But he felt the cold too. In the pulpit he might wear three vests, two jackets, an overcoat and a cloak – and this was in high summer.

MacKenzie's preaching was of a mystical stamp. His reprimands against immorality and godlessness have entered into Highland folklore. Being of a practical turn, and shocked by the excess of whisky consumed at local funerals, he once composed and issued a set of detailed rules for the precise circumstances under which mourners might take spirits, and up to what quantity. He also had an eerie prophetic gift, and would prophesy in the short term too: he foretold the death of some who opposed him (and in each case they were dead within a week) and even that the day would come when only one communicant would sit at the Lord's table in Lochcarron. This also came true, over sixty years after his death. He was a man of profound spirituality and his sermons are still in print and still read. Bold in the pulpit, he could be timorous outwith it. MacKenzie was quite terrified of sailing. He would only ride a horse if he had a man to lead it by the bridle.

Rev Lachlan MacKenzie's preaching was also, in the context of the day, heavily political. He loathed the Moderates and preached against them. He despised the 'intrusion' of godless ministers, imposed on poor congregations against their will, and preached against that. And he was enraged by the Sutherland Clearances. No other preacher made such devastating use of 'covenant theology' in their witness against the wicked scourings in the north. Covenant theology is a complex business but, to the lay mind, it may be quickly summed up as an overall scheme of biblical teaching, linking every word and thought of Scripture, from Genesis to Revelation, in one consistent order of salvation wrought by God in Christ for man. And, among the practical teaching of the Old Testament, still made relevant in this biblical view, there is a great deal of teaching about land. Land is to be occupied. It is to be cherished. It is to be well tilled and made fruitful, and it should be kept in your family for all generations.

'Woe unto them that join house to house, that lay field to field, till there be no place, that they may be placed alone in the midst of the earth,' cried the prophet Isaiah; and on this verse Lachlan MacKenzie preached a celebrated sermon, with pitiless and minute application to the landlords and sheep-farmers now clearing northern Scotland.

Lachlan MacKenzie died in 1819. By then John MacDonald, forty years old, was minister at Ferintosh and a celebrated preacher. He not merely ministered in Ferintosh, but spent many weeks – sometimes half the year – from 1816 preaching throughout the length and breadth of the Highlands. He favoured, especially, Highland Perthshire; he made no fewer than four visits to remote St Kilda. And he preached to vast congregations; at one communion weekend in Ferintosh, it is recorded that 10,000 people assembled in the open air to hear him. All this aroused the ire of the Moderates. They even sought to try him at the General Assembly for preaching outwith the bounds of his own parish.

The Evangelical Awakening was in full swing. Through repeated waves of revival it swept the Highlands and Islands. It transformed and renewed the Highland culture; it gave a whole new arena to Gaelic – in hymnody, in preaching, in prayer and oratory – and it greatly encouraged literacy and self-improvement. As the Clearances oppressed the people of the glens, coasts and isles, and as famine and upheaval destroyed old ways of society, Evangelicalism created a new class of leaders and a new framework for understanding the world.

The origins of Highland Evangelicalism, humanly speaking, lie in that continuing Gospel flame of Easter Ross, where a live evangelical tradition was preserved through the seventeenth and eighteenth centuries. From thence, in due time, towards the latter part of the eighteenth century, it spread outwards to the west, north, and the islands. The movement was, initially, more lay than clerical. And it was greatly aided by the advent of Gaelic education. The splendidly named Society in Scotland for Propagating Christian Knowledge had been formed as long ago as 1709. As founded, a key aim of this SSPCK was anglicisation. Gaelic was not to be taught in its schools and English was to be the medium of all instruction. It rapidly became apparent that this was a massive cultural barrier to making any improvement in the lot of the Highland people. So the SSPCK began to encourage Gaelic-speaking teachers to teach core subjects in Gaelic – providing, of course, that they also taught English, in effect as a foreign language. From 1811 its work was greatly augmented by the Edinburgh Society for the Support of Gaelic Schools, its 'sole object being to teach the inhabitants of the Highlands and Islands to read the Sacred Scriptures in their native tongue'. Many schools were established by this organisa- tion – by 1828 there were eighty-five of them – and by its ancillary branches in Inverness and Glasgow; as it was funded largely by respectable gentlewives, they are still remembered as the 'Ladies' schools'. By 1830, crippled by maladministration and a chronic shortage of funds, these societies were in decline, but the Free Church assumed the burden after 1843, and took over many of the school buildings. Yet the Edinburgh Society survived, still useful, until 1892.

For such schools to prosper, it was important not to threaten the parish ministers. So teachers at these Highland schools – which fast multiplied in the Hebrides and in the north – were explicitly forbidden to preach. They were permitted to read the Scriptures publicly, of a Sabbath, but no more. Many teachers, though, found themselves unable to abide by this rule. How could they withhold the Gospel when the local minister might be a useless article of a Moderate, who seldom preached, and when he did gave the people stones rather than bread? So men such as John MacLeod, a teacher in the Galson district of the Barvas parish, in Lewis, began to comment on the portions of the Bible he read. Soon people flocked to his Sabbath meetings. The parish minister, Rev William MacRae – he was actually one of the better Moderates, sorely embarrassed by the Clearances – took exception. MacLeod was at length sacked by his society and evicted from house and schoolhouse. But the people built him a new school, a new house, and employed him as master (and missioner) at their own expense.

In 1801 translation of the Gaelic Bible was completed. The SSPCK had overseen production of the New Testament in 1767, in good Gaelic of the Argyll dialect, replacing the inferior (and incomplete) Irish versions which had hitherto been the sole Scriptures available. This complete version, incidentally, owed much to the energy of one Dugald Buchanan, a native of Kinlochrannoch in Perthshire, and whose celebrated Gaelic hymns are still sung. (There is a fine monument to Buchanan in that village, but few in modern Perthshire have ever heard of him.)

Other factors gave the movement impetus. Some landlords were themselves of evangelical sympathy. The Hon Mrs Stewart Mackenzie of Seaforth, who owned much of Lewis (until she sold it to Sir James Matheson), appointed evangelical ministers to such livings as fell vacant in her day. The Mackenzie family of Gairloch were not merely evangelically inclined; in 1843 they actually joined the Free Church. Osgood Mackenzie, who planted the famous gardens of Inverewe, was raised in the evangelical tradition and writes well of it in his wonderful memoirs.

There was even a hand from parliament (which, in a decade or two, would calamitously lose its grip on Scottish Church affairs). The lack of meaningful church services in huge parts of the Highlands had become a disgrace. That parish of Barvas, for instance, ran some thirty miles down the coast of Lewis, from the Butt to Shawbost, and was served by only one minister and one very small church. So parliament, under pressure from articulate Lowland evangelicals such as Thomas Chalmers, sanctioned the creation of new *quoad sacra* parishes, exclusively for church purposes. Thomas Telford (who won fame in building the Caledonian Canal) designed a plain and attractive prototype church which could be erected quickly and cheaply. Quite a few of those were run up in the Highlands: Lewis gained two, at Cross (in the north end of Barvas parish) and at Knock (on the Eye Peninsula east of Stornoway). These populous new parishes became sanctioned charges and attracted able new ministers. They were supported not by the landlords but by special funds, and this was a good test run of the machinery for the future Free Church.

The evangelical movement was not solely Presbyterian. The Haldane brothers, James and Robert, evangelised in Argyllshire, though the Congregational movement they helped to found never took off in the Highlands. Baptist preachers roamed the area too; at one time there were quite a few Baptist congregations in the Hebrides – even in the north of Lewis – though only that on Tiree survives. But, in the main, Evangelicalism fired in the Established Church, which had at last firmed its grip on the Highlands: it drew the great mass of the people into the Presbyterian fold, and into the historic tradition of the Scottish Reformation, its doctrine and practice.

Evangelicalism should be defined. It rests on three pillars. First: an absolute and unquestioning adherence to the Bible as the inspired, infallible and inerrant Word of God. Second: acceptance that Christ alone is the road to salvation; that there is no other way to eternal life; that, without Him, there is only everlasting and conscious torment in eternal punishment. And, third, the need for *personal* salvation, for a personal experience of Christ as one's own Lord and Saviour. In its Calvinist form, which the Highlands knew, the utter sovereignty of God in salvation is stressed. The sinner cannot come to God of his own volition, nor be converted when he feels like it. He must be drawn to God by irresistible grace through the Gospel; the Spirit alone can convert him.

So, at last, the Reformed cause exploded into the Highlands just as, inexorably, it began to ebb in lowland Scotland, edging away before the tide of Roman Catholic immigration and a slow creeping secularism. But Highland Evangelicalism differed from mainstream Scottish Presbyterianism in some key respects. For one, it was tinged with anti-clericalism. Even in an age of superb Gaelic ministries, the Clearances – and their experience of the Moderates – left the Highlanders with an innate distrust of all ministers. Godly laymen – elders, the 'separatists' – were venerated, and often esteemed in authority (and in their manifold prejudices) over the man in the pulpit.

For another, Highland Evangelicalism is prone to what one can only describe as 'Calvinist monasticism'. In Lowland Scotland, converted men and women were actively encouraged to establish Christian 'dominion' in every legitimate field of life – politics, municipal affairs, education, commerce, the arts. In the

Highlands all was tarred as 'the world'. A cultural norm rapidly evolved, demanding that those claiming to be born again repudiated all that was of 'the world'. Of course, men were free to prosecute a trade or a business. And there was continuing regard for education. But instrumental music, traditional Gaelic song, folk-tale – these were now shunned. Many actually destroyed fiddles and other instruments when revival came to their district. Sports, too, were frowned on.

Too much has been made of this by writers hostile to the Gospel. In the balance, Evangelicalism did far more good than harm. But in this aspect its influence often threatened to be negative, baleful and unbiblical. And that tendency in the Highland Churches still survives. A well-known Free Church elder, who died only in 1993, boasted of drowning his bagpipes after his personal experience of Christ; a minister is still alive who, recording one Lewis revival of 1938, noted with satisfaction that, when the Spirit came with power, 'adherents, too, were nonplussed as to what all this would come to, since football, badminton, concerts and dances had lost their most ardent supporters.' Oddly enough, disapproval of 'the world' did not extend to the shunning of tobacco and alcohol. Most godly men enjoyed both in happy moderation, and only a few highly individual ministers frowned upon their discerning use. Such, even today, remains the case.

One Lochaber woman of last century, 'Red Kate', was a staunch Moderate; with whisky she had the better of two ministers. They were passing by her house one day when she hailed them, and they felt obliged to come in and visit her invalid husband. Prayer was offered, and afterwards they could not refuse her offer of liquid hospitality. Then Red Kate produced a packet of mighty peppermints. 'Now,' she said, 'you will put these in your mouths, and they'll not know anything on you when you reach Strone.'

The prohibition on dancing remains one of the most puzzling taboos in the Highland Church culture. There is no explicit biblical ground for it. Dances in the few Highland communities where Evangelicalism retains any force are, certainly, associated with excessive drinking, immorality, and occasional violence; but that is probably because no respectable or religious folk dare to attend them. Even so, in the cracks of history some wonderful light appears to remind us how recent some of these human prohibitions are. Dr MacDonald of Ferintosh enjoyed innocent pleasures. Evander Maciver recorded: 'I used to see as merry dancing in Dr MacDonald's house as anywhere, when many folks thought it was a sin to dance.'

The rigour of the Highland Sabbath has been exaggerated. Many who mock its totality – every shop and business closed, all indoors, emerging only to attend church services – are ignorant of its origins, in the grim days of a subsistence economy, when all toiled from dawn to dusk in the weary and wretched labour of gaining just enough food to survive. The Sabbath was not unique to the Highlands; it came north, with Evangelicalism, much later than to the rest of Britain, and as the Sabbath and the Gospel were late in coming they are late in leaving.

It is in its celebrated communion seasons that Highland Evangelicalism found its unique character. They still survive, though the attendances are now much smaller; as recently as the early 1960s, communion services still had to be held out of doors in certain districts, so great were the attendant crowds.

In most parishes the sacrament of the Lord's supper is only held twice a year, but on these weekends a series of special services takes place, kept by guest preachers, and the ablest and most eloquent ministers are in much demand for these. Visitors come from churches far and wide; many 'go round' the communions, which within Presbytery bounds follow each other on successive Sabbaths, so the Christian enjoys the Sacrament a good deal more than the southern visitor might realise. Throughout the communion season, a holiday is kept in the district, with no work done for the duration; even today, local schools in the Western Isles shut for the Thursday and Friday of a communion weekend, and all shops and bars close on the Thursday. Morning prayer meetings are held, before breakfast, throughout the weekend.

Thursday is the 'Fast Day', a day of humiliation and prayer, kept virtually as a Sabbath, and the preaching is of a penitential character. Friday is the day of self-examination, when believers are exhorted to search their souls for the true marks of saving grace. It is also known as 'Men's Day', because the first service of the day is the Question Meeting. In this extraordinary liturgy – its origins are obscure, but it was probably incorporated into

the communion weekend as a concession to the Separatists – the
ministers preside over a laymen's discussion of some portion of
Scripture. After the opening exercises of worship, the ministers
leave the pulpit and chair the meeting from the floor. The
presiding cleric asks for a 'question' – a verse of Scripture,
suitable for examining for the 'marks of grace' to be volunteered
by any male communicant present. By long custom it is a
member of the local congregation who stands to announce a
suitable text – and it may be anywhere between Genesis and
Revelation – and by long custom no warning whatever is given
to the minister of this verse. He must immediately rule on its
suitability for discussion – he usually accepts it – and then, *ex
tempore*, must briefly preach on the verse, setting it in context.
Then (supplied with a list of male communicants present,
compiled by one of his eagle-eyed colleagues) he calls on a
succession of men to stand and 'speak to the question'.

Traditionally, these men bring out such points of saving faith
as love for the brethren, love of the Lord's Day, conviction of
sin, etc, etc: they generally illustrate their remarks with anecdotes from their own experience, and in Lewis (by tradition)
they simply give their spiritual autobiography, often much
repeated (and honed) over the years. When all is done, the
minister must 'close the question' dealing with interesting points
that have been made, gently clarifying any matter of doctrine
an ill-educated elder might have confused; and at length the
member who proposed the verse is invited to conclude in prayer.

The opportunities such a meeting affords – particularly in
times of fraught Church politics – for digs, barbs, rebukes, and
pointed texts of Scripture will be evident. Many stories – some
funny, others appalling – are told of colourful characters on
various 'Men's Days' in the communions of old. It was darkly
remarked that, when the Gospel came to Barvas in Lewis, the
men of district ceased to brawl at the fank – the folding of sheep
– and fought at the Question Meeting instead.

Friday night has a sermon of similar searching, introverted
character. Saturday is the day of preparation when the weak
and timorous are encouraged to seek grace for the Lord's table.
The kirk session meets for the last time on Saturday to
interview any wishing to profess faith for the first time. All
intending communicants remain behind to collect tokens – little

pewter things, sometimes very old – to identify them as professing Christians. (In the days of 10,000 hearers at Ferintosh, such tokens were evidently necessary.) The deacons lay white cloths on the church pews and prepare the communion vessels – silver, decanter, plates – and the elements, plain white bread and red port wine.

The Sabbath morning service can be inordinately long. In the Free Presbyterian Church of Scotland – the most Highland, and Calvinist, of all Scottish denominations – it may last for over three hours. The minister most senior in ordination always presides. He preaches an 'action sermon', devoted to Christ's death on the Cross for His people. The table is then 'fenced', when he specifies – with much biblical reference – those who may, and may not, sit at the Lord's table. The believers then come forward to take their places, dropping their tokens into an elder's palm, as a suitable Psalm is sung – normally Psalm 116 or Psalm 118, part of the 'Great Hallel' sung at the Jewish Passover. Sometimes there are two or even three 'tables' with separate batches of communicants; each table is exhorted, before and after, in warm and encouraging terms, by a different minister. Finally the table is cleared. The minister of the parish will often give a brief address himself, specifically directed at those who have not professed faith, nor sat at the Lord's table that day.

On Sabbath night the junior minister preaches a specifically evangelistic sermon, addressed to the unconverted. A prayer meeting is held after this service. On Monday morning the thanksgiving service is conducted by the senior minister, and so the weekend is over. It is customary for visitors to stay in the parish throughout the weekend, in the homes of friends; they are royally entertained, with much good food, and fellowship and the singing of praise may continue into the late night.

There is a well-known Highland dread of superficiality in religion; a fear of a presumptuous professing of faith when one is not truly converted. Even today, many in a Church of Scotland congregation in the Western Isles are not full Church members: this is true of the majority in a typical Free Church congregation, and overwhelmingly true of the still more 'careful' Free Presbyterians. So, despite the traditional fear of 'the world' the Church has a substantial 'shell' of adherents able to penetrate secular affairs at various levels, while attend-

ing regularly and playing a significant role in congregational
life.

But the problem has also distorted the dispensing of sacraments. Adherents still require baptism for their children. In the
historic Scottish Church, what qualified for one sacrament
qualified for both. In the Highlands a rather curious theology
has evolved, in effect making the qualification for baptism more
lenient than for the Lord's table. To qualify for baptism the
parents must merely be regular attenders, of known good
character, willing to indicate full assent to biblical doctrine
and to express the knowledge that Christ alone is saviour of
sinners. To become a full member – a step taken with special
seriousness in the Free Presbyterian communion – you must be
minutely examined, by the kirk session, on your spiritual
experience.

The day is now past, even in the Western Isles, when the only
greater disgrace than being refused baptism was in wickedly
failing to seek it. Many now are content to leave their little ones
unchristened, and only in one district – the Isle of Scalpay, off
Harris – is church attendance still socially obligatory; it probably exceeds 90 per cent of the able-bodied population. In that
island one dreadful baptismal custom probably survived longer
than anywhere else. If baptism was sought where the child had
been clearly conceived out of wedlock – to an unmarried
woman, say, or born within the nine months following a
wedding – it was granted on condition that the couple first
were publicly rebuked in the face of the congregation. For this
disgusting (and profoundly unjust) ritual a special service was
held, midweek, and of course the church was always packed to
capacity by an eager crowd, and the wretched parents were
harangued by the minister, in terms often as lubricious as they
were ferocious. Robert Burns endured similar rites in Ayrshire
in the 1780s. It was last held in Scalpay – the first and last time
that their new minister did it – around 1978. Today such
baptisms are intimated, as normal, with merely the dark addition, 'The church discipline necessary in this case has been
carried out by the kirk session.'

The veneration of communion is one cultural hangover from
historically recent Roman Catholicism. So is the phrase 'chris-
tening', still used in Lewis to refer to baptism. Another Roman

relic is the high importance of clerical dress; ministers, in all
denominations, are still expected to wear black or very dark
clothing and a distinctive clerical collar when about their duties.
Some features of Highland Church life are plain superstition.
All but specifically religious events are barred in many districts
from taking place within Church buildings. The site of a new
church can be influenced by regard for a supposedly holy site; a
Free Presbyterian congregation in South Harris split, seventy
years ago, when one township insisted on erecting its meeting-
hall on the site of the home of a famous nineteenth-century
elder. Then there is 'the secret of the Lord', a phrase seeking to
spiritualise the gift of prophecy, to which many godly believers
have attained – and there is an abundance of incontestable
anecdote of Highland Christians, who made astonishingly
accurate predictions. But is this any more than the second
sight by another name?

What cannot be denied is that, where the Gospel came in
power, life at every level of society was greatly improved. The
misery of drunkenness, violence and so on would vanish for a
season. Crime and immorality would be much reduced. It may
vex the visitor to Harris, for instance, that he cannot buy petrol,
postcards, ice-cream or whisky on the Sabbath. That is the effect
of the Gospel. But Harris people can go to bed at night without
locking their doors; many would only lock their houses if they
were off the island. Children can play on island roads from dawn
to dusk, without fear of molestation. That is the effect of the
Gospel, even in 1996.

The Highland Separatists were characterised by lives of great
personal holiness, much prayer, and an incredible facility in
Scripture: many of them, indeed, knew the Bible as only those
who read nothing else can know it, word for word. But their
relationship to the Church was ambiguous. They were reluctant
to cut themselves off entirely from it, and so such lay movements
as the Plymouth Brethren – which made great inroads in
Scotland's north-east Lowlands – never took root in the Highlands. The Separatists valued the Church for baptism and for
communion. But they had utter contempt for the clergy and –
while they had much reason to despise the Moderates – their
language was apt to be vituperative, and some of the godliest

ministers the Highlands ever saw were likewise victims of their venom. 'A bag of sand,' said one Norman MacLeod of the Apostle of the North, and of the saintly Rev John Kennedy of Killearnan, 'he has no more grace than a horse.'

This Norman MacLeod was a native of Assynt, and by the early nineteenth century had built up quite a following in the north-west, who deserted the settled ministry for his exhortations. Born in 1770, he abandoned divinity studies in Aberdeen and by 1815 was schoolmaster at Ullapool. Two congregations formed of his followers, at Ullapool and in Assynt. MacLeod was gifted in many directions – resourceful, brave, eloquent, farsighted – but inclined to malice and of overweening arrogance. By 1817 he had so antagonised the Lochbroom minister that his salary was stopped. MacLeod drummed up some 400 of his admirers and, at the head of them, led them in emigration to Nova Scotia. They settled at Pictou. In a year or two he had fallen out with half of them, and took the other half away to sea again, hoping to settle at Ohio. They settled, instead, at Cape Breton, where in 1826 these 'Normanists' built the first Presbyterian church in the colony. They were remarkable folk. They lived in a co-operative, communal society characterised by what can only be described as Christian socialism. And their leader was at length licensed and ordained to the ministry by a Presbyterian church in New York.

Thirty years later hundreds of Normanists travelled again, for New Zealand, by way of Australia, where MacLeod's son had settled. Norman himself at last went with them, now in his eighties, and formed a new community, at Waipu, where he died in 1866, mourned by all – except the ministers of Scotland, whom he excoriated to the end of his days. He is still quite a hero in Cape Breton and New Zealand.

Alexander – 'Sandy' – Gair was a noted Separatist, of rapier wit. Many tales are told of this Caithness man of God. In old age, in quaint Highland garb and of most biblical appearance, he made his way to the General Assembly in Edinburgh. At its doors he attracted the mocking of some self-consciously sophisticated divinity students. One by one they struck dramatic attitudes, pointed, declaimed, 'Behold – Abraham!' 'Behold – Jacob!' 'No – behold Isaac!' Sandy Gair wheeled on them. 'No,' he said smoothly, 'in truth, I'm Saul the son of Kish, sent in search of his master's asses. Seems I've found them.'

Then there was David Stephen, of Watten in Caithness, and the tale of how he forsook dancing is still regularly trotted out in pulpits and church magazines. This David Stephen, for a time, dared simultaneously to follow devotedly the Lord's people to prayer meetings and, on alternate evenings, to play the fiddle at assorted happy social occasions. Then one day he met a woman on the road of notorious profanity and godlessness, so wicked that she had acquired ('we know not how') the awful nickname of Maggie Hell. She showered scorn upon him for his hypocrisy and ambivalence. 'Has it come to this,' wondered poor David Stephen, 'that I must be reproached by Maggie Hell?' That was the end of the fiddle, and of David Stephen's part in dances.

And there was John Grant, who set off on a tour of the Highlands and Islands in a quest to find men who were Christians *indeed*. He found two.

The Disruption brought most of these souls into the fold of the Free Church. But their culture, and influence, survive. The heirs of 'the Men' still hold Churches, and communities, to spiritual blackmail, blocking many useful and innocent amenities and entertainments, insisting on the continuance of Gaelic preaching where not a soul under forty can understand it, conducting prayer meetings on a Sabbath night in some village meeting-house while the minister, simultaneously, preaches to a half-empty church some five minutes' drive distant. Such have done much to weaken the Church's hands, especially in Lewis, whose status as a uniquely Christian stronghold in Scotland is, today, more imagined than real.

Of quite another stamp was that remarkable evangelist, Finlay Munro, who roamed the Highlands in the early nineteenth century as an intinerant evangelist. Munro, a native of Tain, had little by way of education – he was, in fact, illiterate in Gaelic; he would read an English Bible and translate it aloud to his hearers – but had great gifts of communication and was entirely free of a censorious or malicious spirit. He made some memorable visits to Lewis, and once met a cow-herd on the moor between Ness and Tolsta. As he gratefully accepted a draught of milk, Munro noticed the ring she wore. He turned it

Monument to the Park Deer Raids, by Balallan, Lewis. Here the men assembled before their march into Lady Matheson's deer forest.

Ruins, Dalmore, Lewis. This township was cleared by Sir James Matheson last century, about 1850. As clearances go, it was relatively humane. Those who declined his offer of assisted passage to Ontario were resettled elsewhere in Lewis. Dalmore was revived as a community after the First World War, when some Shawbost families were allotted crofts there.

Salvation and sin, *c.* 1970.
Behind: the Church of Scotland,
Cross, Ness, Isle of Lewis.
Before: a thatched *bothan* – an
illegal drinking club, for the
parish was then 'dry'. As this
bothan stood on Board of
Agriculture land, its legal
owner was the Secretary of
State for Scotland.

Inside the *bothan* at Cross, 1970.
The Ness district now has a public
house and a licensed social club,
but one *bothan* still survives.

Free Church, Lochs, Lewis; one of the very few original churches of
the Disruption period. Most were replaced by new, more elaborate
buildings later in the nineteenth century.

'Poet's Pub' by Alexander Moffat. Sorley MacLean, with moustache, stands at the back; before him, bespectacled, is the Lewis-born poet Iain Crichton Smith.

Old Garenin, Carloway, Lewis. This cluster of black houses is typical of the old clachan settlement – hard by the shore, houses huddled together. Old Garenin's last inhabitant left in 1973: the buildings are now being restored, as a 'living museum' of Lewis life many, many years ago.

At the peat cutting, Lewis, *c.* 1970.

After the service: Free Presbyterians, Ness, Lewis, March 1996.

Above: a Harris Tweed weaver.

John Finlay MacLeod, boatbuilder, Port of Ness, in old age. MacLeod's heroism in the *Iolaire* disaster saved many lives.

Marion Campbell, Plocrapool, Harris at her spinning wheel. Miss Campbell practised all the arts of sheep-to-suit wool production – dyeing, carding, spinning, weaving, waulking – and presented tweed to the Queen. Hard as she worked she could never quite meet demand.

Stornoway Provost Alexander Matheson accepting, on behalf of the town, the bell and engine-plate salvaged from the *Iolaire* by divers, *c.* 1966. Three survivors of the tragedy look on.

Bringing water from the well, at Ness, Lewis.

Marjorie Kennedy Fraser by John Duncan.

MV Hebrides at Tarbert, Harris. On this station until 1985, this much-loved vessel was the first of the modern car ferries to revolutionise transport in the Western Isles.

Donald Stewart, the first Scottish National Party MP to win his seat at a General Election, campaigning in North Uist in 1970.

The unattractive headquarters of Comhairle nan Eilean, the Western Isles Islands Council, at Stornoway. These corridors were shaken by the BCCI debacle in August 1991.

Stornoway youngsters. Beyond the harbour is Lewis Castle, 'built on opium' by Sir James Matheson.

gently in his fingers. 'How like eternity a ring is,' said Finlay Munro, 'it has neither beginning nor end.' The thought struck home; she was soon a converted woman. It is said that in a glade by Glen Moriston, being mocked by scornful men, Munro prophesied that his footprints would remain in the ground where he stood, to the end of time, as a witness that the Gospel he preached was true.

Two or three of the ministers of this period are worth examination. Rev Alexander MacLeod we have met before. He was the first evangelical minister in Lewis in the modern era, presented to the parish of Uig by the Hon Mrs Mackenzie in 1824. MacLeod, born in Assynt in 1786, was the son of a humble crofter. The local minister was an alcoholic, and in permanent debt. But he acquired as assistant the Rev John Kennedy, later of Killearnan, and under his preaching MacLeod, then a lad of fourteen, was converted. It is recorded that he was extremely clever – he did well at university – but exceedingly shy, and rather aloof. In the zeal of youth he was associated, for a time, with Norman MacLeod's cult. Alexander MacLeod had expressly to repudiate the great Separatist when he was licensed to preach by the presbytery of Tongue in 1818.

By then he was married, and that in itself is a good story. At the end of his studies Alexander MacLeod was engaged for a time as tutor to the sons of a wealthy Skye farmer. (There was an abundance of probationers and divinity students in those days; a charge could be a long time in coming.) He fell in love with this man's daughter, and she with him. So they eloped. They lived for a time in Edinburgh, then in Assynt, in a lowly black house. His in-laws were far from overjoyed. Mrs MacLeod's father sought to keep the young man from parish preferment. Her brother armed himself to the teeth with pistols and confronted Macleod on the road. It was all made up, in time, but it set the steel in Alexander MacLeod's soul.

He worked for a time as assistant to Rev Lachlan Mackenzie, in the last months of that notable cleric's life. We have heard of his gifts and his eccentricities, and his idea of encouragement was novel too. After he had preached a sermon, Alexander MacLeod repaired to the manse to find Mackenzie in much woe. 'Oh, I'm in distress. I found your sermon so interminably long and uninteresting that I feel myself as a vile wretch. I have just been thinking what a woeful future I shall have if I found eternity as long as I found you!' And it is one of the oddest features of MacLeod's career that, by all accounts, he was a very average preacher.

Alexander MacLeod was finally ordained at Dundee, then ministered in Cromarty until the Hon Mrs Mackenzie presented him with the Lewis living. His reputation preceded him to Uig. The folk of that parish heard that he was a most narrow minister, and tight with baptism. By the time MacLeod reached Uig a large number of families had tramped over to Harris, *en masse*, where the Moderate minister sprinkled their host of offspring without demur. MacLeod had already run the gauntlet at Stornoway. A good man accosted him on the pier and questioned him sternly about his business. What was he to do at Uig? 'To give the people the simple Gospel in all its glory and wonder.' 'It's sorely needed there,' mused his interrogator, 'for there's none in Uig knows anything about it, save one poor herd-laddie, and they call him stark-mad.'

His new congregation numbered some 800 souls, and they were little more than pagans.

They thought there were seven sacraments. At morn and evening they would bow in homage to the sun. After church on the Sabbath, they would buy whisky from one hawker and tobacco from another, within yards of the door itself. MacLeod sent them flying with plenty to think on. He then introduced a midweek meeting, and called an elder to lead in prayer. This man implored the Almighty to cast a good shipwreck soon on the shores of Uig, as they were running short of timber. He called another elder. This man condoled with the Lord on the death of His son, surely the most dreadful calamity there ever was. 'Stop, stop, man!' said MacLeod, aghast. 'You have said enough.'

It is said that this drove him to secret prayer. And by the end of the year something was in the air. His commonplace preaching remained commonplace preaching, but an unseen quality lent it new power. People began to weep under it. More and more folk crammed the church to hear him. The great Revival had come to Lewis.

Almost every adult in the parish was on the communicant roll, and so many were manifestly unfit for the sacrament that

MacLeod simply cancelled the communions, for his first year. In his second year in Uig he cancelled them again. This time there was an outcry, and not merely from his people. The Moderate ministers of the presbytery were angry too. The Stornoway minister at length despatched a servant to Uig with a bag of communion tokens, and the invitation to come and take the sacrament in town. Word reached the Uig manse, and MacLeod consulted with two good friends, Francis MacBean, who was then in charge of public works, and John MacRae, who was parish schoolmaster. MacBean was later an esteemed minister, and we shall hear more of this MacRae. As he and MacLeod were both under presbytery jurisdiction, they were powerless to stop this messenger. MacBean was not. He advanced into the moor with a stout cudgel, met the fellow, and roared, 'Your tokens or your life, sir!' The man dropped the bag and took to his heels.

MacLeod was had up at presbytery for withholding communion and for his disturbing sermons, but escaped censure in comic circumstances. Under interrogation, he declared that he cared only for the approval of *am Ministear Mor*, the great minister, by whom, of course, he meant Jesus Christ. But the large and drunken Moderator, Simson of Lochs, immediately took the remark to apply to himself. 'I'm with you, MacLeod, and we'll set them at defiance!' And Simson promptly pronounced the benediction. Presbytery was over and the case was never heard of again.

In his third year MacLeod did hold a communion. Only five dared to come forward and take their seats. By 1828 the parish was convulsed in a huge revival, so great that that year is still known in Lewis as 'the year of swooning', for many literally fainted under the preaching of the Gospel. (Mass hysteria always seems to accompany the symptoms of genuine revival.) It is said that on the Sabbath hundreds walked twenty miles and more to church. It is said that every night men wailed in prayer on the open hills. It is said that, from the length and breadth of Lewis and Harris, people tramped hill and dale to reach Uig and sit under MacLeod's preaching. It is said that, on one Sabbath of a communion, a crowd of no fewer than 9,000 stood in worship on the Ardroil sands, and that the Gaelic singing of Psalms rang out to sea for miles, in a vast and celestial

chorus. For five years this work went on. The movement flooded
through Lewis. The life of every parish was renewed and
transformed, and more ministers of MacLeod's stamp came
to minister: Robert Finlayson to Eye, then Knock; Finlay Cook;
then John MacRae to Cross; Duncan Matheson to Stornoway.

And yet this man, Rev Alexander MacLeod, gained his glebe
at the expense of families cleared to make room for it; his letters
to the proprietrix are remarkable for their ingratiating, fawning
quality, and, though he ministered elsewhere, and lived until
1869, he never presided over a revival movement again.

There came the Disruption.

The Disruption of 1843 was forced because the continuing
imposition of patronage had become insufferable. A nationwide
evangelical movement had taken hold in Scotland, and the
evangelical party grew close to a majority in the General
Assembly. They began, increasingly, to resist the filling of
parishes with useless and lazy Moderates, despised and un-
wanted by the people. So presbyteries dominated by evangelicals refused to ordain or induct such ministers. And landlords
and patrons began to sue the Church courts at civil law. In a
succession of cases the Court of Session found against the
Church. Nothing would persuade the Queen, the Prime Minister or the government to abolish patronage. This was an age of
laissez-faire politics, an age fearful of social upheaval and
revolution. So in May 1843 – having exhausted every concei-
vable avenue for redressing the matter – the evangelicals quit
the Church of Scotland and set up the Church of Scotland,
Free.

The Free Church leaders made plain they still wholeheartedly
endorsed the Establishment principle. The state was obliged,
under God, to support and maintain a Christian ministry in
every parish. But the state had no authority whatever to
command the Church in its own spiritual affairs. Nor had it
the right, even by parliamentary law, to deny congregations the
right to pastors after their own hearts. Thence the Disruption,
which the Free Church leaders sought to portray not as a split in
the Church but as a most reluctant divorce of Church from
establishment.

A good third of ministers, and probably a majority of the
Scottish people, adhered to the Free Church. In the Highlands –

save only for the parish of Strath, in Skye – the Established Church was almost wholly abandoned. For nigh on a century only a handful of people, in almost every parish, would worship in its fold. Within living memory the congregation in the parish of Cross, in Lewis, consisted of the minister's housekeeper, the minister's farmservant, and one man who attended when he was sober, which was seldom. This was the fruit of the Clearances. The Moderates had destroyed themselves in the eyes of the folk by their connivance in the work of eviction.

The Free Church left all the churches, all the manses, all the money and all the livings. It had only the ministers, the people, and a good deal of careful planning behind the final divorce. But a Sustentation Fund was quickly established so that ministers, for the first time, would be directly paid by voluntary givings from the people. Arrangements were made for training new ministers. New Free Church schools would be built. New churches and manses would be erected in every district.

The landlords, as one can imagine, were far from pleased. Many did their best to frustrate the movement. The people from Kilmallie were driven from the churchyard. They repaired to the shore, where at length they were driven below the high tide mark – the line where the landlord's jurisdiction ended. So for some time their worship was dictated by the movements of the sea. It was a long time before Cameron of Lochiel – an Episcopalian, of course – would grant a site for a Free Church. When he did at last give a plot, it was deliberately in one of the worst pieces of land in the Lochaber district, a Corpach bog so swampy that the people used to trap wild horses in it. The building was never stable, and had to be demolished in 1976.

In Strontian the landlord refused to grant any site anywhere. At length friendly folk in the south started a fund and built a remarkable floating church, of iron, in a Clydeside shipyard. This was towed to the Argyll coast, up Loch Linnhe, and duly anchored. It was in use for many years, until a new laird granted land, and it is said that for every hundred people on board it sank one inch in the water.

The Highland people, of course, needed exhortation in Church principles. Besides, there was a chronic shortage of Gaelic pulpit supply. So a ship, the *Breadalbane*, was acquired to carry deputies up and down the western seaboard: later, she carried relief to districts hit by the potato famine. One of the ministers released from his parish for a season, to go about the region and lecture on Free Church affairs and needs, was that John MacRae we met as parish schoolmaster at Uig. He was now minister at Knockbain and a most remarkable man. Born in Kintail, in 1794, John MacRae was a man of awesome build and inhuman strength. He was of formidable appearance, with broad shoulders and great hands and a dark, craggy face. It is said that there were two lines of MacRaes in the Kintail district, and that someone once asked John MacRae to which he belonged, the 'Fair' or the 'Black'? 'The Fair,' replied MacRath Mor. 'Then God have mercy on the black.'

He was a wild youth. He had a strong head for drink and there are many tales of his savage feats in brawling. Even, after conversion, MacRae's temper was quick. When someone bashed a dent in his hat, as he came from church, MacRae had the man on the ground at once. 'Oh, John, remember grace!' wailed his companion. 'But for grace,' said MacRae darkly, 'the beggar would never breathe again.' When he was parish teacher at Uig, he once marched over the moor to Stornoway for a barrel of herring. The storeman, winking at onlookers, offered him a huge barrel free – if he could carry it away in his bare hands. 'Really?' said MacRae, beaming. He threw one mighty arm around the barrel, and another mighty arm about another, and went off with them both. On another day he met a poor man whose heavy cart was stuck in a ditch. The horse had, despite valiant efforts, quite failed to shift it. So MacRae set to and, after some huffing and puffing, had the wagon back on the highway. 'Well, I'm not surprised the poor horse was stuck. I could hardly shift it myself.'

Lachlan Mackenzie had prophesied that this wild youth would be a great minister. So it proved. After long and terrible depression, under much conviction of sin, MacRae was converted. He did well in study – showing particular skill in mathematics – and was ordained to the ministry of Cross, in Lewis, in 1833. He successively ministered at Knockbain, Greenock, Lochs and Carloway. He was a spellbinding preacher of much oratorical gift. In other respects he might have been less acceptable today. Even in old age he wore a bright auburn wig. He chewed tobacco in the pulpit, and spat lumps of this on the floor as his sermon proceeded. (It is said that, afterwards, one church officer would dry them out and smoke them.)

So, in 1843, he toured the Highlands. At a Lochcarron meeting, he roused the ire of the parish minister, a Moderate, unworthy heir to Lachlan Mackenzie. 'Well might you lecture us, MacRae,' he heckled, 'I mind fine the day when you were hunting foxes on the hills above us.' 'Indeed,' roared Big MacRae, 'and it seems I did not get them all.' In Lochaber – preaching to the Fort William congregation, as they huddled in the parish cemetery – he went even further. 'People of Lochaber,' cried Big MacRae, 'seed of the thieves and murderers, you are there sitting on the graves of your fathers, where their bodies are rotting and their souls are roasting in Hell.' Not a hand or voice was raised against him, proof of the mighty change in the Highlands within a century of the '45.

MacRae was minister at Lochs when Lewis was shaken by its second great revival, in 1859. His parish was huge and divided by great arms of the sea – Loch Seaforth, Loch Erisort, Loch Leurbost – and friends clubbed together to buy him a little yacht, the *Wild Duck*. He was delighted with it. Many are the tales told of Big MacRae, and throughout the Highlands there are still dozens of places named for him – MacRae's Knoll, MacRae's Dell – where, once, he had preached in the open air. And there are tales too of great kindness, and much humour, to match those of physical might and barbed sarcasm.

A famous history of Highland Evangelicalism, *The Days of the Fathers in Ross-shire*, appeared in 1861, written by the minister of Dingwall, John Kennedy. He was the son of that Kennedy of Killearnan and perhaps the ablest and most learned Highland cleric of them all; he was certainly the last to be a serious force in the counsels of the old Free Church. For the great days of Highland Evangelicalism were already ebbing – in the Scottish mainland at least – and the Free Church was drifting steadily away from its roots. Instrumental music and uninspired hymns were seeping into its worship. The Free Church had grown grandiloquent, and aggressively denominational. Its leaders now sought union with the more liberal United Presbyterian Church, in the hope of creating a new super-Church, that would quite eclipse the continuing Established Church. Kennedy opposed this movement vigorously and, as he was held in great awe throughout the region, had the Highland people at his back.

He was an educated man, a man who devoured the plays of Shakespeare (though he would never have darkened the door of a theatre); he had a kindly streak (on his last sick-bed he was found making up a bow and arrow for the little boy of the house). But he was a man who, though a Doctor of Divinity, was self-consciously and proudly at the heart of Highland Evangelicalism, who would defend it in all its glories and curiosities, who already knew it was within a spiritual minority in the Free Church and within Scotland.

John Kennedy died at Bridge of Allan in 1884, returning to Dingwall after a Mediterranean holiday, in a vain attempt to alleviate the diabetes which killed him. But he had lived through that movement which, in the end, had restored dignity, literacy and cohesion to the Highland people. And they, like he, were already turning their understanding of the Bible to confront their own practical oppression.

Writing of the rising Gospel fervour in the north, Dr Kennedy wrote:

the body of the people in the Highlands became distinguished as the most peaceable and virtuous peasantry in Britain. It was just then that they began to be driven off by ungodly oppressors, to clear their native soil for strangers, red deer, and sheep. With few exceptions, the rulers of the soil began to act as if they were the owners of the people, and, disposed to regard them as the vilest part of their estate, they treated them without respect to the requirements of righteousness or to the dictates of mercy. Without the inducement of gain, in the very recklessness of cruelty, families by hundreds were driven across the sea, or were gathered, as the sweepings of the hillsides, into wretched hamlets on the shore. By wholesale evictions wastes were formed for the red deer, that the gentry of the nineteenth century might indulge in the sports of the savages of three centuries before. Of many happy households sheepwalks were cleared for strangers, who, fattened amidst the ruined homes of the banished, corrupted by their example the few natives who remained. Meanwhile their rulers, while deaf to the Highlanders' cry of oppression, were wasting their sinews and their blood on battlefields, that, but for their prowess and their bravery, would have been the scene of their country's defeat.

By Kennedy's death many of his admirers, in townships throughout the Highland region, already strove to turn that tide. Evangelicalism had brought them confidence, literacy, a new sense of popular consciousness. Like Israel of old, they felt called from Egyptian bondage.

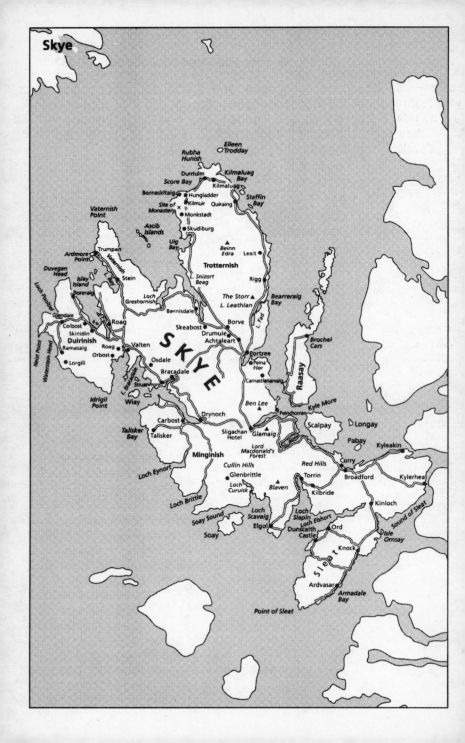

CHAPTER NINE

When I Was Young

―――――――――――――――――――――――

Moch's mi 'g eirigh air bheagan eislein
Air madainn Cheitein 's mi ann an Os
Bha spreidh a geumnaich an ceann a cheile
'S a ghrian ag eirigh air Leac an Stoir
Bha gath a' boillsgeadh air slios nam beanntan
Cur tuar na h-oidhche 'na dheann fo sgod
Is os mo chionn sheinn an uiseag ghreannmhor
Toirt 'na mo chuimhne nuair bha mi og

Nuair chuir mi cuairt air gach gleann is cruachan
Far 'n robh mi suaimhneach a' cuallach bho
Le oigridh ghuanach tha nis air fuadach
De shliochd na tuath bha gun uaill, gun gho
Na raoin 's na cluaintean fo fhraoch is luachair
Far 'n tric a bhuaineadh leam sguab is dloth
'S nam faicinn sluagh agus taighean suas annt'
Gum fasainn suaimhneach mar bha mi og

Rising early with little sorrow
On a May morning when I was in Ose
The cattle were lowing together
And the sun was rising on Leac an Stoir
A ray of sunlight shone down the side of the mountain
Quickly banishing the shade of night
And over my head sang the lively skylark
Reminding me of when I was young

When I went round each glen and knoll
Where I used to be serene, herding cattle
With merry young people who now are scattered
Seed of country folk without vanity, without guile
Fields and pastures under heather and rushes
Where often I cut sheaves, handfuls of corn
And if I were to see people and houses put there
I would be as contented as when I was young

From 'Nuair Bha Mi Og', 'When I Was Young', by Mary MacPherson, bard of the Skye land
agitation in the late nineteenth century.

THE CLEARANCES, on the notorious scale of the first half of the century, ceased in the 1860s. Sheep-farming was no longer the lucrative deal for landlords it had proved forty years before. Nor was there the same pressure of population. Highlanders were once more free, voluntarily, to sail overseas; and they did so in large numbers. Many more moved to Lowland Scotland in search of work. Work there was in abundance, in the docks, and on the Clyde ferries, and such steamer lines as the fleet of David Hutcheson (whose company was at length taken over by his protégé, David MacBrayne). Glasgow, especially, was a growing city, with plenty of work in construction. Women, too, could readily find employment in domestic service. Until the Second World War this would afford great opportunity for Highland girls.

And then there was the fishing. The massing population of the cities needed food, and a good source of cheap protein was salted fish – particularly herring. There was also a valuable trade in salt herring to the ports of Russia and the Baltic. So Highland men and women followed that trade too: the men on the boats, and the women in the gutting. As the herring shoals moved down the coast of Britain, so these Gaels moved after them: Stornoway, Lerwick, Buckie, Peterhead, and so on, as far south as Lowestoft and Yarmouth, following the work in such great numbers that the Highland Churches would send ordained deputies after them, to hold Gaelic services on station.

The spread of education, and increasing funding for lads of ability – scholarships, bursaries, endowed schools – brought many Highlanders from poor backgrounds into respectable, often urban professions. Highland youths became ministers, doctors, lecturers, engineers; they attained high positions in the military, in local and national government. But there was a sadly aleatoric element to such advancement. The higher education of a child meant much sacrifice for the parents: a pair of labouring hands lost for the croft, an extra income deferred for some years. Few families, then, could allow – or afford – the schooling of more than one child. It was seldom the oldest boy; he was heir to the croft. Girls, of course, were almost never permitted to continue study. Generally the second son, and he alone, was permitted to advance himself; if he was not in truth the ablest, that was unfortunate.

Emigration continued, the new colonies – Australia, New Zealand, Hong Kong, South Africa – gaining advantage over the Americas. The empire as a whole – its civil service, its trades, its policing, its armed forces – soaked up thousands of Highlanders. Overseas, liberty and opportunities were afforded that were denied at home. At home was subsistence living, the grim labour to wrest some living from poor soil. At home was insecurity, oppression.

But, as the century advanced and Highlanders continued to pour from the region, thousands of visitors poured in. More and more the region integrated into the wider British Isles, by tourism, by a popular fascination with its landscape and culture. This enchantment with things Highland and Celtic, though, was as misinformed as it was specious. It was founded on a cottage industry of colourful writing and given a huge boost by the leaders of society, even by the royal family itself.

The cult of the Highlands began with the work of one James MacPherson, born in the Badenoch district of Inverness in 1736. He was of the local gentry, but from a family of modest means. If he was witness to the outrages that followed Culloden – and the little boy must have been; Badenoch and its MacPhersons suffered greatly – James MacPherson never sought to avenge it. He was raised as a Gaelic speaker but, like many in the post-Culloden world, broke with the popular culture of his infancy. MacPherson went south and made his way in the world. He became a civil servant, a propagandist for the government. He sat for a time in parliament. He was London consul for an Indian prince; it was, however, a book published in 1760 – when he was still a young man – that made James MacPherson rich and famous.

It was called *Fragments of Ancient Poetry Collected in the Highlands of Scotland*; it was followed by two other books in much the same vein, in 1762 and 1763. These, MacPherson led readers to believe, were remnants of the verse of the celebrated, semi-mythical Ossian, a Gaelic bard of the early Celtic period, who was thought to have flourished even before Columba. The books were an astonishing success. They attracted a huge following in the cities of the empire. By the turn of the century they had been translated into almost all European tongues. They sold well in America. More than anything else, these cod-Homeric effusions of 'Ossian' made the Highlands known and famous. MacPherson's work has coloured, to a remarkable degree, perceptions of the region ever since.

It is a little too strong to say that the work was faked: MacPherson had a deep and genuine knowledge of Gaelic tradition, and collected much ancient rhyme and legend; in the excitement he triggered, many scholars headed northwards to continue the work. Samuel Johnson and others, though, plainly accused MacPherson of fraud: the writing, they insisted, came from his own fertile imagination, and he had no business passing it off as the work of the great Ossian. This was unfair. MacPherson's *oeuvre* was heavily indebted to genuine, and ancient, Gaelic myth. He certainly had access to some ancient manuscripts. But the work was not Ossian's, and it was indubitably polished, styled and finished to the tastes and dictates of MacPherson himself. History was adjusted for artistic licence. He laid claim for Scottish Gaeldom what belonged more properly – certain sagas and legends – to Ireland. Though he dated his discoveries at the third century AD, the Vikings were introduced to the tale for some additional blood and thunder. The debate on MacPherson's integrity has never been resolved. But, as Derick Thomson puts it, he 'was neither as honest as he claimed nor as inventive as his opponents implied'.

Tradition or fiction, it was spooky stuff. MacPherson's Highlands are a world of mist, damp, gloom, misery, a general sense of past tragedy, present trouble and impending doom. It is a world where the sun never shines, the trees are always bare, the hunter is always alone and the grave is always haunted. It is quite foreign to the cheerful, leafy world of most traditional Gaelic poetry. But it appealed hugely to a world now beginning to weary of Enlightenment sophistication. By the last decades of the eighteenth century, intellectuals across Europe were in full revolt against the 'smile of reason'; men such as Jean-Jacques Rousseau challenged the flattening, denaturing influence of civilisation itself. The ideal of the 'noble savage' took hold. As the Romantic movement – with its love for drama, nature, the wild, all things irrational and Gothic – struggled for birth, men seized on the works of James MacPherson as proof of past reality for their present beliefs.

By 1818 the English essayist William Hazlitt listed the highest attainments of human literature – in all seriousness – as 'Homer, the Bible, Dante and, let me add, Ossian'. Men such as Goethe were unstinting in their admiration for MacPherson's work. His creation's influence can be seen in much subsequent endeavour: the writing of Herder, Schiller, Hugo, Byron and Yeats; the etchings of Alexander Runciman, the music of Brahms and Mendelssohn. In our own era J. R. R. Tolkien's *Lord of the Rings* shows the unmistakable influence of 'Ossian'. And so on. But the fantasy landscape MacPherson had engineered was soon deployed by a Scottish writer, Walter Scott. His popular romances, his florid poetry, his swashbuckling dramas seized repeatedly on Highland history and Highland settings. He took MacPherson's universe to new extremes. In Scott's stage-setting, birch trees wept, stags mourned, bloodhounds bayed and hills lamented. His characters delighted (if that is the word) in lost causes, last stands, noble resignations and forlorn hopes.

What men like MacPherson and Scott had created – and the tradition was continued, in increasing vulgarity, by such execrable writers as 'Fiona MacLeod' (William Sharp) and William Black – was a Highland, Gaelic universe of the past. It bore no relation, of course, to the lot of Highlanders in their own day. And it lay far and safely beyond much more recent, and meaningful, Scottish history, like the Wars of Independence and the Jacobite Risings. These books were devoured by men and women who had done well out of the Union. Their investment and security was in the British empire; at the top of their social pyramid reigned the House of Hanover. They had, if anything, a positive fear of Scottish nationalism. Yet the Lowland gentry were still eager to find anything that might grant a Scottish identity, and the more remote and mysterious such romance was the better. The Highlands no longer threatened anyone, after all. Cumberland had seen to that.

It became a craze. And then, in 1828, it was granted a stamp of high approval, from the highest authority of all – King George IV himself. Cumberland's godson had come to the throne late, after the long and increasingly senescent reign of his father. George IV was obese, drunken, lecherous, and dissipated; his features, ravaged by years of living not too wisely but too well, were smeared in rouge and powder. But King George came to Scotland, the first reigning monarch so to do for many a decade; it was a visit staged by Walter Scott himself, and it was a play bedecked in tartan.

As word spread of the coming theme-party, Scots nobles flocked to their tailors to be appropriately clothed for the event. A few, of course, could lay claim to genuine tartans. Many others could not, and most of Scotland's spurious clan patterns date from this royal visit. Many were devised, in fact, by two eccentric brothers who lived on an island in the River Beauly and claimed to be grandsons of Charles Edward Stuart. These 'Sobieski Stuarts', as they styled themselves, were pretenders in every sense of the word – had Charles fathered a legitimate son, he would certainly not have concealed the fact, and an exhaustive inquiry by Napoleon for such a Stuart claimant had failed. But they were harmless enough.

The king came to Edinburgh, and the visit was a great success. It is hard now to convey just how hysterically fashionable the Highlands became. Scott's long and effusive poem, *The Lady of the Lake*, sold 20,000 copies in its first year. Loch Katrine in the Trossachs, where it was set, became a magnet for visitors. In the first seasons after the book appeared, every guest-house and inn in the region was packed with tourists. In the late 1820s, Lord Cockburn – whose intuitive sympathy for the crofters of North Uist is one of the first bright notes in the Clearance saga – still found the district thronged.

> The inn near the Trossachs could, perhaps, put up a dozen, or at the very most, two dozen of people; but last autumn I saw about one hundred apply for admittance, and after horrid altercations, entreaties and efforts, about fifty or sixty were compelled to huddle together all night. They were all of the upper rank, travelling mostly in private carriages, and by far the greatest number strangers. But the pigs were as comfortably accommodated. I saw three or four English gentlemen spreading their own straw on the earthen floor of an outhouse with a sparred door and no fireplace or furniture . . .

Scott himself was amused – later, embarrassed – by the new mania for Scotland. 'Every London citizen makes Loch Lomond his washpot and throws his shoes over Ben Nevis.' But what he and MacPherson had done was to overturn entirely conventional notions of beauty in landscape. The Hanoverian officers after Culloden had, to a man, detested the region; it was 'wild' and 'barbarous'. Its mighty hills were 'monstrous excresences'. Words like 'horrible', 'frightful' and 'awful' recur frequently in the Highland travelogues of the eighteenth century. A hundred years later, romantics of every class and stripe exulted, now, in 'majesty' and 'magnificence', among 'lofty peaks' and 'frowning glories'.

George IV died in 1830; in 1837 his niece, Victoria, ascended the throne, and shortly took as consort her cousin, Prince Albert of Saxe Coburg-Gotha. He came from a wooded, rugged part of Germany; both he and Victoria were great admirers of Scott (as a little girl, the queen had actually met him) and soon visited Scotland to see these wonders for themselves. The outcome, famously, is Balmoral Castle, in the Deeside region of Aberdeenshire, which particularly reminded Victoria's consort of his childhood home. The castle itself is of somewhat vulgar architecture, but it has remained the summer haunt of the dynasty ever since, with its attendant lodges and shooting-boxes – Birkhall, Abergeldie and the like.

The queen adopted a piper for her household; ever since, wherever the monarch resides, the pipes are played at twilight. Their growing family wore kilts, and the princes and princesses were photographed in them. Edwin Landseer painted the royal pets; his most famous work, *Stag at Bay*, is almost an ikon, worldwide, for the Highlands and Islands. The queen actually published a book, culled from her diary, recounting innocent pastoral adventures at their Highland retreat. When she was widowed, in 1861, she withdrew for a long time from public life, and spent much of her inordinate mourning at Balmoral; her attachment to one rough-and-ready retainer, John Brown, grew so strong that, upon his death, she was inconsolable, and had an enormous statue erected of him on the Balmoral estate. It was even rumoured that queen and servant had secretly married. Queen Victoria's third daughter, Princess Louise, defied precedent by marrying, for the first time in many generations, outwith the cosy circles of European royalty. She tied the knot with the Marquess of Lorne, heir to the Duke of Argyll, premier Highland noble.

So the Highlands became not merely fashionable, but an essential place of retreat, refreshment and interest to any of social aspiration in nineteenth-century Britain. There were three striking results of this in the nineteenth century. The first was an accelerated anglicisation of the existing Highland gentry. Many – such as the Argylls – defected from the Kirk to the Episcopal Church. Many more began to marry into the English aristocracy, or seek wives from it. And so on. Second, a huge new industry came to the region – that of sporting estates. Those who could not afford to buy some acres of hill and wood, with suitable and grandiloquent accommodation, would happily rent. Those who had the money – such as George Bullough, who bought the Isle of Rhum – spared no extravagance in their residences. (Rhum's Kinloch Castle, now in the hands of the National Trust for Scotland, boasts elaborate baths, with whirlpool and shower attachments; an internal telephone system, with the instruments made of inlaid rosewood; and an extraordinary organ, combined with all manner of percussion instruments in a sort of one-player band.)

New sports were devised, such as deer-stalking, which appealed to the wild romantic in every high-born gentleman. Fly fishing became almost an essential accomplishment for young men. Visitors began to shoot at almost everything that flew or ran. The environmental consequences – not least in the pressure put on gamekeepers to eliminate certain 'vermin' – were dire. But huge numbers of people were brought into employment in this sphere – as gamekeepers, ghillies, bailiffs, boatmen, carriers, house servants and so on – and it remains a significant sector in the Highland economy to this day.

The third innovation was the coming of new, and most efficient, transport links. The Crinan Canal was dug, allowing West Highland passage from the Clyde without need for sailing around the long Kintyre peninsula. The Caledonian Canal soon linked Loch Linnhe to the Moray Firth. Now the new steamships could carry a traveller from Glasgow to Inverness in less than two days – much faster than he could travel by road. By century's end railways were striking deep into Highland territory. The line reached Inverness first, then westwards to Strome on Loch Carron, and north into Sutherland (where its crazy, wandering route, still followed, was dictated by the insistence of the Duke of Sutherland that the iron road link his shooting-boxes). Later the line was extended to Kyle of Lochalsh. The West Highland Railway eventually gave direct transport from Glasgow to Oban, Fort William and Mallaig. The steamers of David MacBrayne operated a service of such efficiency that many foot-passengers in, say, 1890 could accomplish journeys much more readily than they can today.

There was much absurdity in all this. The *nouveau-riche* of Yorkshire strutted in kilts. The Skye Ball was (and remains) an event barred to most native Skyemen. Queen Victoria was flattered to be told she bore some resemblance to the Young Pretender; once, quite unconscious of paradox, she declared she was in truth 'a Jacobite at heart'. In time, this integration would benefit the Highlands; it would mean, by the 1880s, that almost everyone who mattered in high places had visited the area and knew something of it. For now, the ordinary folk of the islands and glens were seen as no more than hired help; often, a positive nuisance, sometimes even as but the savage descendants of a once-great civilisation. And the very landscape of the Highlands itself was distorted in popular imagination. It became more dramatic, much wilder, even steeper and ever more grotesque than was truly the case. Scott's Highland scenes, lovingly described, resemble nothing as much as the covers of modern fantasy fiction. Many paintings of the Victorian era exaggerate height, depth, gradient and precipitousness; if you know the scene they purport to describe, the effect is most disconcerting.

And still the biggest export of the region was its people. The crofting culture had matured from the sub-division, chaos and famine of the 1840s. It was now widely accepted that only one child of a family should stand heir to the croft – in its entirety – and the rest should go forth into the world, to fend for themselves. As they were able they would send funds home, to feed the little mouths for which their parents were still responsible, to provide for such sophistications as had now caught on in the Highland culture – tea, tobacco, crockery, clothes of softer fabric than wool, mirrors, clocks, and the like. Increasingly, too, they sent back new ideas, new ways of thinking and acting, from the wider political realm of the day.

It was, however, in the Isle of Lewis that popular resistance to proprietorial excess now began to set its teeth. Over years the people of the island had endured much from their ruling class. They were among the last Scots to suffer thirlage, a feudal custom whereby a tenant's grain had to be milled at the mill operated by his superior – usually, in Lewis, the tacksman, though sometimes it was the minister – and a charge of meal exacted for the privilege, mill dues or multures. If he declined to use the approved mill, the tenant had to pay a 'dry' multure, in money or in kind. Further, the ordinary people had themselves to maintain mill, lade and dam at their own expense. Many islanders, then, kept hand-mills – querns – but they had still to pay dry multures. Factor and tacksman, naturally, disapproved of querns. One tacksman in the Laxay township is said to have searched every home, seized all the querns and dumped them in a loch. It was a wicked system, not least because approved mills were few, and islanders had often to walk a good many miles to reach them. Yet the custom endured. The Moderate minister of Barvas, Rev William MacRae, complained bitterly in 1833 when the bounds of his thirlage were restricted to the Barvas village itself.

Even the timber cast up by a bountiful sea was not their own. Lewis is largely treeless; this wood was precious, for roofing their dwellings, and men were known to kill for it. Yet, in the days of the Seaforths, men were employed to mark all substantial pieces of driftwood found on the shore with the letter 'S'. It then became estate property, and if it were thereafter found in the roof of a house the luckless tenant faced eviction. Houses were regularly searched by a factor's men for this purpose.

Lewis had escaped the worst of the Clearances and, through the middle decades of the century, had been under the benevolent landlordship of Sir James Matheson. Even so, many townships in the large parishes of Uig and Lochs were swept of their tenants. They were not compelled to emigrate – though Matheson offered assisted passage overseas – and, by and large, land was found for them elsewhere. New townships were formed in north Lewis for such. Inevitably, though, there was much inconvenience and hardship. A pre-Matheson clearance, in 1828 – when the island was still owned by a Mackenzie scion – dumped a good many people in Aird Tong, a hamlet north of Stornoway. The weather was bad, no housing had been provided, and they were without decent materials for building proper accommodation.

Until I saw the actual situations of the new lotters in the Aird of Tong, [wrote a troubled official to his proprietor] I had no idea of the great hardship and privation that the poor people endure who are forced into new allotments, without matters being previously arranged for their moving. The situation of the new lotters in the Aird of Tong, at this moment, beggars description. It is worse than anything I saw in Donegal, where I always considered human wretchedness to have reached its very acme. The roofs of the present hovels on the Estate might, in general, stand for a few years if they were let alone, but the act of taking them down breaks and injures them so much that they are of comparatively little value in roofing their new homes – fresh timber is therefore necessary, and the exorbitant price demanded is so great as to more than exhaust their means.

I am therefore deeply of the opinion that whenever a general move of the people is ordered by you from one part of a farm to another, you ought to present them with the timber necessary to roof their buildings, and besides, good access should be made to the site of the proposed habitations before they be required to leave their old: for lack of such an arrangement at Aird of Tong, the poor people at the new lots there are suffering the greatest hardship, many of them dead, I am told, from disease brought on, I have no doubt, from the unwholesome situation in which they have been forced to plant themselves. To erect their cabins, the sward has been taken off the whole line of the intended road which has now become a morass, dangerous for both man and beast to set their foot upon: how the children contrive out and in of their cabins baffles my comprehension, for the men have literally to step up to the knee in mud, the moment they quit their threshold.

Matheson cared genuinely for the welfare of his people, and spent a good deal of money on the island; even so, his endeavours were only as good as his detailed knowledge of a place or problem – settlers at New Shawbost, around 1850, faced just the same problems as the 1828 settlers at Aird Tong – and, more importantly, as good as his staff. And, by 1874, Sir James had largely given up hands-on management of his affairs, and delegated the running of Lewis, and the treatment of his people, to one Donald Munro.

This Donald Munro was factor – or, as he preferred to describe himself, Chamberlain – of Lewis. He was also Justice of the Peace; Notary Public; Commissioner of Supply; Commissioner under the Income Tax; Head of Militia; Vice-chairman of the Stornoway Harbour Trustees; Director of the Stornoway Water Company; Director of the Stornoway Gas Company; Chairman of the island's four Parochial Boards; Chairman of the island's four Parish School Boards; Legal Advisor to those same boards; Commanding Officer of the Local Volunteer Force; and Procurator Fiscal. The locals nicknamed him 'the Shah'.

In these irresponsible, malignant hands were concentrated all the significant posts of secular power on the island. Munro's name is still detested on Lewis. The ordinary people of the island he held in the same contempt as Patrick Sellar had regarded the 'aborigines' of Sutherland. Eviction was Munro's weapon, and 'I'll have the land from you!' his favourite threat to any who threatened the least resistance or inconvenience to the estates of the island. One man would later insist to a parliamentary commission that Donald Munro's policy 'from the first day of his factorship to the last, was to extirpate the people of Lewis as far as he could'. Another went even further. 'The Commandments of our Great Master are only ten in number, and a reward is offered if we keep them; but those of our well-meaning and easy insular tyrants are impossible of being observed; and all we can expect is to live as slaves and die as beggars.' And a local poet, John Smith of Earshader, pilloried the monstrous factor in verse. Even the Chamberlain of Lewis, ran the lines of 'Spiorad a' Charthannais' – 'Spirit of Charity' – had to submit to his Maker, who gave all their deserts; when the great one died, he would be left but with a plain shirt and six feet of earth. Donald MacDonald's translation gives its flavour:

> An sin molaidh a' chnuidh shnaigheach thu,
> Cho tairceach 's a bhios d'fheoil;
> 'N uair gheibh i air do charadh thu,
> Gu samhach air a' bhord.
> Their i' S e fear miath' tha 'n so,
> Tha math do bhiasd nan cos,
> Bho'n rinn e caol na ciadan
> Gus e fein a bhiathadh dhhoms'.

Then shall the crawling maggot praise
The bulkiness of your carcass
When it finds you stretched
Lifeless in the grave
It will say, 'Here's a corpulent body
Whom the crevice creatures will enjoy
Since he beggared hundreds
To fatten himself for me.'

Earshader, in the parish of Uig, is within sight of Bernera, a
large island on the Atlantic coast of Lewis, separated only by the
narrowest of channels from the main island. (It is still inhabited; in
the early fifties a road bridge was built.) In 1872 the local crofters
were told, to their dismay, that their summer grazings were to be
taken from them; it was the second transfer in two decades, for in
1850 they had lost good pastures to the Uig deer forest. A new
estate was being formed for some sporting tenant. But they were
offered new land, of inferior quality. There was little the crofters
could do. They reluctantly accepted these grazings and, as
ordered, built a long stone dyke to separate this land from the
old. It was weary and, from their point of view, pointless toil.

This dyke was seven miles long and took the poor men two
years to build. It had just been completed when Munro sent word
peremptorily to announce that their grazings had been changed
again. All their trouble had gone for nothing. The Bernera men
were furious, and the factor's messengers retreated hastily before
their vocal abuse. The island was soon seething with unrest.
Munro responded as many a colonial governor before and since.
He donned one of his hats – as Commanding Officer of the
Volunteers – and sent in troops. They were to howl threats of
eviction (though not one Bernera crofter was in arrears of rent).

Munro drafted fifty-eight papers of eviction, to be served on all
the families of two townships of which he wanted particularly an
example made – Tobson and Breaclete. So his officials descended
on Bernera and stomped about the place handing these documents out to surprised tenants; nothing untoward happened until
evening, when they encountered a crowd of children – young boys
and girls – who had their own opinion of these dignitaries. The
estate officials came under a shower of little turves and peats. 'If
I'd a gun with me,' snarled the sheriff officer, 'there'd be women in
Bernera tonight lamenting their sons!'

Next morning a deputation of crofters surrounded these estate officers. Who, they demanded to know, had dared to threaten their children? A scuffle broke out. The sheriff officer had his coat ripped. Back they fled to Stornoway, with a pretty tale, and a warrant was issued for the arrest of three Bernera crofters on charges of assault. The men, naturally, were not minded to appear, and so Munro resorted to another device of the colonial governor through time, and Scots kings in their day. He would take a hostage. The first Bernera crofter sighted in Stornoway after these incidents, some weeks later, was arrested and jailed. Now scenes broke out on the streets of Stornoway. As an increasingly irate crowd flocked about the local nick, the Riot Act was read. With difficulty the folk were dispersed. Word quickly reached Bernera and a procession of Bernera men marched, *en masse*, to town demanding an audience of Sir James Matheson himself.

The proprietor agreed to meet them. He was astonished to learn that Munro had gaily decided on the eviction of fifty-eight Lewis households without his knowledge or consent. Why? demanded Sir James. Munro said he had not thought the matter of sufficient importance for his employer's attention.

Two crofters (and a town baker who had sought to help them) were acquitted at trial. But the sheriff officer was fined twenty-one shillings for a vicious assault on a man in the Stornoway police station. The defence, and the bench, had much to say about Donald Munro and his conduct of the affair. So the Chamberlain of Lewis was sacked by his mortified boss.

Donald Munro ceased to be Chamberlain of Lewis, Baron Baillie, Procurator Fiscal, Justice of the Peace, Commander of Local Volunteers, Commissioner of Supply, Chairman (and Advisor) of all Lewis school boards, Commissioner for the Revenue, Director of the Gas Board, Director of the Water Board, Collector of Poor Rates, etc, etc. He lived for many more years, stripped of all authority and standing, and as an old man he would shuffle miserably through Stornoway streets, the urchins dancing about him and crying his old taunt, 'I'll have the land from you! I'll have the land from you!'

The year preceding Munro's downfall, 1873, saw the first issue of a radical newspaper, the *Highlander*; it lasted eight years, despite several bouts of legal action by enraged landlords

assailed on its pages. The editor and proprietor was John
Murdoch, a native of Nairn. He had spent much of his life
in the service of the government, as an officer of the Inland
Revenue, and in that calling Murdoch spent many years in
Dublin. There he was drawn in to the turbulent world of Irish
nationalist politics. He now used his newspaper to further the
cause of land agitation.

Murdoch denied that there could be any absolute property in
land, which was 'not the creation of man', to be treated in the
same way as 'houses or furniture or ships or manufactures'.
Gaelic tradition, he pointed out, recognised Highland land only
as belonging to a clan, not its chief, who was but head of the clan
or family. Spurious charters had, of course, been granted by the
crown to these chiefs, and in time their people had been
'degraded into feudal tenants'. But, though they had become
landlords, they had no right to indefinite enjoyment of that
status. The *Highlander* became celebrated for its ferocious
attacks on landlords and landlordism. It was forced to close
down in 1881, but its radicalism was taken up – for a spell – by
the *Oban Times*.

There were two other figures in this movement worth noting.
One was a woman, Mary MacPherson, and she is remembered
not as a politician or leader in agitation but rather as a composer
of radical Gaelic songs; she was ample in figure, and is still
remembered as Mairi Mhor nan Oran – Big Mary of the Songs.
She was born in Skeabost, in the Snizort parish of Skye, in 1821.
By profession she became a nurse, and while in that service in
Inverness, in a private household, she was falsely accused – and
convicted – of theft from her employer. The trial had heavy
political overtones; her late husband, whose death had left her
struggling with the care of a young family, had been active in
trade unionism. Proceedings were rendered all the more unjust
by the accused's inability to speak English. Mary MacPherson
was jailed for a crime of which she was innocent. This humiliation she never forgot nor forgave, but it was in the prison of
Inverness that she began to make songs.

After that, she made her way to Glasgow, and a new career
for herself as a midwife; but MacPherson's ordeal bound her
thereafter to the cause of the wronged, the maltreated and the
misunderstood. So, on her retiral to Skye – after many years'

absence – Mary MacPherson allied herself with the land agitation, and this became a dominant theme in her lyrics. She sang at noted crofters' rallies; she sang on electioneering rounds through Skye with pro-crofter candidates. Her best songs celebrate the landscape and weathers of Skye, with much reference to suffering – that of herself and her people.

There was also Rev Donald MacCallum – a minister, remarkably, of the Established Church – who became the most prominent clergyman in support of popular aspirations in the Highlands and Islands. He was a native of Craignish, in Argyll. MacCallum's real skill was in oratory; he excelled in blending the rhetoric of radical socialism with redolent biblical imagery. His parishes, too, always seemed to coincide with periods of local anti-landlord passion: Morvern, in Argyll; Waternish, on Skye (which included Glendale); Heylipool, on Tiree; and Lochs, in Lewis, which included that district called Park. He was invited to Waternish in 1884 by a group of radical crofters (who would have been Free Church to a man). Two years later his own Church censured him for 'inciting class hatred'; he was even briefly jailed (though never charged) in Portree. 'The land is our birthright,' MacCallum declared, 'even as the air, the light of the sun, and the water belong to us as our birthright.'

'*Chunnaic sinn bristeadh na faire, is neoil na tralealachd air chall an latha sheas MacCalium laimh rinn*,' Big Mary remembered; 'we saw the dawn break, and the clouds of thralldom flee away, the day MacCallum stood beside us at the Fairy Bridge.'

Park was scene to a new bout of resistance, inspired by events unfolding on Skye. Much of the Park area had been cleared earlier in the century, and taken over for sheep-farming. Repeatedly Lochs men begged for crofts on it. The estate insisted that Park was unsuitable for crofting; this was ridiculous. Rather, it suited the estate much better as a sheep-farm paying good rent. Many were still alive who remembered the fine living Park land had given its tenants. At the end of 1881 the lease of the Park farm was due to expire, and thirty-two Lochs fishermen petitioned Lady Matheson – who now managed Lewis; her husband had died – for the letting of the lands of Orinsay and Steimreway on such terms as she might see fit to grant. Further, they undertook to abide by all estate regulations.

There was no reply. They wrote to her chamberlain. There was

still no answer. And they wrote yet a third time, in December
1882, expressing now the hope that they might not be led,
reluctantly, to take such steps as others of their unfortunate
countrymen had been forced to take. Now Her Ladyship waxed
wroth. She sent back a chilly refusal; further, she made very plain
her anger at the very cheek of the peasants in daring to ask.

> Her Ladyship regrets that the above named respectable class of
> Lewis men should have been led to address her on a subject of
> such importance as that contained in their petition by adding to
> it a letter which causes her to set aside their request, as Lady
> Matheson is too devoted to her Queen and the laws of which Her
> Gracious Majesty is the representative, to listen for one moment
> to a petition accompanied by a threat from them to infringe the
> law by which all are governed, and by the support of which, as
> individuals, the well-being of the land and its communities at
> large can alone be promoted . . .

Lady Matheson, that winter, was well aware of the lengths to
which Highland people were now prepared to go. The year now
ending had seen dramatic events in Skye, in two districts: Braes
and Glendale. Glendale was typical of the more unhappy
crofting community of that time, and is worth a passing
look. It was one of the most fervent centres of Evangelicalism. The Free Church had the great mass of the people; they
were gracious, godly folk, and in 1893 would be at the centre of
the Free Presbyterian movement (as, indeed, would be the men
and women of Braes). As the Hebrews suffered Pharoah,
though, so had the people of Glendale suffered their landlord. As elsewhere, more and more of their sad land was seized
for sporting use – deer park here, grouse moor there. As
elsewhere, the Glendale folk were refused even the most basic
measures to protect themselves against vermin – fences, dykes
and so on. (Things were even worse on rabbit-ridden Raasay. By
now the grazings were so stripped that Raasay people were
going hungry. Mr Wood imported more rabbits.)

But, in January 1882, even the amenable people of Glendale
were pushed too far. A notice was hammered up at the village
store, 'for all the world as if it were an Act of Parliament',
remarks Hunter. Dogs were now banned. All driftwood cast up
on the shore was henceforth the exclusive property of the estate.

'Notice is hereby given that the shepherds and herds on these lands have instructions to give up the names of any persons found hereafter carrying away timber from the shore, that they may be dealt with according to law.'

Now, according to law, a landlord's rights cease at the hightide mark, as early Free Church congregations had demonstrated. And, in the treeless isles of the west, driftwood was their sole source of roofing for their houses. But the only law that now ran in these islands was the whim of a landlord, the grudges of a factor. And in their hands all civil and secular power was concentrated. This was no longer law; this was despotism, of a kind that bordered on vicious and irrational anarchy.

Another notice now appeared in the Glendale store, from good men who had borne more than enough. But the first blows in this struggle fell in Braes.

Braes is that land on the Trotternish peninsula, running south of Portree and along the shore of the Narrows of Raasay. It is beautiful country. From such townships as Penifiler, the Ollachs, Gedintailor, Balmeanach and Peinchorran are lovely views of Raasay itself, of the mountains of Kintail, of the jagged rock of northern Skye, of the Red Hills. The climate is mild, the landscape undulating, and there is much soft woodland, with copses of birch and hazel. Today it is a desirable residential area, and some of the wealthiest families in Skye have their homes there. But, last century, it was not regarded as good land at all. It was peopled largely by Skye folk evicted from sweeter and better ground elsewhere – such as had escaped forced passage overseas. The people of Braes were poor, by Skye standards, and needed every scrap of land they could use, so thin and begrudging was the soil. For some years, at least, they had enjoyed the grazings on the slopes of Ben Lee, the high hill rising from Loch Sligachan. Then this ground was taken from them, for a tenant and his hordes of sheep.

At length this fellow's lease ran out, and the crofters conferred together and sent a polite proposal to Lord MacDonald's factor. Could they have this land back for their own use? They would pay a better rent. The factor, and Lord MacDonald himself, were most displeased. The men of Braes were told to mind their own business. On no account would this land be returned to their use.

Now, by the winter of 1881, new notions were abroad in the
Highlands, and in Skye especially. Many of the young men were
off fishing during summer, and did much of their fishing in fleets
off the shores of Ireland. Naturally, they frequently landed in
Ireland, and soon they brought word home of the exciting events
in that country. A Land League had been formed. The Irish were
demanding rights. They were organised in agitation against their
landlord class. They had initiated rent strikes – and got away with
it. They were denying services and labour to landlords in a new
practice known as 'boycotting'. Already the Irish, and their rising
clamour for home rule, were wringing concessions from the
nervous Liberal administration of William Gladstone.

In November 1881 the crofters of Braes were due to pay their
annual rent. But the monies did not come to the factor at
Portree. Instead a dignified little deputation confronted the
factor, Alexander MacDonald, and told him there would be
no rent that year, nor any year, until the grazings of Ben Lee
were restored to them. And they returned home to release their
own sheep on the hill.

Lord MacDonald was shocked. Very shocked indeed. He
promptly asked the sheriff officer to serve exemplary notices
of eviction on twelve Braes crofters. The deputy sheriff officer
complied, for he was, after all, that same Alexander MacDonald,
factor of the MacDonald estates; and, in addition, like Donald
Munro, held all the posts of power that mattered, and more
besides – local agent for the Bank of Scotland, Distributor of
Postal Stamps, and so on.

MacDonald sent a deputy, and two heavies from Portree, to
serve these papers. They were met by the women of Braes, large
and vocal and hostile. The three men soon quaked in the midst
of this angry huddle of wives and mothers. The papers were torn
from their hands and burned before their wide eyes.

Word of this was soon brought to Sheriff William Ivory, a
Border Scot of good family, and if Donald Munro had beheld
himself as a colonial governor, this Ivory – sheriff of Inverness –
thought himself a veritable viceroy. To him the very empire was
threatened by these insurrectionists. And, as viceroys through
time have decided, he felt the situation called for a full-blown
expeditionary force. Nothing would impress the natives like a
good show of strength. So Sheriff Ivory began to organise a

formidable army of policemen from Glasgow. Word of this came to Braes. The men readied themselves to fight, and posted sentinels along the road to Portree. The chief constable gave the sheriff a quiet word on tactics. Why take the risk of falling upon Braes in winter, when all the young men were at home? Why not wait until April, just within the legal time-limit for serving a summons – and by which point the vigorous manhood of the district would have headed off for the Kintyre fishing fleets?

Ivory agreed that this was sensible. He continued to plan his expeditionary force, and declared that he himself would be at the head of it. In the end, on the morning of 19 April 1882, he was actually at its tail, bumping up the road in a cosy carriage, behind sixty Glasgow policemen, wet and miserable under lashing heavy rain. They moved before dawn, and reached the southernmost village, Peinchorran, as the sun rose. The Braes folk were quite taken by surprise; their sentries had long since been stood down. The constables rapidly accomplished their mission. Half a dozen men were arrested and bundled on the north-going road to Portree. But southern Braes has two roads, looping. Above this shore road is a high road, and a hundred men and women of Balmeanach and Peinchorran were already out of bed and angrily rushing along it – in true Wild West fashion – to cut the invaders off at the pass.

At the narrow bridge over Allt nan Gobhlaig, furious women railed curses; the braver battered the Glasgow policemen with flails. The police fought back with truncheons. Had the young men of Braes been home, dead bodies would have lain in Braes that night. But they were not, and the police were determined. They made a grim baton-charge, and broke clear. In the meantime Sheriff Ivory, and his prisoners, had escaped in the confusion.

Then the policemen fell under the high road. There, months before, stones had been heaped in a makeshift munitions dump. Now the Braes people streamed about these piles. Jagged lumps of rock hailed down on the officers. More men were scurrying thither from the gorge of Allt nan Gobhlaig, and women too. The wretched policemen, with great difficulty, and much blood, somehow survived this assault. They fought their way to open ground in a desperate rush – had they stayed below this fusillade, they were surely dead men – and battled, hand-to-hand, with the men and women, finally breaking clear of the enraged people, and made for Portree as fast as they could. A local minister sallied forth to dissuade the Braes men from falling upon the town. Meanwhile, in sorry state, bruised, some badly injured, the policemen made the safety of Portree.

The nation was soon in uproar. But Skye seethed with rage too. No one in any position of authority felt safe. Even the bench in Inverness grew nervous. When the prisoners of Braes went on trial, the authorities dared not risk a prison sentence. They were released on payment of fines – immediately settled by the subscriptions of public admirers. London, meantime, decided that this was the end of civilisation as it knew it. Troops and gunboats were sent to Skye, with all the more urgency when Whitehall heard the news from Glendale.

For that new notice in the store had read, 'We, the tenants of the estate of Glendale, do hereby warn each other to meet at Glendale Church on the seventh day of February, at about one p.m., for the purpose of stating our grievances publicly.' The men of the district duly did. Their leader was a man called John MacPherson, already namely as an agitator for crofting rights. 'It would be as easy to stop the Atlantic Ocean,' MacPherson declared, 'as to stop the present agitation until justice has been done to the people.' The men of Glendale signed a compact, and petitioned their landlord for a return of bitterly missed grazings at Waterstein. Their crave was refused; who did these common folk think they were? So they went on rent strike. And drove their beasts on to the Waterstein farm. Writs were quickly obtained by the estate from the Court of Session in Edinburgh. But against such a solid front the documents could not be served. A party of policemen was driven from Glendale too.

Sheriff Ivory was quick, again, to call for armed action, for the arrest and exemplary treatment of ringleaders. But Ivory's credibility was fast thinning. Already, under pressure from Cameron of Lochiel, the Braes folk had been granted Ben Lee – if at a steep rent. A local, Gaelic-speaking official was despatched to Glendale, where he persuaded the leaders of the movement voluntarily to attend trial in Edinburgh. And they left on the McCallum Orme steamer, *Dunara Castle*; not on HMS *Jackal*: 'a victory for tact and common sense'. Three men were given jail terms of three months, earning MacPherson the soubriquet of 'Glendale Martyr'. The dismay in that place was shortly offset by startling news from London.

The government of William Gladstone was, at heart, humane and wise. And the ministers were rapidly repairing a sublime ignorance of Highland affairs. They had begun to sense the truth, as W. H. Murray writes, 'that since 1746 there had been a gross dereliction of government, both local and central'. The rule of law was in utter disrepute throughout the Highlands and Islands. Besides, public opinion was outraged. There were manifest injustices in need of correction. It was, therefore, in 1883 announced that a royal commission was to tour the Highlands and Islands and examine all crofting grievances.

The commission was headed by a Scotsman, Francis, Lord Napier, who had served as Governor-General of India. He was joined by Cameron of Lochiel. The Liberal MP for Inverness Burghs, Charles Fraser Mackintosh, also joined; the commission had been granted in large part because of a memorial he and twenty other Scottish Liberal MPs had signed and laid before the Home Secretary. Sir Kenneth Mackenzie of Gairloch served – of the house of Osgood. There was the Professor of Celtic at the University of Edinburgh, Colonsay-born Donald Mackinnon. And there was Alexander Nicolson, Skye-born sheriff at Kirkcudbright, and a pioneer of climbing in Skye; Sgurr Alasdair, highest of the Cuillin, is named for him. The Gaelic speaker who had mediated in the Glendale conflict, Malcolm MacNeill, was appointed secretary to the royal commission. Napier was its only non-Highland member. Half their number spoke Gaelic. But Donald Mackinnon, to his credit, refused to serve until he was permitted to minute his protest that three landlords had been granted seats, which he (and many others) felt most inappropriate. There were no crofting representatives, after all.

But the Napier Commission was still manned by men of substance and ability, men determined to pursue truth and press for justice. They convened for their first hearing at Braes, in May 1883. Over the months that followed, through all manner of conditions and difficulties – they even suffered shipwreck, off Stornoway – Napier and his colleagues travelled the length and breadth of the Highlands. Skye, the Outer Isles,

Orkney, Shetland, western Sutherland, and Ross and Inverness-shire and Argyll. They went to the North Highlands and the East Highlands and to such remote islets as St Kilda and Foula. Their work was accomplished in simple fashion. In each district they intimated a public meeting, and all who wished to attend were free to come and make complaint or bear witness. An interpreter was always on hand for those who preferred to speak – or could only speak – in Gaelic.

The volumes of evidence gathered by the commission – a fine facsimile edition was published in Ireland, some years ago – still make fascinating reading. Many tales of exploitation and woe are recorded in them. Much of the detail of daily life of the time is minuted for posterity. The fear of landlords and their agents is manifest; at Braes, and in other districts, some refused to utter a word until a factor present had been bound by the chair to undertake no mischief would befall them for speaking their minds. It is tempting to plunder these records for detailed accounts of the Clearances, but this must be done with caution. The mass evictions were long over, the tales had been apt to improve in the telling, and few of those who spoke of them to Napier and his colleagues had actually witnessed such events with their own eyes.

Within a year the Napier Commission had concluded its business, and presented its compiled report to parliament, disclosing 'a state of misery, of wrongdoing, and of patient longsuffering, without parallel in the history of our country'. The report was published on 28 April 1884, with five volumes of gathered evidence. The royal commission called for regulated crofting townships, their bounds recorded and fenced, their roads half paid by the landlord. Full free access was to be granted each tenant to the gathering and use of peats, thatch, heather and seaware. If a sheriff were persuaded, in due process, that a township was overcrowded, he could compel the landlord to enlarge its bounds. If it seemed more fitting to create new townships, government grants should be made available for this purpose. Most of all, a crofter must be granted compensation for all permanent improvements, should he relinquish (or be evicted from) his tenancy.

The Napier Commission did not, however, believe in security of tenure, save for crofters on large holdings, paying over £6

annually in rent and holding a thirty-year lease. On this issue
alone the members of the commission were sharply divided.
Fraser Mackintosh wanted this rent capped at £4. Sir Kenneth
Mackenzie sought the abolition of common grazings. Cameron
of Lochiel thought the landlord should have greater powers to
reform the bounds of crofts and townships.

Great disappointment was felt in the Highlands and Islands
when the commission's thoughts were made public. People had
hoped for more. So crofters renewed their campaigning through
a new agency, the Highland Land League. Modelled on an Irish
organisation of similar concept, branches were established
throughout the region, local committees elected, enthusiastic
meetings convened. John MacPherson, the most prominent
'Glendale Martyr', was in great demand for his oratory. Great
crowds gathered whenever he spoke. At a critical rally in
Dingwall, Land League activists rejected the conclusions of
the Napier Commission. They demanded security of tenure
for all crofters and they demanded fair rents and they demanded land courts to assess these rents and they demanded
these things now. To this end they would mount candidates to
contest the parliamentary seats in the Highlands. The franchise
had just been massively extended by the Gladstone government,
and for the first time Britain approached universal manhood
suffrage. Candidates in the crofting interest could win.

In the meantime huge rent strikes began, coinciding (conveniently) with a worldwide slump in the price of beef. There
were more land raids, in Skye and in the Uists. Unrest grew
quite serious in the Kilmuir parish, north of Portree on Skye,
and at the end of October 1884 local police, marching in posse to
restore order, were met, rebuffed, and jostled all the way home
by jeering crofters. The government, this time, genuinely panicked, and responded in a way that must have gratified Sheriff
Ivory. Fifty policemen, toting revolvers, were despatched to
Skye, and over a hundred marines. Their ship anchored in Uig
Bay and they proceeded to shore and to march north through
the Kilmuir district. But the crofters were ready for them. This,
they knew, was not a time for trouble and affray, nor could such
an armed presence be readily despatched with divots, stones and
sticks. So the astonished invaders found themselves proceeding
through village after village in an atmosphere of mocking,

pastoral calm. Women fed their chickens. Cows lowed. Children smiled at them shyly. At Glendale 600 Land League activists were rallied; but all they did was talk and vote. They dispersed, once their meeting had been closed, in a word of prayer. Some revolution.

The marines left Skye in the summer of 1885. The later general election of that year saw the ousting of three local members and the return of three triumphant Highland Land League MPs to Westminster. Fraser Mackintosh quickly cast in his lot with their cause. Irish home rule was now the issue of the day; the Liberal Party was badly divided on the issue, in parliament and beyond, and the government needed all the Commons support it could muster. The new Highland members were happy to grant it – if their demands were met. Legislation was quickly drafted, using the Irish Land Act as a model.

On 25 June 1886 parliament passed the Crofters Holding Act, popularly known as the Crofting Act. It went beyond the hopes of Napier. All crofters paying less than £30 rent a year were granted the same benefits: security of tenure, the right to bequeath the tenancy to a family heir, compensation for all improvements were the tenancy relinquished, and a new public body – the Crofters' Commission – with the power to fix fair rents. Into the hands of that body were invested all powers of management over all crofting estates. There would be no more doublings or triplings of rent, no more wholesale evictions or contrived emigrations. A crofter's house was even free of rates. And it could not be seized for debt. Nothing was wrought for cottars, nor others with no crofts of their own. Nor – yet – was land empty, but for sheep and deer, recrofted and repeopled. But it made existing crofters secure, at last, in what they held, and at fair, fixed rents.

When the commission was formed it soon uncovered further injustices. Reductions were made in croft rents throughout the Highlands, at an average of 50 per cent. Arrears were written off, up to 70 per cent. The Crofting Act is still on the statute book, and may be heavily criticised. Security of tenure, as Napier foresaw, can be a mixed blessing, encouraging complacency, making it most difficult for newcomers to gain crofts, engendering lazy and damaging land use. But it made crofting safe, and the Act has done much to keep a fair population in most districts of the Highlands.

Yet still, in Park, Lewis crofters were denied the grazing land they had patiently sought for years. In 1887 the former sheep-walk became a deer forest; the old townships the fishermen had sought in 1881 were now added, in a gesture of almost studied insolence, to the policies of another farm at Crobeg. Anger boiled over in the Lochs parish. They soon found a leader, a newly appointed schoolmaster in the Balallan township. And they resorted to a dramatic demonstration of their feelings. Early on the morning of 22 November, over a hundred men from all over the parish – Crossbost, Ranish, Grimshader, Keose, Balallan, Laxay, Gravir, Kershader and so on – marched in solemn procession into the heart of this new deer forest, some armed with ancient guns (these, it is said, concealed in thatched roofs since Culloden). The sporting tenant was away, but his wife was in residence, Mrs Platt, and with assorted ghillies and gamekeepers began berating the men, who simply chorused, 'No English, my lady; no English, my lady', though they understood every word she said.

They held a deer drive. Beasts were shot and, towards evening, tents were erected in the long-deserted village of Stromas. Great fires were lit and on these the men cooked their venison. A patriarchal old elder, from the Gravir township, said grace.

Estate staff took careful note of faces and names. There was little else they could do. Mrs Platt frantically wired her agent in Edinburgh; he, in turn, demanded that the Lord Advocate despatch soldiers. The Stornoway sheriff was despatched to read the Riot Act. For a day or two the Park deer raiders camped in the heart of the forbidden land, until the weather broke, and then – having made their point – they went home. The next day, eighty troops of the Royal Scots arrived in Stornoway. A ship with 400 marines aboard sailed from Greenock, but was disabled *en route*. But HMS *Jackal* turned up, followed by HMS *Seahorse*. Each of her forty marines was issued with a hundred rounds of ammunition. It was an absurd, and dangerous, show of strength. A wise local policeman, with many assurances of good treatment, eventually persuaded some of the ringleaders to submit to arrest. They were sent for trial to distant Edinburgh, but to no avail. The men were acquitted by an amused court, carried about the streets before cheering crowds on the shoulders of Highland students, and were royally entertained by the city before returning in quiet triumph to their native island.

Orinsay was, at length, recrofted and resettled.

It was not long before the public demanded the break-up of more great sheepwalks and deer forests. Under new pressure, parliament in 1897 passed another measure, the Congested Districts (Scotland) Act. The Congested Districts Board had the power, and the money, to put crofters on land, to grant stock, fencing, houses and seed. In a decade or two, the benefits of all this would be seen. The quality of Highland sheep and cattle improved beyond recognition. Houses, now that there was no fear of abiding eviction, began rapidly to improve. Existing black houses were upgraded, given windows, gables and chimneys. Later, on generous fifty-year loan terms, crofters began to erect houses of the approved 'Board' type – the classic, one-and-a-half-storey, storm-windowed Highland cottage.

Poverty remained. Simplicity was prevalent, but the days of bondage and slavery had gone for ever.

By the Second World War the west side of Harris lived again. The people, under the auspices of the Congested Districts Board, settled once more on the Atlantic shore. Today Luskentyre, Seilebost, Borve, Scarista and all the old townships are again crofted and peopled. Lights shine at night from the windows of good houses. Cattle stand on the tidal flats; poppies flutter on the machair land. The empty, sheep-ridden desert of the Clearances is forgotten.

The Bays of Harris are a declining district, full of empty houses and half-dead townships, but Scalpay – despite manifest problems: Church troubles, local feuds, and a fishing industry in present decline – remains a populous community, humming with children and young people, still with high percentages of church attendance and spoken Gaelic, still a seething, lively place of human life and human conflict. The people have adapted well. Quite a few Gaelic songs have been written in praise of the island. The wealth harvested from the sea, over generations, has been ploughed into fine houses and big cars. Soon the little ferry from Kyles will be history, as a new road bridge takes shape over Scalpay Sound. Recently the islanders built a fine new community centre. Money was invested in the herring fishing, and as that failed the Scalpaich turned to prawn fishing, and the harvest of velvet crabs, and today to static gear fishing generally and the dredging of scallops from the ocean floor.

Scalpay has a shop, a filling station, a knitwear co-operative, two churches, a district nurse, a clinic, a primary school and a junior secondary school.

Pabbay, from whence the Scalpay people came, has never been repeopled.

There are still some very old women on Scalpay who have never left the island in their lives. In 1991 a Scalpay lady died who, almost certainly, was the last true Gaelic monoglot in Scotland – a woman who never spoke, and appears never to have learned, a word of English. But some day even such must leave their native island.

For Scalpay has no burial ground. And, when a Scalpach dies, and the obsequies of funeral worship are done, a hearse drives on and over the Kyles ferry, and away through Harris to the cemetery at Luskentyre, in the west. Here the Scalpaich are laid to rest, by white sands and open blue ocean and rolling dunes of marram and the flower-strewn sward of the machair. It is terrain quite alien to Scalpay; but it is the same landscape from which their hapless forebears were driven, one and a half centuries ago.

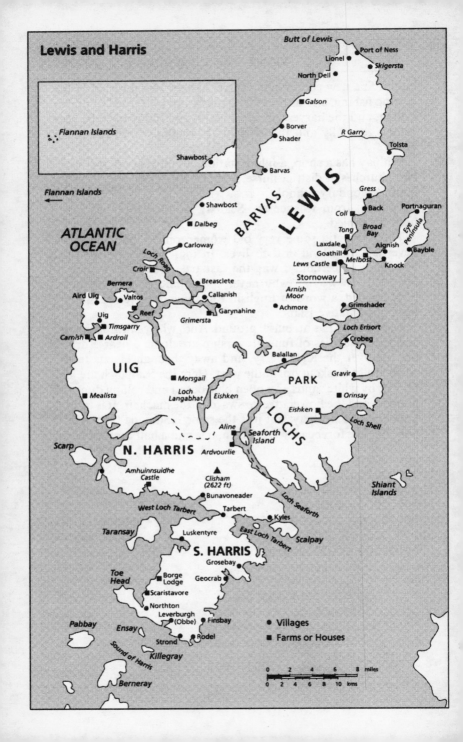

CHAPTER TEN

To An Honoured Rank

Togaibh i, togaibh i, canain ar duthcha
Togaibh a suas i gu h-inbhe ro-chliutich
Togaibh go daingean i 's bithibh rith baigheil
Hi ho-ro togaibh i, suas leis a' Ghaidhlig

'S i canain na h-oige, 's i canain na h-aois
B' i canain ar sinnsir, b 'i canain an gaoil
Ged tha i nis aosd tha i reachdmhor is treun
Cha do chaill i a cli, 's cha do striochd i fo bheum

Exalt it, exalt it, language of our country
Lift it up to an honoured rank
Praise it hard and treat it with affection
Hi ho ro, lift it up, up with the Gaelic

It is the language of youth, the language of great age
It was the language of our fathers, language of love
Though it is old now it is mighty and noble
Not stripped of its vigour, not overcome by aversity

From 'Suas Leis a' Gaidhlig', 'Up With the Gaelic'. The anthem of An Comunn Gaidhealachd,
sung at the closing of Mod sessions and other events. Words by Donnchadh Raoideach.

BY THE END OF THE nineteenth century popular awareness of the Highlands had at last moved away from the fantasies of MacPherson and Scott to some genuine interest in the language, music and culture of the Highland people. From the enthusiastic adoption of tartan, bagpipes, dancing, and Highland field sports, a good many proceeded to explore the real folk traditions, to study the language, to try and record song, story and fable before it was lost for ever. There also rose, in the Victorian period, much interest in the mystical; in the supernatural and the occult. Spiritualism became fashionable. Arthur Conan Doyle and others began to dabble in seances and necromancy. Even Queen Victoria, it is said, tried to contact the shade of the blessed Albert; some attribute to the supposed abilities of John Brown in this field of communication the hold he established over the queen.

The Neo-Raphaelites, and others, grew fascinated by the 'uncanny'. It was an age, after all, when the theological certainties that had bound British thought for centuries began to crumble. The work of Darwin – and the most inadequate response of the Churches to his ideas – had, many thought, disproved the authority of the Old Testament. So the Christian faith was increasingly stripped of its supernatural elements; as man is incurably superstitious, men and women were eager to find mystery and wonder in other fields. The rich pastures of Highland lore – its witches, its fairies, its incantations, its tales of enchantment, second sight and Tir nan Og, the land of the ever young – were greatly tempting.

Besides, too, there was now a considerable number of

Highlanders in the Lowlands, and in the great cities of the empire. Many had 'done well'; they occupied prosperous positions in urban society. But such had a deep-rooted need to maintain some identification with their culture. So from every great city arose local Highland societies. Glasgow alone had a Skye Association, and a Lewis and Harris Association. Inevitably these organisations developed a most rosy view of the world they had left. They sang Gaelic songs to piano accompaniment. Or they formed choirs to sing in four-part harmony. The dances, too, were the prettified, simplified products of the age, owing more to Balmoral than to the native jigs and reels of the north. It is easy to mock such bodies, or their surviving heirs in our own day – the men in full Highland dress, the ladies in ankle-length tartan skirts, the suppers of scones and jam, potatoes and herring. But, in their own sweet and sentimental way, they did much good.

Take Marjory Kennedy-Fraser. Today she is widely derided for her labours in popularising Gaelic song – the melodies much simplified, lyrics reduced to the banal and the self-consciously fey, all harmonised to shimmering accompaniment on the pianoforte and fitted best for singing by large ladies in metropolitan parlours. Born in Perthshire in 1857, Kennedy-Fraser came from a large and musical family. Her father was a noted singer, and she used to go about with him as a girl; through these tours, she developed an interest in Gaelic and in Gaelic music. She studied Gaelic under a noted Lochaber poet, Mary Mac-Kellar, and in middle age took under her tutelage the young Kenneth MacLeod, a native of Wester Ross. He collaborated with her in her life's achievement, *Songs of the Hebrides*, a mighty collection of Gaelic songs strained and softened through their musical tastes and served up for public enjoyment and edification. For raw material, Kennedy-Fraser travelled widely in the islands, listening to all sorts of singers, noting every tune and verse that took her fancy. But each was determinedly processed and adapted for publication in her folios.

It is easy to laugh at these songs today. They are pigeon-holed with naïve efficiency in the indexes – 'Love Songs', 'Working Songs', 'Uncanny Songs', 'Lullabies', and so on. Many are archetypal of the worst era of 'Celtic Twilight': dark, arch, simplistic, redolent of haunting and tragedy that happened really too long ago to bother anyone very much. A very few have survived, and are still sung in schoolrooms the world over – the 'Eriskay Lovelilt', and so on. They sing 'Kishmul's Galley' too; but one noted singer, John Macinnes of Daliburgh in South Uist, used to entertain his friends by singing 'Kishmul's Galley' in both styles. He would sing the authentic, native version, as it is sung in Barra – complex, fluid, utterly Gaelic – and then, with just the right hint of exaggeration and satire, Marjory Kennedy-Fraser's manicured version.

Most are mercifully forgotten. But Kennedy-Fraser's real achievement, and which should not be mocked, lay in all that indefatigable recording. Though she had little time for the traditional songs as she found them, and grimly ironed out their elaborate metres, their lively humour, their intricate grace-notes and plain pentatonic melody, she preserved every one of them, neatly inscribed in her files, notes and words and all. True, she gave many a false impression of what Gaelic song is really like; but she also gave the world a good many wonderful songs to sing that it would otherwise never have known. She herself never passed off her versions as the real thing, and freely acknowledged their modification for the ears (and prejudices) of those brought up in a different musical tradition.

She did it well: Kenneth MacLeod, in the thirties, joked in Glasgow of critics who had unhesitatingly dubbed 'most ancient' melody lines he had written himself. Purists are too hard on them. Thanks to Marjory Kennedy-Fraser, and Kenneth MacLeod, a great deal survived to the present day that must otherwise have perished.

In 1891, in Oban, the mother of all Gaelic associations was formed, *An Comunn Gaidhealachd* – the Highland Society. Oban is a true creation of the Victorian era: a town which sprang to life from transport links – the railway to Glasgow, the complex steamer services of David MacBrayne – and is a place of mighty villas, respectable hotels, and many a light entertainment; Oban has been dubbed the Charing Cross of the Highlands. It was a fit cradle for the organisation still, to this day, most identified with the Gaelic language. Today the aims of An Comunn – and they have little modified over the years – are to encourage and support the teaching, learning and use of Gaelic; the study and cultivation of Highland literature, history, music, art and traditions; the social and economic welfare (in 1891 it was 'native industries') of the Highlands and Islands; and the wearing of Highland dress.

The very fact of An Comunn's birth demonstrates how, by 1891, lovers of Gaelic and Highland tradition already felt that culture threatened and in decline. Gaelic had suffered a severe blow in 1872 by the advent of compulsory education under state control. The parochial and Free Church schools had been voluntarily transferred to the public spheres, and the Gaelic-medium teaching which had characterised them – at least for infant entrance-classes – promptly vanished. English became the sole language of education. From the day that a Highland child entered school – supposing he had not a word of English – he would be addressed, instructed and taught in that tongue. If he responded in Gaelic he was rebuked. Many teachers beat children they heard speaking Gaelic even in the playground.

An early concern of An Comunn, then, was education. Gaelic, in 1891, was permitted as a 'specific subject'; but the Highlands and Islands have long been unfortunate in their teachers, and many were themselves entirely strangers to the language. Many, by all accounts, would have been unemploy-able as teachers anywhere else; in the Hebrides, alcoholics, morons, sloths, perverts and plain psychopaths regularly found place as schoolmasters. One teacher in South Uist – a Roman Catholic, from Birmingham – is still remembered, partly be-cause he was an exceptionally good teacher, but largely because he kept a fascinating diary of his thirteen years in the island, with much detail of the life of his school and the world of his pupils, and published much of this in a 1927 volume of reminiscences.

But Frederick Rea spoke not a word of Gaelic when he was met on Lochboisdale pier in 1889 by Father Allan MacDonald – a celebrated collector of Gaelic folklore – and Rea still had not a word of the language when he at length left South Uist, after thirteen years of service in its schools. On his first day he found only the temporary schoolmistress, who greeted him, had any command of English; his pupils wore neither shoes nor stock-ings, and most of the younger boys wore homespun kilts. On an evening walk Rea was startled by 'weird sounds': it was the merry chant of women singing at the waulking, the fulling of newly woven cloth. He loved South Uist – he returned after a decade-long absence to carry on teaching – and concluded his memoirs by paying tribute to the people of that island, 'brave, enduring, generous, warm-hearted, true and faithful friends'. But he remained as ignorant of Gaelic as ever.

So An Comunn lobbied vigorously for recognition of Gaelic in schools. Readers and song-books were published under its auspices. It was not, however, until the Education Act of 1918 that all schools in Gaelic-speaking districts were required, by law, to include the language in their curriculum.

An Comunn, though, has never been radical and at times has appeared almost introverted. This is rather a pity. In 1884, when the Earl of Dunmore – landlord of Harris – had dared to condemn the prevalent agitation in the Highlands before the Gaelic Society of Inverness, he was howled down. 'The Gaelic language has never been put to a more unworthy and unpatriotic or wicked use,' declared he, 'than when it was employed, not as a means of tranquillising the poor people by reasoning with them in a spirit of pacification and conciliation in their own tongue, but on the contrary, in urging them to rebellion and crime.' The hall erupted in laughter; there were loud cries of 'Rubbish!' But few of that spirit entered An Comunn, which was determinedly cultural, and benevolent to a fault.

An Comunn's most celebrated manifestation is the annual Mod, modelled on the Welsh *Eisteddfod*: a week-long competitive festival in speech, literature, singing, instrumental music, drama and so on, with senior and junior sections. Oban played host to the first Mod, in 1892, and – apart from the years of world war – it has been held every year since, growing more and more in ambition and scope, its programmes and contests covered by the press and the broadcast media. In most categories of competition there is a requirement for contenders to have some fluency in spoken Gaelic, though this is leniently interpreted. Glasgow, Oban and Inverness have been the favoured venues, though there are determined efforts to hold the Mod in such unHighland spots as Motherwell and Airdrie; there was even a serious proposal, in the 1980s, to stage the Mod in Cape Breton. The huge numbers who participate, and the many more who attend performances, require a large town or resort with much and varied accommodation; yet there must be a considerable Gaelic community in the locale of the venue, to help raise funds and co-ordinate the arrangements. Inevitably there are hiccups, difficulties and squabbles, eagerly highlighted in the press.

As Gaelic has declined in Scotland, from 210,000 in the 1891 census to under 70,000 a hundred years later, so many would say that standards in Gaelic song and music have fallen. Certainly the given pool for talent is much reduced and few recent Gold Medallists – the Mod's highest award for a Gaelic singing soloist, in the trained classical tradition – have matched the ability and warmth of medallists even in the 1950s. Much more valued by the discerning are the Traditional Gold Medal competitions; winners are not publicly fêted, nor widely noticed, but this contest – in untrained singing by native speakers – is a much more valuable measure of Gaelic vigour in Highland communities.

Since 1905 the Mod has been supplemented by an extensive programme of local or provincial Mods, with greater emphasis at these on training children in music, song and the Gaelic language itself. In recent years An Comunn has developed a federal structure; there are now four regional councils within Scotland: North, South, Argyll, and Western Isles. In its early years it largely financed itself, often in such spectacular ventures as the 1907 Feill (bazaar), and its Highland clachan set-piece at the 1911 Scottish Exhibition – a somewhat idealised replica of a little Highland community. The clachan was restaged for Glasgow's Empire Exhibition in 1938; there was another Feill in 1927, and again in 1950. Today An Comunn wins much of its funding from voluntary and statutory bodies; it has many local branches, and the support of various affiliated societies. There has, since 1905, been a regular An Comunn journal. The organisation invented Gaelic drama, and did much to foster Gaelic choral singing. It has sponsored many Gaelic plays as well as many useful manuals and courses for those who wish to learn Gaelic.

An Comunn also did its bit for the Highland economy. Senior activists identified – or created – markets for local crafts. In 1929 an inner organisation was formed, a hardcore of dedicated activists, all fluent in Gaelic, called Clann an Fhraoich, Children of Heather. It in turn sponsored the Comunn na h-Oigridh movement, for children, with local branches; its main activity was the organisation of summer camps, which still survive, though now under the auspices of local authorities. An Comunn has never lacked in zeal for the Gaelic language or in much useful effort for its furtherance. Its weakness lies in its own bureaucracy and love of regulation – activists are prone to wax passionate over the precise rules governing a contest in Gaelic song – and the tweedy, be-tartaned respectability of its public image. But it would be very many years before the most passionate advocates of Gaelic would start to further their cause beyond the bounds of An Comunn Gaidhealachd.

The accelerating decline of Gaelic would be one of the most sobering aspects of the new century for Highlanders. In 1871 the German linguist Ernst Ravenstein defined 'Gaelic Scotland' in geography, indicating those areas where Gaelic was spoken by at least a quarter of the population (and, apart from some little pockets along the line he drew, Gaelic speakers exceeded 50 per cent of folk in the region). The Ravenstein Boundary follows the Highland Line from Helensburgh on the Firth of Clyde, heading north-east into Angus before curling back and north through the county of Nairn on the Moray Firth. It also eliminates most of little Caithness, where Gaelic was never strong. Gaelic, then, was massively spoken in the Highland counties – Sutherland, Ross and Cromarty, Inverness, Argyll, and all the Hebrides – but, in 1871, was still found in northern Dunbarton, a piece of Stirling, half of Perth, and western districts of Angus, Aberdeen, Banff, Moray and Nairn.

There are no native speakers alive in any of these latter counties today. We can even name some of the last survivors: Petrine Stewart, who appears to have been the last native speaker in Perth – she came from Kinlochrannoch, the home of Dugald Buchanan – died in 1991. Throughout the twentieth century Gaelic has beaten a steady retreat north and west in the Highlands. As a spoken living language, heard in shops and on the street and in the home, the medium of public worship, it survives only in the Hebrides (strongest in Skye and Islay, and massively strong only in the Western Isles, excluding Stornoway). Gaelic speakers can still be found, though, in Lochaber and Wester Ross, and most communities around the seaboard to Strathy in the far north of Sutherland. Some speakers are still

living in certain East Highland pockets, such as Balintore in
Easter Ross and Embo in Sutherland. If Ernst Ravenstein drew
his boundary today, by the same criteria, it would enclose only
the Western Isles, Skye and Raasay.

In October 1900 the Free Church of Scotland merged with
another body, the United Presbyterian Church, to form the
United Free Church of Scotland, creating the biggest Protestant
body – the biggest Church – in the land. It was the culmination
of a process which, in some regards, had much in common with
the secularising trend of the nineteenth century; the new Church
was avowedly liberal, and permitted a wide breadth of theological opinion within its bounds. The union was greeted with
much anguish throughout the Highlands, and led to a good deal
of trouble. After a century of advancing integration, most
Highlanders now found themselves increasingly isolated in
religion from the majority of Scots. There was a cruel paradox: the union, which had sought to blend two Churches into
one across Scotland, resulted in most West Highland parishes
supporting four Presbyterian denominations where, in 1890,
there had been but two.

The Crofters' War of the 1880s had shown up sharply a subtle
change in the character of the Free Church since 1843. It had lost
the popular touch. Things had come to a pretty pass when it was
a Free Church minister who ordered the heroes of Braes to
return to their homes; when it was an Established minister, Rev
Donald MacCallum, and not a Free Church cleric who lent the
radical movement ecclesiastical endorsement. But the Free
Church had grown respectable. It had become rich; it had built
mighty churches, grand divinity colleges, well-equipped missions the world over. In its pews worshipped many of Scotland's
most influential citizens – lawyers, judges, academics, leaders of
society. The Free Church even had high political contacts.
Principal Robert Rainy of New College, Edinburgh – who,
by the 1880s, was the dominant figure of the denomination –
was related to William Gladstone himself; Rainy was closely
tied to the Liberal Party, and had many a friend in high places.

The Free Church had undergone subtle change in religious as
well as spiritual character. Its worship grew increasingly anglicised. As founded, only metrical Psalms were sung in worship,

without instrumental accompaniment. Further, it adhered rigorously to Scripture as the inspired, infallible, inerrant word of God, and to the Calvinist doctrines of the Westminster Confession of Faith, which all its ordinands – ministers, elders and deacons – were expected to homologate *simpliciter*, as confession of their own faith. And it was still, in testimony, committed to the principle of religious Establishment. The 'civil magistrate' – the state – was duty-bound, before God, to support and maintain true religion in the land; to erect and maintain churches, to pay the ministers, to recognise the Church's authority in the spiritual realm, to recognise the Church courts as of equal standing to its own.

From 1870 onwards, organs and hymns crept into the Free Church, though these were vigorously resisted in the Highlands as unedifying innovations, blurring the simplicity of plain biblical worship. Lowland congregations became more and more enmeshed in pleasant – but scarcely religious – activities, such as concerts, sales of work, sporting events, cycling clubs and so on. The Free Church had long made a cult of learning, and an idol of intellectual attainment and academic qualification. The ablest divinity students were more and more inclined to finish their studies abroad, at the most fashionable theological colleges on the Continent, particularly in Germany. They came back with new and radical ideas, from a school of biblical interpretation known as Higher Criticism. Higher Criticism taught the study of the Scriptures – hermeneutics – on precisely the same lines as one would address a piece of ordinary human writing. Its graduates began to question traditional matters of biblical authorship. The prophecy of Isaiah, for instance, they ascribed not to Isaiah but to two different writers – neither of whom was Isaiah himself.

The supernatural, at every turn, was discounted, because 'science had disproved it'; if a book of the Bible predicted a future event, and if that had really taken place, then one immediately discounted prophecy and assumed that portion of truth had been written subsequently. Ministers of the Free Church grew uncomfortable, too, with the darker aspects of Calvinist doctrine. They did not like the idea that man was utterly unable, by his own strength, to lay hold on God's salvation. They wanted to believe that Christ had died for all men, and that the Atonement covered, in some sense, every human being. These notions were encouraged by the advent of American-style evangelism in Scotland, by preachers such as Dwight L. Moody, whose tour of the land brought forth scenes of dramatic – but short-lived – revival.

Principal Rainy and his like-minded brethren, in the high places of the Church, began to see the Free Church as important in secular Scottish terms as in its spiritual power. They dreamed of heading a new, large, super-Church, one that would entirely eclipse the Established Church. They resented the privileges of the latter, and campaigned unsuccessfully for its disestablishment. Patronage was abolished at length; but there was no thought of returning to the Establishment's fold. Rainy and his colleagues were no longer convinced of the Establishment principle. In short, they drew into Voluntaryism – the belief that, as in America, Church and state, the religious and civil orders, should be entirely separate. And, in their quest for building their super-Church, they began to pursue union schemes with the United Presbyterian Church.

This body was the merged bulk of small, liberal denominations in the old Secession tradition, strongest in west central Scotland; the United Presbyterians had long been innovators in worship and doctrine. Uncomfortable with binding subscription to the Westminster Confession of Faith, the United Presbyterians had passed a Declaratory Act. This amended subscription of ordinands to the Confession. It allowed, in particular, two popular United Presbyterian views – Voluntaryism, and the double-reference theory of the Atonement: belief that Christ had, in some sense, died for all men. So Principal Rainy began, from 1890, to lead the Free Church to a Declaratory Act of its own; an essential step if union were to be achieved by the end of the century.

By then the ministers and men of the Highlands were almost alone in their opposition to Rainy's schemes. Free Church people, north of the Highland Boundary Fault, were overwhelmingly attached to traditional ways of worship, conservative Calvinist theology, and the principle of Establishment. Great tension arose in the Church. Pamphlets began to circulate. Highland presbyteries repeatedly expressed violent disapproval of innovations in liturgy, of Higher Criticism, of Voluntaryism, of the United Presbyterians. Pulpit stars such as Rev Murdo MacAskill – who had succeeded Dr John Kennedy in Dingwall – declared they would leave the Free Church in a second Disruption if the tide went much further. But such were in a minority; the last great ministers of like mind in the Lowlands were dead. The Highland votes could not muster anything like a majority in the General Assembly. In many parts of the Highlands, particularly in Caithness and Sutherland, the Separatists found new life again, and began holding separate services in such communities as Wick.

The Free Church Declaratory Act was passed in 1892, though it had – under a mechanism called the Barrier Act – to muster a majority of presbyteries in support before it could effect a change in the constitution of the Church. Through summer and winter, into 1893, the Free Church in the Highlands was in uproar. The Declaratory Act was a clever, subtly phrased piece of writing; it bore the mind of its maker, Rainy himself, whose smooth and impenetrable oratory was once described as 'golden mist'. All might look into it and see whatever they chose to see. But, in law and in deed, it wrought key amendments. It subtly distanced the Church from the hardcore Calvinism of the Confession of Faith. It repudiated the Establishment principle. It took from Scripture, and conferred on the General Assembly, full power of determining and shaping doctrine, which ceased now to be a constant of the inspired Word and became whatsoever the Supreme Court of the Church might, in its wisdom, see fit to dictate. It was, too, an enabling Act, allowing full liberty of conscience in the Free Church to all ordinands, providing that they adhered 'to the substance of the Reformed faith'. That substance has never been defined; by the middle of the next century, it would be plain that clergy in Declaratory Act churches could believe whatever they liked, or not, as long as they kept within recognisable bounds of liturgy and dispensed the sacraments of presbyterial order.

The Highland conservatives – the Constitutionalists – were neatly outmanoeuvred by Rainy, and they split. Most now took cold feet and, in May 1893, found themselves able after all to remain in the Free Church fold. These included Rev Murdo MacAskill, whose denunciations of the Declaratory Act had been among the most extreme (though in 1900 he was able even to enter the United Free Church). Only two ministers – Rev Donald Macfarlane of Raasay, and Rev Donald Macdonald of Shieldaig – quit the Free Church. They were followed by some 17,000 people, including many elders, deacons and communicants, and the new Separatist groups fell in with them. Macfarlane and Macdonald convened a relief body, the Free Church Presbytery of Scotland, to head the movement; it was their adamant belief, and the conviction of all their followers, that they and they alone preserved, and continued, the tradition of the Reformed Church of Scotland and the testimony, pure and entire, of the Disruption Free Church. And they instructed lawyers to draw up a remarkable Deed of Separation, endorsement of which was required of future ordinands in their cause.

Both men, and their congregations, suffered greatly. Though their presbyteries were dominated by other Constitutionalists, they were driven from their manses and their followers denied the use of any Free Church buildings or a penny of any Free Church funds. Yet they persevered, preaching in the open air, in all weathers; it is said that Macdonald often had to brush snowflakes off his Bible. The movement was strongest in Skye, Harris, the north-west Highlands, and in the larger communities of the East Highlands; substantial congregations were formed in Edinburgh and Glasgow. By the end of 1894 the denomination had a name, the Free Presbyterian Church of Scotland. It was – and remains – an overwhelmingly Highland body.

The scale of the exodus discomfited Rainy and his party, but they sought to laugh it off; after all, the Free Presbyterian Church had drawn very few away of significant wealth and standing, and its people were among the poorest in the Highlands. (In its lay following it attracted much support, oddly enough, in certain areas namely for pro-crofter agitation: Glendale and Braes became strongly Free Presbyterian townships.) But Rainy was shrewd enough to postpone further reforms in the Free Church, like a planned amendment to the 'questions and formula' put to a minister at ordination or induction. So he succeeded, somewhat, in defusing the crisis.

But, in October 1900, twenty-seven Free Church ministers refused to enter the United Free Church. More: when the Assembly majority marched out of the Assembly Hall to meet with the United Presbyterians for the joyous nuptials, the

Constitutionalist minority continued to sit, declaring that it and
it alone was the true Free Church of Scotland, and its General
Assembly continuing. On the following day the Assembly Hall
was barred to them, the gates locked, the little group met by an
insolent janitor and stout policemen. The minority repaired to
another hall, and instituted legal proceedings. They would sue
the new United Free Church for the name, rights, properties and
funds of the Free Church.

The minority were backed by the mass of Highlanders; they had
a far stronger following, among the common folk, than the United
Frees. In every parish of Lewis, for instance – though only one
minister had declined to enter the union – the majority of the
people cast in their lot with the Free Church continuing. The
United Frees responded, at first with mirth and ridicule, then with
anger. It refused any share of the assets, any part of Church funds,
any joint use of church buildings. It tried to evict Free Church
congregations from churches, and Free Church ministers from
manses. It denied them the very right to use the Free Church name.
Retired missionaries and ministers, who associated themselves
with the minority, were stripped of their pensions, and so on.

The next four years were taken up with a celebrated law suit.
The majority argued that, having entered freely into union, by
all regular process, they took with them the name of the Free
Church and all its assets; further, the Church had every right to
alter its constitution, doctrine and practice as it pleased. The
minority opposed those points. The United Free Church was
fundamentally different, in key respects, from the Free Church
of the Disruption. It had no right to occupy buildings, or to
spend funds, acquired from the givings of Christian people who
had supported ends and concepts the United Free Church had
repudiated. But the case did not, at first, go well. The minority
lost in both houses of the Court of Session. They then took the
case to the House of Lords. It was on the point of conclusion
when one of the Lords of Appeal in Ordinary died, and the case
had be taken again from scratch. In 1904, in a sensational
judgement, the House of Lords declared for the minority.
They, and they alone, were the true Free Church and entitled
to the entirety of its assets, to every church, every manse, every
college, and every penny of the money.

The United Free Church now wheeled and screamed. Rainy

had his friends in high places; his cause had widespread support
in the ruling orders of Scotland and in the Scottish press. Having
refused even the most minimal division of property to the
minority, the United Frees now wailed their own sufferings,
their great wrongs endured to the skies. The Free Church was
widely pilloried; it was dubbed the 'Wee Frees', a nickname it
has never since shed. In an astonishing intervention of the
executive, the government itself was persuaded to step in and
overrule the Lords. A parliamentary commission was established, and a division of the properties forced. This had some
practical sense. The Free Church had no surviving following in
the Borders, or in much of southern and eastern Scotland; it had
no use for many churches and manses. But the House of Lords
had granted it title to it all and its disposal in this manner was
profoundly unjust. The Church was granted almost all its
manses and church buildings in the Highlands. But it had
great difficulty securing buildings in Glasgow and Edinburgh;
the United Frees tried to claim every single one, even where they
were but a vocal minority in a congregation. The United Frees
got all three divinity colleges, and the libraries, and the Assembly Hall; the Free Church won but the old offices, on the Mound
in Edinburgh, for part use as a divinity school.

The case wrought very great bitterness. There were grotesque
disputes throughout Scotland, and especially in the Highlands.
In the parish of Cross the United Frees insisted on possession of
the church, and refused even to share it. Then it was occupied, at
night, by a party of Free Church youths; they smashed a door to
gain entry, and the damaged panel can still be seen. The United
Free minister and office-bearers won a sheriff order against
them. The Secretary of State panicked, as tales reached him
of uproar in North Lewis, and sent the inevitable gun-boat, an
utter overreaction. Traditions both colourful and fantastic have
come down of this particular dispute. It has been retailed that
Free Church thugs sought to ambush the United Free minister
in Cross; they would cripple his pony with scythe-blades, as he
rode by, and then kill him. But, at the critical moment (it is, of
course, one of United Free descent who retails this story) the
minister appeared, pony and trap and all, surrounded by a blaze
of light and a chorus of angels . . .

In the meantime the Free Church had refused to pursue what

might seem a logical course of action: reconciliation with the Free Presbyterians. The issues of the *Free Presbyterian Magazine* immediately following the union show much interest in, and deep sympathy for, the minority cause. The succeeding years of legal wrangle cost the Free Church any real chance of union with the former brethren; the more so because it was not until 1904 that the Free Church got round to abolishing the Declaratory Act. Resentment in Free Presbyterian circles was still keen, after their sufferings in 1893. Some now foremost in the Free Church had been active in persecution of the 'seceders'. Men now rising to leadership in the Free Presbyterian Church – such as Rev Neil Cameron, minister of their huge congregation in Glasgow – were opposed with every fibre of their being to any return to a Free Church they could no longer trust, and whose practice was still dubious on certain points. The Free Church did not outlaw hymns and instrumental music until shortly before the First World War. And it was most reluctant either to admit the wrongs done in 1893 or that the Free Presbyterian separation had, after all, been justified.

Still, it wooed; and though all approaches and blandishments failed, the Free Church did succeed in luring away some of the ablest and most prominent Free Presbyterian ministers: there were significant departures in 1905 and 1917. These losses were keenly felt by Free Presbyterian people: but, while some of those clergymen were much beloved – such as Rev Alexander MacRae in Portree – scarcely a soul followed them into the Free Church, though the latter did gain some small Free Presbyterian groups which had not qualified as ministerial charges.

Shortage of ministers was to bedevil both Churches for much of the century. It would be the 1970s before either finally attained a healthy complement of clergymen. They were heavily dependent on lay preaching, by elders and salaried 'missionaries', and divinity students had a weary burden of pulpit supply, with much travelling laid on them, in addition to their classes and course-work. To the outsider, both denominations seemed weirdly similar; indeed, they were – and still are – frequently confused, both in the popular press and many an author's Highland travelogues. Both were evangelical in their ethos and Calvinist by profession and doctrine. Both practised 'purity of worship'; unaccompanied Psalm-singing, standing for prayer, exclusive use of the Authorised Version. Both had their heartland in the Highlands, though the Free Church covered the area much more comprehensively, and in only a few districts – Harris, Raasay, Torridon, certain Lewis townships – were the Free Presbyterians superior in numbers.

But the Free Church had a significant Lowland presence, especially in central Scotland, whereas there were only four Free Presbyterian congregations beyond the Highland Line, and from 1921 only three. Save for Caithness, virtually all Free Presbyterian ministers had Gaelic, and principal services even in Glasgow and Edinburgh were held in that language. There was a significant Lowland minority in the Free Church, different in culture and ethos from the Highland brethren, and these the Free Church had to accommodate. It was really a coalition of different strains and interpretations of Reformed Evangelicalism. The Free Presbyterians were much more of one mind, and much less required to compromise for the sake of internal unity. In succeeding years, partly from the dynamic of the distinctive Highland outlook, and partly to establish clear water between itself and the Free Church, the Free Presbyterians took up ever harder policies on such questions as Sabbath observance, Scripture translation, Freemasonry, the conduct of funerals and the styling of women's hair. These were enforced in Church discipline; the Free Presbyterian communion grew stricter than that of the Free Church. It took – and still takes – a remarkably high view of the communion table. Very few of those born in the Free Presbyterian Church ever publicly profess faith, though they attend loyally, contribute to its funds and are readily granted baptism for their children, if their lives are free of open fault and their adherence judged faithful.

By 1920 the division between the two estranged sisters was set as in concrete. It has never been bridged. There were no exchanges of pulpit; few Free Presbyterians ever heard a Free Church minister or attended a Free Church service, and those who did were liable to – and frequently suffered – church discipline, suspension from ordinances for six months being the general penalty. As a plurality of Highlanders adhered to these two bodies, the region was newly distanced from the rest of Scotland. The twentieth century would see much mocking of Highland Presbyterianism in popular culture, with the 'Wee

Frees' regularly attracting attention for their forthright pro-
nouncements, and as regularly ridiculed.

The United Free Church maintained, with much difficulty, some
presence in almost all Highland parishes, though it had to go to the
great expense of erecting churches and manses in place of those lost
to the Free Church. In its Highland manifestation it had a distinctive character. Gaelic was preached from its pulpits, and they
preached evangelical truth, with great stress laid on the necessity of
personal salvation. But it was a distinctively middle-class Church,
strongest in the Highland towns: its pews were filled with grocers,
doctors, schoolmasters, and the minor gentry of the isles and glens.
Its theology, though, was not Calvinist, but its antithesis: it was an
Arminian Gospel, essentially humanist, with great stress on man's
ability, as well as responsibility, to seek after God.

It was inclined to take a naïve view of human nature; there was
much of sunny Edwardian optimism in the United Free Church,
a sense of human perfectibility, of the inexorable and beneficial
march of progress, of the wondrous blessings of science. Many in
the United Free Church were attracted to a social gospel: they
involved themselves in good works, in missions to slums and
districts blighted by poverty. They were politically active. Many
who played an important role in the rising Labour movement
adhered to the United Free Church. It had one eccentric aspect: a
vigorous teetotalism. Temperance was widely preached and
practised. Most United Free congregations adopted non-alco-
holic wine for communion services.

The Highland faithful had been torn apart in the quest for a
unity irrelevant to them; the United Presbyterians had only a
handful of congregations in the region. 'First we had two
churches,' ran a bitter saying, 'then we had a union: now there
are four.' It was true of too many Gaelic-speaking communities.
Robert Rainy, worn out by his trials and exertions, over eighty,
died suddenly in 1906. Tributes were paid to him in the House of
Commons: he was accorded a magnificent funeral, memorialised in a two-volume biography, and described – quite cor-
rectly, and with little dissent – as the greatest Scotsman of his
day. By the end of the century he was all but forgotten.

The Congested Districts Board toiled on, doing its best to
alleviate the poverty of many in areas hugely overcrowded by

the turn of the century. It is tribute to the vacuity of Clearance logic – and to the great advances in nineteenth-century medicine – that islands such as Barra and Lewis actually harboured more people in 1900 than they had in 1840, notwithstanding the famine and evictions of mid-century. Even if overpopulation were accepted as justification for the cruelties of that era, it had all been for nothing. What Highlanders clamoured for was a programme of resettlement: the recovery of deer forest and sheepwalks, and the resurrection of old crofting communities. The Congested Districts Board greatly preferred – and was better endowed with the appropriate powers – to create employment opportunities, in fishing, agriculture and industry. Like all such bodies, then and since, it was quite capable of significantly improving the Highland standard of living; it failed, utterly, to address the region's fundamental problems.

It tried. A resettlement programme began in Harris, where Scalpay and the Bays were desperately overcrowded. Northonton was resettled early in the new century; Scarista would follow, and by the Second World War all the sheep-farms along the Atlantic machair of Harris were recrofted, and reborn as communities. (The autobiographical novels of Finlay J. MacDonald give a good impression of this exhilarating period.) Of wider economic significance for the Harris people, though, was the growing trade for their robust native cloth. In 1911 the Harris Tweed Association was formed to regulate its production and promote its sale.

All the Highlands were well known for coarse woollen cloth, made universally throughout the region and of formidable durability. The people of Harris, however, were especially famed for their skills in weaving, and the introduction of Blackface sheep to the islands, in the nineteenth century, had at least this virtue: their wool was ideally suited for the production of durable textiles. In 1844 the Earl of Dunmore, first non-native proprietor of Harris, was keen to see his tartan – Murray – produced locally. His enterprising countess commissioned two sisters, the Misses MacLeod, in the Strond township to weave the cloth. She and her husband were taken aback at its beauty and quality.

The Dunmores recommended Harris tweed throughout their social circle; they suggested improvements, and set up classes in spinning and weaving on their estates. What really made Harris tweed was the rising importance of field sports in the Highland economy. The cloth was perfectly suited to arduous outdoor pursuits in the wettest, wildest conditions. It was all but thorn-proof. It had high water resistance; even when at length wet, it retained ample warmth. And Harris tweed takes a very, very long time to wear out. By 1857 it was for widespread sale through an Edinburgh agent, who placed regular orders in Harris. By 1888 the same lady moved to London and opened a depot for tweeds, so popular and celebrated had the cloth become. But it had a mystical value too, rather like the burgeoning cult of Scotch whisky.

Each web of tweed was unique, by colour and sett. It was made at home in what London society dreamed of as delight-fully romantic conditions; all the processes were carried out by hand. The wool was washed in streams outside the weaver's cottage; it was dyed from natural colourants – mosses, lichens, soot – in big black three-legged pots, set on open peat fires by these same streams. Carding, spinning and weaving were like-wise done in the native black house, lending every tweed the faint but recognisable whiff of peatsmoke. There were other subtle hints in that aroma which, fortunately, most customers did not recognise: weavers conserved stale urine in great tubs, as the ammoniacal liquor was the best thing to hand for 'fulling' – tightening – the finished cloth.

Local merchants in Harris, and in Lewis too, seized on the trade. Shopkeepers led many island communities, and through Stornoway could develop mainland contacts and outlets. Their role in the trade was important, but they were apt to abuse their position. One Lewis merchant, in the Shawbost township, was most reluctant to pay his weavers in cash: rather, he paid them in kind – pressing upon them groceries and goods – and, of course, they were charged at the retail price for those, though only paid wholesale terms for tweed. Lewis was slow to enter the industry; employment opportunities, after all, were much more abundant than in Harris – the various schemes and public boards under Sir James Matheson, the many service industries of Stornoway. But, inevitably, Lewis was brought in, for demand for Harris tweed now far exceeded the available supply.

The new industry – the first successful enterprise of its kind in the West Highlands – had two disadvantages. While much of the appeal of Harris Tweed lay in the domestic cosiness of its manufacture, it was a most inefficient way of producing cloth in large quantities. Further, Harris Tweed's fame had led to widespread imitation, throughout Scotland and indeed the Empire: much of the copied cloth was of greatly inferior quality, and this threatened the product's reputation. Harris Tweed needed trademark protection; further, without sacrificing its traditional appeal, some way had to be found of simplifying and expanding its production. Carding was the slowest, and most unpleasant, part of its manufacture. So wool was sent across to the mainland for carding; it quickly became clear, though, that this damaged the Hebridean image of the cloth. In 1900, then, the new Harris proprietor, Sir Samuel Scott, opened a water-powered carding mill at Tarbert. Three years later a similar plant was built at Stornoway. In the meantime, various charitable and benevolent agencies – the Scottish Home Industries Association, the Crofters' Agency, An Comunn Gaidhealachd – encouraged the creation of more depots for distribution and sale of tweeds. The Congested Districts Board appointed a peripatetic instructor, under whose aegis weaving was greatly improved. Imaginative and appealing setts of cloth were devised. The 'flying shuttle' made weaving much simpler (on the traditional wooden loom of the islands, the shuttle was only a sheep's shin bone, thrown by hand).

The Board awarded grants for better looms. To Uig, too – where a depot had been established to foster the industry in west Lewis – great black pots were despatched, paid for by Board funds. These allowed the uniform dying of much larger quantities of wool, and thus more consistent pattern in a large web of cloth. More and more, Lewis was drawn into the industry, which had long since outstripped the available time and energy of Harris weavers. In 1899 there were only fifty-five looms in Lewis. In 1906 there were 161. By 1911 there were 300. Enterprise, alas, was not confined to Lewis: 1906 saw the conviction of a Londoner selling as 'Harris Tweed' cloth unmistakably woven on a power loom.

Now carding was not the brake: the problem was spinning, for island women could not produce sufficient yarn from their traditional wheels. The import of cheap mill-spun yarn was resorted to;

further, Lewis weavers, new to the industry, were falling far short of Harris skill. Lewis tweed of this era was distinctly inferior, so much so that the name 'Stornoway Tweed' was coined for the poor cloth. The position was untenable, and threatened the reputation of the whole industry, so strenuous measures were taken to supply better yarn. The spinning was brought to Stornoway, with a big carding and spinning mill opened. Product quality improved, and Lewis Tweed recovered its integrity.

What had been strictly a domestic craft in Lewis now became a major source of employment; it also became increasingly a male employment, for though the flying shuttle greatly speeded the work, the loom's operation demanded much more strength. Weaving was now done largely on a commission basis: producers in Stornoway supplied yarn (bought locally or on the mainland) and ordered tweeds from pet weavers, the yarn and tweed remaining at all times their property. In the meantime the cottage industry in Harris continued on traditional lines. Both were marketed as Harris Tweed, but the Harris cloth was widely judged the better, and it was also much more expensive to produce: Francis Thompson costs Lewis tweed at twenty-one shillings per web, and perhaps thirty-six shillings for the Harris product, still largely made from hand-spun yarn. It was hard lines for Harris, and the Harris merchants clamoured for regulation and a properly policed trademark.

They had great difficulty in persuading the Board of Trade that there was a need for greater control; Harris, then as now, has a much smaller population than Lewis, and much less of a noise in the world. In 1909, in alliance with the non-profit-making associations who had done so much for the industry, they applied to the authorities for a trademark, defining Harris Tweed as 'tweed, hand-spun, hand-woven and dyed and finished by hand in the Outer Hebrides'. The isle of manufacture should be added to the mark as appropriate. This demand the Board of Trade accepted. Hence, in 1911, the Harris Tweed Association was born. It consisted of representatives of each Harris merchant, the Crofters' Agency and the Scottish Home Industries Association. In 1912, it was expanded to include representation of certain Stornoway merchants who could satisfy the association that they produced good, reputable cloth in terms of the trademark. The Harris Tweed Association still exists, and all cloth sold as Harris tweed must bear its distinctive trademark, an orb surmounted by a cross; it is stamped, by association inspectors, on every three yards of finished cloth. But there were many more battles to come.

The reign of Edward VII saw a continued expansion of the Highland population in Glasgow and other parts of the Lowlands. Of course, there had been southern migration for centuries, with a significant drift under constant way since the reign of James VI. Many then found employment as casual labourers, particularly as carters and sledders in city ports. Glasgow increasingly offered seasonal employment as it enlarged its coasts in the eighteenth and nineteenth centuries. Some Lowland communities became almost Highland towns: Greenock is a striking example. By the end of the eighteenth century over a quarter of its population were of Highland birth. Gaelic services were held in Greenock churches, and would survive until long after the Second World War; the town even supported a healthy Free Presbyterian congregation.

Migration, as Michael Lynch points out, met the needs of the two distinct zones of Highland society. Large-scale farming came into the East Highlands, particularly Easter Ross and eastern districts of Inverness, and migration allowed much more commercial management of the area's rich farmland. For most West Highland communities, migration was a necessity. In the Hebrides and along the western seaboard, life was always precarious; into our own century, many lived on the very margin of subsistence. A wet summer, and a bad harvest, meant hunger and hardship through winter. The less mouths to feed, the better, and – added to the shortage of crofting land – there was great social pressure on the young and single to migrate south for work. But this movement remained, for a long time, stubbornly seasonal. Many found work on Lowland farms at harvest time, but returned home for winter. Others followed the fishing; women found good work in the herring trade. It was a merciful providence that saw the worst years of Highland famine coincide with new job opportunities, particularly canal and railway construction. There were as many Highland navvies in the 1840s as Irish. Labouring jobs of every variety abounded in the cities and along the docks and quays.

So the young and unattached worked for a few months in the south, and returned home, bringing presents and precious cash for their families. By the end of the nineteenth century, however, a growing number had begun to settle in the Lowlands: there they married, obtained cheap housing, and made their homes. The Church was good to them: all the Presbyterian denominations created Highland charges with Gaelic ministries. They had their Highland societies, as we have seen. One district of Glasgow, Partick, attracted huge quantities of Gaels, and became as Highland in character as London's Kilburn is Irish. Partick was well placed in the city for the major fields of work: it was at the centre of Glasgow dockland, where men found employment as stevedores, lightermen, warehouse labourers, and the crewing of puffers, steamers and river ferries. And it bordered some of the most prosperous residential districts – Hillhead, Kelvinside, Hyndland – where Highland girls, demure and courteous and industrious, and often of highly religious character, were much sought after as domestic servants; they found work, too, like Mary MacPherson, as nurses and midwives in the hospitals near that area of the city.

They not only spoke Gaelic, so did a good many of their children; and these Glasgow Highlanders can still be found, born and raised in the second city of the empire, but fluent Gaelic speakers. Most tried to return home once a year, usually in the last fortnight of July, the 'Glasgow Fair', when all the city's industries and trades traditionally shut up for two weeks' holiday; so many city Gaels joined this exodus that Highland congregations all but collapsed in this brief period, and resorted to holding their services in small adjoining halls. Some, though, did not go home: home had unhappy associations, with hardship, hunger, and disease. All, if they had close relatives in the islands and glens, sent money, and this was quite important to the economy of small Highland communities.

And overseas emigration continued. Land was still cheap and plentiful in Canada. East Highland migrants favoured Upper Canada, the prairies; Hebrideans were apt to make their way to Nova Scotia, where there was a thriving fishing trade – the great cod banks, the lobster-creeling – and, too, coal-mining.

In the wider Highland region there was employment. Jobs of every variety could be found in the prosperous mainland burghs: Inverness, Dingwall, Fort William, Oban and so on. A most important industry had begun to develop in Lochaber, the processing of aluminium. The British Aluminium Company, advised by Lord Kelvin, one of the great Victorian scientists, had seized upon Kinlochleven, at the head of Loch Leven – a ten-mile inlet of Loch Linnhe – as ideally placed for the refining of aluminium from the raw ore, utilising a new source of energy, hydro-electric power. An option was taken out on the chain of lochs above the hamlet in 1894. In 1906 they began to build their plant, at times hiring as many as 3,000 men: they included Irish and English and Lowland labourers, but most were Highlanders. David MacBrayne Ltd provided a launch to ferry men and supplies from Ballachulish; there was still no road along the southern shore of the loch. (This boat, the *Comet*, was the first MacBrayne ship propelled not by steam but by internal-combustion engines, another innovation of the age.) The labourers were accommodated in wooden huts. A shop was opened for them in 1904 by a Ballachulish firm, who later added a bakery; in 1905 there arrived a post office.

A mighty pier was built. The Narrows of Loch Leven, at Ballachulish, were dredged, widened and deepened to permit passage of ships carrying ore to and finished aluminium from Kinlochleven, as well as larger passenger vessels. And work proceeded on the new factory, on the elaborate system of dams and sluices and pipelines that would direct water, empowered by gravity, into the new Blackwater Reservoir and down to the factory at Kinlochleven for the running of its formidable machinery. There was much blasting. There were accidents; some men were killed. Others died of exposure on the hill, lost and disorientated in storms and blizzards; some were buried where they were found long after, unrecognised and unnamed, and gravestones can still be found in that country.

Around this plant grew a sizeable community: the Kinlochleven name survived a serious proposal that it be named, instead, Aluminiumville. Housing presented a serious problem. Land was scarce and the landlords reluctant to sell at a realistic rate. In 1913 the Kinlochleven Co-operative Society, aided by the Scottish Housing Commission of that year, managed to buy thirty-five acres of ground at the cost of £4 per acre. It was thought fit to create a separate body to deal with the housing problem, administered by directors both of the Co-operative Society and the British Aluminium Company, and the Kinlochleven Village Improvement Society was born, to supervise construction. Later developments in 1914 brought a temporary interruption to house construction in the village.

Ballachulish, too, had its trade – the quarrying of blue-black slate, of which there were considerable deposits in the Ballachulish hills. Nearby Bonawe was namely for granite; later, Lochaline would be quarried for a special sand, high in silica and of use for manufacture in optical glass. The Argyll and Lochaber region is the only part of the Highlands where minerals are found in commercially viable quantities – even gold has been panned, at Tyndrum, just over the border in Perth – though coal was once mined at Brora, in eastern Sutherland.

Kinlochleven sees not a ray of sun from November to January, so high are the surrounding mountains. It had another difficulty besetting it for much of the century: though initially in Argyll, it expanded across the boundary into Inverness, and this dual control spawned a host of squabbles and problems. At length the community appealed to the Secretary of State to be incorporated in an enlarged county of Argyll, but there were years of obfuscation and delay, and the county border remained fixed. After a public inquiry in 1927 statutory provision was made for united action in Kinlochleven by the adjoining local authorities. Kinlochleven still supports a fair community, and there is still an aluminium plant; the company had long a paternal relationship to the community, and until the advent of a public electricity supply in the Highlands wired all the village homes for free power from its plant.

Many of its people are of West Highland, even Hebridean descent, seed neither of Argyll nor Lochaber. 'Throughout the years Kinlochleven has never lacked seasonal workers,' writes Kinlochleven's memorialist in the Inverness volume of the *Third Statistical Account of Scotland*. 'These included crofter-fishermen from the Isle of Lewis, strong and willing workmen, independent and trustworthy, content with simple pleasures like angling or going to *ceilidhs*. Entire families from Lewis have taken up permanent residence in the locality – MacLeods, MacLeays, MacKenzies and Morrisons . . . The mingling of peoples of differing history and language makes for tolerance, a liberal outlook, and receptivity to new ideas.'

Fishing prospered, in that Edwardian summer, as never before in the Highlands. Vast shoals of herring swam round the coast, and great fleets followed them, with their crews, and the herring-girls – the gutting crews – and the curers in their train. Castlebay, in Barra, saw memorable scenes at the height of this boom. Even the old fortress of MacNeil, Kishmul Castle – strategically built on an islet in the bay – was used as a curing station. Stones vanished from its tumbled walls, purloined as ballast for boats returning 'light' to the mainland, having delivered salt and barrel-staves. The bay was thronged with herring drifters from every port in Scotland; curing was done all over the village and about the harbour, with hundreds of women toiling late into the night. On the Sabbath the hundreds of douce Protestant fishermen could not hope to fit into the tiny kirk on this massively Roman Catholic island; but, undeterred, they would sail their drifters into the middle of the bay, and climb the rigging, and sing hymns at top volume. At its height, it was said that the Castlebay of the herring boom saw drifters packed in so tightly one could walk right across the harbour on their decks and bulwarks.

Scotland, in 1914, has been described as the most prosperous and happy realm in the British empire. Despite the social divisions, and the grim poverty still readily found if one looked for it, there is much to bear this out. Certainly, by and large, there was prosperity in the Highlands and Islands as not known for many a long year. The homes continued to improve. Agriculture standards rose: cash poverty remained, but hunger grew infrequent. People still sang old songs and told old stories, even in the most religious of communities, even the most staunch Free Presbyterian adherents. And, in summer in the Western Isles, women and children still drove cows into the moor, to the grassy shielings, there to rest for some weeks and rest the croft land of the township itself, while the men rethatched the houses and tended the growing potatoes and the rising corn. It was a most ancient social custom, the last form of transhumance agriculture in Europe.

The shielings ceased and died, like so much else, with the outbreak of the First World War.

CHAPTER ELEVEN

Seas Too Great to Swim

Gur duilich leam mar tha mi, 's mo chridhe 'n sas aig bron –
Bho'n an uair a d'fhag mi beanntan ard a cheo,
Gleanntanan a' mhanrain, nan loch, nam bagh 's nan ob,
'S an eala bhan tha tamhann gach la air'm bheil mi'n toir.

A Mhagaidh na bi tursach, a ruin, ged gheibhinn bas;
Co am fear am measg an t'sluaigh a mhaireas buan gu brath?
Chan eil sinn uileadh ach air chuairt mar dhithean buaile fas;
Bheir siantanan na bliadhna sios 's nach tog a' ghrian an aird.

Oidhche mhath leat fhein, a ruin, nad leabaidh chubhraidh
    bhlath;
Cadal samhach air a chul 's do dhusgadh sunndach, slan;
Tha mise n'seo san truinnsidh fhuair 's nam chluasan fuaim
    a' bhas,
Gun duil ri faighinn as le buaidh – tha'n cuan cho buan
    ri shnamh.

Sad I am, and my heart filled with grief
Since when I left the lofty, misty mountains,
Glens of music and talk, of lochs, bays and creeks,
And the white swan to be found whenever I seek it

Do not mourn, Maggie love, if I die;
Who of us all the people can live forever?
We are not here fixed, but pass as the wild flowers that grow;
A year's storms blow them down and the sun cannot revive them.

Goodnight to you, my secret, in your fragrant warm bed;
Rest gently upon it, and awaken refreshed and well;
I am here in the chilly trench, and in my ears the noise of death,
Without a chance of good escape – the seas too great to swim.

From 'An Eala Bhan', 'The White Swan', by Donald MacDonald of North Uist, written from
the Flanders mud during the Great War. This fine writer did survive the conflict, and returned to
his native island. Known as Domhnall Ruadh Choruna, Red Donald of Coruna, MacDonald's
collected poems were published in 1969, two years after his death. 'An Eala Bhan' is easily his
best-known song.

THE GREAT WAR of 1914 to 1918 was the worst disaster of British history in the twentieth century. Paul Johnson has described it as the ultimate Darwinian conflict: a war between self-appointed master races. Certainly its focus was otherwise obscure and the issues uncertain. Its waging was characterised by grotesque military incompetence and a blithe disregard for human life. It left Britain traumatised, heavily in debt, lost in the world and already on the decline in which she has remained. But the war was peculiarly calamitous for Scotland. Scots made up a disproportionate number of the casualties, and in the new economies of peacetime her traditional industries – shipbuilding, coal, steel and so on – found themselves at a disadvantage.

The war is a colon in history. It ended the imperial dream, Britain's self-image as mightiest power of the globe. Retreat from empire followed hard upon the Armistice; within four years, the Irish Free State was established, Britain's first emancipated colony. Russia had turned Bolshevik, and socialism in Britain – especially in Scotland – took on new confidence. There was much fear, in high places, of proletarian revolt. New rigorous gun laws were introduced, in an attempt to oversee the holding and use of arms in private hands. Tanks were sent to quell unrest in Glasgow, in 1919. America had emerged on the world stage; around the same time, she pulled the shutters on mass immigration, and Highlanders – like everyone else – could no longer move, with readiness, into new lives in that great country.

Grief, anger, aspiration, sudden destitution, despair – these were the states of Highland society in the years immediately following the carnage of Flanders. The

experience of Lewis is worth outlining in some detail: in that
populous island the issues of emotion and change stood out with
great clarity, typical, if with special vividness, of wider Highland
history in the post-war years. For the Lewis people are the most
vigorous and practical of Highlanders, characterised by strong
emotion and considerable aggression and energy. There are few
more buoyant or considerable communities: and yet, within a
decade of the Great War's end, the island's society and soul was
brought to the brink of collapse.

The war had ended, for Lewis, with a blow of peculiar cruelty. At
the end of 1918 a large number of islanders in the forces – mostly
naval ratings – were released from service, and headed joyfully
for home in the last days of the old year. The Admiralty was
in charge of transporting them, and arrangements were careless
and slipshod. On New Year's Eve hundreds of Lewismen were
disgorged by trains on Kyle of Lochalsh pier, far more than the
Stornoway mailboat, the sturdy little *Sheila*, could carry. Tele-
graphs flew back and forth across the Minch; the *Sheila* duly left
for Stornoway, laden with excited men, and the rest of the great
crowd were told another ship, the Admiralty steam-yacht *Iolaire*,
had been called from Stornoway. She was coming at once; even
so, some would have to wait a day or two for passage.

The *Iolaire*, a rich man's yacht requisitioned for war service,
reached Kyle late that night, and sailed again for Stornoway in
the early minutes of 1919; 284 men were piled on board, jammed
into her saloons and crowded on her decks. There was a strong
southerly wind, and a fair swell on the Minch, but conditions
were uncomfortable rather than dangerous. Ahead, the *Sheila*
had reached Stornoway to an exuberant welcome. It was New
Year, a time of traditional mirth and merriment, and all the
happier in 1919, the New Year of peace. Every home in Lewis
tingled with anticipation. Tables were spread for the returning
heroes, some of whom had not seen home for four years. There
was still a large crowd on Stornoway pier, watching as the
Iolaire's lights appeared, distant and flickering, beyond the
harbour mouth. Then they vanished, behind the jutting peninsula of Goat Island, and the waiting friends watched expec-
tantly, but the lights did not reappear.

The *Iolaire*, badly off course, had slammed into a reef a little before two a.m. – the Beasts of Holm – in heavy seas by the harbour entrance. Within minutes, her back broken, the ship sank, taking with her over 200 men, who had survived all the terrors of the Great War to perish on the rocks of their native island. No officers appeared to give orders; lifeboats were launched by men on their own initiative, and all were immediately swamped. In any event the ship had not nearly enough for her complement of passengers, the greater part of whom were trapped below deck. Desperate men jumped overboard, to swim for their lives, but most were dashed to death on the rocks of the nearby headland. One man, John Finlay MacLeod, did make it; with him he had dragged a line, and so was able to pull across a hawser, and it was on this that most of the seventy-nine survivors eventually struggled.

It was New Year, well into the small hours, and darkness, confusion, lack of telephones, and drink all combined to frustrate any organised attempt at rescue from land. A car could not at first be found to bring breeches-buoy apparatus; the navy, incredibly, did not have a vehicle of its own. It was dawn before any ordered party had reached the shore above the Beasts, and by that time there was nothing that might be done. A navy boat took off the last survivor, at ten a.m., a boy clinging to the ship's masthead, all that remained above water. His brother had been up there with him, and, benumbed, had lost his grip and sunk from sight before the boat arrived.

Two hundred and six men were dead; there were bodies on every cove and shore about the harbour, or bobbing in the tide, and bodies were still being recovered, beyond identification, months later. One youth, Donald MacPhail, never forgot the sights of that New Year; half a century later, he recalled them for Gaelic radio. His memories lose little in translation.

I was only a young lad at the time – I was seventeen – in the high school in Stornoway, and I remember well New Year's Day . . . A man in the next house, next door to me, he came home across the moor – how he got ashore I do not know – but he was like a man out of his mind. And those in the village who had lost men – the mothers and the wives – they were coming in to ask if he had seen any sight of Donald, or Angus, or John, but he could only look at them and the tears coming down his cheeks; and he had two words, I remember that, he had two words that he said often: 'Good God . . . Good God . . .' as though he had caught on to

those words on board and they had followed his mind, and he had
no other words. It was a very sorrowful business for those who
were waiting. As the bard said: *home awaited them warm, and all
was best prepared.* All had been got ready – food and clothing for
those who were expected; friendship and warmth, the families at
home; then the awful news that they would never come . . .

I left for Stornoway – I remember it was dawn – with a horse and
cart, myself and two other boys, and the father of one of the lads
who had been lost, and we went down to the Battery, where the
bodies had been laid out for identification. I remember they had
tickets on them . . . Leurbost . . . Shawbost . . . Tolsta . . . and the
man from Shawbost who went over with us, his son was there and I
remember he was so handsome that I would have said he was not
dead at all. I remember the colour in his face. I remember that fine
yet . . . His father went on his knees beside him and he began to take
letters from his son's pockets, and there was money, I remember,
silver and paper money, in the pocket of the trousers. And the
father was reading a letter that he found and the tears were falling
from him, splashing on the body of his son. I think it is the most
heart-rending sight I have ever seen, and that was only one of many
to be seen at the Battery that day – and for days afterwards.

One distraught woman hurried from town to the shore, to join
those searching for their dead. She picked up a naval cap,
floating in the surf, and there was stencilled her husband's
name – JOHN MACKINNON. She went home weeping; shortly, a
telegram came from Kyle. Her husband was still there, safe and
well. Another MacKinnon was lost.

Carts and lorries, half a dozen or a dozen coffins on each, were
soon trundling into the scattered townships of Lewis with their
grim burdens. Stornoway ran out of coffins; a ship had to come
from the mainland with a cargo of them. The Admiralty
behaved with an astonishing lack of sensitivity. The crew of
one boat, commissioned by the navy for the task, was almost
lynched in Stornoway harbour, when aghast townsfolk beheld
them dumping bodies on the quayside by crane and sling. The
Admiralty resisted the view of Admiral Boyle, the local commander, that a court-martial be held – he was in no doubt that
the *Iolaire*'s officers were responsible, though none had survived
– and instead ordered a privy investigation. Of that inquiry, held
in Stornoway on 8 January, nothing was made public. Then it
became known that the Crown had put up the sunken wreck for

sale, only fifteen days after the disaster, when eighty-eight bodies had still not been recovered. Calls for a public inquiry became a clamour. The Lewis people were in no doubt that the Royal Navy was wholly culpable. It was widely maintained that the *Iolaire*'s officers had been drunk.

A public inquiry was at length granted by the Lord Advocate, and held on 10 February, taking evidence from all survivors, local seamen, and senior officers of the Royal Navy. It was greatly hampered, of course, by the absence of the only men who knew the truth – the *Iolaire*'s lost command – and the yacht's charts and log were also lost. No evidence was given of drunkenness on board. The inquiry's main concerns were the incompetence of the land-rescue efforts, and the evident lack of lifesaving direction on board after the ship struck the Beasts. The verdict of the seven jurors was unanimous. They found that the officers in charge did not exercise sufficient prudence; that the vessel did not slow down, and that a lookout was not on duty; that the number of boats and life-belts was insufficient; that no orders were given by any officer on board with a view to saving life; and that there was a loss of valuable time between the distress signals and the arrival of lifesaving apparatus in the vicinity of the wreck. They were satisfied no one on board had been under the influence of intoxicating liquor, and that there had been no panic. They recommended drastic improvement in the conveyance of lifesaving equipment to the scene of a ship-wreck, the construction of a light on the Holm side of the harbour entrance, and that the government should in future make adequate and safe arrangements for the transport of ratings and soldiers. John Finlay MacLeod was recommended for an honour, in token of his bravery.

No one can ever explain why the *Iolaire* had drifted so badly from the correct passage into Stornoway harbour: engines and steering were all in perfect order to the moment of impact. A noted skipper of the Stornoway mailboat, Captain John Smith, many years later, came up with the most convincing explanation. He argued that the inexperienced officers of the *Iolaire* had confused the Lewis light-houses, and taken a course too far north of Stornoway; on realising their mistake, as the ship neared the coast of the Eye Peninsula, they had steered south, hugging the shore, and been clumsily feeling their way down the coastline when the *Iolaire* smashed into the Beasts of Holm.

The tragedy scarred Lewis for a generation; it would be the last decade of the century before all survivors of the disaster had gone to their rest. All of any age to remember the events of that black New Year never forgot it; it was made all the more bitter, perhaps, in this island of seafarers, by the certain knowledge that among the *Iolaire*'s many dead were dozens of men who could have sailed her into Stornoway blindfold. More lives were lost in the disaster than in any other peacetime British sinking; and yet, beyond the Hebrides, few have ever heard of it.

David Lloyd George, Prime Minister of victory, had promised a Britain with 'homes fit for heroes'. It was a foolish promise, one government could never honour, but it was eagerly seized upon in Lewis as assuaging the general hunger for land, for the island was swollen with people: in 1911, the population – including Harris – peaked in excess of 35,000. Even the Crofters' Act had failed to end landraids. The Park deer raid had been followed, within weeks, by a raid on the large and fertile farm of Aignish: a party of Royal Marines were in attendance, and – but for a well-timed Gaelic joke by a wise sheriff – it might have ended in tragedy, for both troops and crofters were armed, and a single shot would have ignited a shooting-match. Tempers were ebbing when a party of Royal Scots troops arrived, and the crowd dispersed. Eleven men were later convicted of mobbing and rioting, and sentenced to terms from twelve to fifteen months of imprisonment.

Aignish Farm was duly crofted in 1905. By then there had been further raids, skirmishes, and bouts of dyke-toppling and midnight vandalism – at Galson Farm, at Orinsay in Park, and so on. The Small Landholders (Scotland) Act reached the statute book in 1911, which further empowered the Congested Districts Board in the creation of new crofts: over 800 people, in Lewis alone, had applied for crofts of their own. The Great War had put a hold on Board of Agriculture plans for Lewis; the Board had, in 1914, drawn up schemes for the crofting of the rented farms at Gress on the Broad Bay coast, at Galson in the parish of Cross, at Carnish and Ardroil in Uig, and – at long last – at Orinsay and Steimreway.

In 1917, with the approval of the Secretary of State, the board finalised the details of the immediate implementation of the scheme, to be carried through on cessation of hostilities. They were not greatly alarmed when Lewis was sold in May 1918, by the last of the Mathesons; Government plans for Lewis were eminently sensible, and the new proprietor would surely grasp the importance of satisfying the widespread longing for land. They immediately opened negotiations with William, Lord Leverhulme – and found themselves against a wall of implacable opposition. Lord Leverhulme was no despot, nor a man out for the rape of Highland estate. He had great plans for Lewis, plans that would remould the island's economy and create thousands of jobs, plans in which he would invest much of his considerable fortune. But William Hesketh Lever, who would die as Viscount Leverhulme of the Western Isles, had no interest at all in agriculture and little understanding either of crofters or of crofting psychology.

Leverhulme's ill-fated enterprises in the Hebrides are all the more tragic because he was a man of great ability and benevolence. He had made his fortune from soap and household cleansing agents – the islanders soon dubbed him, in Gaelic, the Wee Soap Mannie – and proved himself one of the great and paternal Victorian capitalists. And he had built a model village for workers in Cheshire, and named it Port Sunlight, after his best-known product. It was Lord Leverhulme who first sold soap in packaged bars, rather than loose by pound-weight, and so – by the consistent quality of the product, and the appeal of its bright packaging – created and maintained a huge market. It was Leverhulme, too, who first remarked, 'half my advertising is wasted, but I don't know which half,' though it is often attributed to Henry Ford. He was a man of grand visions. Leverhulme was bluff, friendly, energetic and kind. But his discussions with islesmen were hampered by his acute physical deafness. And he simply could not understand the Highlander's craving for land. Lewismen wanted crofts; further, the crofting life was incompatible with full-time toils on the sea.

Leverhulme's dream was to make Lewis the base for a massive fishing industry. Stornoway would be a new super-port, where his ships and crews would land fish by the ton, and where great new factories would process and can the same fish. From the island, ships and lorries and vans would bear fish throughout Britain, the main outlet being Leverhulme's very own 'MacFisheries' chain of shops. The scale of Leverhulme's dream still makes one reel. Not a detail had escaped him. Stornoway was to be largely demolished, levelled and rebuilt, with arcades and parks and libraries and every kind of improving amenity. Nor would the islanders merely fish, or can: he proposed such further, ancillary industries as land reclamation, reforestation, handloom weaving, basket making, poultry farming, the building of a railway network, the construction of new roads. Leverhulme 'wanted to have a happy and prosperous resident population, with each family earning, as a result of his development schemes, as many pounds as they then earned in shillings', writes Donald MacDonald. 'He was horrified to discover that the women carried eighty lb. creels of peats when the women of the Congo were only allowed, by law, to carry forty-four lb . . .' Leverhulme had the foresight, too, to see a looming change in national taste, and that soon the British would no longer eat salt herring – hence his interest in canning fresh fish.

Leverhulme, in short, planned to turn Lewis to an urban economy, the great mass of her population concentrated in Stornoway, at the heart of a booming and largely self-sufficient community. He disagreed violently with the board schemes for the crofting of Galson and Gress, for these were the very farms he had identified as most suited to producing milk for the people of the brave new town. The board's schemes, he argued, would cost £75,000 – a huge waste of public money. Barely 150 crofts would result, all of them uneconomic, all of them without abiding value to the community, and in any event not nearly enough crofts to meet present demand. So the peer refused to co-operate with the Board. And the soapbaron made plain that, should they proceed with their proposals, he would forthwith abandon his plans and withdraw from Lewis. After much thought, the Board of Agriculture decided to go along with him. Leverhulme was, after all, preparing to invest vast quantities of money in the island. So the crofting plans were deferred; but no one in government had reckoned with the intensity of veteran feeling.

Leverhulme is a woeful figure, because he had a genuine interest in the island's good, and sought nothing for himself save the glory and satisfaction of regenerating the fortunes of

Lewis. He was much maligned for his pains, and remains much misunderstood. The early phase of his Lewis project shows the scale of his ambition. Fine new houses were built on the outskirts of Stornoway. A road was begun to Arnish, and from Tolsta to Ness. Much was spent on the upgrading of harbour facilities. Construction of the canning factory began. On an island where horse and gig remained near universal as wheeled transport, cars and lorries began to land in large numbers. There had never been so many islanders engaged in lucrative employment. But a minority of veterans – a couple of hundred – continued to chafe. Land settlement programmes were in full swing throughout the Highlands. Areas of Skye long cleared were being recrofted. There were land raids under way in other islands – Raasay, Vatersay – and although retribution was swift, treatment of offenders was markedly lenient. It mattered little to such that Leverhulme was spending tens of thousands in Lewis – £200,000 in 1919 alone – or that so many island men now had jobs. They were aware of nothing but their own hunger for crofts.

There was talk of land raids, especially near the lush swards of the machair farms on the Broad Bay coast, Tong and Coll and Gress. And some put their names to a menacing letter, which was shortly laid before the concerned Sir Robert Munro, Secretary of State for Scotland:

Sir,

We thought it necessary to inform you of our firmly Determination concerning small holdings in the Island of Lewis. Shortly there is going to be a Lawful or Illegal action to be taken by us regarding Coll Farm. Of course we would rather have it lawful but time and space can't allow us to wait any further, and we are determined to take it by force, without Delay to Fulfil the promise granted by the Government to Demobilised soldiers and sailors, the land ought to be in wait for us we are anxious to know where does the Obstacle Lay's as we are in wait on the land. As propitors are not willingly to give us land suitable for Cultivation we inform you that there isn't a landlord or even a Duke in the British Isles that will keep the land from us, that has been promised to us by the Primier and the Country at Large without bloodshed. As is in your power we sincerely hope that you will grant and fulfill the promise made by the Government and at the same time giving us our wish and saving us from any trouble that's liable to come round concerning small holdings.

We desire every farm great or small to be cut down as long as there is any of us without a piece of Land able to call his own with Fair Fixity of tenure and compension for improvements we have forwarded a copy of this letter to the Prime Minister and Dr Murray, MP for the Western Isles.

The letter is scarcely literate, but the native language of its authors was not English. What is striking about the epistle is its tunnel vision. Such a man as put his name to this could see nothing but a croft of his own as all that might be aspired to; further, it was something to which he now felt he had a God-given right. It was more than economics. A croft was a link with your past, with ancestors. It was a badge of manhood. It was a psychological anchor in a fast-changing, alarming world. Crofting was the only life these men had ever known, or would ever expect. They could not comprehend the world Lord Leverhulme sought to build; they desired no place in it.

Nor was Sir Robert Munro in a position steadfastly to deny them. The coalition government of David Lloyd George was not stable; though the Prime Minister himself was Liberal, it was backed largely by Conservative and Unionist MPs, and the Liberal Party had split on its formation, with a bloc of 'Asquithian Liberals' in opposition under Lloyd George's ageing predecessor. The Western Isles had, in fact, bucked the national trend by returning an Asquithian Liberal candidate, Dr Donald Murray, in 1918. (In true Highland fashion he lost his seat to a Lloyd George Liberal in 1922, just after the coalition had collapsed.) The Liberals, of both camps, still looked on Scotland as their heartland. They were a party noted for their interest in land economics: since Gladstone's day, they had courted the crofting vote. The government – certainly the Liberals within it – could not be seen to resile on their promises.

In March 1919 the first land raids began, on the Broad Bay farms. Leverhulme, alarmed and hurt, hurried down to Gress to meet the raiders, and delivered himself of an orotund but passionate speech. He outlined the wonders he looked to bring to Lewis, the great rich future that awaited them all in fishing. There was an enthusiastic ovation when he finished. But one of the leading land-raiders, Allan Martin – the sort of man who delights in easy applause, and has not the responsibility of affairs – followed the peer, speaking in Gaelic. 'Come on men, this won't do! That man with his silver tongue would make us think that black is white and white is black! We're not concerned with his fancy dreams that may or may not come true. What we want is land, and that's the question I put to the landlord. Is he willing to give us the land? And is he willing to give it to us now?' The large crowd roared happily. Leverhulme stood and said, quickly, 'The answer is *no*.' He launched again on his grand vision, but was interrupted by another crofter, who asked permission to speak.

'We give credit to your lordship for your good intentions in this matter. We believe you think you are right, but we know that you are wrong. The fact is, there is an element of sentiment in the situation which is impossible for your lordship to understand. But for that we do not blame you . . . You have spoken of steady work and steady pay in terms of veneration, and I have no doubt that in your view and in the view of those unfortunate people who are compelled to live in smoky towns, steady work and steady pay are very desirable things. But in Lewis we have never been accustomed to either – and, strange though it must seem to you, we do not greatly desire them. We attend to our crofts in seed-time and harvest, and we follow the fishing in its season – and when neither desires our attention we are free to rest and contemplate. You have referred to our houses as 'hovels'. But to us they are homes, and I will venture to say, my lord, that, poor though these homes may be, you will find more real happiness in them than you will find in your castles throughout the land. I would impress on you that we are not in opposition to your schemes of work; we only oppose you when you say you cannot give us the land, and on that point we will oppose you with all our strength. It may be that some of the younger and less thoughtful men will side with you, but believe me, the great majority of us are against you – because we want to live our lives in our own way, poor, it may be, but clear of the fear of the factory bell, and free and independent.'

It was an impasse: a collision between two very different cultures, locked in mutual incomprehension. Too late, Leverhulme began to sense the psychological importance of land to the people of Lewis. But he was a stubborn man, and – partly from the natural pride of the self-made success, partly from his sunnily optimistic nature – he persuaded himself that, given but ten years of prosperity under his schemes, and when they saw all

the wealth and comfort brought to Lewis by his efforts, the great
mass of islanders would unite behind him. The government was
in a difficult position. It had promised land; it was embarrassing
to be seen to back down from an electoral commitment. But this
man was enriching Lewis at absolutely no expense to the
Treasury. So the Scottish Office leaned not on the crofters,
but on Leverhulme, and Munro and his colleagues did their best
to persuade the tough little entrepreneur to grant some division
of Lewis farms. Leverhulme refused. He was adamant. He had
to have those farms to provision the new Stornoway with milk.
And it must be said that very many – the great majority –
islanders were in full support of Leverhulme and his projects.
Thoughtful men were in no doubt that, if he was defeated and
withdrew from the island, the economy of Lewis would collapse
and there would be no recourse but mass emigration.

The dispute grew, by the month, ever more entrenched and
bitter; 1920 saw more land raids, better organised, and determined.
Fifty men staked out plots at Coll and Gress, and began to build
houses. Leverhulme's farm managers were terrorised: property
damaged, horses and machinery interfered with. Leverhulme took
out interim interdicts on the raiders: they were ignored. When they
were cited to appear in court for breach of interdict, the men failed
to turn up: they were busy planting potatoes. Warrants were issued
for their arrest, but no arrests were made. Opinion rose quite high
in Lewis against the miscreants: many feared that their antics
imperilled the future of the island. In fact the Scottish Office had
interfered, dissuading Leverhulme from serving the warrants.
Munro feared an embarrassing confrontation. He also made
subtly plain to Leverhulme that, if these men were seized, the
government would quickly secure their release.

Leverhulme, vexed, furious at the vacillation and cowardice
of the politicians, now made a dreadful mistake. His temper –
always brittle – snapped, and as an awful warning to the people
of the Broad Bay district he ordered the dismissal of sixty estate
employees who hailed from that district They would get their
jobs back, he declared, when the land raiding ceased. The move
was as cheap as it was pointless. Overnight Lewis opinion turned
savagely against Leverhulme: he was just like other landlords,
after all. His enemies were quick to publicise it as an example of
what might befall anyone foolish enough to fall into the Wee

Soap Mannie's total power. The Board grew alarmed. They continued efforts to mediate. Could Leverhulme not give over certain other farms in Lewis, those over which the board had no compulsory powers of recrofting, in return for a total withdrawal by the land raiders? Leverhulme, with some justification, demurred mightily. He sought an unconditional retreat from Broad Bay: he pointed out that he was offering free quarter-acres sites all over Stornoway for houses, and loans on benevolent terms for up to four-fifths of building costs. But things were spinning out of control. By April 1920 defiant men had seized plots in the Uig farms, and in Park. And the Coll raiders sent another of their eccentric letters to the Secretary of State:

> Right Honourable,
>   A crowded meeting of landless ex-servicemen was held at Coll on 19th inst. and the meeting was unanimously agreed to give the land to the landless ex-servicemen without delay and unanimous. Protested against the one-sided meeting that was held at Stornoway on the 14th inst. The said meeting was formed by Crofters, Drapers, and Fishcurers, and a great many of Con-Objectors and many was blind and lame, and full of consumption until the war was over but after the Peace was Proclaimed they were all right. Now after we fought and bleed for King and Country and conquer the enemy on account of the great Victory won and the promise was made to be fulfilled that is to say to give land to Soldiers and Sailors and proper Homes but as we took 4 1/2 years . . . conquering the Germans it seems to us it is going to take longer before the British Government shares out the land for the few was left to tell the tale. But our main object is this. We took possession of Coll Farm on account of our extemities circumstances and more than that we only claim our rights as matters is not in such as it was anticipated. We have to help ourselves the best way we can.
>   Now the Government bear in mind that the land was promised to Sailors and Soldiers and also was passed by Act of Parliament as you are well aware of, if it goes by votes from ex-servicemen we are sure to get the majority . . . We hope the Government will look into our circumstances without delay and get the Land Act to work in Lewis.

But Leverhulme had already had enough. That same month, without warning, he abandoned all his Lewis operations, throwing hundreds of bewildered islanders out of work. A month later, a troubled Provost of Stornoway telegraphed Robert Munro: DESPERATE SITUATION IN LEWIS COMPELS ME TO WIRE YOU; ABANDONMENT OF LORD LEVERHULME'S DEVELOPMENT SCHEMES CAUSING WIDESPREAD DISCONTENT; HUNDREDS DEMANDING EMPLOYMENT AND OUT OF WORK BENEFIT; FISHING ALSO FAILURE UP TO PRESENT; CAN YOU DO ANYTHING TO GET LORD LEVERHULME TO RECONSIDER HIS DECISION?

And still the haggling went on: the land raiders defiant as ever; Leverhulme at times belligerent, and at others confused; the politicians watching their backs at every turn. Relations between Leverhulme and the Scottish Office rapidly deteriorated. They began to threaten him – that they would press ahead with compulsory recrofting if he did not revive his enterprise forthwith – and he demanded then assurances against further land raids, which they would not give. But the Lewis public again rallied to his cause: they held meetings, and signed bonds, many pledging – even in the Broad Bay communities – not to indulge in further land raids for at least ten years. A partial scheme of resettlement placated the chief raiders. So, on the basis of elaborate and brittle compromise, and amid a general atmosphere of impending doom, work started again on Leverhulme's Lewis empire, in April 1921, but on a greatly reduced scale. For Leverhulme was now financially pressed – at this critical juncture he was short of cash. Then the wretched raiders, when they saw their newly built black houses, so lately abandoned for the sake of peace, being tumbled on the Broad Bay farms, struck again. They reoccupied their plots. It was the last straw. On 31 August, Lord Leverhulme announced the 'indefinite suspension' of the works. Foolishly, the Secretary of State immediately threatened him, warning that he now felt entirely free to begin compulsory land settlement.

By the end of the year, Lewis was in deep distress: unemployment and destitution so widespread that some literally starved, and the Free Presbyterian Church opened a Lewis Destitution Fund. In Edinburgh and Stornoway, of course, among comfortable folk well removed from the suffering, recrimination and bitterness were widespread. Despite his recalcitrance on the Broad Bay crofts, one must feel great sympathy for Lord Leverhulme, and the great mass of islanders supported him throughout. The blame lies with the ignorance of a few veterans, the irresponsible selfishness of the land raiders, the feetdragging of local leaders and the cynical manoeuvres of the Scottish Office.

Leverhulme, with remarkable generosity of spirit, in 1923 donated, to a specially formed trust, his former residence – Lewis Castle – and all the lands of Stornoway, Broad Bay and the Eye Peninsula; the freehold of crofts was offered to each tenant, save for the pointed exception of those crofts occupied by land raiders. The rest of Lewis, beyond Stornoway, was offered on similar terms to the Lewis District Committee. They declined his offer, but the Stornoway people gratefully accepted, and the Stornoway Trust functions to this day, local residents regularly electing its governing body, and in effect directing their own landlord. But only forty-two crofters, in all the island, took his offer of freehold. The rest preferred to remain as crofting tenants, with all the customs and rights that implied.

Leverhulme repaired to Harris, and drew up new plans for a fishing industry there. He focused on the lagoon of the Obbe, in South Harris, well placed – to the lay map-reader, at least – for exploitation of the grounds both in the Minch and the Atlantic. Good houses were built, piers constructed, kippering-sheds erected, lighthouses planted, reefs and islets obscuring the harbour entrance blown up. He built miles of new road; he built, too, a fine new tweed mill at Geocrab. His scheme was flawed in some respects – the Obbe is a poor harbour, and the Sound of Harris among the most treacherous straits in the West Highlands – but great things were expected of the enterprise. Obbe village was even renamed Leverburgh, in honour of the new founding father, and the Harris folk united about Leverhulme in cordial welcome. The place rapidly prospered. So much fish was landed in 1924 that men had to be brought over from the mainland to help in curing and packaging.

Then, in 1925, Lord Leverhulme suddenly died. All work was immediately abandoned. His executors sold the Leverburgh facilities, the sheds and stores and houses, for a knock-down price; much of it was demolished and sold for scrap. Only the houses, some lights and harbour-works, the water-tower, the concrete floors of his flattened sheds, and the Leverhulme Hall stand as physical monuments to the Wee Soap Mannie. There have been calls over the years for the name of Leverburgh to be restored to Obbe. It would be most unfair; this lively, charismatic figure has as much right to be remembered in the islands as the dozens of Vikings commemorated in the names of creeks, hills and townships.

Ail the Highlands suffered, in decades following, from Leverhulme's failure: it badly coloured political perceptions of the region, and the Gaels were widely painted as a feckless, irresponsible race who could not unite around even the most bountiful scheme in their own community interest. And yet, if Leverhulme had succeeded in Lewis, and continued with his plans, his sudden death could still have ended it all – and perhaps with Stornoway itself levelled to nothing, in the hiatus of a dead man's dream.

What Lewis now inherited was bad enough. In 1922 the island was hammered by a terrific storm, causing widespread damage, even loss of life. Huge emigrations began, to Canada, and a whole generation of young islanders sailed out on great ships whose names are still vividly remembered: the *Metagama*, the *Marloch*, the *Canada*. Most never returned. Some died in mining and tunnelling disasters; some starved to death in the Depression; some simply disappeared, or re-migrated – illegally – into the USA. At the worst of the Depression, many families came home to Lewis, where at least there was some subsistence agriculture.

Harris had the tweed industry; the recrofting of the west side did much to ease the population pressure. There were also remarkable migrations within the Hebrides, under the auspices of the Board of Agriculture. A large number of Harris families were removed to the Portnalong township, in Skye, and took much of their Harris culture with them: the Free Presbyterians were able, after the war, to recognise the Bracadale district as a sanctioned charge. Others removed to Lochportain, in North Uist, where a new trade – in the processing of seaweed for alginates – gave some industrial base.

Little Scalpay, on the east coast of Harris, underwent a wondrous rejuvenation, largely due to that most rare of figures, a local Hebridean of initiative who wins the confidence of his community. Captain Roderick Cunningham had established his own fleet of coasters, run from his Scalpay base; these tramps and puffers traded all round Britain, and even on occasion to the Continent, carrying coal and heavy goods and livestock and so on. Cunningham was a shrewd businessman, and his profits were considerable. He invested them locally, in the fishing industry, offering loans on the most benevolent terms to any who wished to acquire a boat, building jetties in Scalpay's magnificent natural harbours, encouraging the establishment of a fishermen's co-operative. It was a condition of these loans that all members of a boat's crew took an equal share of the catch, save only that the boat's owner took an additional share to cover his overheads. The traditional seniority system – where the youngest hand got least – had long discouraged boys from going to the fishing. Now they were attracted to it in large numbers. Scalpay's industry boomed. By the 1960s the islanders were widely believed to enjoy the highest *per capita* income of any community in Britain. Their island still retains a considerable population.

Cunningham's leadership carried over into the affairs of God's house, and this was significant in 1929, when the great mass of the United Free Church of Scotland returned to the Establishment fold. It was a move widely hailed as a reversal of the 1843 Disruption; but in reality it was a response to advancing secularisation of society, and also the continuing decline of Calvinism and Evangelicalism in the mainstream of Scottish ecclesiastical life. Both great denominations were desperately short of ministers, and acutely so in the Highlands, where Gaelic-speaking clergymen were still in many areas essential. United Free agents even went about schools, trying to identify bright young boys for the ministry, and offering bursaries for further study at such centres as Stornoway, Kingussie, Dingwall or Inverness. Ability seemed more valued than piety; some unfortunate ministries resulted, and some (like the young Finlay J. MacDonald) advanced so far in studies with an eye to the ministry, and then followed another calling.

The union negotiations were protracted and amicable. The Free Presbyterians were invited to join discussions, but – predictably – refused. So did the Free Church. As union involved some delicate legal manoeuvres – to win over some susceptible United Frees, it was necessary both to weaken the bonds of Establishment and to win for the new General Assembly greater autonomy to determine doctrine – the Church leaders were eager to keep the Free Church silent, lest it make great protest and fight the necessary Parliamentary

legislation. Its silence was bought, with a secret deal that in
Highland areas where it remained dominant the Free Church
would be granted a portion of the 'patrimony' – funds from the
various trusts, feu-duties and teinds that had hitherto supported
only the Established ministry. The Free Church kept obliging
silence, but the promise was not afterwards honoured; there was
no written agreement, and – no doubt mindful of the inevitable
Free Presbyterian derision – the Free Church hierarchy could do
no more than quietly seethe.

A significant minority of United Frees – largely ministers and
families of United Presbyterian background – made plain they
would never return to any form of Establishment. Rather than risk
a recurrence of the 1900 litigation, a split was generally acknowledged as inevitable, and friendly division made of property and
funds, though inevitably there were some bitter local disputes. A
continuing United Free Church survived the union, very much
reduced, and with only a minimal Highland presence – a congregation in Fearn, another at Fort William, stations in Ballachulish and Kinlochleven. Almost all their Highland people entered the
union, and so became part of the new 'national Church' – not
Established, but enjoying state recognition – known, thereafter, as
the Church of Scotland. In the Highlands and Islands, Church of
Scotland congregations retain a strong ethos, and body of tradition, from the old ways of the United Frees.

There was some local confusion. The great bulk of Scalpay
people, hitherto loyally United Free, declined to enter the union.
Captain Cunningham and some office-bearers led them into the
Free Church, who acknowledged them as a sanctioned charge;
Scalpay, formerly a station of Tarbert, soon enjoyed a minister of
its own. So the Free Church had again a presence in Harris, at both
ends, for a Free Presbyterian schism after the Great War had led to
the formation of a small but viable congregation in Leverburgh. In
Uig, Lewis, where the great revival had ignited a century before,
the majority of the Established Church congregation – who had
actually returned to its fold in the 1870s, repudiating the Free
Church – now declined union with the liberal United Frees. They,
and their minister, Rev Roderick MacInnes, applied for admission
to the Free Presbyterian Church; he later repented, but the
congregation would not follow him, and the Church of Scotland
refused MacInnes ministerial status thereafter. He was graciously

allowed his pension. Another United Free congregation, in Portree, also joined the Free Church. The group at Ballachulish joined the Free Church for a time, then had second thoughts, and returned to the continuing United Free communion. These were strange and cynical times. Personality, more than principle – and the perennial hope of settled ministries – came into these local situations.

Even fishing came, increasingly, under threat, from an alien culture employing new and highly destructive technology. Ring-netters and trawlers – many from Scotland's north-east Low-lands, as well as such ports as Fleetwood, Grimsby and Hull – increasingly raided West Highland fishing grounds, having fished their own to near-extinction. They fished well within the twelve-mile limit; they terrorised local boats; they deliberately destroyed long-lines and static gear where they found them. Long-line fishing – submerged lines with hundreds of baited hooks – was prevalent in the Hebrides; seagoing boats employed drift-nets, designed only to catch mature herring as they shoaled, and a sustainable means of fishing. For years Hebrideans lobbied. John Lorne Campbell, of Canna – a noted Gaelic scholar – and Compton Mackenzie, the Barra-based novelist, set up the Wes-tern Isles Sea League, committed to obtaining better fishery protection, with exclusion zones around areas where fishing was the sole support of the local economy. For all their endea-vours, they failed. Politicians ignored the League. The devasta-tion continued. After the Second World War, the ring-netters themselves would be fighting for their livelihood against still more savage and wasteful means of fishing.

Hunger, and malnutrition, and endemic unemployment, and ongoing emigration, haunted the Highlands for many more years. Poverty was rampant until after the Second World War; tuber-culosis remained a scourge until the fifties; as late as 1947, beyond the bounds of Stornoway, most Lewis families still lived in black houses, without piped water, sanitation or electricity.

In 1923 the BBC broadcast its first programme in Gaelic; only a very few more followed, however – mostly religious services – until 1935, when the corporation appointed its first Gaelic producer. But, even as the nation floundered in recession and depression, and the aspirations of Great War veterans quite

failed to be addressed, and as the world of politics remained in
turmoil – there were repeated periods of minority and coalition
government – something of a renaissance flowered in Highland
culture. For the first time, writers appeared in a new tradition of
Gaelic realism. The banalities of the 'Celtic Twilight' fell from
favour. A new generation of young men, educated, articulate,
from most ordinary backgrounds, showed that Gaeldom could
produce more than Neil Munro's tales of feckless, lazy Para
Handy and Alasdair Alpin MacGregor's meandering, maudlin
travelogues.

Two are worth profiling in detail. Neil Gunn was born in
Dunbeath, Caithness, in 1891; and his first novel – *The Grey
Coast* – was published in 1926. Gunn wrote in English – he was
not raised as a Gaelic speaker – but is one of the definitive, and
most accessible, writers the Highlands has produced. He had a
mastery of that pure, plain style we might call 'Highland
English'; his novels are all of Highland setting, and explore
themes, and fears, of Highlanders in that mid-century period.
Gunn was a prolific novelist, writing many books between 1926
and 1956, and on that account alone deserves to be hailed as the
greatest Scots novelist of the century. Instead he has been largely
eclipsed by the work of Leslie Mitchell – 'Lewis Grassic Gibbon'
– who wrote but three novels, only the first an undisputed
masterpiece; Mitchell had the additional advantage of dying
young. Gunn's work is variable – not all his novels succeed, and
some are distinctly patchy in quality – but the book that made
his name, *Morning Tide*, the classic epic *The Silver Darlings*, and
the later *Highland River* should by themselves win him recognition as a master of fiction. His reputation underwent a recovery
in the late eighties, but Gunn novels were never all in print at the
same time, and copyright is not even held by the one publisher.

Neil Gunn worked in the Excise division of the civil service
until he felt able to support himself by writing. He then resigned
from his Inverness position – thus throwing off the certainty of a
good pension – and committed himself to full-time writing. He
celebrated this turning point in his life by cruising round the
Hebrides in a little launch, and later wrote up this experience in
the very funny *Off In A Boat*. His wife, Daisy Frew, went with
him, and loyally endured the various storms, breakdowns and
mishaps, never betraying fear to her husband, although she later

admitted to a friend that she had been 'terrified'. She had a vital catalytic role to Gunn's muse: he wrote little of account before they married, and virtually nothing after he was widowed, though he survived her by a decade. The marriage had its moments. After a longed-for child was stillborn – they had no other issue – there was a period of great coolness; Gunn for a time took a mistress, who unpleasantly told all after his death.

It was an uncharacteristic aberration. Neil Gunn was the archetypal Highland gentleman: very quiet, soft-spoken, gently witty, very careful with money – he had a reputation for meanness – and enjoyed physical pleasures in moderation: a little whisky, a little pipe tobacco, plain good food – Baxter's Royal Game Soup, roast beef, buttered oatcakes. He was an enthusiastic salmon fisherman. All his life Gunn walked, and he delighted in being fit and trim. Like many creative people, he had a restless streak. The Gunns repeatedly moved house, though it was at Braefarm, in Ross, that he produced perhaps his finest work. The author was an enthusiastic, and lifelong, Scottish nationalist, and active in the early counsels of the Scottish National Party, formed in 1934. Gunn enjoyed quiet friendship; he had a long and valued relationship with the poet Christopher Grieve – 'Hugh MacDiarmid' – and MacDiarmid's encouragement, and efforts in promoting the new Highland talent, did much to advance Gunn's career. MacDiarmid, though, was an odd, aggressive, and at times extremely nasty man; jealousy later turned the poet against the novelist, and this badly damaged Gunn's standing in his last years.

The Grey Coast, set in a north-east fishing village in deep depression, was a bitter launch to Gunn's career, born from the widespread despair of the Highlands in the twenties. *Morning Tide* appeared in 1930, and was immediately Book Club Choice; it made his name, and introduced much that would come to symbolise his wider work: its hero a boy on the verge of puberty, its setting another coastal community (where the sea is perilous and women-folk always in dread of its power to bereave), and where epic battles to land salmon, caught with bare hands, are translated into a wider, subversive Highland struggle against poverty, landlords, and the forces bearing down on traditional culture. In *Butcher's Broom*, Neil Gunn wrote a novel of the Clearances. *Sun Circle* was another historical tale, set in the Norse days.

The individual was important to Gunn; his heroes tended to be loners, rebels, somehow isolated within their communities – orphaned (like Finn in *The Silver Darlings*), reluctantly shackled to the feudalism of the sporting estate, exiled in the city, on bad terms with parents, schoolmaster, minister. Two recurring nightmares feature heavily in Gunn's novel: a young man returning home from failure and disgrace (a rusticated student, a sacked employee of an urban office); and 'ghilliedom', which to Gunn was the worst fate that could befall a Highlander. He had an intense notion of privacy; that the hero (himself) should guard his inner self at all costs. The writing of Gunn is remarkable for its masculinity, for its stress on men engaged in arduous, dangerous activity: at times he is almost homoerotic. The books do, on occasion, show sexual awareness – in *Morning Tide* the hero, young Hugh, is oddly stirred when he happens on his brother courting a local girl – but there is no explicit physicality.

At Gunn's best, his novels hit the mark with a vigour and insight that the years have not dated. *The Green Isle of the Great Deep* anticipates the nightmare of a totalitarian world captured, much more famously, in Orwell's 1984. *The Silver Darlings* is, indubitably, Gunn's finest work: a brilliant portrayal of nineteenth-century Highland culture, and of epic scale, the narrative spanning the first two decades of a man's life and ranging from Sutherland through Caithness to the Outer Hebrides. It includes splendid action writing: an epic storm at sea; a desperate cliff-climb, on the Flannan Isles, for vital fresh water. There is also intimate writing of deep empathy and tenderness; the past is present in the landscape (the ruins of the 'House of Peace' where little lost Finn is found and restored to his mother); the violent past is very near (the Clearances only a decade or so behind) and frightening psychological forces threaten to overwhelm the hero, as when he is irrationally enraged by his mother's remarriage. *The Silver Darlings* is a true epic novel, somehow capturing all the emotions and drama of later Highland history. But it is also an incisive human account of maturing manhood, of how – through the rites and perils of manhood – Finn comes to terms with his world and his own emotional reactions to it.

Some novels are strikingly flawed. *Second Sight* tries to address the cultural conflict between Lowland observers and

Highland native; it fails, though Gunn finally cracked the formula in *The Key to the Chest*. *The Drinking Well* is an interesting novel, because it abandons the Caithness coast (Gunn's favoured landscape) for the world of sheep-farming in the Central Highlands. There are passages in *The Drinking Well* as fine as anything Gunn ever wrote – such as a wonderful description of the young shepherd's fight to save himself and his flock through a violent April blizzard – but the novel as a whole fails, because of its absurdly optimistic ending: Iain Cattanach, much misunderstood and mistreated, is finally knocked down by a young relative of the laird, and on recovering from this mishap the laird himself takes up Cattanach's advice on how to rejuvenate the agricultural economy of the district, thus saving the community and granting Cattanach final apotheosis.

Highland River reprises some of the themes of *Morning Tide*: it is a heavily autobiographical book, but already showing touches of the Zen-tinted mysticism that renders much of Gunn's latter work bewildering and unreadable: salmon, hazel-nuts and boys are laden with portentous significance, as symbols of wisdom. *Blood Hunt*, almost a thriller, is his last well-plotted novel; thereafter, plain story seems beyond him, and narratives, starting hard, break down into fey speculation and odd, almost hallucinogenic conclusions. *The Atom of Delight* – an autobiography, of sorts – was Gunn's last book. He was widowed a few years later; his health broke, and by his death in 1973 his work was generally out of favour.

Gunn was not consistently brilliant, but his output was considerable and the worst of his writing as competent as it was original. His real weakness, perhaps, was an inability to portray evil convincingly; he was too given to inventing ghastly English colonels, terrorising some shooting lodge or township, and making these totemic of all that is infernal. Yet Neil Gunn deserves wider recognition than he has won; *The Silver Darlings*, at least, should be read by anyone with an interest in the Highlands and in Highland people. Had he been able to write in Gaelic, he would be much more famous – if a good deal less read – than he is at present.

The twentieth century saw the rise of a major Gaelic talent: Sorley MacLean, Raasay's most famous son, can in all seriousness be labelled not merely the finest Gaelic poet of all time but, arguably, the finest poet writing in any language today. Born in 1912, son of a tailor, and raised in a loyal Free Presbyterian family, MacLean showed early promise at school, and won admission to university: he was eager to study Celtic, but by that time family fortunes had ebbed and it was essential that MacLean be able to contribute to the upbringing of younger siblings.

There were no jobs in Celtic, and so instead he dropped the subject after one year and majored in English, becoming a teacher. He taught in Mull – where he was shaken beyond measure by the evidence of Clearance – and in Portree, and in Edinburgh. He was called up in the Second World War, and badly wounded in the North African desert, being invalided home in 1943. Thereafter MacLean taught all his working life, retiring in 1972 as headmaster of Plockton High School in Wester Ross. MacLean removed to Skye, making his home on the croft of his great-grandfather in Braes – Alexander Stewart had been the very first witness to testify to the Napier Commission – and was still writing poetry in his eighties. He also deserves recognition for his essays, which include important studies of Mary MacPherson, realism in Gaelic poetry, and the contemporary verse of the Clearances. In the field of educational politics, he did much for the recognition of Gaelic as a language to be taught, to learners, in Scottish secondary schools.

The core of MacLean's output was written in the thirties, with perhaps his most intense and remarkable work in the four-year period up to 1941. It deals with politics – a gentle socialism had hardened, by 1937, to an idealistic Communism, though he had always a strong sympathy for Scottish nationalism – and with love; two intense and painful affairs, with women he adored, drove the young MacLean to the brink of insanity, and both coalesce in his work, to some extent, as the one love-interest. Current affairs attract the poet's agonised mind: he hated Fascism, he longed to fight in the Spanish Civil War. There is much allusion to the Clearances: anti-landlordism is a recurring theme, and a hint at times of anti-clericalism. Yet, to those familiar with the Highland pulpit, the influence of Free Presbyterian preaching, and the cadences of the Gaelic Bible, are immediately apparent. MacLean's studies in English literature, especially in the verse of the English metaphysical poets, is also evident.

MacLean did not consciously write in Gaelic; poems came to him that way, and his attempts to write in English were not pleasing to him, though he did once write, 'I do not see the sense of my toil, putting thoughts in a dying tongue.' His Gaelic was of the highest order, with a vast and precise vocabulary. He was heavily influenced by Hugh MacDiarmid, and so admired the long and wide-ranging *A Drunk Man Looks at the Thistle* that he began a very long poem of his own, *An Cuilithionn*: a Marxist, anti-Fascist, essay on European affairs and human tragedy through time, with the Cuillin ridge of Skye as an enduring thread. The poem was never published in its entirety. 'It was in the spring or early summer of 1939 that I started what was meant to be a very long poem radiating from Skye and the West Highlands to the whole of Europe,' MacLean wrote many years later.

> I was regretting my rash leaving of Skye in 1937 because Mull in 1938 had made me obsessed with the Clearances. I was obsessed also with the approach of war, or worse, with the idea of the conquest of the whole of Europe by Nazi-Fascism without a war in which Britain would not be immediately involved but which would ultimately make Britain a Fascist state . . . The poem stopped abruptly with the conclusion of the second part in late May or June 1939 . . . the concluding lyric came to me in sleep in the last days of December 1939 . . .
>
> When I was invalided out of the army in 1943, there was talk of publishing it, but W. D. MacColl's objections to almost every line of my own translations of it delayed that until the behaviour of the Russian government to the Polish insurrectionists in 1944 made me politically as well as aesthetically disgusted with most of it. I reprint here what I think tolerable of it.

MacLean later wrote poetry of his wartime experiences, and these deserve wider recognition among the verse of the Second World War: they are lucid, angry, without bitterness, and marked by profound humanity. In later years he drifted into more symbolist verse, of which 'Hallaig' – inspired in the lovely, empty setting of a long-cleared Highland township – is perhaps the best example. Advancing responsibility in his career left him with little time for poetry, but 'Screapadal' (written around 1980) draws on the experience of Clearance, and the beauty of a Raasay setting, for an energetic polemic against nuclear warfare.

To understand MacLean's importance, one has only to check earlier Gaelic poetry of the century, generally banal and much of it rubbish: there is more merit in Gaelic folksong of the period, and indeed MacLean himself acknowledged traditional song as an influence, though cheerfully admitting he himself was tone deaf. Apart from the wide vision of his work – there is a hard, realistic quality utterly foreign to the 'Celtic Twilight' frothings – it brought much of European influence into Gaelic writing. Of the art of poetry he once remarked that rhythm was the tightrope linking two thoughts, the first and the last; his metrics in Gaelic poetry were largely traditional. He had a good deal more respect for the values of his background than was generally recognised. He had no time for those who slated Calvinism as the dark demon of Scottish culture, who attacked such as Free Presbyterian elders. He often praised one celebrated Free Presbyterian minister, Rev Ewen MacQueen – a son of Braes – for his wonderful, vividly colloquial Gaelic. 'There's been an awful lot of exaggeration of a kind of self-righteousness,' MacLean told Donald Archie MacDonald, in an interview for a 1986 symposium on his work, 'because these people were not self-righteous. I mean, in all fairness, there might have been some cases of hypocrites and all that, but there would be in anything. So you see . . . especially in the Thirties when a lot of people were talking and finding all the faults of Scotland in Calvinism, I was saying, "What the devil do all these people, writers and all those, know about Calvinism?"'

MacLean made a most happy marriage, to Renee Cameron of Inverness; it was in his last decades that widespread recognition finally befell him, largely due to the indefatigable promotion of Iain Crichton Smith, another fine Gaelic poet, who worked selflessly to win MacLean's work the attention it deserved. At length the world discovered Sorley MacLean. A fine film, named after the poem 'Hallaig', was made by Timothy Neath about the poet's life; released in 1985, it was beautifully shot in Skye and Raasay, with traditional music and a good deal of verse read by the poet himself. The film won four international prizes. The poet's seventy-fifth birthday, in 1986, attracted worldwide notice. A complete edition of MacLean's verse, including his own English translations, was at long last published by Carcanet in 1989. Honours were heaped on him and MacLean was in much demand for public appearances, especially in his energetic readings of his own work, accomplished with true bardic dignity, and delivered in his inimitable style. For another symposium in 1992, to mark his eightieth birthday, MacLean contributed a rare contemporary poem.

There are aspects to MacLean's conduct as a poet and a public figure worth noting. He respected the dignity and privacy of others: he never discussed, or named, the women who inspired his early and aching work. He repudiated Communism when it became ethically indefensible in the Stalinist era, but honestly never sought to hide his youthful regard for Marx's doctrine. He was loyal to his own culture, refusing to attack 'Wee Free' values, or publicly to embrace atheism; he resisted a passionate desire to fight in Spain because his family were in desperate need of his earnings as a teacher. And he ruthlessly edited his own work; MacLean's reputation is all the greater because he refused to publish anything he considered rushed, cheap or below an exacting standard. Much of his verse he simply destroyed. MacLean was more than a good poet: he was a good and humble man, gently enjoying fame, but always – somehow – surprised by it. Sorley MacLean, like Iain Lom MacDonald, should have died as Poet Laureate to his sovereign.

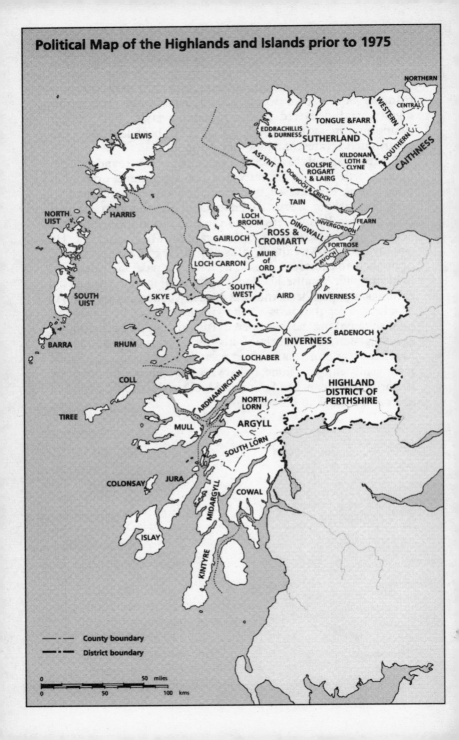

Political Map of the Highlands and Islands prior to 1975

NORTHERN

WESTERN

CENTRAL

SOUTHERN

CAITHNESS

TONGUE &FARR

EDDRACHILLIS & DURNESS

SUTHERLAND

KILDONAN LOTH & CLYNE

ASSYNT

GOLSPIE ROGART & LAIRG

DORNOCH & CREICH

TAIN

LEWIS

HARRIS

NORTH UIST

LOCH BROOM

LOCH GAIRLOCH

ROSS & CROMARTY

INVERGORDON

FEARN

DINGWALL

FORTROSE

MUIR of ORD

AVOCH

LOCH CARRON

SOUTH WEST

SKYE

AIRD

INVERNESS

SOUTH UIST

BARRA

RHUM

INVERNESS

BADENOCH

COLL

LOCHABER

ARDNAMURCHAN

TIREE

MULL

NORTH LORN

HIGHLAND DISTRICT OF PERTHSHIRE

ARGYLL

SOUTH LORN

COLONSAY

JURA

MIDARGYLL

COWAL

ISLAY

KINTYRE

—·—·— County boundary

━·━·━ District boundary

0   50 miles

0   50   100 kms

CHAPTER TWELVE

The Land Where
I Was Born

━━━━━━━━━━━━━━⟊⟐⟊━━━━━━━━━━━━━━

Chi mi 'n tir san robh mi nam bhalach
Tir na suinn, Leac a Li nam shealladh
Chi mi 'n tir san robh mi nam bhalach

A tir nan Suaineach a rinn sinn gluasad
'S i leinn an uair sin tigh'nn tuath air Scalpaigh
Chi mi 'n tir san robh mi nam bhalach

Nam faighinn ordugh gur mi bhiodh deonach
A gheola 'lo' radh' 's a seoladh dhachaigh
Chi mi 'n tir san robh mi nam bhalach

Chi mi 'n iasgair aig ceann nan lion
Is gum b' e mo mhiann bhith 's a chiar gan tarraing
Chi mi 'n tir san robh mi nam bhalach

Chi mi Manais is Ceann an t-Saile
Caolas Bhearnaraidh is traigh an Phabaidh
Chi mi 'n tir san robh mi nam bhalach

I see the land where I was born as a boy
Land of heroes – Lackalee in my sight
I see the land where I was born in boyhood

Out for Sweden we departed
Nearing the north end of Scalpay
I see the land where I was born in boyhood

If I'd an order from the bridge
To 'lower the boat', I'd sail home
I see the land where I was born in boyhood

I glimpse the fisherman at the end of his set net
It would be my joy to join him at the lifting
I see the land where I was born in boyhood

I see Manish and Ceann an t-Saile
The straits of Berneray, the beach of Pabbay
I see the land where I was born in boyhood

From 'Chi mi 'n tir', 'I see the land', an old song by John MacInnes of Lackalee, in the Bays of
Harris. It has been described as the Harris National Anthem.

$\mathcal{T}$HOSE WHO GOVERN Britain have long regarded the Highlands as a 'problem'. In the period after the Glorious Revolution, the problem was stark: the north of Scotland was a realm largely beyond effective government and a perennial base of armed support for the Jacobite cause. The brutal occupation after Culloden eliminated the threat to the ruling order. The Highlands, however, remained for many years a place of disorder and lawlessness. Afterwards, in the nineteenth century, overpopulation, famine and unrest posed new difficulties. It took the Crofters' War to change government attitudes. After the agitation, the state began at last to recognise the wrongs done the Highland people, to give them their due place as British citizens, and to try and remedy their ills.

The latter half of the twentieth century saw unremitting efforts, by governments of both parties, to deal with the 'Highland problem'. Its modern terms were plain. The region was now fast depopulating. Unemployment was a constant difficulty; the great mass of Highlanders were on low incomes, and their housing standards were generally deplorable. The bulk of the population were still denied safe, clean, running water, electricity, and most modern conveniences. Roads were poor, or non-existent; sea routes were more and more obsolete in a world of motorised transport. Voices were now rising, too, in concern both at the deteriorating environment – the great expanses of empty moor and bare hillside – and the remarkably swift retreat of Gaelic. Highlanders themselves felt these ills deeply; they were also increasingly resentful of their popular image in the world. The people of the glens, straths, towns, villages and Hebrides were weary of being, at various turns, romanticised, belittled, mocked, despised, marginalised, and misunderstood.

The Forties saw significant books, and important developments. One Gaels could have done without was the wreck of the large cargo-vessel *Politician*, in the Sound of Eriskay in 1941. The ship, famously, bore 24,000 cases of whisky, a good deal of which was swiftly rescued by local men. The episode inspired Compton Mackenzie's novel *Whisky Galore*; it was not as good a book as the later *Rockets Galore*, and it was not even as good as Alexander McKendrick's hugely successful film. Both film and book, though, glamorised an episode which was a good deal more squalid than romantic. In truth the bounty triggered much drunkenness and suffering, and envy over other spoils caused much ill-feeling and dispute in local communities. Story and film did much to encourage the unflattering view of Highlanders widely held in high places; there were, too, ludicrous touches. The film shows island men watching helplessly the wreck on a lovely day, refusing to raid because it is the Sabbath. Eriskay and Barra, though, are staunchly Roman Catholic communities, with little regard for the Lord's day. Such would have rowed out, Sabbath or no Sabbath.

They distracted, too, from a more serious question: where was the *Politician* going, and who was to benefit from her considerable cargo? Her bounty included bathroom fittings, large quantities of cash (in Jamaican bank-notes), luxurious clothes, furs and furniture, and dozens of bicycles. The episode was a great embarrassment to the British government and to this day certain papers on the *Politician* affair remain classified. It has been suggested that the assorted goodies were for a very important person – an American statesman whose support was vital in Washington, or President Roosevelt himself; even the Duke of Windsor has been named as an intended recipient. In any event, little of the cargo was officially recovered; and the wreck was deliberately blown up. What survives lies under the deep, shifting sands of the Sound of Eriskay. A highly publicised salvage effort in 1990, organised at huge expense by a gung-ho English entrepreneur, recovered only a few intact bottles of perhaps the world's most celebrated whisky.

Compton Mackenzie's role is to be regretted, because he adored the islands, and spent much of his career on Barra;

he is buried at the Eoligarry cemetery, and he twice married women from the Outer Isles. His later novel, *Rockets Galore* – set against insensitive real-life Ministry of Defence efforts to build a rocket-range in South Uist – is a much more sympathetic and incisive portrait of Highland dilemmas. The people of Todday are to be evacuated from their homes, because rockets are more important to Britain than crofters; then, brilliantly, they hit on the notion of dyeing seagulls and seagull chicks pink. Ornithologists discover this new species. There is national hysteria to the threat facing this feathered marvel; the rocket-range is abandoned, and the people of Todday are permitted to return. The irony of a ruling order that cares for birds more than crofters has good basis in fact; most Hebrideans prefer this book to its predecessor, though most cinema-buffs despise the latter film.

Mackenzie, as we have seen, fought with others – unsuccessfully – to defend the interests of Hebridean fishermen. He had no time for fools, and he especially disliked the fools who often descended on the Hebrides, to write up its landscape and people in the most absurd reams of rose-tinted, ethereal twiddle-twaddle. One of Mackenzie's funniest creations – writings and character are regularly quoted in his Highland comedies – is Hector Hamish MacKay, author of *Faerie Lands Forlorn*, a 'well-known topographer', a little fellow 'in a kilt with slightly shrivelled but well-weathered knees, a prim Edinburgh accent, and spectacles'. MacKay's prose, solemnly retailed by Mackenzie, majored heavily on lapping wavelets, crooning seals, sleepy shores, weeping mist and numinous sunsets. He used words like 'forbye', 'forsooth' and 'fornent'. MacKay appeared, seriously, to believe in fairies, brownies, gnomes, elves and pixies, and saw them behind every tussock of 'roseate moor', every rock upon which keened the exiled seal-maiden . . .

Mackenzie's skit on the genre was hilarious: unfortunately, it was true, and immediately recognisable to the informed as a pastiche of the persona and writings of Alasdair Alpin Mac-Gregor, who made much money after the First World War in churning forth fey, nonsensical books about the Hebrides as never-never land, written in the most extraordinary blend of pantheistic rhapsody, laden with arch Scotticisms, painting a landscape as by mescaline and peopled with a folk of spells and visions. Mackenzie's choice of target was quite deliberate. 'My complaint as a reader, as a critic, as an inhabitant against some of the numerous works published during the last decade about the Western Isles,' he wrote in 1946, 'is not so much of their superficiality as of their effort to make the islands and the islanders conform to a sentimental preconception in the minds of their authors.' No one, after Mackenzie's Highland novels, could take Alasdair Alpin MacGregor seriously again; his books are long since out of print, and worth acquiring second-hand only for the eliciting of great gales of derisive laughter.

Compton Mackenzie was the natural choice to portray the Western Isles in Robert Hale's *County* series, and by great misfortune he had to refuse the commission: the novelist was, as ever, floundering in unmet deadlines. The job, calamitously, went to a bitter and vengeful Alasdair Alpin MacGregor, who gleefully set to at his base in that most Hebridean suburb of Chelsea. *The Western Isles* appeared in 1949 and is remarkable for its vicious portrayal of island people. The landscape is still exalted, if in more sober and acceptable terms, but its inhabitants are libelled – there can be no other word – in sweeping statements so nakedly malicious, so manifestly unjust, that even the uninformed reader is apt to revolt.

James Hunter's summary of the most offensive parts of the publication shows admirable restraint.

The people of the Western Isles, MacGregor now tells his readers, are as unattractive and reprehensible a set of folk as are to be met with anywhere. Their 'morals in the sexual sense' are 'extremely lax'. There is much 'early and indiscriminate mating'. It follows that 'bastardy' is 'common' and 'interbreeding' even more so – though quite what it is that the two island sexes see in one another is a little bit mysterious in view of MacGregor's account of their respective characters. Island women are 'plain . . . many of them exceedingly so'. Island males are 'indolent', 'dilatory', 'vindictive' and given to 'drunkenness'. To get off the steamer at Compton Mackenzie's Barra, which MacGregor had previously described as next best thing to paradise, is immediately to meet with islanders who 'stand, in furtive groups, against the post office walls and door, chatting, chaffing, smoking, spitting, swearing, blaspheming and not infrequently giving off alcoholic fumes'. This would be slightly more tolerable, MacGregor observes, were islanders not so dirty. As it is, he comments, men and women alike believe a bath to be a 'piece of nonsense'. Many are 'perpetually in a verminous condition'.

James Hunter draws parallels between this character assassination of a people and the attitude of many American conservationists to the native inhabitants of the land's loveliest wildernesses. MacGregor's book caused outrage in Lewis. Community leaders published a pamphlet answering its most damning charges. They predicted – and, sadly, for some years it proved true – that MacGregor's work would ruin islanders wherever they went, that young Hebridean men and women might find great difficulty in securing mainland employment. It was said that, if MacGregor dared land in the Outer Hebrides, he would surely be lynched. The tale went the rounds of two young men suddenly noticing a man by the rails of the Stornoway steamer as it chugged over the Minch; his briefcase bore the name, 'A. A. MacGregor'. Without hesitation they flung him overboard. His book remains perhaps the vilest portrayal of Highlanders in the modern era, which is saying a good deal.

Of a very different stamp was a book published five years earlier, in 1944, *Island Farm* by Frank Fraser Darling. It was sequel, in a measure, to his earlier *Island Years*, detailing adventures on the Treshnish Isles and North Rona. Fraser Darling was not a Highlander, or even a Scot – he came from Yorkshire – but he was a bright young naturalist with an intense interest in the ecology and environment of north-west Scotland. His work on the sociology of red deer, and later of Atlantic Grey seals, remains definitive; in one of life's pleasant ironies, he was funded in his early field studies by a grant from a foundation established by Lord Leverhulme. He was most disappointed in the autumn of 1938, when he was compelled to accept evacuation from North Rona at the height of the Munich crisis, on the brink of completing a full year's surveillance of the island's considerable seal population.

Island Farm is a memoir of Fraser Darling's experiment on Tanera Mor, largest of the Summer Isles, in the wider reaches of Loch Broom, Wester Ross. He bought Tanera Mor shortly before the war and lived there for some years with his wife and young son. His experiment was one of near self-sufficiency, to explore the possibilities both of regenerating the island's environment (including tree cover) and of successfully farming the island, in a manner more enriching – and less destructive – than generally seen in the West Highlands. It was a murderous chore. 'This book,' he recorded in the preface, 'is part of two people's journey from days of much gaiety and reasonable leisure to a present in which leisure seems immoral . . .'

The last chapter of *Island Farm* – 'Towards a Highland Agriculture' – is one of the best brief summaries of the 'Highland Problem' ever written. The impoverishment of the land Fraser Darling attributes to history, and the resulting Highland society – the destruction of the patriarchal clan system, the failure of the Gaels to produce a significant middle class, the reluctance of Highlanders to become leaders. The excessive pietism of Highland Churches, the individualistic ethos of crofting townships, and the paternalism of the Department of Agriculture all combine to repress initiative and advancement, though Highlanders are in themselves most able; removed from their native society, in business or commerce in the south, they rise rapidly.

The most destructive change in Highland land use, asserts the author, was the widespread shift to intensive sheep-farming after 1780. The old economy was one of cattle husbandry, producing hardy beasts, keeping hills free of old, decaying herbage, evenly grazed, enriched with good dung. Cattle did not threaten established areas of birch wood, and so on. Then came the Clearances. People and cows were removed, and in came great herds of sheep, requiring cleared ground. Most surviving woodland was destroyed. The selective grazing of sheep – and their destructive taste for budding trees – prevented its regeneration. Without cattle, fertility and lushness of verdure rapidly declined. By Fraser Darling's day the days of large-scale sheep husbandry were gone, never to return, for the capital of soil nutrients was spent. Erosion on deforested land made matters even worse.

And still the problem grew. The grazing would no longer support hardy sheep, so lambing ewes were left not on the hill but brought into the bye-land around the croft in spring. This delayed ploughing; if they were allowed to remain until May, it was then late in the year before one could harvest a good hay-crop. So there was more to militate against crofters keeping cattle, and less manure for the hill thereafter. During the Forties, as Fraser Darling wrote, fresh milk in winter had become a great rarity in the West Highlands, so human nutrition suffered. The export trade was largely in under-average lambs and under-average calves, which required months of fattening before they could be butchered by Lowland graziers. 'The prices obtained are low, at the very bottom of the agricultural ladder, but the things which come in, whether food, clothes or furniture, are highly manufactured goods with high transport charges, and are sold at the highest retail price.' A crofter, wrote Fraser Darling, was perhaps among the most privileged agricultural class, for he was 'the one type of land-holder who cannot be evicted for bad husbandry or made to work his land better'. And his food was desperately poor. Nowadays he ate bad, woolly Glasgow bread – invariably stale – not oatcake or barley-bread. Little fresh fish was landed on the West Highland mainland. There was scarcely any dairy produce, save in some of the southern Hebrides, like Islay. Things tinned, packaged, processed, and laden with sugar made up the bulk of the crofter's larder.

Bad diet, low incomes, and, above all, the increasingly wretched state of the Highland land itself were, to Fraser Darling, key elements of the 'Highland Problem'. But it was not the fault of the environment as created. The climate was by no means inimicable to, say, the growing of vegetables. The coastal climate, on low ground, was indeed most mild and kindly, with excessive rain and ferocious wind the only real disadvantages. It was the ideal place for growing grass. The extreme length of daylight in summer at northern latitudes compensated for the lateness of spring and, in general, the late planting of crops.

Windbreaks were Fraser Darling's first solution – walled kitchen-gardens, and the organised planting of suitable trees to form protection belts around a crofting township and its land. The West Highland soil itself – generally poor and acidic, save for such areas of volcanic geology as north-east Skye – needed lime and phosphates; calcium carbonate, in the form of shell-sand, was the best source of lime, and abundantly found in the

region. Basic slag, a waste from steel production, was a cheap
source of phosphates. Seaweed was another excellent supply,
and Fraser Darling lamented the great decline in its application
by crofters.

He preferred digging to use of the plough. He recommended
the growth of swedes and mangolds for cattle fodder; all sorts
of garden surplus would happily feed a cow. On Tanera Mor
the Fraser Darlings had successfully grown a wide range of
vegetables – cauliflour, carrots, peas, sprouts, in addition to fine
potatoes and the larger roots. He had also made interesting
experiments with the plough and harrow, and so on. Oats were
an excellent grain-crop, resistant to the extremes of weather, but
he frowned on the use of hay. Fraser Darling suggested greater
ensilage of grass, and in addition grass could be packed for
silage even in wet weather – a great advantage. Silage was more
nutritious for beasts than hay, and well-worked land should
produce two silage crops a season. Cows winter-fed on silage
produced more manure and this could be used to force early
potatoes.

Many of Fraser Darling's insights were developed over the
next few years. 'The West Highland problem is one of long
standing,' he wrote, though 'many politicians . . . have given
attention to it in moments of political fervour, but not in later
periods of administrative office . . . It is the perfect example of
the social problem on which everyone considers himself a pundit
but which has received little detailed investigation by anybody.'
One statesman, though, was interested; he began to follow
Fraser Darling's writing, and then insisted on a meeting. His
name was Tom Johnston, one of Scotland's most notable
Labour politicians, and he was Secretary of State for Scotland
in Churchill's wartime coalition government.

Johnston, in his spell at Dover House, had already done much
to advance Scottish development, and not least to address the
'Highland Problem'. In 1943, by Act of Parliament – following
his Cooper Commission of 1941 – he established the North of
Scotland Hydro-Electric Board; its members 'so far as their
powers and duty permit, [to] collaborate in carrying out any
measures for the economic development and social improvement of the North of Scotland district, or any part thereof'. Its
remit was to bring 'power to the glens'; the ideal was to generate

this from running water, and though most of the Board's output was by century's end from fossil fuels, its task was accomplished with remarkable dedication and vigour. The Board was empowered to initiate and plan all major developments of water-power, and to improve existing establishments and enlarge the areas they served. It was also empowered to sell extra electricity beyond its northern bounds, the revenue accrued being used to subsidise the grossly uneconomic distribution of electricity to the most far-flung parts of the mainland and the Hebrides.

Through the Forties and Fifties thousands were employed laying cable, erecting poles, building power-stations and transformers, constructing dams (some, on salmon rivers, with the thoughtful touch of fish-ladders). Power was brought to many communities with such speed that they actually enjoyed electricity before they enjoyed piped water; the sight of an elderly woman filling her electric kettle at the well was a common incongruity of the fifties. By 1965 the Hydro Board, as it was popularly known, had built fifty-six major dams and fifty-four principal power-stations. Two mighty pumped-storage schemes were constructed at Cruachan and Foyers; to these vast reservoirs water was pumped up by surplus electricity, effectively storing the power; release of this water released, through the turbines, this packed electricity. By 1985 it was claimed that the Board had reached 99 per cent of its potential customers, and attracted new industries to the Highlands employing over 16,000 people.

Tom Johnston and Frank Fraser Darling struck an immediate rapport. Under the statesman's encouragement, Fraser Darling began to spread his views, in a series of weekly newspaper articles filled with common-sense advice on croft management and husbandry. These were later collated into a book, *Crofting Agriculture*, and the first edition of this – 5,000 copies – was sold out within six weeks. Fraser Darling, though, had an even bigger idea: he wanted to launch a major 'social and biological investigation', to identify the environmental roots of the 'Highland Problem'. The Secretary of State agreed, and in 1944 Fraser Darling won funding for his monumental *West Highland Survey*. In the course of its accomplishment he and his young Highland-born assistants visited hundreds of Highland townships, and his conclusions – deforestation, abusive sheep husbandry, and so on – were confirmed and backed by a mass of evidence. He called for Government initiatives to encourage fundamental changes in land use, the immediate step being a massive reduction in the numbers of sheep. Fraser Darling looked for an 'integrative' programme, drawing on an American parallel, the Roosevelt administration's Tennessee Valley Authority, a public agency with massive economic and planning powers.

But times had changed in the course of Fraser Darling's work: 1945 had brought in the Labour Government of Clement Attlee, whose concerns were primarily urban, whose immediate purpose was – apart from the continuing complexities of foreign policy, from India to the defeated and ruined Germany – to build a comprehensive welfare state. Insofar as it took any interest in land use, the new government, and its successors for the next quarter of a century, were intent on maximising British food production, on encouraging ever more intensive farming. Whitehall had been badly frightened – again – by Britain's inability to feed herself in a time of world war with a naval power. To men with such an obsession, the creation of environmentally friendly crofting was grotesquely irrelevant. Worse: Tom Johnston was no longer Secretary of State. His place had fallen to Arthur Woodburn, MP for Clackmannan and East Stirling, and who had ruined Labour's name in the Highlands by his treatment of the Knoydart raiders.

Knoydart is one of the remotest and wildest parts of the Highlands, on the west coast of Inverness, some miles north of Mallaig, and even today largely inaccessible, its coast riven by two great sea lochs, Hourn and Nevis, its road-link poor and ill-maintained. It was owned by the ghastly Lord Brockett. Brockett was an admirer of Adolf Hitler, and had actually met the dictator on several pre-war occasions; at Hitler's personal invitation, the young peer had attended a variety of Nazi events and rallies. His Knoydart estate was to him little more than a playground, and so badly did Lord Brockett manage his lands that in 1940 starving Britain's government requisitioned the estate, to make sure at least that it pastured a good number of sheep. How Lord Brockett avoided internment in the war years is a mystery, so notorious were his Nazi sympathies. Yet, when the guns fell silent, and Hitler's

Germany was destroyed, Knoydart was restored to its landlord. By 1947 its grazing stock had fallen even below its 1940 level. The government was considering requisition again – food shortages remained acute; Elizabeth would be on the throne before rationing was abolished – when a number of local men formally requested a resettlement scheme. There was no shortage of land in Knoydart, they pointed out, for the creation of new crofts.

By November 1948 it was plain that Woodburn's Scottish Office, despite Lord Brockett's plain deficiencies in estate management, was not prepared to grant the crave or sanction a resettlement. So the men of Knoydart launched a land raid. Several of Lord Brockett's best – and least utilised – fields were staked out and occupied as crofts. All the earlier land-settlement legislation was still in force, which the government had happily wielded after 1918. And only a madman could equate the lazy, racist Lord Brockett with the philanthropic Leverhulme. But the Scottish Office was furious. A majority Labour government was as determined as a Nazi landlord to deny the Knoydart men their claim. The raiders were arrested, charged and imprisoned.

Such a regime in Edinburgh, and London, was no longer of a mind to listen to Frank Fraser Darling. In 1950 he despatched his completed *West Highland Survey*. It was ignored. 'Do you know,' remarked the ecologist in amazement to a good friend, 'that I never received an acknowledgement when I sent the final report of the Survey to St Andrew's House? Six years' work and not even an official paid postcard in reply!' Fraser Darling went on to other things. In North America, in Africa, he became a figure of great influence in environmental circles. He was Britain's biggest influence on ecological thought; he died in 1979 as a sometime Reith Lecturer, heaped with international honours, universally solicited for his views and wisdom on land use. The finest mind ever to study the Highland rural economy has been justly called 'the father of British conservation'. But the Scottish Office, which never developed an effective Highland policy, never again sought his advice, or made any real effort to take advantage of his formidable experience.

The wartime coalition, and the succeeding Labour Government with its massive majority, created a wholly new governance of

Britain. The corporate state was born, funded by heavy taxes, coddled through two decades of consensus politics – with little real change in direction, despite periodic changes of government – big on regulation, on scrutiny, on grand expenditure, on retaining a vast number of white-collar employees on the public pay-roll. After years of austerity, Britain from the early fifties to the mid-sixties enjoyed a considerable consumer boom. They were the years of final retreat from empire, of a massive rise in general living standards, of the universal embrace of the welfare state, the National Health Service, Family Allowance, Public Assistance. Acres – hundreds of acres – of public housing were built. More and more could afford a private car. And so on; the Highland people, as everyone else, benefited from the comfortable wonders of the modern world.

The Forestry Commission – born after the Great War – expanded its work considerably, covering dozens of glens and hillsides in plantations of uniform conifer. Dounreay, in far Caithness, was chosen as the site for Britain's first atomic plant. Remote and sparsely inhabited, the Highlands were well placed for the siting of unpopular, dangerous, noisy or noxious developments. The military had established a considerable presence during the Second World War – throughout the conflict vast tracts of the West Highlands were closed to visitors, and even residents moved in and out only with great difficulty. After the war, the Ministry of Defence retained a considerable presence. So did other NATO forces. The Holy Loch, by Dunoon, became an American naval base, bristling with nuclear submarines, and they stayed until the last decade of the century: had a nuclear war been fought with the Soviet Union, that serene corner of Argyll would have been the first target for thermonuclear assault in Britain.

Lossiemouth in Moray, Aultbea and Mellon Udrigle in Wester Ross, South Uist, Benbecula, Stornoway, the Lewis parish of Uig, the Sound of Raasay and Kyle of Lochalsh, Faslane and the Gareloch, Brora: all, in the decades following the war, played host to a variety of soldiers, sailors and airmen, and all their technology and toys. They enjoyed good things too. In Benbecula, the military did much to boost the local economy: they shared their amenities with the resident population, and started an apprenticeship scheme in various technical trades for local youths. Other areas enjoyed similar blessings. But at times the military caused a good deal of inconvenience. Much happened, too, that has been covered up, or was not known at the time. It will never be known how many commandos died in training (they used live bullets) in the Second World War in the hills of Lochaber and Knoydart. Few Lewismen are aware of biological warfare experiments in Broad Bay in the Fifties. With insufferable arrogance, successive governments refused to do anything about Gruinard, a Wester Ross island not very far from Tanera Mor, where anthrax spores had been hailed far and wide in a wartime biological bomb experiment. For decades it remained a forbidden island, the anthrax still highly dangerous, its bog inhabited only by strikingly large rabbits. It took the 'Dark Harvest' tactics of the early eighties – these ecowarriors posted samples of Gruinard soil to assorted government buildings – finally to trigger action. Gruinard was decontaminated in 1986. The end of the Cold War, and the collapse of the Communist bloc, saw a considerable reduction in 'Fortress Scotland' during the Nineties.

The military presence required good transport links. During the war, to link South Uist and Benbecula, a causeway was at last built over the tidal flats between the islands; in 1960 the North Ford road was opened, between Benbecula and North Uist. Improvement in regional transport – and road transport in particular – became an obsession with successive post-war governments. Roads in the Highlands were generally deplorable; only the A82, the Glasgow to Inverness highway, was without need of massive post-war upgrading. Many minor roads remained unmetalled. They were largely single-tracked, winding, unevenly surfaced; they tended to go around obstacles like headlands, rather than through or over them, and some roads were unnecessarily high, and thus much more likely to be blocked in winter.

There was also the frequent barrier of the sea itself. The journey from Glasgow up the West Highland coast to the far north-west required the crossing of three ferries, at Ballachulish, Strome and Kylescu. These little craft were of the turntable type, carrying, at their largest, no more than six cars at a time, and as tourism boomed in the late Fifties and Sixties, and more and more went on 'motoring' holidays into the Highlands, the ferry-crossings became considerable bottlenecks. In the East Highlands, too, the Dornoch and Beauly Firths greatly limited intercourse between the northern coastal communities and Inverness, which was growing in importance as a centre of commerce and direction in local affairs. The obvious solution was bridges, or at least a more rapid roadloop (there was no road at all round Loch Carron or Kylescu). But claims in the south came first; and even so it took decades of campaigning before a road bridge was built over the Forth, at Queensferry. By the Seventies another bridge spanned the Clyde, at Erskine, supplemented by a new road tunnel at Whiteinch and another new bridge in the city centre.

It was 1970 before a road was built round Lochcarron, and only Applecross and Lochcarron itself felt the subsequent (and unfortunate) closure of the Strome Ferry, though Applecross was cheered by the final opening of a coastal road from Shieldaig, as the high road over the Bealach na Ba was frequently snowbound. At the end of 1975 the Ballachulish ferry – by then notorious for long summer delays – was replaced by a bridge of remarkable ugliness; 1982 saw the opening of a sturdy, earthquake-proof bridge at Kessock, spanning the straits between the Moray and Beauly Firths, and finally integrating the Black Isle closely to Inverness. The end of the decade saw a new road bridge at Dornoch, and the two combined greatly cut the journey time from Inverness to Sutherland. The Queen in 1984 opened the Kylescu bridge, ending that ferry (which, until 1975, had actually been free). A ferry still survived on the Corran narrows of Loch Linnhe, saving travellers from the south to the Ardnamurchan peninsula a forty-mile round trip about Loch Eil. A tiny car ferry was also introduced on the narrows of the Cromarty Firth, largely for the convenience of fabrication workers at Nigg.

The West Highland shipping line, David MacBrayne Ltd, had almost collapsed in 1928. David MacBrayne himself, a most industrious patriarch, had been a rising star in the steamship firm of David Hutcheson (whose role as a pioneer in Highland seaways is commemorated by a monument on Kerrera, off Oban). From 1879 David MacBrayne operated the concern in his own name, latterly aided by his adult sons; he did not retire until 1906, at the splendid age of ninety-two, and it was only then that a family firm became a private limited company. It remained a profitable concern for only two more decades: the rising price of coal, and wages, and the growing demand for shorter hours and better conditions, destroyed the West Highland trade as a profitable enterprise. Financial difficulties coincided with renewal of the all-important mail contract, and there was a parliamentary debate on West Highland steamer services. Then, as now, many resented the near-monopoly operated by the company. But not a sole competitor came forward to take over its services. The company was reconstructed as David MacBrayne (1928) Ltd – the date was dropped in 1934 – under the shared ownership of the London, Scottish and Midland Railway Co and Coast Lines Ltd of Liverpool. Apart from various minor ferries – of which the most important was the Skye ferry at Kyleakin, a solitary Highland outpost of the Clyde's Caledonian Steam Packet Co Ltd – MacBraynes continued to dominate the coastal trade.

Four new motor-driven mailboats were built – the main working vessels, carrying passengers, and light cargo by crane. They operated elaborate routes: the *Lochmor* (1930) spent her long career on the spectacular Outer Isles mail run, sailing from Mallaig to Armadale (Skye), Eigg, Rhum, Muck, Canna, Lochboisdale (South Uist), Lochmaddy (North Uist), Rodel in Harris, Tarbert, Scalpay, Portree, and Kyle of Lochalsh; she performed this grand tour twice a week, circumnavigating Skye in both directions. Bulky cargo was carried by dedicated cargo-vessels from the Glasgow docks to their various Hebridean destinations. Elegant steamers – sleek turbine vessels, splashy paddlers – served for many more years, though the internal combustion engine was increasingly pushing such out. Launches and rowboats tendered to the mail vessels ports and islands lacking suitable piers. There were one or two 'puffers' – the tiny, much-loved rough steamers celebrated in such films as *The Maggie* – but most were run by private firms, such as Roderick Cunningham (Scalpay) Ltd.

MacBraynes had a unique place in Highland culture. The livery of their ships – black hull with red underbody and white waterline, red funnels with black tops – was part of the Highland landscape itself. The crews were local, largely Gaelic-speaking, and MacBrayne masters included such celebrated characters as Donald 'Squeaky' Robertson. Once this inimitable skipper of the *Lochmor* refused to sail from Armadale in Skye to oblige an irate and self-important shooting tenant. This man promptly wired a complaint to MacBrayne's Glasgow office, and shortly a peremptory telegram was delivered to Robertson: WHAT HOLDS LOCHMOR AT ARMADALE? His response was swift: TWO ROPES – ONE AT EACH END.

Though it was the late Sixties before MacBrayne ships ceased to sail on Christmas and New Year's Days, the company traditionally refused to operate Sabbath sailings. MacBrayne's boats, too, were apt to attain venerable age. On the day the company displayed its latest acquisition, the 1931 *Loch Fyne*, she was exhibited at Glasgow's Broomielaw alongside the veteran paddle-steamer *Glencoe*. Built originally for Sir James Matheson in Stornoway, this ship was now eighty-five years old and still sailing; she was finally scrapped that autumn. The well-loved cargo-boat *Hebrides*, long famous in the service of a minor cargo company – she took part in the evacuation of St Kilda in 1930 – was acquired by MacBraynes in 1948, when she was fifty years old. A Lewis wit solemnly assured readers of the *Stornoway Gazette* that, despite her many years, the *Hebrides* had not in fact taken part in the Battle of Lepanto, 'nor was Vasco da Gama ever captain of her.' She sailed on until 1955.

By the end of that decade it was clear to the authorities that radical new investment was required in the company. More and more tourists were driving into the Highlands and Islands, and MacBrayne's traditional mailboats were ill-suited to the carriage of cars. The cargo-runs, too, were grossly uneconomic. The road lobby now dominated public transport policy and the government was eager to promote the use of roads for tourists and haulage. The Scottish Office decided to finance the construction of three large car ferries, to be chartered long-term to MacBraynes; these were to develop new short sea crossings, encouraging maximum use of Highland roads. Great care was taken in the planning of routes and the design of the vessels themselves: the first, a new *Hebrides*, was launched in November 1963, the largest ship (in gross tonnage) MacBraynes had ever sailed. The *Hebrides* was a squat, beamy boat, with beautifully furnished passenger lounges, and some oddly obsolete but endearing touches: teak decking, traditional upholstery, brass-works on the bridge including compass, chronometer and real old-style ship's telegraph. She was certificated for 600 passengers in summer, and 400 in winter; there were sleeping berths for fifty-one. Toilet facilities included even shaving power-points; the lounge had writing desks, and the bell of the previous *Hebrides* displayed on a stand. Her garage space could accommodate fifty motor cars, and this could be adapted for mass transport of cattle on the hoof. Vehicles were loaded by a hydraulically powered hoist, which ran the breadth of the ferry forward of her superstructure, with ramps at each side. The driver drove on; the hoist descended; he drove to his allotted bay on the car deck. Thus she could side-load cars at any conventional pier, whatever the state of tide; the system had been introduced on the Clyde by the CSP in the fifties. Twin diesel engines gave the *Hebrides* a speed of fourteen and a half knots. She was the first MacBrayne boat to be built with stabilisers, and the first to have a bow-thrust unit, to assist in manoeuvring at piers.

Less publicised at the time was the fact that this government-built ship, and her sisters, were deliberately designed to serve – in nuclear emergency – for urban evacuation. The car deck could be sealed by watertight doors and porthole covers, to guard against fallout; there were iron rations stored aboard, and decontamination kits. In a time of crisis the ships were expected to sail to Leith, Glasgow and so on, to remove certain passengers. The interned happy few were, no doubt, men and women of importance; fortunately, the new ferries never had to enact this curious (and, one suspects, rather optimistic) role.

In April 1964 the *Hebrides* began her new route, from Uig in Skye to Tarbert and Lochmaddy, displacing the old *Lochmor*. Thanks to the Uist causeways, she accordingly opened almost all the Outer Isles to motorists. She was an immediate success, and the people of Uist and Harris took her to their hearts. The identical *Clansman* followed her in June, operating a car ferry service from Mallaig to Armadale, in summer only; her real role was to relieve her two sisters, the last of which, *Columba*, began a new Mull ferry service in July, from Oban to Craignure, and also to Lochaline in Morvern.

The ships had minor but vexing design flaws. Though single-screwed, they had only one rudder, enlarging their steering circle. Skippers found the design a little top-heavy; they were reliable in heavy seas, but not comfortable. The biggest problem was the car-carrying equipment. The design was a cost-saving expedient, to save the expense of installing adjustable tamps – linkspans – at West Highland piers, thus allowing much more efficient end-loading. Side-loading ships like the *Hebrides* could not handle vehicles longer than their beam; vehicle weight was restricted by the hoist to twenty-two tons, and headroom on the car deck proved rather too low. Only a decade after their launch, all three ships were already outdated, and their very success made this painfully apparent, especially at extreme low tide, when hoist-loading took a long time and caused great delay.

A small timber ship took over the Small Isles route; a second-hand turntable ferry began a quick service to Scalpay from the Harris mainland. MacBraynes otherwise retained a traditional fleet and network. Inevitably, a private operator took advantage. Western Ferries Ltd sprang up with a most modern car ferry service to Islay, using vessels and terminals of Norwegian design. These ships were drive-on ferries, with bow and stern ramps, using tide-adjustable linkspans. Crews were minimal, and other costs were pared to the bone; the only catering aboard the *Sound of Jura* (1967) was a sweet-dispensing machine. The competition proved a serious embarrassment and Islay soon became a celebrated theatre of car ferry debate. MacBraynes tried to buy over Western Ferries; they tried to withdraw from the Islay ferry service; they tried to drive Western Ferries out of business. The Islay folk, naturally, wanted service by both concerns, although the MacBrayne operation – with all its passenger comforts, and longer route, and service of outlying islands such as Gigha – was wholly unprofitable. Western Ferries did at length abandon Islay, in 1981, though they continued a lucrative route across the Firth of Clyde from Gourock to Dunoon.

By then David MacBrayne Ltd no longer existed.

In 1969 the Labour government created the Scottish Transport Group, uniting the large bus companies in public ownership with the Clyde shipping arm of British Rail, the Caledonian Steam Packet Co Ltd. (Most unjustly, the STG were not granted the veritable goldmine of the Stranraer to Larne ferry link, which British Rail retained.) The STG also gained British Rail's share in David MacBrayne Ltd, inherited from the LMS; by year's end they had bought the other half-holding from Coast Lines Ltd. Both shipping concerns were run almost from the start as one joint operation, with the two head offices – MacBrayne's at Glasgow, the CSP's at Gourock – jousting for supremacy. Gourock won: in 1973 the CSP was renamed Caledonian MacBrayne Ltd, operating all car ferries, and also the four surviving pleasure steamers. The new company – CalMac, as it was quickly dubbed – was confidently expected to run at a healthy profit. David MacBrayne Ltd retained only the old-fashioned passenger and cargo-boats, and a solitary car ferry at Scalpay; it would be the 'subsidy junkie', running only hopelessly unprofitable routes in need of state support. Inflation, and huge hikes in the price of oil, put paid to dreams of profitability: David MacBrayne L'd was abolished in 1980, with all vessels and their operation transferred to CalMac.

A Hebridean transport revolution took much time to effect. The public spending crises of the Seventies did not permit the building of adequate new, modern tonnage. Two big drive-through boats were built for the Kyleakin service; two stern-loading ships for the West Highlands; three stern-and-side-loading boats for the Clyde. CalMac had to modernise things as best it could by adapting or converting older boats, a grossly uneconomic course. Besides, the result was never entirely successful: the conversion of the *Clansman* in 1973 to drive-through operation, and her lengthening by thirty feet, left her badly underpowered and with a nasty roll at sea. Catering standards declined; publicity and promotion deteriorated badly. Some new boats proved of bad design: the *Iona* (1970) was cramped, uncomfortable, and abundantly flawed in her fittings.

Nevertheless, new and successful routes were created – Stornoway acquired a much shorter ferry run to Ullapool, eliminating the long haul to Mallaig and Kyle – and a most useful fleet of eight little bow-loading ships was built, the 'Island Class' ferries, serving small islands such as Raasay, Gigha and Lismore, as well as opening back-door routes to islands such as Mull and Arran. These ships were so successful that six were still running for CalMac over twenty years after their construction.

In the Eighties, under the able management of Colin Paterson, Calmac found its way. Paterson greatly expanded promotion and, while ruthlessly trimming costs, found favour in the Scottish Office – and, too, with funding in the European Community. He won the construction of new route-specific ships; elderly, inefficient vessels were sold off, and all boats built after 1979 were of drive-through design. These new ships were very large, well fitted, and fast. Piers everywhere were upgraded; in real terms, nevertheless, CalMac was able to cut its dependence on state subsidy. By the Nineties it was opening entirely new routes – a car ferry service across Loch Fyne, another over the Sound of Harris.

But it was 1985 before the *Hebrides*, now as much an island institution as she was an antiquated has-been, would retire from the Uig triangle. And 1994 before the last hoist-loading run, to Armadale, would be upgraded. And CalMac was not allowed to upgrade its Kyleakin service (where the 1970 boats were now too old and small) until the Skye Bridge had been approved, on controversial toll-levying terms; nor were they allowed to continue the Kyleakin service once it opened in October 1995.

The Sixties and Seventies were the last decades of big government, corporate planning, trade union hegemony, and a general coddling of public life from wider economic realities. They were also years of class breakdown and a corresponding fluidity in national politics. From the early sixties, Labour and Conservative alienated more and more floating voters. The Liberal Party captured the first boom, and in the 1964 election it seized, simultaneously, three Highland seats. By the end of the decade, though, Liberalism was squeezed off the centre-park of Scottish politics by the Scottish National Party. Nationalism presented excitement, and a new danger to the ruling order.

The SNP had won its first parliamentary seat in 1945, in a by-election during the coalition truce; in the absence of any other major party, Dr Robert MacIntyre seized Motherwell from Labour. He lost it several weeks later in the general election, and for twenty years the SNP remained out of parliament. Its strength became largely small-town, local; it did modestly well in counties such as Stirling and Perth. In the early sixties, though, commentators began to note a rise in SNP support in parliamentary by-elections. In 1962 the SNP actually ran second to Labour's Tam Dalyell, candidate in a supposedly solid Labour seat. (Their candidate, Billy Wolfe, fought Dalyell in no fewer than six successive general elections. He lost every one.) Then, in 1967, they won a sensational victory, Winifred 'Winnie' Ewing, a Glasgow lawyer, demolishing a massive Labour majority in Hamilton. The party scored a high poll in local elections the following year. Then the tide ebbed badly; inexperienced councillors attracted unwelcome attention, and SNP policies could not withstand sustained attack from the old established parties. In 1970 the Nationalists contested almost all Scottish seats – many more than in 1966 – but actually did worse in real terms. Winnie Ewing was easily overthrown in Hamilton.

The party was largely a Lowland phenomenon; unlike Wales, its nationalism was economic and practical, rather than cultural. Though warmly pro-Gaelic, it was scarcely a Gaelic party, and indeed has always been determinedly anti-intellectual. It has also been prone to spats, divisions, and ferocious debates on policy and strategy; at times the Scottish National Party has resembled nothing so much as a secularised doppelganger of the Free Presbyterian Church. Yet, in the 1970 disaster, it scored one sweet and startling success: Donald Stewart won the Western Isles from Labour.

In some ways it was a sad result. The Labour MP, Malcolm MacMillan, was one of the ablest members the Highlands has ever produced, and no one did more for crofters or to advance the Highland interest. He himself had been an unexpected recruit to the Commons: when he won the seat in 1935, MacMillan was a twenty-two-year-old undergraduate. But he had been around rather too long, and he was an absentee member, living in Lanarkshire; able as he was on the Highland interest, he was not greatly thought of as a constituency MP, for Western Isles voters seldom saw him. Stewart was in a different mould. A former Stornoway provost, he occupied a senior position in a major tweed-mill firm, and was known to weavers throughout Lewis and Harris, where live the mass of the Western Isles electorate. Stewart was gracious, affable, and benevolent; he was not as dull as his ponderous television air was apt to suggest. Though very popular in the House of Commons, he was never feared; he lacked the wits, and perhaps the ethical flexibility, vital for high political manoeuvre. As solitary SNP member until 1974, he was natural choice as Parliamentary Group Leader when they scored barnstorming success that year, boosted by the discovery of North Sea oil, most of it in Scotland's territorial waters. In 1973 they won Glasgow Govan in a by-election; in February 1974, seven SNP MPs were returned – including Iain MacCormick for Argyll – and in the October election, eleven. Winnie Ewing in February had the sweetest victory of all: in Moray and Nairn she humiliatingly ousted the Secretary of State for Scotland, Gordon Campbell.

In the October general election the SNP won over 30 per cent of the Scots vote and came second in most other seats. They came close to winning two more Highland divisions, Inverness, and Ross and Cromarty. Many feared them as the Jacobites in 1745: Nationalist advance appeared inexorable, and the advent of home rule seemed vital if they were not to sweep Scotland at a future poll. By the summer of 1976 the Labour government had not even an overall majority in the House of Commons. But, incredibly, it all collapsed. Many Scots feared the SNP. Few outwith its ranks wanted an independent Scotland. Some thought it tainted with Fascism: though it always eschewed violence and xenophobia, certain fervent figures could easily whip up an SNP conference into something resembling a Nuremberg rally. (Rather unfairly, many Nationalists found themselves under the intrusive surveillance of the Special Branch, MI5 and other arms of the 'secret state'.) Though Donald Stewart insisted the SNP was a 'radical party with a revolutionary aim', it was in some respects very conservative; Billy Wolfe – leader until 1979 – described it as 'social democratic', but its leading personnel were largely small businessmen and, like Stewart himself, most conservative in social affairs. The SNP of the seventies was anti-nuclear and anti-European, but it was also pro-monarchy and pro-NATO; Stewart himself – a Free Church adherent – was, in addition, anti-abortion, pro-Sabbath and pro-hanging. Other SNP leaders, such as former Govan MP Margo MacDonald, were assertively left wing. It was easily dismissed as a coalition of cranks, opportunists and empire-builders.

Devolution was emasculated in the House of Commons; a bewildered Scots electorate supported Assembly plans by an inadequately large margin in a 1979 referendum (though their endorsement of Common Market entry had been accepted on a lower poll) and the SNP, with a divided leadership and some very unimpressive representatives in Westminster, floundered.

When Callaghan's Labour government failed, after all, to save the Assembly legislation, Donald Stewart boldly tabled a motion of no confidence in the government. It was followed swiftly by one from Margaret Thatcher. Callaghan, with prophetic wit, described the march of SNP MPs into the hostile lobby as 'turkeys voting for an early Christmas'. He lost the vote. There was a general election, and SNP support fell back to 17 per cent; nine of their eleven MPs lost their seats.

Nationalism slowly recovered in Scotland – in 1994 the SNP managed to win a full third of votes in elections to the European parliament, and two of the eight Scottish seats – but the SNP had lost its capacity to frighten, and its evenly spread support was a great disadvantage under the British electoral system. It was now a much more left-wing party; indeed, by the Nineties its continuing anti-nuclear, public sector, collectivising radicalism was an embarrassment to Labour activists; and it could still win the odd by-election, in 1988 or 1992, and it could still at times intimidate the Labour Party, desperately dependent on its Scottish strongholds. But it seemed incapable of producing leaders who combined judgement, gravitas and charisma, though there were certainly able Nationalists with one or two of those virtues. (One of its finest orators, Kenny MacAskill – a very rich and very left-wing lawyer – had a Lewis grandmother; he inherited a croft there.) Though Winnie Ewing had established the Highlands and Islands Euro-division as her personal fiefdom, the Nationalists had by 1987 largely lost the Highlands to the Liberal Democrats. And Labour recovered the Western Isles easily when Donald Stewart retired that year. The SNP remained a threat in the Western Isles, and in Argyll and Bute, and East Inverness, Nairn and Lochaber. But few expected the last general election of the century to award them many additions to the four seats they held in the spring of 1996. If Scotland ever won independence, it seemed the SNP would be a catalyst, rather than a true national movement that could sweep the land.

The 'Highland Problem' largely defied the patent remedies of the corporate state. When Labour returned to power in 1964, it promised the Highlands a new body to regenerate their economy. For too long, said their new Secretary of State, William Ross, in a sage speech to the House of Commons, the Highlander 'had been the man on Scotland's conscience'. So he presided over the establishment of the Highlands and Islands Development Board, which was credited even with powers of compulsory purchase, as well as many of the devolved powers of the Scottish Office. Yet it was never granted anything like the funding necessary to realise its impressive remit. The HIDB set up shop in a block of hideous new offices in Inverness, and embarked on a far from impressive career. It became apparent that the HIDB favoured massive, high-profile industrial developments, induced to start up with generous grants and subsidies, carefully located in strategic areas.

The ideas were not, in themselves, bad. Corpach, by Fort William, seemed the ideal site for the vast saw, pulp and paper mills opened by Wiggins Teape in 1966. It had rail connections, good road links; it was the west-coast mouth of the Caledonian Canal. Loch Linnhe offered fine deep-water anchorage. The Highlands abounded in suitable forest. The area offered a high standard of living. Yet its immediate impact was unfortunate. The fumes from the plant were plentiful and all-pervading. The local labour pool was too small, and workers were attracted from all over Scotland: a good many, as Calum MacLean viciously described them, were 'the scum of the Lowlands', and brought an interesting variety of social problems. Huge expanses of new and ticky-tacky housing had to be built, destroying much of Corpach's Highland charm. Ecologists reported that wood-pulp wastes were lining the seabed with non-biodegradable solids.

The actual technology was, in fact, corrosive and antiquated, and very expensive. Clients seeking pulp found it cheaper to import it from Scandinavia. The commitment of Wiggins Teape did not survive the withdrawal of public subsidies, and in 1980 – with, inevitably, a calamitous result on the local economy – the pulp mill closed though the surviving Arjo Wiggins concern still operates a paper-mill, and Lochaber's morale has recovered in diversification. The following year, British Aluminium suddenly shut down another HIDB showpiece, its big plant at Invergordon, casting hundreds of Easter Ross workers on to the dole queue. A factory built at Breasclete in west Lewis, for processing fish-meal, folded soon after launch.

Another Labour government continued the party's poor record on Highland affairs. The Heath administration had prepared legislation permitting – indeed, encouraging – crofters to buy their own holdings and take their land entirely out of crofting tenure. To widespread astonishment, Labour simply dusted this most unsocialist measure down and passed it into law in 1976. The new Crofting Reform Act provoked the resignation of significant Highland activists; it was not even popular. Few crofters bothered to exercise the new privilege, which would cost them valued rights of subsidy and common grazing. Those who did generally regretted it. Many crofters simply sought to buy their land for housing or commercial development. Croft land is a finite resource; once crofting tenure is lost, it can no longer be restored.

The HIDB was humiliated in Raasay in the early seventies. The island had no car-ferry link – it was served by the elderly Small Isles mailboat, with infrequent runs – and was in great decline. CalMac were willing to supply a boat. A good terminal was available at Skye. But when the HIDB tried to purchase a site at Churchton, on Raasay – the most sheltered and suitable cove – permission was refused. The necessary quarter-acre of land for a ferry slip and connecting roadway belonged to the dreadful Dr John Green, a retired medical man who now speculated from the safety of Hove in Sussex. In circumstances that have never been satisfactorily explained, Dr Green managed in the early Sixties to buy from the Scottish Office the most important publicly owned properties on Raasay: good houses, fine cottages, the Raasay home farm, and Raasay House itself, once the mansion of MacLeod, laden with antiques and surrounded by magnificent wooded gardens. Dr Green refused to sell cottages to local couples desperate for housing. He paid only one or two brief visits to Raasay. He neglected Raasay House completely, and failed even to ship away its valuable contents; they were swiftly looted and vandalised by tourists, to the huge distress of Raasay people.

It transpired that the HIDB's powers of compulsory purchase were insufficient even to acquire a little piece of land for a ferry slip. They were forced instead to build facilities at the most unsuitable and exposed spot, by the old pier at Suisnish, and it was not until 1979 that the Board bought out – at great expense – Dr Green's entire interest in Raasay. By then, the glories of Raasay House were beyond economic restoration. The Highlands and Islands Development Board applied to the new Secretary of State, George Younger, for greatly expanded powers of compulsory purchase. He refused, on the sly grounds that they had never, after all, deployed the powers they had.

None of the HIDB's four chairmen were Highlanders, none spoke Gaelic, and none was as good as the first one, Sir Robert Grieve, who in his dry understated way achieved a great deal. It could do nothing about the fundamental problem, land ownership, the terms of which remained indefensible. In 1985 it was said – more, it was true, and could be proved – that one-tenth of 1 per cent of Highland people owned over two-thirds of the Highlands. At times HIDB personnel seemed quite unable to understand how Highland minds ticked. The amount of funding and support awarded to incomers grew so notorious that a joke spread widely: all one needed for an HIDB grant was a crazy scheme and an English accent. Its energy was latterly dissipated into a thousand very small local projects, and such occasional set-pieces as the importantly trumped Highlands and Islands Telecommunication Initiative, a grand description of the digitalisation of local telephone services and the deployment of power lines to carry computer data and permit 'telecottaging'. The HIDB died, at length, in the 1990s; it was succeeded, in the same grim concrete premises, by Highlands and Islands Enterprise.

A great restructuring of local government in Scotland came in 1975. The most significant reform for the Highlands, apart from the rise of the mighty Highland Regional Council, was the detachment of the Outer Isles from mainland control under the aegis of a new single-tier authority, the Western Isles Islands Council – Comhairle nan Eilean. The new body had much to do. Lewis had not done badly under Ross and Cromarty – it had a major population base, and a good body of councillors – nor had Harris, which had long been favoured in Inverness. But the Uists and Barra had been deplorably neglected. Many black houses were still inhabited. (One North Uist minister, in the late seventies, almost died from a rare disease he caught in a parishioner's hovel.) Schools in the Southern Isles still had no better toilet amenities than outdoor earth privies.

The linkage had obvious difficulties. The Southern Isles were massively Roman Catholic; north of the North Ford, Calvinism was dominant. Many in Barra and South Uist had never seen Stornoway, and never would. They even preferred the *Oban Times* to the *Stornoway Gazette*; Barra, in particular, had close links with Glasgow and Argyll. Children were schooled in Lochaber; many married Glaswegians, and especially Glaswegians of Irish Catholic stock. Yet the Comhairle had a good start. Its first convener was a Presbyterian minister; his deputy was a Roman priest. It enthusiastically embarked on big spending programmes, and built up a formidable amount of debt. New schools, good council housing, road improvements, a better ferry link to Scalpay, car ferries for the first time to Berneray and Eriskay . . . those were good and useful things.

Its policy on Gaelic was less successful. Gaelic was recognised as an official council language, and simultaneous translation was introduced to the Comhairle chamber for such members as could not follow a Gaelic speech. Less defensibly, English road signs, and village signposts, were replaced not by bilingual but by all-Gaelic signs; as such things are, really, for the benefit of visitors, they bewildered many a tourist. Mindful of the need to preserve Gaelic in the young, the Comhairle introduced a 'bilingual' education policy in primary schools, with Gaelic taught virtually as a foreign language. It was a thoroughgoing failure.

In the late Eighties signs of trouble began to arise. Under pressure from vocal Lewis Sabbatarians – and eager not to be outmanoeuvred by a heavy CalMac offensive to start Sabbath sailings to Uist and Harris – the Comhairle adopted a strict Sabbatarian policy, forbidding any council work on the Lord's day. This caused much ill-feeling in the Catholic islands; it also led to such difficulties in the north (Free Church Sabbath schools generally used council properties) that it had to be abandoned. Opinion in the Southern Isles was further enraged by school closures; a good few local primary schools shut their doors, but not a single school closed in Lewis.

Hospital provision in the Uists became a political minefield.

The Daliburgh Hospital was a public NHS hospital; certain difficulties arose in its surgical cover. It made every sense to build a new and better hospital in Benbecula – more central, more modern – but this was angrily resisted by local priests, for Daliburgh was to all intents and purposes a Roman Catholic hospital, with an uncompromisingly Roman Catholic chapel and big murals of the Virgin Mary. The Comhairle, and the Western Isles Health Board, had acute difficulty in extricating themselves; there were even calls in the Catholic Hebrides for a return to local government under Inverness. But popular support for the Comhairle was stronger than it seemed. Daliburgh Action Group candidates were resoundingly defeated in every ward they fought in the 1994 council elections. It seemed that respect for vocal priests had repressed the real views of the people, most of whom were eager to see a new and better hospital.

The greatest humiliation in the Comhairle's brief history came in 1991. In August the Asian-dominated Bank of Credit and Commerce International went bankrupt; in its fall it took some £22 million of money from Comhairle nan Eilean; worse, money the council did not own, but had on loan from the Scottish Office. The practice of on-lending was illegal, and the council had been repeatedly warned about it; but the lure of new capital generated even by overnight banking with BCCI (which paid good interest rates) had proved irresistible. The BCCI débâcle was a painful episode which brought a blush to every islesman, and was made far worse by the evident chaos and panic at Comhairle headquarters when the news broke. The Comhairle did not even employ a press officer, and its public relations were farcical; its chief executive, a pleasant but awkwardly spoken individual, came across as inept and ridiculous.

There was, of course, an inquiry. The director of finance was scapegoated, and sacked. The chief executive argued his way to early retirement on remunerative terms. The real fault lay in the councillors themselves. The politics of the Western Isles were not party politics. Further, as the Comhairle was by far the biggest employer, and as its employees could not stand for election, there were not very many able candidates available. They were generally elderly, retired, and ill-educated, or small businessmen, sometimes of dubious background; it was widely joked that most eminent councillors were Freemasons. They stood without labels, as Independents; many were returned unopposed, and on occasion a Comhairle ward attracted no candidates at all. In such a council all councillors share responsibility, and there is no party administration to reproach or blame. Not a single councillor, then, saw fit to admit his own liability for the BCCI failure, though some certainly knew of the on-lending, and the others had been too lazy to take a real interest in finance. Some senior councillors were wise enough to stand down in 1994. The electorate were in no doubt where the blame lay. Most defending councillors lost their seats. The new Comhairle, for the first time, included a group of members elected in the Labour interest. Subsequent debate became a good deal more violent and heated; island administration did not noticeably improve. The cloud of BCCI, and the spending restraints it imposed, remained.

The last decades of the twentieth century were dominated by a long period of radical Conservative government, under Margaret Thatcher and John Major, and much cultural change. The decline of Gaelic seemed inexorable. But radical new activists sprang up, like the group *Ceartas* – Justice – who daubed Gaelic translations on English road signs. A Gaelic rock group, RunRig, at last won mainstream success on the Chrysalis label in the nineties (though most of their lyrics were English). In 1986, a new type of Primary One class opened in the primary school at Breasclete – Gaelic medium. The infant entrants were taught reading, writing and everything else entirely in the Gaelic language. In Primary Three English was introduced; thereafter, they joined 'mainstream' classes. The success of the policy was immediately apparent. Gaelic-medium teaching spread throughout the Highlands, and even into the larger Lowland cities, though greatly hampered by a shortage of suitable teachers. For the first time in a generation, and despite the residual suspicion of parents (who feared little ones might be 'held back'), small children fluent in Gaelic were again heard in the Hebrides.

Gaelic radio expanded greatly, despite the BBC's sudden transfer in the mid-Seventies of all its Gaelic output to VHF; many parts of the Highlands still lacked VHF transmission, an

they were given only a few weeks' notice. In the late Eighties a
new group, Comunn nan Gaidheal, or CNAG, splintered from
An Comunn Gaidhealachd and began to lobby for greater
recognition of Gaelic. They were rewarded, in the Nineties,
by the establishment of the Gaelic Television Committee,
Comataidh Telebhisean Gaidhlig (CTG), with an annual £9
million of government funding from an oddly generous Scottish Office. The work of the CTG was, after a few years from its
launch in 1992, plainly winning. Good high-quality Gaelic
programmes were carried by BBC Scotland, Scottish Television
and Grampian. They included fine children's programmes,
cheerful music shows, excellent educational output, a super-
lative current affairs magazine, and – in true TV tradition – a
lovably dire soap-opera. Yet there was no sign of what would
still truly advance the Gaelic language: universal Gaelic-medium
teaching, and a national Gaelic radio station. Indeed, Gaelic
television soaked up funds and personnel that might otherwise
have gone to radio, or into Gaelic teaching, or the university
Celtic departments that train Gaelic teachers.

   The end of the century was noted for an evident, and
disturbing, secularisation. Church attendance even in Lewis,
once a stronghold of Presbyterian worship, declined steeply;
Stornoway apart, most Free Church pews emptied. The Sabbath, for the first time, was openly defied by sportsmen,
restaurateurs, and trippers – and most of these were local.
The trend can only have been accelerated by Church divisions. In 1989 the Free Presbyterian Church was rent apart
by the Lord MacKay affair. The Lord High Chancellor, Lord
MacKay of Clashfern, an elder in the Edinburgh congregation,
was suspended for attending Requiem Mass in memory of a
dead Scottish judge. His supporters appealed the case from
Presbytery to Synod; it collided there with another dispute, over
a Sutherland minister who, in his capacity as a local councillor,
had asked a priest to pray at an education committee meeting.
The bid to restore these unrepentant men to Church privileges
failed: they, and their supporters – largely middle-class Free
           in the Lowlands and East Highlands – left the
        orm the self-consciously progressive Associated
        Churches. A newly ordained APC minister in
     escribed the new body as lying on the ecclesiastical

spectrum 'between the Free Church and the Church of Scotland'.

So the Free Presbyterian Church lost a third of its ministers and people. It remained, more coherent now, more united, but exceedingly small, a marginalised if still vocal force in Highland life. The Free Church too, was soon torn in dispute and strife; few expected, by the mid-Nineties, that it would survive to the next century without major schism.

Skye became a place of new interest. In the Eighties the island began to attract large numbers of incomers, many English, most people of drive and enthusiasm, and a good few deeply sympathetic with local culture: such put their children into Gaelic-medium classes, joined local churches, opened useful and innovative businesses (such as the Skye Serpentarium, probably the best reptile centre in the Hebrides). In 1985 Broadford became the base for the new Scottish Crofters Union, an exciting new organisation which, in 1992, developed an imaginative friendship with the Royal Society for the Protection of Birds: conservation and environmental issues now increasingly dominated Highland politics. Skye was the home of RunRig, whose success continued. It had also, in 1972, seen the birth of the *West Highland Free Press*, a radical community newspaper, run by a group of very young and vaguely Marxist ex-students. The *Free Press*, at times, seemed to combine *Morning Star* with *Private Eye*; it was intolerantly pro-Labour, very hostile to the SNP, inclined to pursue strange vendettas, and too prone to mix news and comment. Yet it survived, and hardened into a mature newspaper, a great asset to modern Highland culture.

It seemed to many, at the end of the twentieth century, that the future of the Highlands lay not in further industrial development, nor embalmment as some sort of pure, empty theme-park, but in its regeneration by a new wave of settlement. Why should estates long since given over to grouse and deer not be recrofted? Why might not empty straths, deserted islands, again see habitation? James Hunter and others warned that such incomers would not, for the most part, be Highlanders, nor even necessarily Scots. But a new world might be wrought: a new, post-Gaelic, world of the Highlands and Islands, where the soil was again tilled, where children again sang in serene summer mornings.

A culture of space, beauty, freshness and tolerance might again
revive in the north and west of Scotland. The Isles of the
Strangers would embrace strangers once more. It was a beguiling
vision; one, you fancied, that would bring a smile to the faces of
past Celts, Picts, Norsemen. Columba himself would welcome
the new and interesting mission-field; the heart of the Gael, with
all its secret thoughts, might again leap in a dream.

BIBLIOGRAPHY

✠

Barron, Hugh, (ed.), *The Third Statistical Account of Scotland: Vol XVI – The County of Inverness*, Scottish Academic Press, 1985.

Beaton, Donald, *Some Noted Ministers of the Northern Highlands*, (1929), Free Presbyterian Publications reprint, 1985.

Cameron, Nigel M. de S., (ed.), *Dictionary of Scottish Church History and Theology*, ed. Nigel M. de S. Cameron. T. & T. Clark, 1993.

Domhnallach, Tormod Calum, *Call na h-Iolaire*, Acair, 1978.

Duckworth, C. L. D. and Langmuid, G. E., *West Highland Steamers*, (1935), fourth edition, Brown, Son & Ferguson, 1988.

Fraser Darling, F., *Island Farm*, G. Bell & Sons Ltd, 1944.

Fraser Darling, F. and Boyd, J. M., *Natural History in the Highlands and Islands*, (The Collins New Naturalist Series, 1963) Bloomsbury reprint, 1989.

Grant, James Shaw, *Highland Villages*, Robert Hale, 1977.

Gregory, Donald,*History of the Western Highlands and Isles of Scotland*, (second edition, 1881), John Donald Publishers Ltd, Scottish Reprint Library, 1975.

Hume Brown, P., *A Short History of Scotland*, Oliver & Boyd, 1926.

Hunter, James, *The Claim of Crofting*, Mainstream Publishing, 1991

Hunter, James, *Scottish Highlanders: A People and their Place*, Mainstream Publishing, 1992.

Hunter, James, *On the Other Side of Sorrow*, Mainstream Publishing, 1995.

Kennedy, John, *The Days of the Fathers in Ross-shire*, (1861), Christian Focus Publications reprint, 1979.

Kermack. W. R., *The Scottish Highlands: A Short History*, W. & A. K. Johnston & G. W. Bacon Ltd, 1957.

Lawson, Bill, *The Teampull at Northton and The Church at Scarista*, Bill Lawson Publications, 1993.

Lawson, Bill, *The Teampull on the Isle of Pabbay*, Bill Lawson Publications, 1994.

Lynch, Michael, *Scotland: A New History*, Century, 1991.

MacAulay, John, *Silent Tower*, The Pentland Press Ltd, 1993.

Macaulay, Murdo, *The Burning Bush in Carloway*, Deacons' Court of the Free Church of Scotland at Carloway, 1984.

MacCulloch, Donald B., *Romantic Lochaber, Arisaig and Morar.* (1939), third edition, W. & R. Chambers, 1971.

Macdonald, Donald, *Lewis: A History of the Island*, Gordon Wright Publishing, 1978.

MacKinnon of Dunakin, Charles, *The Scottish Highlanders: A Personal View*, Charles MacKinnon of Dunakin. Robert Hale, 1984.

MacLean, Malcolm and Carrell, Christopher, (ed.), *As an Fhearan: From the Land*, Mainstream Publishing, 1986.

Macleod, John, *No Great Mischief If You Fall*, Mainstream Publishing, 1993.

McLynn, Frank, *Charles Edward Stuart: A Tragedy in Many Acts*, Routledge, 1988.

McPherson, Alexander, (ed.), *History of the Free Presbyterian Church of Scotland 1893–1970*, Free Presbyterian Publications, 1975.

Murray, W. H., *The Islands of Western Scotland: The Inner and Outer Hebrides*, (The Regions of Britain Series). Eyre Methuen, 1973.

Ross, Raymond J. and Hendry, Joy, (ed.), *Sorley MacLean: Critical Essays*, Scottish Academic Press, 1986.

Smith, Angus, *An Eaglais Mhor (The Large Church)*, Deacons' Court of the Free Church of Scotland at Cross, 1992.

Thompson, Francis, *Harris and Lewis – Outer Hebrides*, (1968) Second edition, David & Charles, 1973.

Thompson, Francis, *Crofting Years*, Luath Press, 1984.

Thompson, Francis, *The Western Isles*, B. T. Batsford, 1988.

Thomson, Derick S., *The Companion to Gaelic Scotland*, (1983), second edition, Gairm Publications, 1994.

INDEX